# The Shiites of Lebanon under C

*The Shiites of Lebanon under Ottoman Rule, 1516–1788* provides a new perspec̶t̶i̶v̶e̶ ̶o̶n̶ ̶t̶h̶e̶ previously ignored history of the Shiites as a constituent of Lebanese society. Winter presents a history of the community before the nineteenth century, based primarily on unpublished Ottoman Turkish documents. From these, he shows how local Shiites were well integrated in the Ottoman system of rule, and that Lebanon as an autonomous entity only developed in the course of the eighteenth century through the marginalization and then violent elimination of the indigenous Shiite leaderships by an increasingly powerful Druze–Maronite emirate. As such the book recovers the Ottoman-era history of a group which has always been neglected in chronicle-based works, and, in doing so, fundamentally calls into question the historic place within 'Lebanon' of what has today become the country's largest and most activist sectarian community.

**Stefan Winter** is Professeur régulier at the Université du Québec à Montréal (UQÀM). His previous publications have included a number of articles for various journals including *Oriente Moderno* and the *Journal of Near Eastern Studies*.

**Cambridge Studies in Islamic Civilization**

*Editorial Board*
David Morgan (general editor)
Virginia Aksan, Michael Brett, Michael Cook, Peter Jackson,
Tarif Khalidi, Chase Robinson

*Published titles in the series are listed at the back of the book*

# The Shiites of Lebanon under Ottoman Rule, 1516–1788

STEFAN WINTER

*Université du Québec à Montréal*

CAMBRIDGE
UNIVERSITY PRESS

CAMBRIDGE UNIVERSITY PRESS
Cambridge, New York, Melbourne, Madrid, Cape Town,
Singapore, São Paulo, Delhi, Mexico City

Cambridge University Press
The Edinburgh Building, Cambridge CB2 8RU, UK

Published in the United States of America by Cambridge University Press, New York

www.cambridge.org
Information on this title: www.cambridge.org/9781107411432

First published 2010
First paperback edition 2012

*A catalogue record for this publication is available from the British Library*

*Library of Congress Cataloguing in Publication Data*
Winter, Stefan, 1970–
The Shiites of Lebanon under Ottoman rule, 1516–1788 / Stefan Winter.
  p.   cm. – (Cambridge studies in Islamic civilization)
Includes bibliographical references.
ISBN 978-0-521-76584-8
1. Shi'ah – Lebanon – History.   2. Shiites – Lebanon – Political activity.   3. Lebanon – Politics
and government.   4. Lebanon – Ethnic relations.
I. Title.   II. Series.
DS80.55.S54W56   2010
956.92´03408829782–dc22

                                                                    2010000071

ISBN 978-0-521-76584-8 Hardback
ISBN 978-1-107-41143-2 Paperback

Dedicated to Safuh Murtada, 'Abir Bassam,
Bernard Heyberger and Mafalda Ade

# Contents

# Lists of illustrations and maps

## Illustrations

## Maps

# Acknowledgements

Research for the present book began in Istanbul in the summer of 1999 and has taken me to many places, literally and metaphorically, over the years. It is a pleasure to finally acknowledge those who have offered me their time, support and criticism and contributed to seeing this work to fruition: Nabil Al-Tikriti and Charles Wilkins, my stalwart companions in the archives of Istanbul, Damascus and beyond; Ridwan al-Sayyid, Talal Majdhub and especially 'Abir Bassam, who helped guide my research in Lebanon; and Marco Salati, Astrid Meier, Stefan Knost, Erdem Kabadayı and Sabine Mohasseb Saliba for their aid and suggestions. I am also grateful to the directors of the Başbakanlık archives in Istanbul, the library of the Lebanese University and Qasr Nawfal in Tripoli, the Archives Nationales in Paris and the Sächsische Landesbibliothek in Dresden for permission to use their collections. Institutional support was provided by the Institut Français du Proche-Orient in Damascus, the German Orient-Institut in Beirut and of course the University of Chicago, where an early version of this study was accepted as a doctoral thesis in 2002; warm thanks are due to my advisor, Cornell Fleischer, as well as to John Woods and Jim Reilly. The Fonds québécois de la recherche sur la société et la culture (FQRSC) generously supported both the initial and later research for this project. I owe a particular debt of gratitude to Bernard Heyberger for his counsel and for inviting me to present my revised findings at the École pratique des hautes études (EPHE) in the summer of 2007, and I have also benefitted from Ussama Makdisi's insightful comments as well as from Marigold Acland's professionalism in guiding the final draft through publication. For all the remaining shortcomings I alone am to blame. Most of all, I express my thanks to Mafalda Ade, for preparing the maps for this book, for her shared scholarly interests and many critical discussions of my work and for so much more than can be put in words.

# Note on transliterations

This study draws on source materials in Turkish, Arabic and several western European languages. Modern Turkish spelling has been used for administrative terms and names of officials of the Ottoman Empire, whereas the modified *International Journal of Middle East Studies* system for transliterating Arabic has been used for people and most place names in Lebanon and Syria. The point of the study, however, is that many individuals and institutions were proper to both contexts, so that I have thought it best to alternate between systems, and by the same token to use modern standard Kurmanci orthography for names of identifiably Kurdish groups and individuals, depending on the context or on the sources being quoted. This entails a certain number of subjective choices and inconsistencies, for which I ask the reader's indulgence.

# Abbreviations

| | |
|---|---|
| AE | Affaires Étrangères |
| MD | Mühimme Defteri |
| MM | Maliyeden Müdevver |
| ŞD | Şikayet Defteri |
| TD | Tahrir Defteri |

# Introduction

This book is a history of the Shiite community of what is today Lebanon in the early modern period. It traces the rise and fall of the Hamadas, Harfushes and other Shiite notable families as *mukataacı*s, agents invested by the Ottoman state to tax and police the rural highland districts of Tripoli, Damascus and Sidon that were not otherwise amenable to government control. Their co-optation by the authorities of the nominally Sunni empire beginning in the sixteenth century, and their displacement through other sectarian groups by the late eighteenth century, raise a number of important questions about Shiism in both Ottoman and Lebanese history.

From the standpoint of Ottoman Islamic law, Shiites were seen as *Rafizi*s or heretics. The consolidation of imperial rule and the systematization of both *shari'a* and imperial administrative (*kanun*) jurisprudence in the late fifteenth and sixteenth centuries, and the revolt by heterodox Kızılbaş tribesmen in Anatolia against this same process of state centralization, resulted in a legal position on Shiism that legitimized the killing of sectarians as Rafizis or Kızılbaş and thereby provided an official basis for the proscription of non-Sunni enemies both within and outside the Empire. The Ottoman chancery would in fact apply this vocabulary against refractory Shiites in Lebanon and elsewhere into the nineteenth century, denouncing them as 'accursed Kızılbaş whose elimination is a religious duty' whenever they ran foul of the state authorities.

The campaigns against Anatolian and other 'Kızılbaş' and the persecution of individual scholars and deviant sufis are well documented and provide a dramatic, but essentially one-sided picture of heterodoxy in the Ottoman Empire. The following attempts to complement and nuance this picture with a more long-term, socio-political examination of a Shiite community under Ottoman rule. Historians of the state's central institutions have tended to ignore the day-to-day experience of Ottoman administrative practice – especially in the Arab provinces which are often apposed to the so-called 'core provinces' of the Empire. Yet the Shi'a of Lebanon, abundantly cited not only in state archival sources but also in a wealth of local chronicles and foreign reports, was probably the best documented of any heterodox population in Ottoman history. The fact that these Shiites, in particular their tribal leaderships, could be integrated into the structures of Ottoman provincial government, but became progressively marginalized in the competition with other feudal lords in an era of imperial administrative reforms, suggests that long-term processes of state rationalization and modernization were more central to the fate of heterodox minorities in the Ottoman Empire than timeless religious or legal ideologies.

If tax farming, tribal control and administrative reform set the general parameters of the Shiites' range of action under Ottoman rule, how families such as the Hamadas and Harfushes managed to establish themselves and exercise authority within these parameters must ultimately be explained in terms of local society and politics. The principal aim of this study is therefore to resituate the Shiites with respect to the emerging polity of Lebanon. Nationalist historians have traditionally traced Lebanon's origins back to the 'Druze emirate', the feudal rule of the Ma'n and Shihabi families in the province of Sidon which gradually also encompassed the Maronite community in Tripoli and which has therefore stood as a model of inter-confessional cooperation in the face of Ottoman Turkish tyranny. This romanticized vision of the country's roots, however, ignores the fact that the expansion and consolidation of the Druze emirs' power by the end of the eighteenth century occurred primarily at the expense of the region's Shiite feudatories; these have in effect been written out of the national narrative. The problem this study attempts to address is thus not one of simply reinserting a community that has always been a little under-represented into the overall story of Lebanese nationhood, but of using its specific evolution to question the very foundations on which this story has been written.

## Sources

The basic premise of this book is that the conventional sources for the history of 'Lebanon' in the Ottoman period (for the most part Maronite narrative chronicles and nineteenth-century positivist histories that project Lebanese autonomy back into earlier times) inherently served to legitimize the rule of Druze feudal lords and must therefore be supplemented with other sources in order to gain a more complete understanding of the local realities of Ottoman rule. The principal source used in the following study are Ottoman administrative documents pertaining to the provinces of Syria (Tripoli, Damascus, Sidon) between the late sixteenth and the late eighteenth century. These records can be divided into three broad categories: executive, fiscal and judicial. The first consists of extraordinary decrees (sing. *hüküm*) issued by the Sublime Porte to the provincial authorities in reaction to specific petitions or reports of fiscal abuse, banditry or rebellion. The largest corpus of these decrees is that comprised in the *Mühimme Defterleri* (MD; 'registers of important state affairs') at the Başbakanlık Archives in Istanbul, which on account of the insight they afford into both local conditions in the provinces and the central government's response are among the best known and most popular Ottoman archival materials. Several collections of selected *Mühimme* documents pertaining to heterodox Shiism in the Empire and to the Ottoman administration of Syria have already been edited or translated.[1] However, as the choice of documents that were included or not included in these collections already betrays a certain editorial position (and as the translations are not always entirely correct), we have referred only to the original registers for this study. A unique *Mühimme* register found to contain the earliest known Ottoman reference to the Hamadas (see chapter 3) was consulted at the Sächsische Landesbibliothek in Dresden. Further collections of executive decrees, most notably the Cevdet and Ali Emiri classifications, were researched using the Başbakanlık's printed and computer catalogues; the extraordinarily rich series of *Şikayet Defterleri* (ŞD; 'complaints registers') remains uncatalogued and only a small sample has been used here. Individual decrees in Ottoman Turkish are also interspersed between the Arabic-language proceedings of the Islamic court in Tripoli or Sidon (see below). Interestingly, none of these match exactly the orders copied in the imperial chancery registers.

While executive decrees can provide important and sometimes colourful detail on salient political events, the fiscal records preserved by the accountancy division (*Maliyeden Müdevver*; MM) offer a more structural, long-term picture of revenue raising in the provinces. Ottoman tax cadastres (*Tahrir Defterleri*; TD), which exist mainly for the sixteenth century, have been taken in the past as comprehensive economic and demographic statistics; both types of document, however, are closely tied to specific revenue sources and in fact provide little usable information on actual government or local society. Individual documents and registers from these collections have been used here only when they make explicit reference to villages or persons relevant to the Shi'a.

The third category of documents to be used are *shari'a* court records from the provincial capitals Tripoli and Sidon. Court documents constitute one of the premier sources for Ottoman social history and have proved particularly useful for recovering individual stories of peasants, women, non-Muslims and other reputedly voiceless minorities. Their value for our purposes lies in their presentation not of contingent government directives or of anonymous fiscal structures, but of regular, institutionalized contacts and negotiations between local Shiite notables and the Ottoman state. Copies of Tripoli's court records, which are extant from 1666 onward, are preserved at the Lebanese University as well as by the Municipality of Tripoli and have been used in numerous studies of the province's history in the Ottoman period.[2] The following draws especially on *iltizam* (tax

[1] Ahmet Refik, *Onaltıncı Asırda Râfızîlik ve Bektaşîlik*, new edn by Mehmet Yaman (Istanbul: Ufuk Matbaası, 1994); Baki Öz, ed., *Alevilik ile ilgili Osmanlı Belgeleri* (Istanbul: Can Yayınları, 1995); Cemal Şener, ed., *Osmanlı Belgelerinde Aleviler-Bektaşiler* (Istanbul: Karacaahmet Sultan Derneği, 2002); Cemal Şener and Ahmet Hezarfen, eds., *Osmanlı Arşivi'nde Mühimme ve İrade Defterlerinde Aleviler-Bektaşiler* (Istanbul: Karacaahmet Sultan Derneği, 2002); Uriel Heyd, *Ottoman Documents on Palestine, 1552–1615: A Study of the Firman according to the Mühimme Defteri* (Oxford: Clarendon Press, 1960); Abdul-Rahim Abu-Husayn, *The View from Istanbul: Ottoman Lebanon and the Druze Emirate* (London: I. B. Tauris, 2004).

[2] A series of unpublished Lebanese University (Tripoli) Master's theses supervised by Khalid Ziyada in the 1980s provide indices to some of the early registers; for a partial listing see *Cahiers du CERMOC* 11 (1995), 78–9.

concession) contracts awarded to the Hamada family in Mt Lebanon as well as on sales deeds, lawsuits and other notarial documents. For the province of Sidon, a single original register from 1699–1703 as well as a fragment from 1763, only recently discovered and salvaged by Talal Majdhub,[3] were consulted at the city's Sunni Shari'a Court. This material does not appear to have been used elsewhere and still awaits a thorough examination. Several single documents from the court registers of Damascus and Hama, preserved at the Centre for Historic Documents in Damascus, have also been used where they pertain to the Lebanese Shiites.

Ottoman administrative documents of course present an ideal, normative picture of the state's government and are not inherently more 'objective' than the local narrative chronicles. Every effort has therefore been made to understand both types of text in the historical context in which they were written and to cross and compare them with other available sources, including a number of imperial histories, Ottoman religious treatises, oriental and European travel accounts, and published Maronite Church documents. In particular, this study draws heavily on French consular reports sent from Tripoli and Sidon in the late seventeenth and the eighteenth centuries, which despite France's stated interest in protecting the Maronite Catholic community provide detailed and surprisingly equitable appreciations of different aspects of local society. Selections from this correspondence were published in the 1970s (see chapter 5); the documents used in the present work were researched at the Archives Nationales (Affaires Étrangères; AE) in Paris.

This study cannot pretend to have exhausted all the possible sources on Lebanon's Shiites in the Ottoman period; future ones may profit especially from British or other European consular correspondence and Vatican and Roman Catholic missionary sources, neither of which we were able to examine in the scope of the present work. A key source which has not been used here but which likely contains numerous references to Shiite feudal lords are the private archives of Maronite churches or monasteries preserved both in Lebanon and abroad. A number of such documents are looked at in Sa'dun Hamada's recent contribution to the *History of the Shi'a in Lebanon*;[4] many more may still come to light in private collections. If the present work has focused especially on previously untapped archival sources, it is hoped that this will also significantly help widen the documentary basis for future discussion and debate on the subject.

## Argument

This book comprises six chapters. The first examines the Ottoman state's 'policy' on Shiism, contrasting the legal position defined by jurists such as Ebu's-Suud Efendi with the pragmatism of Ottoman rule in Shiite-inhabited regions. The

---

[3] Talal Majdhub, 'Masadir Tarikh Lubnan fi'l-Qarn al-Thamin 'Ashar' in *Lubnan fi'l-Qarn al-Thamin 'Ashar: al-Mu'tamar al-Awwal li'l-Jam'iyya al-Lubnaniyya li'l-Dirasat al-'Uthmaniyya* (Beirut: Dar al-Muntakhab al-'Arabi, 1996), 23–41.

[4] Sa'dun Hamada, *Tarikh al-Shi'a fi Lubnan* (Beirut: Dar al-Khayyal, 2008).

second looks at the Ottoman administration of western Syria beginning in the sixteenth century, and shows that Shiite notables such as the Harfush emirs of Baalbek were among the most sought-after local intermediaries of the state. Chapter 3 traces the rise of the Hamadas, who exercised control over multiple tax farms in the rural hinterland of Tripoli in the seventeenth century through a complex matrix of rapports with both the Ottoman state authorities and the local non-Shiite communities. The fourth chapter shows how this system began to break down in the social and political crisis that engulfed the Empire at the end of the seventeenth century, leading to an unprecedented punitive campaign against the Hamadas and the Harfushes and leaving them increasingly dependent on the Druze emirs of Sidon and on their own Maronite subjects. Chapter 5 turns the focus on the Shiite community of Jabal 'Amil, as they struggle to maintain their autonomy vis-à-vis the burgeoning Shihabi emirate in the new context of decentralized rule in the eighteenth century. The final chapter returns to the Hamadas and Harfushes, the former being eliminated by the Shihabi-Maronite condominium and the latter being reduced to a mere subsidiary of what by the end of the eighteenth century has indeed taken on the form of a single pan-Lebanese feudal regime.

The main arguments of this study can be summarized as follows: that the Ottoman state, contrary to conventional assumptions, was ideologically too heterogeneous and politically too pragmatic to follow an actual policy against Shiism; that instances of persecution by state authorities must be seen in their specific temporal and political context rather than assumed to be part of a universal anti-Shiite impulse; that the designation of individual Druze or Shiite tribal leaders in the Syrian coastal highlands as 'emirs' must be seen in the context of sixteenth-century imperial reforms, primarily the monetarization of the provincial administration, rather than as an expression of timeless Lebanese particularism; that the sectarian, tribal and mercenary character of certain Shiites not only posed no obstacle, but virtually recommended them as government tax farmers over the local population; that the very unfavourable picture of Shiites in contemporary historiography and popular lore reflects not an objective truth, but derives in part from their status as taxlords over the central institutions of the Maronite Church and their embroilment in secular conflicts within the powerful Lebanese Order of monks; that French sponsorship of the Maronite Church and a rising Maronite landed elite in the eighteenth century, allied with the Druze 'princes' of southern Lebanon, caused the more traditional Shiite leaderships to become less viable as state tax agents; that Ottoman social engineering measures, in particular a major tribal settlement initiative around the turn of the eighteenth century, further reduced the autonomy once enjoyed by Shiite feudalists; and that the elimination of the Shiite tax concessionaries in the north and the subjugation of those in the south and the Bekaa Valley under the Druze emirate in the late eighteenth century can hardly be made the starting moment of a single, pan-confessional Lebanese national identity in the modern period.

The story of the Shiites of Lebanon under Ottoman rule is not one of essential religious or national characteristics but on the contrary one of co-optation, social process, political struggle, reform and adaptation over nearly three centuries of profound change throughout the region. It challenges the linear view that the expansion of Shihabi-Maronite rule over what would only be defined retrospectively as 'Lebanon' somehow corresponded to the aspirations of the victims of this expansion, and it suggests, in taking not only the documents but also the institutions and practices of Ottoman government seriously, a new reading of Lebanese history per se. The Shiites form the largest and in many ways the most activist sectarian community in Lebanon today, yet their rapport with the myths and emblems of Lebanese nationhood has always been problematic. Serious reflection on modern-day questions of identity, sovereignty, political confessionalism or communitarianism in Lebanon cannot begin without also coming to terms more seriously with the Shiites' place in this history.

CHAPTER 1

# Shiism in the Ottoman Empire: between confessional ambiguity and administrative pragmatism

The history of Lebanon's Twelver Shiites under Ottoman imperial rule remains for the most part unknown, subject to narrow sectarian perspectives or subsumed under the general mythology of Lebanese particularism. Whereas the Shiite tradition of southern Lebanon (Jabal 'Amil) has preserved the memory of the persecution or exile of a handful of Shiite scholars in the sixteenth century as emblematic of the community's fate under the Ottomans as a whole, modern nationalist historiography, where it remembers the Shiites at all, sees them only as seconding the Druze' and Maronites' creation of a quasi-independent 'Lebanese' emirate. Both share a vision of the Ottoman Empire as something inextricably hostile and alien, over the four centuries of its dominion, to local heterodox society, and neither has made much effort to accept the Ottomans' authority and institutions, their language and chronicles and archives, as valid parameters for the writing of Lebanese Shiite history.

To come to a new understanding of Lebanon's Shiite confessional community in the early modern period, both in terms of its internal dynamics and as an organic constituent of what would later become the Lebanese republic, it is first necessary to consider it not as a unique local phenomenon but within the religious and administrative evolution of the Ottoman Empire as a whole. What was the Ottoman state's position vis-à-vis the non-Sunni Muslim minorities on its territory? Were they subject to discrimination or to toleration, to benign or hostile indifference, on the part of the authorities? Did the imperial bureaucracy defend a particular religious ideology, and did it change over time? And are our conceptions of state and ideology, tolerance and persecution even applicable in a setting such as that of the Ottoman Empire, or are they to some extent modern anachronisms?

Students of Ottoman history have long noted the seeming paradoxes in the definition of its official ideology: on the one hand, the state laid claim to holy war (*gaza*), Hanefi Islamic law and universal Sunni caliphate as its governing principles; on the other, high court officials and even sultans could dabble in astrology or millenarianism and patronized a wide spectrum of antinomian sufi mystics. In the sixteenth century, the Ottoman Empire pursued a fierce sectarian war against the Shiite shahs of Iran and their presumed supporters in Anatolia. Yet the expression of 'Alid loyalties remained an integral part of Ottoman religious culture, shared in by Istanbul's intellectual elite, the urban-based *seyyid* class (descendants of the

Prophet), and countless rural communities from the Balkans to the Yemen. The historical experience of the Shiite feudalists of Lebanon, alternately harassed as 'Kızılbaş' heretics and then reinstated as emirs or *mukataacı* taxlords by the state, epitomizes the ambiguities and contradictions in the Ottomans' position vis-à-vis religious heterodoxy and the heterodox communities of the Empire.

The aim of this chapter is to situate the history of western Syria's or Lebanon's Shiites in the context of the Ottoman Empire's more general experience with Islamic heterodoxy and Shiite sectarianism. It will briefly develop three arguments which, though to some extent already established in modern Ottomanist research, will bear directly on our discussion of the Ottomans' attitude towards the Harfush, Hamada and other Shiite feudal families in the later chapters. First, that the state's very equivocal stance towards Shiites and Shiite heterodoxy is deeply ingrained in Ottoman history, in some ways a necessary by-product of the Empire's development. Second, that religious persecution, or persecution in the name of any formal ideology, was part and parcel of the centralization, consolidation and institutionalization of Ottoman authority, particularly in the sixteenth century. And third, that despite this intensification of state control, there continued to be a considerable amount of ambivalence and leeway about Shiism and Shiites in Ottoman culture, Ottoman learned discussion and Ottoman administrative practice. If the Empire, having formally espoused Sunni Islam, could not explicitly tolerate religious dissidence, the pragmatism sometimes shown in accommodating and indeed integrating deviant groups and individuals is no less a defining feature of its history.

## Shiism in Turkish history

Was the Ottoman Empire fundamentally anti-Shiite? In the first half of the sixteenth century, around the time of their conquest of Syria, Egypt, the Hijaz and Iraq and largely in the context of their ideological and political struggle against Safavid Iran, the Ottomans began to assert their right to rule more pronouncedly in terms of religious conservatism, as caliphs and custodians of the Holy Cities, as champions of Sunni legal orthodoxy and as patrons of Islamicate arts and learning. Yet they also remained heirs to a long tradition of confessional liberalism, if not outright heterodox deviance and 'Alid loyalties, that had inspired the Turkmen adventurers and mystics from Central Asia when they first began to penetrate into and colonize Anatolia more than four centuries beforehand. The heritage of this confessional liberalism remained evident in the Ottoman Turks' reverence for the Imams of the Shiite tradition, in their embrace of Bektaşism, in their respect for the holy cities in Iraq and countless other 'Alid shrines across the Balkans and in Anatolia, or in their observance (of course with many local variations) of the mourning ritual of *Ashura*, and necessarily tempered the state's attitude towards the Lebanese and other Shiites well into modern times.

'Shiism' or partisanship for 'Ali ibn Abi Talib (d. 661) and the succession of Twelve Imams is as old as Islam itself. From the very beginning and throughout Islamic history, an important minority of Muslims has maintained that 'Ali, the Prophet Muhammad's cousin and son-in-law, father of his only grandsons Hasan and Husayn, was also his spiritual successor and should have been his only political heir. The forms this partisanship took, however, could vary widely, from outright rebellion against those seeking to organize and rule the Islamic community according to the Prophet's example and traditions (Sunnism), to quiet acquiescence while awaiting the return of a messiah-like Imam to deliver the world from iniquity. With time, Shiism became both the ideology of the disenfranchised, an intra-Islamic opposition ever ready to channel social protest against the powerful, and a religious sect or church in its own right, with a scholastic and legal tradition every bit as institutionalized as that of the rival Sunni majority.

In rural and tribal-dominated areas such as Khorasan (north-eastern Iran), where the Turkmen of Central Asia first came into contact with Islamic civilization, these differences remained largely academic. Here, 'Shiism' above all entailed a popular devotion to 'Ali and Husayn as the warrior champions and tragic heroes of early Islam. Along with Abu Muslim, who in 749 CE led the revolution from Khorasan that would install the Abbasids in Baghdad, only to be betrayed and murdered by them, and al-Hallaj, the Turko-Iranian sufi philosopher who was executed by the same dynasty for his alleged pantheism in 927, the Shiite martyrs exemplified the valour, moral rectitude and free-spiritedness so highly regarded by the Turkmen tribes. Their conversion to Islam in this period was achieved largely through the efforts not of textual scholars (*ulema*) expounding the finer points of Koranic exegesis and *shari'a* law, but by charismatic sufi dervishes whose cult of Muslim saint worship, mystical divination and millenarianism spoke more directly to the steppe mindset.[1] In this context, Shiite inclinations (*tashayyu'*) and 'Alid loyalties were not an express negation of Sunni orthodoxy but rather the natural mode of a non-literate, non-sectarian folk Islam. The Turkmen whose westward migration in the medieval period would so change the course of world history could very well be formally Sunni and affectively Shiite at the same time.

This dualism or 'confessional ambiguity', to use John Woods' term, was nowhere more in evidence than among the great nomad confederations that dominated Iran and western Asia after the great Timurid conquests of the fourteenth century. Timur himself alternately presented himself as a defender of Sunnism and of Shiism; the leaders of the Karakoyunlu Turkmen who controlled the region from Lake Van to Baghdad were decried by contemporaries as *ghulat* (extreme) Shiites but never actually adopted formal Shiite doctrines; the powerful Akkoyunlu confederation, from whose ranks many of the Kızılbaş would later be drawn, patronized both Sunni and militantly Shiite sufi orders, including the Safavids of Ardabil.[2] Confessional ambiguity was also the norm throughout Anatolia after the Turkmen invasions.

[1] Mehmet Fuat Köprülü, *Islam in Anatolia after the Turkish Invasion (Prolegomena)*. Trans. and ed. Gary Leiser (Salt Lake City: University of Utah Press, 1993), 3–15; Ahmet Karamustafa, *God's Unruly Friends: Dervish Groups in the Islamic Later Middle Period, 1200–1550* (Salt Lake City: University of Utah Press, 1994).

[2] Michel Mazzaoui, *The Origins of the Safawids: Šī'ism, Ṣūfism and the Ġulāt* (Wiesbaden: Franz Steiner, 1972), 63–6; John Woods, *The Aqquyunlu: Clan, Confederation, Empire* (2nd edn, Salt Lake City: University of Utah Press, 1999), 3–10, 83.

Many mid-size artisan and trading towns such as Ankara or Kırşehir were run by the *ahi* brotherhoods, local craftsman corporations which, much like the medieval Islamic *futuwwa* guilds on which they were modelled, adhered to a code of moral conduct and urban self-governance that was replete with Shiite symbolism and values without repudiating orthodox religious practice and *shari'a* law. Among the tribes, the more esoteric (*batini*) Ismaili form of Shiism, as well as the Kabbalah-like Hurufi sect and any number of nonconformist sufi movements, could fuel the periodic millenarian revolts against the Saljuq dynasty in Konya, which would in retrospect be identified with conventional Sunni Islam.[3] 'Maybe the religious history of Anatolian and Balkan Muslims living in the frontier areas of the period from the eleventh to the fifteenth centuries should be conceptualized in terms of a metadoxy,' Cemal Kafadar has written in the most fluid synthesis to date of the Ottoman Empire's religious origins, 'a state of being beyond doxies, a combination of being doxy-naive and not being doxy-minded, as well as the absence of a state that was interested in rigorously defining and strictly enforcing an orthodoxy ... It was much later that a debate emerged among Ottoman scholars and statesmen with respect to the correctness of some of the practices of their ancestors.'[4]

### The Ottoman emirate, the Janissaries and Bektaşi sufism

Of all the Turkmen *beğlik*s (principalities) to crop up in Anatolia in the late medieval period, the Ottomans were destined to play a special role by their geographic proximity to the Byzantine capital Constantinople and to Europe beyond. From their home base in Bithynia (whose capital, Izmid, they captured in 1337), the Ottomans were in constant contact with Byzantium, alternately allying or fighting with one or the other of its rival ruling dynasties. This enabled the Ottomans to cross over and begin expanding in Europe, and then to turn against and supplant one by one the remaining Turkmen principalities of Anatolia, ostensibly to be better able to pursue *gaza* or holy war against the Christians. From very early on, the Ottomans thus found themselves in the slightly ambivalent situation of leading an offensive against Christendom which they would justify in the name of Islam, by attracting and employing the sort of tribal adventurers whose allegiance to any form of Islamic or dynastic authority was by nature volatile.

As in Khorasan and western Asia before, the Turkmen who spearheaded the Ottomans' drive into the Balkans and Anatolia were more inspired by a vaguely Shiite folk Islam than by formal religion. Many times, their campaigns were accompanied or guided by Bektaşi dervishes, spiritual heirs of the thirteenth-century sufi 'saint' Hacci Bektaş Veli, himself a native of Khorasan. Little is known of the historical Hacci Bektaş, whose life is the subject of countless popular

[3] Köprülü, *Islam in Anatolia*; Ahmet Yaşar Ocak, *La révolte de Baba Resul: La formation de l'hétérodoxie musulmane en Anatolie au XIIIe siècle* (Ankara: Türk Tarih Kurumu, 1989).
[4] Cemal Kafadar, *Between Two Worlds: The Construction of the Ottoman State* (Berkeley: University of California Press, 1995), 76.

legends and Turkish poetry and who remains a focus of Alevi piety in Turkey (and parts of Bulgaria and Albania) down to the present day. Like many contemporaries he held the Shiite Twelve Imams in special esteem, but he is also famous in Turkmen lore for his magical abilities, his closeness to nature and his contacts with other leading mystics of the age.[5] Many of the teachings and practices associated with Bektaşism in fact resembled those of Christian folk religion, and Bektaşi missionaries are thought to have played a key role in converting Christians in newly conquered Byzantine lands to Islam. Numerous modern studies have posited Turkish Shamanist as well as heterodox Christian influences in Bektaşism, and have asked whether its 'syncretic' belief system in fact served to integrate the disparate rural Christian and Muslim populations of the Ottoman realm.[6]

Like most such debates, the question of Bektaşism's presumed Turkmen and Balkan roots (ultimately, what universalist religion is not to some degree syncretic?) says as much about the ideological stakes of modern historiography as it does about the Ottomans' socio-cultural origins. Certainly Ottoman scholars and statesmen even of later years saw no contradiction in accommodating and indeed incorporating Bektaşism with all its heterodox overtones into the Empire's foundational institutions. In the fourteenth and fifteenth centuries the Ottoman dynasty supported numerous Bektaşi lodges (*zaviye*) throughout Anatolia and the Balkans by establishing Islamic religious foundations (*vakıf*) in their favour, despite the controversial and unmistakeably Shiite character of some of the order's rituals and cult. The geographic spread of these lodges also corresponded by and large to the areas affected by the Kızılbaş revolts of the sixteenth century, yet the Bektaşi order as such was not implicated in the revolts and is never mentioned in the context of the Ottomans' persecution of other suspected Shiites in this period.[7] The parent monastery at the Hacci Bektaş mausoleum in central Anatolia may have been shut down briefly in 1577–8 but overall the Bektaşis are conspicuous by their absence in Ottoman government documentation (other than tax records). A single order sent to the *kadı* (judge) of Aleppo in 1616, for example, notes that the Baba Bayram *zaviye* just outside the city had been taken over by dervishes who were 'pretending outwardly' to be followers of Hacci Bektaş Veli but who were 'in reality' adherents of apostasy and heresy (*ilhad u zandaka*).[8] The Bektaşi order itself was never seen as insufficiently orthodox or as a threat by the state authorities.

[5]   John Birge, *The Bektashi Order of Dervishes* (repr. London: Luzac, 1994); Matti Moosa, *Extremist Shiites: The Ghulat Sects* (Syracuse University Press, 1988), 10–20; Irène Mélikoff, *Hadji Bektach, un mythe et ses avatars* (Leiden: Brill, 1998); Karamustafa, *God's Unruly Friends*, 83–4.
[6]   Kafadar, *Between Two Worlds*, 75; Yuri Stoyanov, 'On Some Parallels between Anatolian and Balkan Heterodox Islamic and Christian Traditions and the Problem of their Coexistence and Interaction in the Ottoman Period' in Gilles Veinstein, ed., *Syncrétismes et hérésies dans l'Orient seldjoukide et ottoman (XIVe–XVIIIe siècle): Actes du Colloque du Collège de France, octobre 2001* (Paris: Peeters, 2005), 96–8.
[7]   Suraiya Faroqhi, *Der Bektaschi-Orden in Anatolien (vom späten fünfzehnten Jahrhundert bis 1826)* (Vienna: Institut für Orientalistik der Universität Wien, 1981), 38–46; see also Irène Beldiceanu-Steinherr, 'Les Bektaşī à la lumière des recensements ottomans (XVe–XVIe siècles)', *Wiener Zeitschrift für die Kunde des Morgenlandes* 81 (1991), 21–80.
[8]   Başbakanlık Archives: Mühimme Defteri (MD) 81:28. The Mühimme registers and other executive sources, however, do make frequent reference to the Bekdaşlo tribe, which Irène Beldiceanu-Steinherr

The Bektaşis' association with the Janissary corps is perhaps the most striking case of the Ottomans' openness to Shiism or quasi-Shiism. The Janissary (Yeni Çeri; 'New Army') corps was composed mainly of Christian prisoners of war and other converts, often recruited at a very young age, who were all technically slaves of the Ottoman household. Created in the late fourteenth century, it would eventually constitute the Empire's main infantry army and provide most of its military and administrative cadres. Like the frontier *gazis* before, the young men who essentially grew up in the Janissary corps were attended to by Bektaşi sufis and adopted Bektaşism not only as a private mystical devotion, but as a warrior ethos and a code of conduct. In their military ceremonies the Janissaries would invoke Hacci Bektaş as well as 'Ali and the Twelve Imams, and 'Ali's mythical two-pronged sword Dhu'l-Fiqar was emblazoned on all the corps' standards.[9] The Dhu'l-Fiqar symbol in Islam still awaits a thorough heraldic study, but Jane Hathaway's research on the formation of Janissary factions in Egypt suggests that it may indeed have been the Ottoman soldiery who initially disseminated it throughout the Arab Middle East.[10] Today it is the crest of the Shiite sectarian community in the entire region. Again, the Ottoman state in the classical period saw no problem with the use of 'Alid or Shiite-tinged symbols and rituals by its own army; it was only with the suppression of the increasingly mutinous Janissary division in 1826 that it decided the Bektaşi order was too unorthodox as well.

## The Kızılbaş challenge

The confessional ambiguity that was tolerated and in some ways institutionalized in the early Ottoman Empire would fall victim to the centralization of state power in the late fifteenth and sixteenth centuries. If the frontier ethos had previously permeated through the highest echelons of Ottoman authority (and continued to influence some of its maverick princes), after the conquest of Constantinople in 1453 the sultanate became increasingly determined to assert its fiscal but also its juridical and political control over the farthest reaches of the Empire. The resulting Kızılbaş revolts, a series of millenarian anti-state uprisings by the heterodox rural population of Anatolia that culminated in the establishment of a militantly Shiite rival state in neighbouring Iran, forced for perhaps the first time in Islamic history the 'sharp delineation' of Sunni and Shiite doctrinal schools.[11] In doing so, they also changed forever how the Ottoman state would define and treat Muslim heterodox minorities living within its own borders.

---

('Les Bektašī') has connected with the origins of Bektaşi sufism but which has not yet been subject to further investigation. At least in the period presently under consideration, the Bekdaşlo appear as a Kurdish tribe mainly based north-west of Aleppo.

[9] Birge, *The Bektashi Order*, 46–8, 74–6.

[10] Jane Hathaway, *A Tale of Two Factions: Myth, Memory and Identity in Ottoman Egypt and Yemen* (Albany: State University of New York Press, 2003).

[11] The term 'mezhep farkı keskinleştirme' is borrowed from Taha Akyol, *Osmanlı'da ve İran'da Mezhep ve Devlet* (Istanbul: Milliyet Yayınları, 1999), 68.

The Kızılbaş or 'redheads,' so named for the red, twelve-pleated tuque (supposedly for the Twelve Imams) which they wore, were the Anatolian tribal followers of the Safavi sufi order of Ardabil, in what is now Azerbaijan. Like the Bektaşis, the Safavis had long been the recipients of Ottoman subsidies, and it was only in the mid-fifteenth century that their leaders stepped forward with the *ghuluw* ('immoderate') claim of physically incarnating 'Ali and of initiating a new dispensation of divine rule on earth. This was not the first time that Ottoman rule had been contested by millenarian religious revolts in the far provinces, but the sheer number of tribes involved in the Kızılbaş movement, and the magnitude of the state's response, suggest that the dynamics of early modern state-building and centre–periphery relations were as much at issue here as simple religious freedoms.[12] Archival evidence that has recently come to light suggests that the Ottomans did not even refer to the Safavids' followers as 'Kızılbaş' prior to the conquest of Tabriz in 1501, perceiving the revolt as a purely tribal problem and not as a religious or ideological threat to their sovereignty.[13]

This is not the place to delve deeper into the history of the Kızılbaş movement, which has been dealt with in many studies of Ottoman and Iranian history.[14] After 1501 the Ottomans attempted to prevent the Safavids from recruiting more followers on Ottoman soil, deporting numerous Kızılbaş tribes to the Balkans and Cyprus, and closing the frontier with Iran. Naturally this only fomented even more rebellion among the Turkmen, who considered the young Safavid shah Ismail to be an avatar of 'Ali and who were willing to sacrifice themselves for his cause; the Kızılbaş-inspired Şahkulı uprising of 1511–12 led to the abdication of the Ottoman sultan Bayezid II in favour of his violently anti-Shiite son Selim I, who set out to crush the Safavid-Kızılbaş forces in the battle of Çaldıran on the border of Anatolia and Iran in 1514. The consequences of this first Ottoman–Safavid war were far-reaching: despite the defeat and in some ways the discrediting of Ismail as a divine leader, the Safavid regime was now firmly entrenched in Iran with the Kızılbaş forming its military and political elite. Upon seizing power in Tabriz, Shah Ismail had declared Twelver Shiism to be their official state religion, and, as such, Iran would remain the Ottoman Empire's ideological opponent, and very often its real enemy, well into the nineteenth century.

Syria, a term which we will use here in the general geographic sense, as well as Egypt and northern Mesopotamia were conquered and annexed to the Ottoman Empire by Selim in 1515–17, almost as an afterthought to the Çaldıran campaign. The reasons behind Selim's unexpected attack on (and extirpation of) the Mamluk

---

[12] Fariba Zarinebaf-Shahr, 'Qizilbash "Heresy" and Rebellion in Ottoman Anatolia during the Sixteenth Century', *Anatolia Moderna* 7 (1997), 1–15.

[13] Gilles Veinstein, 'Les premières mesures de Bâyezîd II contre les Kızılbaş' in Veinstein, ed., *Syncrétismes et hérésies*, 225–36.

[14] See especially Hanna Sohrweide, 'Der Sieg der Safaviden in Persien und seine Rückwirkung auf die Schiiten Anatoliens im 16. Jahrhundert', *Der Islam* 41 (1965), 95–223; Kathryn Babayan, *Mystics, Monarchs and Messiahs: Cultural Landscapes of Early Modern Iran* (Cambridge, Mass.: Harvard Center for Middle East Studies, 2002).

sultanate were manifold. In Cairo the Ottomans subsequently had Shah Ismail cursed from the pulpit, and circulated rumours, however unlikely, that the Mamluks had been Shiite sympathizers.[15] More fundamentally, however, the integration of 'Arabistan', which included the Muslim holy cities Mecca and Medina, just like the defeat of the Safavids and the incorporation of the autonomous emirates of Kurdistan at the same time, served to consolidate the Ottoman state's dominion over the entire Near East, and would allow the government to turn its attention to controlling, disciplining and integrating the Empire's subject population.

The sharp delineation of Islamic doctrinal schools (*madhhab*; *mezheb*) that resulted from the Kızılbaş revolution went hand in hand with unprecedented measures of social engineering in the Ottoman Empire. Forty thousand Kızılbaş tribesmen (i.e. an indefinitely large number) are said to have been massacred by Selim or subjected to *sürgün*, the practice of deporting entire tribes or village populations to remote areas which they would help populate and develop while at the same time being removed as a threat in their original homes.[16] More portentously, the Kızılbaş and other heterodox groups began to be persecuted on the sole basis of their religious beliefs – a veritable inquisition that is documented by, and that indeed makes tangible, the new apparatus of state control and legal repression in the sixteenth-century Ottoman Empire. The *Umur-ı Mühimme Defterleri* or 'registers of important state affairs', the premier compilation of executive orders sent out to the Empire's provincial authorities to deal with cases of rebellion, heresy, tax evasion or war, began to be kept in the second half of the century during the reign of Kanuni Süleyman. Even more than the imperial chronicles, these detail the near obsession of the central government at this time with finding and punishing Kızılbaş. The *Mühimme* decrees studied by Colin Imber and others mainly focus on individuals suspected of being fifth-column collaborators of Iran, but they also bespeak a new concern on the part of the state with detecting and then sanctioning the very essence of 'Alid religiosity and identity among the Anatolian rural population, such as the holding of mixed night-time religious gatherings, the celebration of *Ashura* in commemoration of the Shiite martyrs and the refusal to name children for the three orthodox caliphs of the Sunni tradition.[17]

Yet the Ottomans' concern over their subjects' inner religious beliefs would be short-lived (and arguably not surface again until the Hamidian period). After the sixteenth century, even in times of war with Iran, the Anatolian tribes' potential

---

[15] Adel Allouche, *The Origins and Development of the Ottoman–Safavid Conflict (906–962/ 1500–1555)* (Berlin: Klaus Schwarz, 1983), 88, 128.

[16] On *sürgün* in the sixteenth century see Hüseyin Arslan, *Osmanlı'da Nüfus Hareketleri (XVI. Yüzyıl): Yönetim, Nüfus, Göçler, İskânlar, Sürgünler* (Üsküdar: Kaknüs Yayınları, 2001). Similar massacres are said to have been committed against Shiites during the Ottoman conquest of Aleppo, but these cannot be substantiated historically and in any event the city counted very few Shiites at the time.

[17] Colin Imber, 'The Persecution of the Ottoman Shiites according to the Mühimme Defterleri, 1565–1585', *Der Islam* 56 (1979), 245–73; Zarinebaf-Shahr, 'Qizilbash "Heresy"'.

heterodoxy no longer features as a subject of concern in the *Mühimme* or other chancery decrees. The Kızılbaş challenge, it seems, was very much about the dialectics of state centralization and religious deviance at a very specific moment in time: the more the Anatolian rural population resisted creeping bureaucratic and fiscal control, in the late fifteenth and sixteenth centuries, in the name of a traditionally nonconformist religious identity, the greater the state's determination to categorize and interdict that identity as heresy. The result, seen over the long term, was not so much the humiliation or even the marginalization of the Empire's non-Sunni Muslim minorities, which continued to thrive under Ottoman rule, as a change in the way the Ottoman state exercised authority over its subject populations. If the Kızılbaş revolts served to polarize Sunni and Shiite sectarian identities and eliminate the grey areas of confessional ambiguity in Ottoman society, they also brought the problematic relationship between heterodoxy, tribalism and provincial governance to the forefront of the imperial state's concerns.

## Ebu's-Suud: the formation of a persecuting society?

Whenever the Ottoman state authorities became enmeshed in conflict with the Hamadas, Harfushes or other Shiite taxlords in the Lebanese highlands, as will be seen in later chapters, they would refer to them and more specifically to their tribal followers as 'accursed Kızılbaş whose destruction is an incumbent religious duty'. Several chancery documents pertaining to military campaigns against the Syrian/Lebanese Shiites in the seventeenth and eighteenth centuries would refer explicitly to 'a noble *fetva*' (Islamic legal ruling) that had been 'given in respect to this sort of people'.[18] Were the Hamadas and Harfushes personally the subject of *fetva*s issued in Istanbul; did the Ottoman authorities perceive them as a religious and political threat akin to that of the Anatolian Kızılbaş? A more likely explanation, in the absence of any Ottoman religious texts dealing specifically with the Lebanese Shiites, is that their categorization as 'Kızılbaş' was a legal artifice, an invocation of a famous but deliberately vague *fetva* pronounced by the Ottoman chief *müfti* Ebu's-Suud Efendi in 1548, each time the state authorities needed to justify shedding the blood of rebellious Shiite subjects.

Heterodox belief, it has been said, becomes heresy only when the authorities find it useful to define it as intolerable.[19] Ottoman theologians had of course always been versed in Sunnism's heresiographical tradition, but it is precisely in the context of the Empire's growing conflict with the Safavids that the condemnation of Shiism became a matter of political import. In a formal legal opinion solicited by Sultan Selim in 1512, the jurisconsult Hamza Saru Görez first declared 'the Kızılbaş faction' to be infidels and enemies of the faith. 'To crush them and disperse their numbers is a duty incumbent on the Muslim community.' The ruling, which bears close similarities to Ibn Taymiyya's and other classical writings

---

[18] MD 105:5, 6, 9, 10; MD 140:311. See also p. 109 below.
[19] R. I. Moore, *The Formation of a Persecuting Society* (Oxford: Blackwell, 1987).

against Shiism, explicitly invites 'the sultan of Islam' to kill all male heretics without accepting their repentance, and to 'divide their wealth, women and children among the warriors of the faith'.[20] A treatise from the same period by the famous legal scholar İbn-i Kemal (d. 1535) is even more universal in its condemnation of Shiites. While repeating the standard injunction that effectively strips all apostates of their Islamic identity, thus permitting their extermination and the seizure of their goods and families, İbn-i Kemal significantly does not utilize the derogatory term 'Kızılbaş' specific to the Anatolian tribes, but speaks instead of the duty to combat 'a faction of Shiites' that has 'conquered many lands of the Sunnis in order to establish their false doctrines'.[21]

The definitive statement on Ottoman Shiism, and that most cited in later centuries, would be the *fetva*s produced by Ebu's-Suud Efendi (d. 1574), the *müfti* of Istanbul whose consecration as *şeyhü'l-İslam* (chief jurisconsult) under Sultan Kanuni ('the lawgiver') Süleyman marked the culmination of efforts to bring Sunni Islamic law in line with Ottoman *raison d'état*.[22] Ebu's-Suud's *fetva*s placed religious sanctions on a wide range of behaviour deemed deleterious to public order, from drunkenness and pronouncing frivolous oaths to public celebrations of the Hızır-St-Elias feast (especially popular among Balkan Alevis) and of course outright denigrations of the faith, claims to be Jesus, or other manifestations of *zandaka* (materialist atheism; heresy). His systematization of the categories of unbelief and apostasy became key to the prosecution of enemies of the state; Ahmet Yaşar Ocak, in his far-ranging study on *zandaka* in the Ottoman Empire, and other historians describe him as the linchpin in the elaboration of the Empire's 'official ideology' of Sunnism in the sixteenth century.[23]

A close look at Ebu's-Suud's *fetva*s on the Kızılbaş, however, suggests that they afforded the state authorities more leeway in the persecution of Shiites than might be assumed. In several related responsa he rules unequivocally that spilling Kızılbaş blood is licit inasmuch as they are generally infidel and have 'drawn the sword against the army of Islam'.[24] However, he skirts the one question that explicitly deals with Shiism: 'The said [Kızılbaş] faction claim they are of the Shi'a and pronounce the statement of faith "There is no God but God." What is to

---

[20]  Turkish transcription in M. C. Şahabeddin Tekindağ, 'Yeni Kaynak ve Vesikaların Işığı altında Yavuz Sultan Selim'in İran Seferi', *Tarih Dergisi* 22 (1967), 54–5.

[21]  Arabic transcription in *ibid.*, 77–8.

[22]  See R.C. Repp, *The Müfti of Istanbul: A Study in the Development of the Ottoman Learned Hierarchy* (London: Ithaca Press, 1986), 272–304; Cornell Fleischer, *Bureaucrat and Intellectual in the Ottoman Empire: The Historian Mustafa Âlî (1541–1600)* (Princeton University Press, 1986); Colin Imber, *Ebu's-su'ud: The Islamic Legal Tradition* (Stanford University Press, 1997).

[23]  Ahmet Yaşar Ocak, *Osmanlı Toplumunda Zındıklar ve Mülhidler (15.–17. Yüzyıllar)* (Istanbul: Türkiye Ekonomik ve Tarih Vakfı, 1998). See also Ismail Safa Üstün, 'Heresy and Legitimacy in the Ottoman Empire in the Sixteenth Century' (University of Manchester doctoral thesis, 1991); Nabil Al-Tikriti, 'Kalam in the Service of the State: Apostasy and the Defining of Ottoman Islamic Identity' in Hakan Karateke and Maurus Reinkowski, eds., *Legitimizing the Order: The Ottoman Rhetoric of State Power* (Leiden: Brill, 2005), 131–49.

[24]  M. Ertuğrul Düzdağ, ed. *Şeyhülislâm Ebussu'ûd Efendi'nin Fetvalarına göre Kanunî Devrinde Osmanlı Hayatı: Fetâvâ-yı Ebussu'ûd Efendî* (Istanbul: Şûle Yayınları, 1998), 173–6.

be made of them?' Here Ebu's-Suud responds that the issue is not whether or not the Kızılbaş are 'of the Shiites',[25] but that they clearly do not belong to the one sect among the seventy-three which, according to a Prophetic tradition, will be safe from hellfire. The implication for other Shiites, whom Ebu's-Suud never expounds on as such, is that they are not necessarily counted among the seventy-two errant sects and not a priori included in the execution order against the Kızılbaş. It would in fact be at the discretion of later Ottoman government officials to label the Lebanese and other rebellious Shiites having no organic link to the Anatolian Turkmen as 'Kızılbaş' when the situation required. More or less defensible from a theological point of view, the assimilation of Twelver Shiites to the sect authoritatively proscribed by Ebu's-Suud provided a convenient legal framework for killing known Shiites guilty of more mundane crimes such as banditry and tax evasion. The decision when to invoke the statutory *fetva* and fight the Shiites as 'Kızılbaş', and when to quietly ignore their confessional identity and reinstate them as emirs and tax farmers, depended on factors other than religious ideology.

## Shiism in Ottoman thought

The legally ambivalent term 'Shi'a' is almost never encountered in Ottoman administrative correspondence; it would arguably not surface again in state discourse until 1736, when Iran's Nadir Shah sought – unsuccessfully – to have the Ottomans recognize Ja'fari (Shiite) jurisprudence as the 'fifth *madhhab*' (legal school) of orthodox Islam as a basis for peace between the two empires.[26] For the Ottomans, the touchstone of Shiism as intolerable heresy was always its quality of *rafz*, or 'rejection' of the Sunni tradition, and identifiably Shiite individuals or groups are consistently characterized by the pejorative term 'Rafizi' in Ottoman texts. The origins of the appellation are complex,[27] but popularly Rafizis (*Rafidi*s, or *Rawafid* in Arabic) were seen as rejecting the Sunni caliphs Abu Bakr and 'Umar, mainly by way of deliberately offensive, public calumniation (*sebb*). What was intolerable about Shiism in a predominantly Sunni setting was thus generally not its abstract theological and doctrinal implications, but real or imagined attacks by its adherents against the majority's communal honour and identity. Persecutions of Shiites in medieval Syria, for example, can be shown to have almost always revolved around the question of whether the two caliphs had been insulted or not.[28] Apart from evident political crises such as the Anatolian Kızılbaş revolts, the Sunni clerical establishment, much less the Ottoman state authorities, rarely made it their

---

[25] 'Şia'dan değil', in other variants 'Şia olmak değil'.

[26] Ernest Tucker, 'Nadir Shah and the Ja'fari *Madhhab* Reconsidered', *Iranian Studies* 27 (1994), 163–79.

[27] Etan Kohlberg, 'The Term "Rāfiḍa" in Imāmī Shī'ī Usage', *Journal of the American Oriental Society* 99 (1979), 677–9.

[28] Stefan Winter, 'Shams al-Dīn Muḥammad ibn Makkī 'al-Shahīd al-Awwal' (d. 1384) and the Shī'ah of Syria', *Mamluk Studies Review* 3 (1999), 159–82; see also Anne Broadbridge, 'Apostasy Trials in Eighth/Fourteenth Century Egypt and Syria: A Case Study' in Judith Pfeiffer and Sholeh Quinn, eds., *History and Historiography of Post-Mongol Central Asia and the Middle East: Studies in Honor of John E. Woods* (Wiesbaden: Harrassowitz, 2006), 363–82.

business to inquire into the hearts and minds of Muslims simply in order to discover and uproot heretical belief.

It is by no means certain that there ever existed, even in the sixteenth century, a single, clear-cut consensus among Ottoman *ulema* (religious scholars) as to Muslims of Shiite persuasion. Historians have identified numerous anti-Shiite polemical treatises written in the context of the Empire's constant struggle with Safavid Iran. Much like the *fetva*s, most of these texts are highly formulaic refutations (*redd*) of the Shiite faith and condemn the Safavids' political venture, but betray not the slightest anthropological interest in the vast population of heterodox subjects living in the Ottoman realm. While they may generally have reflected the opinion of educated Ottomans on Shiism,[29] it should not escape notice either that their authors were all salaried government officials or, in several prominent cases studied by Elke Eberhard, highborn political exiles from Safavid lands seeking patronage and backing at the Ottoman court. This again raises the problem with what sort of sources the history of Ottoman Shiism is to be written. Whereas religious tracts and narrative chronicles are by nature quick to point up opposition and conflict, informal tolerance and reasonable accommodation were far less likely to leave a literary imprint.

There is evidence that other Ottoman scholars whose works have not been utilized to the same degree held more nuanced and indeed controversial views of Shiism. As early as 1589, the bureaucrat and historian Mustafa Âli wrote a treatise which in part criticized his colleagues' preoccupation with the Safavids' religious doctrines and pleaded for greater harmony between Sunni and 'Alevi' Muslims.[30] From the mid-seventeenth century we have indications of an acrimonious but as yet obscure dispute over the nature of Shiite deviancy. Around 1655, a treatise seems to have circulated which defended or at least sought to qualify the heterodoxy of rural Anatolians in sociological terms. No longer extant, the echo of this piece can be found in a rebuttal which itself has attracted very little attention so far. *Al-Yamaniyyat al-Maslula 'ala 'l-Rawafid al-Makhdhula* ('Yemenite swords uptaken against the heretics godforsaken') exists in two versions: as a unique 99-folio Arabic manuscript at the Bibliothèque Nationale in Paris[31] and as an untitled twelve-folio summary in a manuscript compendium at the Berlin Staatsbibliothek.[32] The author of the longer version is identified as Zayn al-'Abidin Yusuf ibn Muhammad al-Kurani (Gorani), an otherwise unknown

---

[29] Elke Eberhard, *Osmanische Polemik gegen die Safawiden im 16. Jahrhundert nach arabischen Handschriften* (Freiburg i.Br.: Klaus Schwarz, 1970); also J. H. Mordtmann, 'Sunnitisch-schiitische Polemik im 17. Jahrhundert', *Mitteilungen des Seminars für orientalische Sprachen an der Friedrich-Wilhelms-Universität zu Berlin; 2. Abteilung (westasiatische Sprachen)* 29 (1926), 112–29.

[30] Cornell Fleischer, 'Mustafâ Âlî's *Curious Bits of Wisdom*', *Wiener Zeitschrift für die Kunde des Morgenlandes* 76 (1986; Andreas Tietze Festschrift), 104, 108. This appears to be the earliest, isolated, use of the term 'Alevi', normally derived from the French mandate authorities' designation of Syrian Nusayris as 'Alawites' (Alaouites) in the twentieth century, for the Anatolian Kızılbaş Shiites.

[31] Bibliothèque Nationale (Richelieu), Paris: Ms. Arabe 1462.

[32] Staatsbibliothek Preußischer Kulturbesitz, Berlin: Ms. Or. 2132. It is wrongly attributed to the sixteenth-century fundamentalist Birgevi Mehmed; see Wilhelm Ahlwardt, *Verzeichniss der arabischen Handschriften der Königlichen Bibliothek zu Berlin* (Berlin: A. Asher, 1889), II:467.

scholar who, judging by his last name, may well have been another refugee from Safavid-occupied Kurdistan. The Berlin manuscript was 'written and composed' by (*katabaha wa-harraraha*) a molla Husayn al-Ghurabi, but is identical in content matter with the longer Paris manuscript. Both versions are dedicated to Sultan Mehmed son of İbrahim, and his grand vizier Ahmed Paşa, dating its composition to the period 1661–76. The text does not dwell on the Kızılbaş as such but seeks to elucidate the beliefs of 'the reprehensible Shi'a' and the transgressions (cursing the caliphs, etc.) for which some scholars excommunicate them from Islam (*takfir*). Other scholars, however, would apparently 'excommunicate the excommunicators ... and think that the occurrence of such crimes is rarer than a vulture's egg or as remote as the night stars'. The author attempts to correct this misperception in a lengthy if rather conventional exposé of the Shiites' foul beliefs and the judgements rendered against them by the classical scholars of Sunnism. The last two chapters defend the *fetva*s of past Ottoman scholars legitimizing the persecution of the Kızılbaş against the criticism of the unidentified seventeenth-century voice of moderation. The nature of this dissent and the resulting controversy become most evident in the conclusion, where the author insists that 'whoever rebukes or finds fault with them over their *fetva*s, like one of our contemporaries, is wrong ...'. He concedes that some respectable scholars defended the older Safavids and their tribal followers, excusing them as 'antinomians' (adepts of *ta'wil*) who nonetheless do pronounce the Muslim attestation of faith (*shahada*) and pray towards Mecca, and noting that 'many of their common folk who live in tents simply do not know the *shahada*, nor how to pray, nor the direction of Mecca, [being] like dumb beasts without religious or moral restraint'. The author himself rejects this relativist argument, maintaining that the Kızılbaş are infidels if only because they hold true Muslims to be such. Even he, however, appears to agree that heresy and unbelief can be mitigated: 'It is certainly correct that those who are ignorant are closer to salvation than those who are in error.'[33]

Colin Imber in his study on 'The Persecution of the Ottoman Shiites' has argued that 'Ebu's-su'ud's distinction between the *shi'a* and the *kızılbaş* would be academic and, in any case, it is virtually impossible to distinguish the various strands of Ottoman *shi'ism*.'[34] This failure to distinguish may be true of the Ottoman judicature in concrete (though inherently rare) instances of organized state violence against Shiites, when it had every interest in including them without qualification in Ebu's-Suud's definition of illegal heretics. However, it is apparently less true of those classically trained scholars who were well aware of the many strands of Shiism (Twelver, Kızılbaş, Zaydi, Ismaili, Nusayri, Druze ...) existing in the Empire, who chose to interpret religious heterodoxy as a sociological phenomenon or who advised against overemphasizing sectarian divisions. And it is hardly true of the many Ottoman government officials, imperial as well as provincial, who were well appraised of the confessional identity of their charges, but chose not to make an issue of it in day-to-day administration. The Ottoman Empire's 'policy' on

---

[33] *Ibid.*, fol. 39a–40b.    [34] Imber, 'Persecution', 245.

Shiism was not fixed for all time in a sixteenth-century *fetva* or any other religious text, but morphed and adapted constantly according to specific, usually local, contingencies.

## The Shiites of Jabal 'Amil and the clerical migration to Iran

How did Shiites and Shiite society fare under day-to-day Ottoman rule? Even at the height of the Empire's tensions with the Safavids and their Anatolian supporters, entire Kızılbaş communities were settled in the Balkans and continued to grow; Twelver Shiite scholars and pilgrims from Iran and elsewhere freely travelled to or settled in Syria and the Hijaz; Shiite notable families occasionally governed important regional centres such as Medina or Lahsa; and in the Yemen, the Ottomans repeatedly had to come to some sort of accommodation with the indomitable Zaydi imams.[35] The most prominent Ottoman Shiite community, at least in terms of historical visibility, was that of Jabal 'Amil in what is today south Lebanon. Jabal 'Amil is thought to constitute one of the oldest Twelver communities in the Arab world and has since the Middle Ages produced an impressive succession of theologians and legal specialists whose works have become cornerstones of the Shiite scholastic tradition. In the course of the sixteenth century, up to a hundred Jabal 'Amil-born scholars emigrated to Iran to benefit from Safavid patronage and help institutionalize Twelver Shiism as the new state religion. Here the "Amilis' and their descendants formed a clerical elite which would have a profound impact on Iran's religious and political history as well as on the evolution of Shiite thought. Their migration, which spawned a vast output of Shiite scholarly and biographical literature down to the present day, has thus also become an essential part of Lebanese Shiite identity – as a source of pride in the community's past significance, as the seed of its social and ideological ties to Iran and the Shiite world at large, and as evidence of its supposed oppression by the Sunni Ottoman state.[36]

There is of course a problem in relying on the stories of individual émigré scholars who rose to fame as Safavid state officials to document the situation of Shiites back in the Ottoman Empire. In an important revisionist essay, Andrew Newman has sought to explode 'The Myth of the Clerical Migration to Safawid Iran' by arguing that all but a minority of 'Amili scholars rejected Shah Ismail's

---

[35] Marco Salati, 'Toleration, Persecution and Local Realities: Observations on the Shiism in the Holy Places and the *Bilād al-Shām* (Sixteenth–Seventeenth Centuries)' in *La Shi'a nell'Impero Ottomano* (Rome: Accademia Nazionale dei Lincei, 1993), 123–32; Abdul-Rahim Abu-Husayn, 'The Shiites in Lebanon and the Ottomans in the Sixteenth and Seventeenth Centuries' in *ibid.*, 107–19; Juan Cole, *Sacred Space and Holy War: The Politics, Culture and History of Shi'ite Islam* (London: I. B. Tauris, 2002), 4–5, 18–24, 31–57; Werner Ende, 'The *Nakhāwila*, a Shiite Community in Medina: Past and Present', *Die Welt des Islam* 37 (1997), 267–91.

[36] Rula Abisaab, 'The Ulama of Jabal 'Amil in Safavid Iran, 1501–1736: Marginality, Migration and Social Change', *Iranian Studies* 27 (1994), 103–22. See also Albert Hourani, 'From Jabal 'Āmil to Persia', *Bulletin of the School of Oriental and African Studies* 49 (1986), 133–40; 'Ali Muruwwa, *al-Tashayyu' bayna Jabal 'Amil wa-Iran* (London: Riad al-Rayyes, 1987); Ja'far al-Muhajir, *al-Hijra al-'Amiliyya ila Iran fi'l-'Asr al-Safawi: Asbabuha al-Tarikhiyya wa-Nata'ijuha al-Thaqafiyya wa'l-Siyasiyya* (Beirut: Dar al-Rawda, 1989).

extremist Kızılbaş brand of Shiism and consistently shunned contact with the Safavid state and clerical hierarchy. Moreover, their migration would have been unnecessary since the Ottomans 'avoided alienating Twelver clerics living in their territory'; the noted 'Amili scholar Zayn al-Din ibn 'Ali was even received in Istanbul in 1545 and appointed to a Sunni *madrasa* (religious college) in Baalbek, where according to his biographers he taught Shiite as well as all four Sunni schools of law.[37] Yet the argument is counterfactual, centred on who did *not* come to Iran and what the Ottomans did *not* do to Shiites. Devin Stewart has rightly faulted Newman for assuming that the neglect of some 'Amilis to emigrate was tantamount to a massive rejection of Safavid Shiism and proffers new evidence that Zayn al-Din ibn 'Ali's companion in fact dissimulated their confessional affiliation in Istanbul by claiming to be Shafi'i.[38] Most important, the Shiite biographical dictionaries recall that Zayn al-Din himself subsequently had to go into hiding in southern Lebanon out of fear of persecution, before being arrested in Mecca and killed on the way back to Istanbul in 1558; it is for this reason that he is remembered as *al-Shahid al-Thani*, the 'Second Martyr' of the Shiite scholarly tradition, to the present day. In another article, Stewart describes the trip of the Safavid high official Baha' al-Din al-'Amili back to his native Syria around 1583, where he had to disguise himself as a simple pilgrim and shunned contact with his admirers in Aleppo for fear of discovery by the Ottomans.[39]

Did the Ottoman state see the Shiites of Jabal 'Amil and their clerical tradition as a threat? The bureaucratic apparatus which would later provide detailed accounts of the Empire's provincial administration was only being put in place in the mid-sixteenth century, and the Ottoman archives offer up little information on the alleged persecution of Shiite scholars in this period. However, some idea of the Ottomans' perception of the Jabal 'Amil Shiites may be garnered from incidental references in little known scholarly texts touching on the question, of which many more no doubt remain to be discovered in Istanbul's manuscript libraries. One such text is the anonymous and undated anti-Safavid polemic *Risale der Redd-i Revafiz*.[40] The format of the *Risale* is fairly conventional: a defence of the Sunni caliphs and Companions of the Prophet, an inventory of the Shiites' heretical beliefs and practices, and a presentation of Ibn Taymiyya's, Hamza Görez's and Ebu's-Suud's *fetva*s confirming them as unbelievers. But the author also displays a

---

[37]  Andrew Newman, 'The Myth of the Clerical Migration to Safawid Iran: Arab Shiite Opposition to 'Alī al-Karakī and Safawid Shiism', *Die Welt des Islam* 33 (1993), 66–112. On Zayn al-Dīn ibn 'Alī's trip to Istanbul, see also Marco Salati, 'Ricerche sullo Sciismo nell'Impero Ottomano: Il Viaggio di Zayn al-Dīn al-Šahīd al-Ṯānī a Istanbul al Tempo di Solimano il Magnifico (952/1545)', *Oriente Moderno* 70 (1990), 81–92.

[38]  Devin Stewart, 'Notes on the Migration of 'Āmilī Scholars to Safavid Iran', *Journal of Near Eastern Studies* 55 (1996), 81–103; Stewart, 'Ḥusayn b. 'Abd al-Ṣamad al-'Āmilī's Treatise for Sultan Suleiman and the Shī'ī Shāfi'ī Legal Tradition', *Islamic Law and Society* 4 (1997), 156–99.

[39]  Devin Stewart, '*Taqiyyah* as Performance: The Travels of Bahā' al-Dīn al-'Āmilī in the Ottoman Empire (991–93/1583–85)' in D. Stewart, B. Johansen and A. Singer, *Law and Society in Islam* (Princeton Papers in Near Eastern Studies 4 (1996)), 1–70.

[40]  Süleymaniye Kütüphanesi, Istanbul: I. Serez 1451. The catalogue title ('Treatise on the Refutation of the Rafizis') does not actually appear in the manuscript.

rare interest in the actual history of Ottoman–Safavid relations and reproduces two lengthy chancery letters, one from Sultan Selim to Shah Ismail and the other from Süleyman to Tahmasb, replete with colourful taunts and threats of war. The treatise ends with a plea to Murad IV to 'abrogate the abominable rule of Shiism' and annex Persia, but makes no reference yet to the Safavids' reoccupation of Iraq; it can thus probably be dated to the early 1620s. What is perhaps most striking about the treatise is the precise reference in the introduction to an 'Amili scholar as the founding ideologue of Iranian Shiism:

> From Jabal 'Amil near Damascus, that quarry of Shiism and fountainhead of heresy, a damned Rafizi by the name of 'Abd al-Al, commander of the pugnacious and high-priest of error, joined Ismail and supported and helped to propagate this false teaching. Calling himself their şeyhü'l-İslam, he became the şeyh of apostasy.[41]

'Abd al-'Ali (d. 1596) was actually the son and successor of 'Ali al-Karaki (d. 1534), an 'Amili scholar resident in Najaf whom the Safavids recruited around 1510 to formulate a distinctively Shiite theory of rule whereby political power would be exercised in the name of the hidden Imam. This revolutionary innovation in Shiism earned both father and son (though the latter was far more moderate than his father) the title of '*mujtahid* [sovereign jurist] of the age', and the lineage known for 'Abd al-'Ali came to dominate one of the leading schools of juridical and political thought in Isfahan.[42] The author of the treatise bemoans that 'over a century later' the venerable Companions were still being 'cursed and defamed from the tops of the pulpits and minarets and in every corner of the bazaar' in Iran; it marks the perhaps first (or the only) time that an Ottoman text clearly traces the Safavid enemy's ideological origins to a 'fountainhead' in western Syria.

It is unclear whether or when this insight, which betrays a certain knowledge of Safavid internal affairs, was widely shared in Istanbul, or what repercussions it might have had. Reports of religious persecution in the Syrian provinces are in fact extremely sparse in this period. A sufi of Anatolian provenance caused a stir in the 1540s by preaching the imminent appearance of the *mahdi* (messiah), but there is nothing to indicate that he acquired a following among Shiites.[43] A document in the Aleppo court archives relates that a group of villagers from the surrounding country in 1555 accused their local *khatib* (preacher) and his followers of being Ismaili Shiites and/or of practising *zandaqa*, but provides no indication how the suit ended.[44] In 1565, '*ulama*' of the four Sunni schools in Damascus accused a

---

[41]  *Ibid.*, fol. 3a.
[42]  Rula Abisaab, *Converting Persia: Religion and Power in the Safavid Empire* (London: I. B. Tauris, 2004), 15–20, 44–6; Said Amir Arjomand, *The Shadow of God and the Hidden Imam: Religion, Political Order, and Societal Change in Shi'ite Iran from the Beginning to 1890* (Chicago University Press, 1984); Ja'far al-Muhajir, *Sittat Fuqaha' Abtal: Al-Ta'sis li-Tarikh al-Shi'a 2* (Beirut: Higher Shiite Islamic Council, 1994), 109–30.
[43]  Cf. Adnan Bakhit, *The Ottoman Province of Damascus in the Sixteenth Century* (Beirut: Librairie du Liban, 1982), 185–6.
[44]  Marco Salati, 'Shiism in Ottoman Syria: A Document from the Qāḍī Court of Aleppo (963/1555)', *Eurasian Studies* 1 (2002), 77–84.

colleague of holding corrupt and *rafizi* beliefs; the Sublime Porte ordered the governor to investigate and imprison the man if this proved true but to 'guard against prejudice and zealotry' otherwise.[45] The most prominent case of actual persecution was the execution in 1610 of a certain Yahya ibn 'Isa, an obscure student from Karak Shawbak, who attracted a large following in Damascus, including senior Janissary officers, with his derision of organized religion and predication of a Shiite-tinged materialist folk Islam. The conservative Damascene chroniclers who reported on – and indeed pushed for – his conviction for *zandaqa* admit that the Ottoman secular authorities at first refused to inculpate him, preferring to commit him to a *bimaristan* asylum and then suggesting to banish him, 'as one usually does with his sort'.[46] The Ottoman government's general attitude to religious deviants is summed up by the executive order sent to Damascus in the unrelated case of a sufi mystic whom local officials suspected of unbelief in 1570: 'Inasmuch as the *şeyh* and his dervishes do not actually behave against the holy law, they are not to be molested.'[47]

The execution of Zayn al-Din ibn 'Ali in 1558 thus remains the only instance where the Ottoman state may have specifically targeted an 'Amili scholar on account of his confessional affiliation. Zayn al-Din was one of the most innovative and broad-based Shiite *'ulama'* of his age, having made a point of studying not only in the Shiite tradition but also with Sunni teachers while on extended stays in Damascus, Cairo and the Hijaz.[48] His expertise in Sunni law and his trip to Istanbul under ambiguous circumstances to seek an official state appointment to a Shafi'i college in Baalbek have already been alluded to. His death and canonization as 'the Second Martyr' apparently inspired a new generation of 'Amili intellectuals to leave their home and seek their fortune under Safavid patronage; but for all their detail on his exemplary life, the Shiite biographical sources are vague and inconsistent on the reasons for his persecution, the date of his apprehension and even the place of his killing: while some maintain that he was beheaded in Istanbul on the sultan's orders, others claim that his death en route was accidental and resulted in the arresting officer's own execution, with Turcoman nomads tending to the *Shahid*'s burial.[49]

The controversy can probably now be laid to rest with the publication by Richard Blackburn of the memoir of a Meccan official who travelled to Istanbul in 1557–8 and there witnessed Zayn al-Din ibn 'Ali's execution first-hand. According to the official, Qutb al-Din al-Nahrawali (d. 1582), Zayn al-Din was

---

[45] MD 6:498, 500.

[46] Muhammad Amin Fadlallah al-Muhibbi (d. 1699), *Khulasat al-Athar fi A'yan al-Qarn al-Hadi 'Ashar* (Beirut: Dar Sadir, n.d.), IV:478; see also Najm al-Din Ghazzi (d. 1651), *Lutf al-Samar wa-Qatf al-Thamar* (Damascus: Culture Ministry, 1982), 698–707. For an example of an accused *zindiq* being committed to a *bimaristan* in Aleppo in 1609–10, see Abu'l-Wafa' ibn 'Umar al-'Urdi (d. 1660/1), *Ma'adin al-Dhahab fi'l-A'yan al-Musharrafa bi-him Halab* (Aleppo: Dar al-Milah, 1987), 66–8.

[47] MD 11:71.

[48] Devin Stewart, *Islamic Legal Orthodoxy: Twelver Shiite Responses to the Sunni Legal System* (Salt Lake City: University of Utah Press, 1998), 86–92, 168–72, 204–5; al-Muhajir, *Sittat Fuqaha'*, 133–86.

[49] For a critical discussion of the conflicting reports, see al-Muhajir, *Sittat Fuqaha'*, 161–71.

decapitated without trial by order of the grand vizier after being extradited from Mecca via Egypt. He had been brought to the attention of the *qadi* (judge) of Damascus several years before, but had been released after convincing him of his Shafi'i credentials and respect for the venerable Companions in a friendly discussion. However, the *qadi*, German-born convert Hasan Beğ Efendi, subsequently heard of Zayn al-Din's stature as a leading Shiite *mujtahid* and author of legal manuals. He resented how Zayn al-Din had managed to extricate himself from his authority and gone into hiding, and immediately ordered his arrest upon being transferred to Mecca in 1557 and learning that Zayn al-Din was now resident in that city too. There appears to have been an attempt by locally based, possibly Shiite merchant notables to purchase his freedom, but in the end Hasan Beğ Efendi, a rising star in the Ottoman religious bureaucracy who would later be promoted *qadi* of Cairo and then of Istanbul, found it preferable to remand him directly into grand vizier Rüstem Paşa's power.[50]

The example of Zayn al-Din ibn 'Ali shows that religious persecution against Shiite individuals was a very real possibility in the sixteenth-century Ottoman Empire. At the same time, the particular circumstances of his embroilment with the *qadi* Hasan Beğ Efendi suggest that such persecution was not systematic and involved factors other than mere confessional divergence. The case of Baha' al-Din al-'Amili (d. 1621), the Syrian-born *şeyh'ül-İslam* of Isfahan who travelled incognito through Ottoman lands for two years at the height of the Ottoman–Safavid conflict, is similar. Devin Stewart has reconstructed in detail how Baha' al-Din disguised himself as a simple ascetic, falsified his genealogy and pretended to be Sunni vis-à-vis most of the people he met along the way; in the Lebanese folk tradition he is still remembered as the ultimate escape artist from Ottoman hands. On the other hand, the same sources also make clear that Baha' al-Din made no secret of his Shiism in more private settings, occasionally asking his Sunni hosts not to broadcast the fact but also engaging in frank theological discussions, including with the famous Damascene scholar al-Burini, himself the friend of a Shiite Iranian scholar who had taken up residence in Syria.[51] The very fact that Baha' al-Din could freely associate with Iranian expatriate scholars and merchants as well as with Sunni notables who knew or strongly suspected he was Shiite suggests that, apart from his status as Iran's leading religious dignitary, there was nothing particularly unusual about his experience as a Shiite travelling in the Ottoman Empire.

Baha' al-Din had of course picked a particularly difficult time for his voyage, and there is some curious evidence that Ottoman officials were precisely anticipating Safavid agents coming to the Empire incognito as pilgrims or merchants in order to stir up trouble. The Ottomans had imposed a total ban on Iranian pilgrim

---

[50] Richard Blackburn, *Journey to the Sublime Porte: The Arabic Memoir of a Sharifian Agent's Diplomatic Mission to the Ottoman Imperial Court in the Era of Suleyman the Magnificent* (Würzburg: Ergon, 2005), 208–10.

[51] Stewart, '*Taqiyyah* as Performance'.

traffic after the resumption of open war in 1578. In February 1581, the governors of Basra and Lahsa in north-eastern Arabia were warned that

some of the Kızılbaş trash are currently disguising themselves and coming your way on the pretext of performing the pilgrimage. They convince those guarding the frontier to let them pass, then join the *hajj* caravan and go to the Holy Sanctuaries intending to foment evil and strife.

After determining the identity of Iranian travellers, all but those entering the 'Well-Protected Domains' for commercial purposes were to be turned back at the border. The orders issued concomitantly to Syrian-area governors, however, were more stringent and bespeak an explicit concern with the Safavids' relationship to local Shiites:

Currently, some Shiite heretics from the east are disguising themselves and travelling as merchants to Damascus and from there to Aleppo, where they mislead and corrupt some individuals devoted to them, and go to the Holy Sanctuaries with the Syrian *hajj* caravan ... Appoint competent spies from among your most trusted men and gather information on these individuals with the utmost care. Investigate their situation openly and in secret, and if it is clear that they have come with evil intentions, imprison them securely, immediately inform my noble threshold, and emphatically warn all emirs, judges and governing officers in the region.[52]

These orders predate Baha' al-Din's trip by approximately two years, but are striking for the way they prefigure his itinerary and especially his meeting Shiites from Jabal 'Amil who came to see him in Aleppo. Did the orders specifically target Baha' al-Din, who had signalled his intent to go on pilgrimage as early as 1575?[53] Or are they indicative of the Ottomans' perception of Iranian Shiite travellers as a general problem in this time? Either way, their very uniqueness suggests once again that the Ottoman state's actions must be placed within a specific, historically circum-scribed context. The persecution or harassment of individual known Shiites such as the 'Amilis followed from textually well-attested but essentially limited political concerns, rather than from a diffuse and universal anti-Shiite animus.

For Stewart and many other western writers, the Shiites' survival in a hostile Sunni environment always depended on their practice of *taqiyya* or 'dissimula-tion'. The principle of *taqiyya* is firmly anchored in Islamic jurisprudence and allows members of stigmatized minorities to conceal their sectarian identity to avoid persecution. Many Iranian scholars in particular have characterized it as the very essence of Shiite religiosity and imagined it as a necessity of life for Shiites under Sunni Ottoman rule.[54] It is therefore interesting to note that Lebanese and Syrian Shiite historians, from those communities who were theoretically most prone to *taqiyya*, rather consistently deny that it was in fact practised.[55] The

---

[52] MD 42:175, 176.    [53] Stewart, 'Taqiyyah as Performance', 8.

[54] *Ibid.*; Etan Kohlberg, 'Some Imāmī-Shī'ī Views of *Taqiyya*', *Journal of the American Oriental Society* 95 (1975), 395–402.

[55] To cite only the most notorious example, the great Syro-Lebanese Shiite scholar Muhsin al-Amin (d. 1952), in his biographical compendium *A'yan al-Shi'a* (Beirut: Dar al-Ta'arif, 1996), IX:241; X:60, has altered text passages where in the original 'Amilis were claiming to be Shafi'i or Sunni.

question merits further investigation. For our purposes, it may be useful to construe *taqiyya* as the Shiites' pendant to Ebu's-Suud's *fetva*: a conceptual framework, used by jurists and scholars to situate conflict between Ottomans and Shiites within a confessional discourse, rather than an actual reason or result of religious persecution. Just as mundane violence against Shiites could always be interpreted as fulfilling Ebu's-Suud's injunction against illegal Kızılbaş heretics, any instance of Shiites not trumpeting their sectarian identity could be labelled dissimulation. The Ottomans' intolerance and the Shiites' conspiracy can always be backed up by particular historical texts; instances of toleration and accommodation, on the other hand, do not make history. The problem occurs when one takes the textual evidence of intolerance and conspiracy as the sole parameters of Shiite life under Ottoman rule.

## The Shiite holy places in Iraq

One of the most delicate balancing acts required of the Ottoman state authorities was governing the Shiite shrine cities of Iraq. After centuries of neglect and destruction wrought by successive Turkmen invasions, Najaf, Kerbela, Samarra, and other places associated with the Twelve Imams all passed under Ottoman control in 1534. The Ottomans struggled to establish their sovereignty in the region, however, due to the problems of distance as well as geopolitical rivalry with Iran. Among Sultan Süleyman's first acts was to order the restoration of the Shiite Kazimayn tombs in Baghdad, in addition to those of famous Sunni scholars, and to re-establish a fresh water supply to the desert towns of Najaf and Kerbela, in an effort to eclipse Shah Ismail's renovations of the two shrines a generation previously.[56] Further renovation work was undertaken in 1568.[57] This all served the Ottomans to conciliate the native Shiite population, but also to appropriate the heritage of 'Alid loyalty and veneration for the Twelve Imams. Inasmuch as Sunni theology did not acknowledge the political significance attributed to them in Shiism, the care shown to their graves or to Shiite shrines elsewhere, and the respect paid to their memory, was a means for the Ottomans to negate confessional pluralism and assert their religious primacy over all Muslims.

However, the Ottomans could hardly pretend to be blind to the shrines' special meaning to Twelver and other Shiites. Provincial law codes from as early as 1526 indicate that the state was aware of 'Rafizis heading from the region of Damascus to visit the sanctuary of Ali' in Iraq – and imposed a travel tax on them to be collected at Hama;[58] Kızılbaş interrogated in eastern Anatolia around 1593 confessed that 'our god is Ali' and affirmed praying in the direction of his and

---

[56] Stephen Longrigg, *Four Centuries of Modern Iraq* (Clarendon Press, 1925), 24–5; Yitzhak Nakash, *The Shi'is of Iraq* (Princeton University Press, 1994), 14–22.

[57] MD 7:862, 864, 865.

[58] Ahmed Akgündüz, ed., *Osmanlı Kanunnâmeleri ve Hukukî Tahlilleri* (Istanbul: FEY Vakfı/Osmanlı Araştırmaları Vakfı, 1990–6), VI:671.

Husayn's tombs rather than towards the Ka'ba.[59] Throughout much of the six-teenth century, the Ottoman authorities appear at odds over how to deal with the flow of Iranians coming to visit the shrine cities. In principle, the Ottomans permitted Iranian pilgrims to go on *hajj* on the basis of a treaty originally signed by Sultan Bayezid (reigned 1481–1512), but insisted repeatedly that they join the Syrian caravan and not travel directly via Baghdad.[60] Even in times of peace the Ottomans were extremely suspicious of Iranian visitors who would come and stay longer than necessary at the Iraqi shrines to distribute food and sweets to the poor; they also tried without much success to interdict the 'corpse traffic', the still-active custom of bringing deceased pious Shiites from abroad to bury near the Imams' graves in Najaf or Kerbela. In 1573, the Sublime Porte issued orders to secretly eliminate 'fifty individuals reciting prayers day and night for the despicable shah', but more usually (and more diplomatically) it granted permission to high-ranking Safavid officials and members of the dynasty to visit or even to live out their retirement in the Iraqi shrine cities.[61]

The problem from an administrative standpoint was that the *Meşhedeyn* (Two Noble Shrines: Najaf and Kerbela) were supported by a massive pious foundation (*vakıf*) since before the Ottoman conquest. As Islamicate rulers, the Ottomans were bound to honour and uphold this foundation, even if that meant having to accept a substantial part of its revenues as well as gifts (such as the carpets traditionally sent to furnish the shrines) from Shiite Iranian sources. So, while the Sublime Porte might condemn individual local *vakıf* officials as Rafizis, to stop the influx of money, pilgrims and goods from Iran would have been to admit the sectarian character of the shrines themselves. The Ottomans were at pains to discourage and disguise Shiite activity while appearing to run things business as usual. Still in 1573, for example, orders were given to build a new caravanserai especially for Iranian visitors in Kerbela – ostensibly because of the lack of accommodation in the city, but in fact so that they would no longer stay at private homes and mix with the local 'Muslim' (i.e. Shiite Muslim) population.[62] Referring to the Safavid shrine at Ardabil, which briefly came under Ottoman occupation in the eighteenth century, Fariba Zarinebaf-Shahr has suggested that religious endowments suffered from being converted back and forth between Shiite and Sunni management.[63] The Ottomans (like the Safavids), of course, did not formally admit that distinction and saw themselves as custodians serving the one true universal religion. The administrative correspondence clearly indi-cates, however, that this entailed the constant, conscious 'dissimulation' of the shrines' Shiite quality on the part of the state itself.

---

[59]  MD 69:59. I am indebted to Prof. Pál Fodor for bringing this item to my attention.

[60]  MD 6:17–18; MD 7:980; MD 12:467–8.

[61]  MD 6:313, 651; MD 12:217; MD 21:278–9; MD 22:339; MD 36:96; MD 48:297.

[62]  MD 23:203–4.

[63]  Fariba Zarinebaf-Shahr, 'The Ottoman Administration of Shiite *Waqf*s in Azerbaijan' in Faruk Bilici, ed., *Le waqf dans le monde musulman contemporain (XIXe–XXe siècles): Fonctions sociales, économiques et politiques* (Istanbul: Institut Français d'Études Anatoliennes, 1994), 234.

## Urban Shiism and the *ashraf*

In appropriating the religious heritage of the *Meşhedeyn*, the Ottomans assumed not only certain functional ties to Iran but also the culture of 'Alid loyalty and saint veneration germane to the shrines. This, we suggested, did not pose any problem to a dynasty with deep roots in non-confessional folk Islam and Bektaşi and other nonconformist sufism as well as a claim to universal Islamic leadership. In the sixteenth century, Ottoman court and polite society still remained very receptive to literary expressions of Shiite or quasi-Shiite devotion; the Iraqi poet Fuzuli-i Bağdadi (d. 1556), who panegyrized Shah Ismail before gaining renown in the Ottoman world for his mystical, anguished verse on the effervescence of love and the futility of existence, was widely seen and accepted as an Imami Shiite sympathizer.[64] The social group with the most tangible link to the Shiite heritage of the Ottoman Empire were the *ashraf* (*eşraf*). As descendants of the Prophet by his daughter Fatima's union with 'Ali, the *ashraf* were genealogically tied to the line of Twelve Imams and in many cities tended the shrines and sanctuaries associated with them. For all that, however, they were not necessarily Shiite in a political sense, and often claimed affiliation with the Shafi'i school of law. The *ashraf* enjoyed social distinctions and tax exemptions that were jealously guarded by their corporation; Ottoman-era court registers are rife with investigations of individuals wrongfully claiming the coveted *sharif* status. In medieval Baghdad, the *naqib*s or heads of the *ashraf* corporation might be leading Shiite theologians, but among their chief social functions was to diffuse tensions between the militantly opposed Hanbali and Twelver Shiite populace of the city. A similar role was performed in Damascus by *naqib*s of the 'Adnan family, themselves scions of a Baghdadi *naqib* dynasty, in mediating between the Mamluk authorities and Druze or Shiite communities and in getting their own followers to tone down anti-Sunni rhetoric and cursing.[65] Alevi popular historian Baki Öz has pointed to the seeming contradiction of a quasi-Shiite office constituted under Ottoman sovereignty,[66] but in many ways the *ashraf* and *naqib al-ashraf* incarnated the continuing tradition of 'confessional ambiguity' in medieval and Ottoman Muslim society.

*Ashraf* with strong Shiite leanings played a prominent role in several cities of Ottoman Syria. The best-known case, thanks to the research of Marco Salati, is Aleppo, where the office of *naqib* was dominated for much of the seventeenth century by the Zuhrawi family. The Zuhrawis had vast landholdings in the countryside around Aleppo, notably in the Shiite villages to the south-west, and contributed heavily to the *vakıf* endowments for the *Meşhedeyn* in Iraq as well as the local Husaynid shrine in Aleppo. Both Shiite biographical and other contemporary sources identify them as Shiite, notwithstanding that the *naqib* post was among

---

[64] Abdülkadir Karahan, 'Fuzûlî' in *Türkiye Diyanet Vakfı İslam Ansiklopedisi* (Istanbul: İSAM, 1996), XIII:240–6.

[65] Winter, 'The Shi'ah of Syria', 153.

[66] Baki Öz, *Aleviğin Tarihsel Konumu* (Istanbul: Der Yayınları, 1995), 78–89.

the most politically important in the city at the time.[67] Less is known of Tripoli, where the *naqib* was also influential in municipal politics. For the most part the post was held by Sunni notables, but in 1713 a deputy *naqib* was accused of constantly siding with and inciting the local 'Kızılbaş' to revolt, and was imprisoned in the island fortress of Arwad.[68]

Perhaps the most illustrious of Syrian Shiite *ashraf* were the Murtada family of Baalbek and Damascus. The Murtadas had been *naqibs* of Baalbek since Mamluk times, with the 'Alwan branch of the family assuming the *waqf* intendancy of the Karak Nuh (prophet Noah) shrine in the southern Bekaa.[69] In 1366, the Murtadas were named supervisors of the newly endowed 'Alid shrine of Sayyida Zaynab near Damascus, a position which they seem to have retained for much of the Ottoman period[70] and indeed up to the present day. They also retained control of the Karak Nuh foundation throughout the eighteenth century, which they had to defend against the interference of the local Druze emirs in at least one instance that was signalled to the imperial chancery.[71] Official documents do not make reference to the Murtadas' confessional identity, though one may speculate that it was part of the reason they never became *naqibs* of Damascus. The famous Damascene scholar 'Abd al-Ghani al-Nabulusi, whose travelogues are anyhow tight-lipped on the non-Sunni culture he encountered during his trips to the Lebanon, eulogizes a *sayyid* Murtada at length on his visit to Karak Nuh in 1700, noting only that they prayed together according to the Shafi'i rite.[72] Despite their clear 'Alid associations, these and the other such shrines in Syria, and the notable *ashraf* families who cared for them, were never as explicitly linked to Shiism in the Ottoman period as some of them have become in modern times.

## Conclusion: what ideology?

Ultimately, it becomes difficult to ascribe to the Ottoman state any definite policy towards Shiism. Even at the height of imperial rule, its heritage of Turkmen metadoxy, the social and cultural diversity of its subject peoples, and the difficulties of governing so vast a territory militated against the imposition of religious uniformity for its own sake. Especially in the sixteenth century, rural resistance against the secular centralization of the state manifested itself and was repressed in

---

[67] Marco Salati, *Ascesa e caduta di una famiglia di Asraf sciiti di Aleppo: I Zuhrawi o Zuhra-zada (1600–1700)* (Rome: Istituto per l'Oriente C. A. Nallino, 1992).

[68] MD 121:1. See also p. 152 below.

[69] Sulayman Zahir, 'Safha min al-Tarikh al-Shami lam Yudawwan Aktharuha', *Majallat al-Majma' al-'Ilmi al-'Arabi/Revue de l'Académie Arabe de Damas* 17 (1942), 445–6. On individual Murtada *naqibs* in the seventeenth–eighteenth centuries, see al-Amin, *A'yan al-Shi'a*, II:324–5, 329; III:401; V:13; VI:182; IX:432.

[70] Markaz al-Watha'iq al-Tarikhiyya, Damascus: Damascus Shar'iyya Court Registers 3 m:54 (March 1690); 59:169 (November 1726); 139:163 (April 1753). I am indebted to Astrid Meier for these references.

[71] Başbakanlık Archives: Cevdet Evkaf 14884, 20088, 22285, 32176.

[72] 'Abd al-Ghani al-Nabulusi (d. 1731), *al-Tuhfa al-Nabulusiyya fi'l-Rihla al-Tarabulusiyya*, ed. Heribert Busse (Beirut: Franz Steiner, 1971), 107–11.

terms of heresy vs orthodoxy, and the legal grammar of persecution deployed by Ebu's-Suud and others would have a direct bearing on the Ottomans' dealings with rebellious Shiites in later times. But even this did not impinge on the space the Empire continued to afford Bektaşi sufism, 'Alid saint veneration and the celebration of *Ashura*, pious foundations for Imami shrines and travel by Iranian pilgrims, or local autonomy for non-orthodox minorities. In many cases, the *tashayyu'* of the *ashraf* or of individual scholars was not really seen to be at variance with Sunnism, the lines of confessional differentiation not yet so clearly drawn, as they are now. But in many other cases, we contend, it was the Ottoman authorities themselves who pragmatically chose to blur, deny and above all ignore the Shiite identities of particular individuals and institutions.

This raises two problems. First, that 'Shiism' was very much a question of definition, even of 'construction' in the postmodernist sense. Not only that religion itself can evolve over time, and that one can debate if 'Alid loyalty necessarily equalled Shiism in the Ottoman era, but also that turning it into Rafizi or Kızılbaş heresy, into an object of *taqiyya*, a reason for persecution or a separate Ja'fari law school, always took an act of definition on the part of some authority or another. The historian is then vassal to that whose definitive texts he has chosen to read. Which leads to the second problem with respect to writing a history of Shiites and Ottomans: reifying, as we are prone to do, the 'state'. If certain religious scholars and jurists provided the discursive and legal elements that have come to be accepted as Ottoman 'ideology' regarding Shiism, it was really up to a constantly shifting lattice of imperial bureaucrats and competing governors, of emulous *qadis* and local notables and heterodox tribal lords, when and how to commission, report, pass on, digest, withhold or act on information regarding Shiite subjects. This is not to belittle the agency or efficacy of the Ottoman administration, for its adaptability and pragmatism were every bit as much a part of imperial 'ideology' as religion and law. It does suggest, however, that the historical experience of individual Shiite communities under Ottoman rule must not only be situated within a broader imperial framework, but that it, in turn, would also have an impact on the continuing evolution of Ottoman government practice and ideology.

# CHAPTER 2

# The invention of Lebanon: Ottoman governance in the coastal highlands, 1568–1636

Since its origins, Shiism has crystallized, or had a reputation for crystallizing, resistance, social protest and revolution within Muslim society. Accordingly, the history of Shiites under a self-professedly Sunni regime like the Ottoman sultanate has almost always been understood as one of opposition, endurance and blood-shed, for which salient events such as the martyrdom of individual free-thinking scholars or the deportation of entire tribes seem to provide ample evidence. Away from the spotlight of *histoire événementielle*, however, the mundane day-to-day experiences of Shiite communities under Ottoman rule testify to the contingency and flexibility of the early modern state's rapport with its heterodox constituency. From Deli Orman to the Tihama, the Ottoman Empire encompassed countless non-Sunni sectarian groups which formed local majorities, participated in rather than protested against the reigning order and were quite often co-opted into the structures of local government.

The coastal highlands of Syria are home to the most written-about examples of heterodox home-rule under imperial dominion (Map 1). Since the Middle Ages, Druze tribal chiefs from the Shuf mountain south-east of Beirut enjoyed formal recognition as 'emirs' in return for their fealty and tribute to the Ayyubid, Mamluk and Ottoman states. Starting in the seventeenth century, the Druze Maʻn dynasty took numerous Maronite and other Christian populations from the Shuf and adjoining parts of the coastal range under its wing, forging an increasingly autonomous commercial and political enclave which the Great Powers would later help detach from Ottoman sovereignty. This alliance of Druze warlords and Maronite peasants and churchmen, amply recorded and memorialized by Christian chroniclers of the day, has become the founding myth of modern Lebanon – generally to the exclusion of other actors and groups whose historical realities did not fit into the narrative of a timeless, uniform, ecumenical Lebanese particularism.

The history of the Shiite communities and their leaderships in the early modern period challenges this narrative in several important respects. In the seventeenth century, the Harfush emirate of the Bekaa Valley and the Hamadas of Mt Lebanon rivalled the territorial extension and power of the Druze emirate of the Shuf. Unlike the Druze, the Shiite emirs were regularly denounced for their religious identity and persecuted under Ebu's-Suud's definition of Kızılbaş heretics, making their

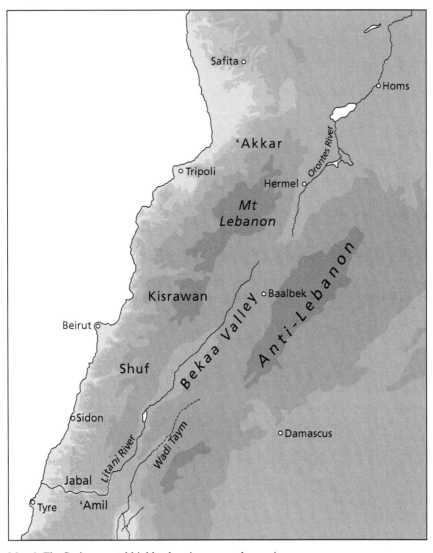

Map 1  The Syrian coastal highland region: general overview

efflorescence under Sunni Ottoman rule perhaps all the more remarkable.
Notwithstanding, the documentation analysed in the following pages suggests
that initially they too carried the Ottoman state's imprimatur as local tax collection
and government concessionaries, and only lost this role in the eighteenth century
with the triumph and violent expansion of the Druze emirate over all of what would
then retrospectively be designated as 'Lebanon'.

This chapter traces the rise the Harfushes, the best-known Shiite emirate under
Ottoman sovereignty, as an alternative to the exclusionist narrative of Druze–Maronite

autonomy in Lebanon. It starts from the argument that continues to be the pillar of Lebanist historiography of the Ottoman period, namely that the rule of the Druze Ma'n emirs constituted a separate political regime grounded in an ancient tradition of mutual tolerance and support against outside interference on the part of Lebanon's different sectarian communities, and resituates the creation of both the Ma'n and the Harfush emirates plainly within the context of Ottoman provincial reforms in the sixteenth and seventeenth centuries. Drawing on both chancery decrees and tax farm (*iltizam*) records, it attempts to show how the imperial government stoked competition among leading notable families as a means to extend its authority into the inaccessible desert and highland periphery. At first the Ottomans valued the Harfushes because of their social pre-eminence among the region's large Shiite population, it will be argued, and withdrew their support in the later seventeenth century not out of religious considerations but because the Harfushes ultimately proved unable to match and contain their Druze rivals on the state's behalf.

## The 'classical system' of rule

There has never been a precise definition of what territory historically constitutes 'Lebanon'. In the Bible and other texts of antiquity, the term is used to denote the highest summits of the Syro-Palestinian coastal range near Tripoli, or the whole part of the range that is home to ancient cedar groves as far south as the Galilee, or the entire mountainous region of western Syria including the Bekaa Valley and the Anti-Lebanon range that today marks the border between the Lebanese and Syrian republics. The appellation fell into disuse after the Muslim conquest and is encountered neither in medieval Arabic histories nor in Ottoman documents from before the nineteenth century. In the period under consideration, French consular reports, which probably reflected local usage, clearly distinguish Mt Lebanon in the province of Tripoli from the Kisrawan mountains (north-east of Beirut) and the Shuf, which were part of the province of Damascus and later Sidon. As a political entity, Lebanon is no older than 1842, when the Concert of Europe enjoined the Ottomans to institute a special administrative district (the twin *kaimmakamiye*, a.k.a. 'the Lebanon' to the Europeans) to protect the interests of the Maronite Christian population in the Levant. This regime would form the basis of the separate province of Mt Lebanon (Cebel Lübnan) in 1861, and of the French mandate state of Greater Lebanon (Grand Liban) in 1920.

The district designated by the Règlements 'organiques' of 1842 and 1861 corresponded not to any natural or historical unit but to the area previously controlled by Bashir II Shihabi (d. 1850), the last and most powerful incumbent of the Druze emirate (though the Shihabis were actually Sunni converts to Maronitism). The removal of this zone from direct Ottoman control satisfied not only European (essentially French) colonialist designs but also an important part of the local Christian population, who, like their co-religionists in Greece and the Balkans, were in the nineteenth century beginning to envision a brighter future as citizens of independent nations under European protection rather than as subjects of continuing

Ottoman imperial rule. Contemporary Christian historians, whose work would also spearhead the Arabic literary revival known as the *nahda*, had every interest in discovering (or imagining) the historical origins and structures of 'the' emirate as a forerunner of the nascent Lebanese polity: Nasif al-Yaziji (d. 1871), a Greek-Orthodox secretary of Bashir II, Haydar Ahmad al-Shihabi (d. 1835) and other historians of the Shihabi family, and especially Tannus Shidyaq (d. 1859), whose two-volume *Akhbar al-A'yan fi Jabal Lubnan* remains the most programmatic description of the Druze emirate as a unified political regime, have provided the basis for an entirely modern nationalist historiography that projects Lebanon's reputed solidarity and independence-mindedness far back into the Ottoman centuries.[1]

The modern historiography of 'Lebanism' – the ideology of Lebanon as a strong central state with a homogeneous historical identity – has several common features as regards the early modern period: the assumption that the Ottomans invested Druze emirs with authority in the area from the very start of their rule; that this authority permitted them to govern, dispense justice and bestow titles independently of, and often in opposition to, the imperial government; and, most critically for our purposes, that this authority somehow applied to the entire population of the coastal highlands, irrespective of family, tax district or confessional affiliations. Under the influence of both nineteenth-century positivism and orientalism, the Ma'ns and Shihabis came to be viewed as 'princes' ruling a nearly independent eastern Mediterranean 'mountain refuge' for Christians and heterodox Muslims on the basis of a 'feudal' hierarchy of shaykhs and *muqaddam*s (headmen) loyal to them. Already forty years ago, the great historian of Lebanon, Kamal Salibi, pointed to the false premises of this 'Ruritanian image of the Lebanese emirate', showing that the investiture of an emir Fakhr al-Din ibn Ma'n 'the First' by Sultan Selim was a legend that originated in the nineteenth century, and suggesting that historians have 'over-emphasized the dynastic principle involved, over-estimated the antiquity and extent of the autonomy enjoyed ..., and generally exaggerated the degree of Christian–Druze cooperation on which this autonomy was based'.[2] And Ahmed Beydoun, writing in the darkest years of the Lebanese civil war, has brilliantly examined the confessionalist underpinnings of this very historiography that purports to describe a pan- or inter-confessional system of rule under the Druze emirs and after: each sectarian community claims a special role in setting up the non-sectarian state for all – and thus feels entitled to dominate this state in the future as well.[3]

---

[1]  See esp. Kamal Salibi, *A House of Many Mansions: The History of Lebanon Reconsidered* (Berkeley: University of California Press, 1988).

[2]  Kamal Salibi, 'The Lebanese Emirate, 1667–1841', *al-Abhath* 20–3 (1967), 1–16; Salibi, 'The Secret of the House of Ma'n', *International Journal of Middle East Studies* 4 (1973), 272–87. See also Salibi, *A House of Many Mansions*; Abdul-Rahim Abu-Husayn, 'The Feudal System of Mount Lebanon as Depicted by Nasif al-Yaziji' in Samir Seikaly, Ramzi Baalbaki and Peter Dodd, eds., *Quest for Understanding: Arabic and Islamic Studies in Memory of Malcolm Kerr* (American University of Beirut, 1991), 33–41.

[3]  Ahmed Beydoun, *Identité confessionnelle et temps social chez les historiens libanais* (Beirut: Université Libanaise, 1984), esp. 540, 548. In the Arabic edition, the word 'confessional' has been dropped from the title.

Historians have in fact brought numerous correctives to bear on our under-standing of 'Ottoman Lebanon' in the past years, showing that *iltizam* tax farming by the emirs should not be compared to medieval European feudalism, that the emirates operated essentially as Ottoman institutions, or that political confession-alism is a product of nineteenth-century Ottoman and European discourses of power rather than deeply embedded in Lebanon's past.[4] Even the most theoret-ically acute of these, however, have largely accepted the postulates and period-izations of Lebanist historiography, and have sought to refine rather than reject the notion that the Druze emirate represents a valid paradigm for all Lebanese in the early modern period. In many cases, contemporary historians of Lebanon, appalled at recent violence in the country, seem preoccupied with proving that socio-economic divisions cutting across the different communities, but not tribal and confessional affiliation as such, determined conflict in the past; too often, the 'classical system' of rule in pre-nineteenth-century Lebanon has been re-embellished as a foil for the negative changes that came thereafter, and rein-vented as a model for the deconfessionalized state one wishes to 'return' to today.

What was the Shiites' place in the 'Lebanese emirate'? Lebanist historiography, as we have indicated, generally ignores their specific experiences under Ottoman rule, absorbing them into the mythology of Christian–Druze cooperation or brand-ing them as simple outsiders. Shiite historians, in turn, have been ambivalent about their community's role as a historical constituent of Lebanese society. Writing on Lebanon in the Middle Ages, Muhammad 'Ali Makki has emphasized the shared experience of persecution among the Christian and heterodox Muslim mountain-eers, effectively bringing the Shiites into the Lebanese 'mountain refuge' com-munity; Muhammad Jabir Al Safa (d. 1945), for his part, has sought to demonstrate the Jabal 'Amil Shiites' participation in Lebanese 'feudalism' and resistance against Turkish misrule in the Ottoman period.[5] However, pioneer revisionist historian 'Ali al-Zayn (d. 1984), and to a lesser degree Al Safa as well, have also insisted on Jabal 'Amil's freedom from Ma'nid and Shihabi control, and argued that the Lebanese Shi'a was able to hold both the Druze emirate and Ottoman sovereignty at arm's length. Wajih Kawtharani, in many ways the most accom-plished Lebanese historian of Ottoman imperial rulership, has likewise argued for the Shiites' relative autarchy before the nineteenth century.[6] There can of course be

---

[4] Dominique Chevallier, *La société du Mont Liban à l'époque de la révolution industrielle en Europe* (Paris: Geuthner, 1971); Abu-Husayn, *The View from Istanbul*; Axel Havemann, *Geschichte und Geschichtsschreibung im Libanon des 19. und 20. Jahrhunderts: Formen und Funktionen des historischen Selbstverständnisses* (Würzburg: Ergon, 2002); Ussama Makdisi, *The Culture of Sectarianism: Community, History and Violence in Nineteenth-Century Ottoman Lebanon* (Berkeley: University of California Press, 2000).

[5] Muhammad 'Ali Makki, *Lubnan 635–1516: Min al-Fath al-'Arabi ila 'l-Fath al-'Uthmani* (4th edn, Beirut: Dar al-Nahar, 1991); Muhammad Jabir Al Safa, *Tarikh Jabal 'Amil* (2nd edn, Beirut: Dar al-Nahar, 1981).

[6] 'Ali al-Zayn, *Li 'l-Bahth 'an Tarikhina fi Lubnan* (Beirut: n.p., 1973); see also Beydoun, *Identité con-fessionnelle*, 229–32; Majed Halawi, *A Lebanon Defied: Musa al-Sadr and the Shi'a Community* (Boulder: Westview Press, 1992), 25–6; Havemann, *Geschichte und Geschichtsschreibung*, 182–8, 223–30.

no question of merely substituting the Ruritanian image of the 'Lebanese emirate' with an equally Ruritanian image of Shiite particularism in the same period. The Shiites of Jabal 'Amil as well as the Bekaa and Mt Lebanon always maintained complex relations with the Druze and other local 'feudal' lords as well as with Ottoman imperial and provincial authorities. Yet the very fact that their history remains relatively obscure, and has not been moulded and pressed into service since the nineteenth century to construct a particular national identity, offers the hope that it may in turn provide a fresh, unencumbered perspective on the workings of Ottoman government in the rural hinterland of Syria.

## Ottoman sovereignty in Syria

The coastal highlands that now form Lebanon, like all of Syria, came under Ottoman sovereignty in 1516 following the defeat of the Mamluks in the battle of Marj Dabiq. The conquest of Syria and then Egypt was sudden and perhaps unexpected, and the Ottomans initially maintained many of the Mamluks' governing officials in place so long as they transferred their allegiance to the Ottoman sultanate. Sultan Selim himself spent an unusually long time in Damascus in order to oversee the restoration of the tomb of Muhyi'l-Din ibn al-'Arabi (d. 1240), one of the guiding luminaries of Turkish sufism. The discovery of the long-lost tomb, predicted by an apocalyptic prophecy current in elite Ottoman circles ('When the *sin* [S, for Selim] enters the *şin* [Ş, for Şam; Syria] will appear the tomb of Muhyi'd-Din'), may go a long way to explaining Selim's personal motivation in the campaign.[7] Selim then left the administration of the entire region in the hands of the energetic and popular ex-Mamluk governor Canberdi al-Ghazali; it was only after Selim's death in 1520 and al-Ghazali's attempt to establish himself as an independent sultan that the Ottomans returned a second time, crushed the revolt and began to incorporate Syria more systematically into the structures of imperial government.[8]

Probably the most serious challenge faced by the Ottomans – and indeed by every regime before them – was how to pacify the desert and mountain periphery. Selim himself had gained the allegiance of the region's two most powerful Bedouin dynasties, the Hanash of the Bekaa Valley and the Tarabays of the Nablus area, and over the next years they served the Ottomans to keep other tribes under control and to secure the all-important *hajj* route southward to the Hijaz.[9] The most rebellious tribes seem to have been the Druze, who were concentrated in the Shuf mountains south-east of Beirut, with smaller populations to the north as well as in the Jabal al-A'la west of Aleppo. A *kanunname* (provincial law code) for Tripoli from Sultan Süleyman's reign makes reference to 'forty un-Muslim Druze *beğs* [tribal chiefs] in the mountains, a misguided folk where each follows his own cult', and

---

[7]   See Ryad Atlagh, 'Paradoxes d'un mausolée: Le tombeau du sceau des saints à Damas', *Autrement: Collection Monde* 91/2 (1996) *'Les hauts lieux de l'islam'*, 132–53.

[8]   Bakhit, *The Ottoman Province of Damascus*, 19–34.

[9]   *Ibid.*, 4–5, 11, 16–17, 204–6, 209; Abdul-Rahim Abu-Husayn, *Provincial Leaderships in Syria, 1575–1650* (American University of Beirut, 1985), 183–7.

from whom collecting taxes proved inherently difficult.[10] The first punitive campaigns against the Druze were launched in 1522 and frequently legitimized as religious war by the Damascene 'ulama'; and the paramount Druze chieftain, Yunus Ma'n, whose tax farms are attested in Ottoman registers as early as 1530, was killed while in Damascus in 1545.[11] The imperial authorities did not categorize the Druze as a religious threat akin to the Kızılbaş but as the ultimate thugs (which is the meaning of 'dürzi' in Turkish to the present day). Beginning around 1565 the Druze began to acquire muskets from the Venetians through the illegal export of grain, which far outperformed Ottoman firearms. Adnan Bakhit and Abdul-Rahim Abu-Husayn, whose extensive research in the Ottoman archives has yielded a detailed tableau of Ottoman rule in Syria at the time, describe a state of nearly constant warfare between Druze and government forces until Ibrahim Paşa's punitive campaign in 1585.[12]

The Ottoman invasion of the Shuf is recounted in numerous local and imperial sources: hundreds of Druze combatants killed, villages razed, back taxes forcibly collected, several tribal chiefs deported to Istanbul, and honours and military awards bestowed on veterans of the 'Druze war'.[13] After the campaign the Ottomans changed strategy in the area, and began to police and levy taxes through the intermediary of local chiefs to whom they granted the title 'emir' (or beğ in Turkish) to set them off from their rivals and make them loyal to, and dependent on, the state. In 1590 the Druze mukaddem Fakhr al-Din ibn Ma'n was officially given the rank of sancak-beğ of the sub-province (sancak) of Sidon-Beirut, marking the beginning of what would later be construed as the 'Druze' emirate. Ottoman backing above all helped the Ma'ns prevail over the 'Alam al-Dins, their most serious rivals among the Druze; through a combination of advantageous trade relations with Italian merchants, reliance on a privately financed army of sekban irregulars, and Ottoman patronage and regular payments to Ottoman officials, Fakhr al-Din was then able to establish himself as the most powerful potentate in the region.

If the 1585 campaign thus certainly constitutes a turning point in Lebanese history, it must also be seen in the wider perspective of the consolidation of Ottoman imperial government. The Ottomans' interest in the coastal highlands in this time stemmed not merely from the local tribes' insubordination but from what may be seen as a general effort to 'territorialize' their provincial rule. After the conquest of Cyprus in 1570–1, for instance, a divan register records the distribution of hundreds of timar prebends in the sancak of Jabala (Cebele) on Syria's northern coast to veterans of that

---

[10] Akgündüz, Osmanlı Kanunnâmeleri, IV:538.

[11] Bakhit, The Ottoman Province of Damascus, 164–5; Abdul-Rahim Abu-Husayn, 'Problems in the Ottoman Administration in Syria during the Sixteenth and Seventeenth Centuries: The Case of the Sanjak of Sidon-Beirut', International Journal of Middle East Studies 24 (1992), 666–8.

[12] Bakhit, The Ottoman Province of Damascus, 165–7; Abu-Husayn, Provincial Leaderships, 76–9; Abu-Husayn, 'Problems in the Ottoman Administration in Syria', 668–70; Abu-Husayn, The View from Istanbul, 14–16, 24–34.

[13] Abdul-Rahim Abu-Husayn, 'The Ottoman Invasion of the Shūf in 1585: A Reconsideration', Al-Abhath 32 (1985), 13–21; Abu-Husayn, The View from Istanbul, passim.

campaign to secure and develop.[14] Around the same time, the Sublime Porte also began to apportion lands along the upper Euphrates valley to both Ottoman soldiers and loyal Bedouin tribes in a bid to extend its authority into the desert interior;[15] the creation of the *eyalet* (province) of Raqqa in 1586 on territory previously under Diyarbekir's jurisdiction answered to the same logic. In 1579 the *eyalet* of Tripoli ('Trablus-ı Şam' or 'Trablus-Şam') was created from the north-western districts of Damascus and Aleppo, which until 1567 had themselves formed a single accounting unit (*defterdarlık*). The new province was essentially a hybrid, incorporating military-appanage *sancak*s such as Jabala, but also ones like Sidon-Beirut, Homs and Salamya, which would be dominated by emirs or local notables who provided taxation rather than imperial military services. Far from reflecting a unique concern with the Lebanese highlands, the administrative reorganization of the region around the turn of the seventeenth century can be said to have followed the more general shift, described by Metin Kunt, from *sancak* commands to *eyalet* revenue farms as the primary unit of Ottoman provincial government.[16]

It is therefore not surprising that the governorship of Tripoli was given to the Sayfas, a family of feudal lords from the north of the province. In the classical military structure, the governor (*vali*) of an *eyalet* would also have been its *beğlerbeğ*, the commander-in-chief of all its *sancak* cavalry divisions (also called *liva*; 'flag') when the Empire was at war. As the provincial cavalry slowly became obsolete, however, the rotative assignment of *timar* prebends and *sancak* posts became less important than efficient tax collection. Provincial governorships were therefore increasingly awarded to high-level palace officers, rather than to meritorious career soldiers, or directly to members of *ümera* households (from the Turkish plural of 'emir'), the families and retinues of past commanders who combined court access and patronage in Istanbul with deep social and economic ties to the province in which they were based. The Sayfas, most likely of Kurdish origin but affiliated with the Zulkadir Turkmen confederation, arrived in the region as Ottoman tribal auxiliaries (*levend*) around 1528.[17] They became feudatories to the 'Assaf Turkmen, who had been established in the Kisrawan since Mamluk times and whose career as emirs of the northern highlands in the sixteenth century will be examined in the next chapter. It was probably this subordinate position which made the Ottomans choose Yusuf Sayfa as *vali* of Tripoli in 1579, rather than the more powerful emir Mansur 'Assaf (who paradoxically remained the Sayfas' taxlord in their home district of 'Akkar). The Sayfas gained a full monopoly of power after eliminating the last 'Assaf emir in 1591, but

---

[14] MD 42, passim.

[15] MD 19:28, 263; MD 23:130; Stefan Winter, 'The Province of Raqqa under Ottoman Rule, 1535–1800: A Preliminary Study', *Journal of Near Eastern Studies* 68 (2009), 253–68.

[16] Metin Kunt, *The Sultan's Servants: The Transformation of Ottoman Provincial Government, 1550–1650* (New York: Columbia University Press, 1983); cf. Klaus Röhrborn, *Untersuchungen zur osmanischen Verwaltungsgeschichte* (Berlin: Walter de Gruyter, 1973), esp. 64–84.

[17] See Kamal Salibi, 'The Sayfâs and the *Eyalet* of Tripoli 1579–1640', *Arabica* 20 (1973), 28–32; Abu-Husayn, *Provincial Leaderships*, 11–22; Juzif Alyan, *Banu Sayfa: Wulat Tarabulus 1579–1640* (Beirut: Lahad Khatir, 1987).

then had to fight constant turf battles against the governors of Damascus and, increasingly, the upstart Ma'n emirs of the Shuf and finally the Shiite Hamadas of Mt Lebanon.

The Ottomans actively fanned these rivalries. From 1598 onward individual governors of Damascus encouraged Fakhr al-Din ibn Ma'n to encroach on the province of Tripoli, often just as a means of putting pressure on Yusuf Sayfa to pay up his tax debts before he was reconfirmed as *vali*. Yusuf Sayfa, in turn, was to lead the Ottoman forces against Fakhr al-Din when he rebelled against the state in 1606, and then intervened in the Shuf in favour of his Druze rivals during his exile in Tuscany in 1613. After Fakhr al-Din returned to Ottoman favour he once more began to occupy individual districts of Tripoli with the help of a rebel Sayfa nephew, the *sancak-beğ* of Jabala.[18] Following the contemporary account of Fakhr al-Din's secretary al-Khalidi al-Safadi (d. 1624), later historians saw these skirmishes as establishing the Ma'n emirate's sovereignty over the entire coast up to Latakia. Istfan al-Duwayhi (d. 1704), the Maronite patriarch whose *Tarikh al-Azmina* would become the mainstay of nineteenth-century Lebanist historiography, wrongly believed that Fakhr al-Din had been invested with the governorship of Tripoli;[19] today even the Ayyubid-era fortress at Tadmur (Palmyra) in the Syrian desert is attributed to him. In fact Fakhr al-Din was merely serving the Ottomans to break a local satrap who had become too powerful, a fate to which he in turn would succumb in 1633. The Sayfas foundered in successive liquidity crises and internecine disputes, largely of Ottoman making, until 1641; their highland fiefs were then awarded to a new generation of smaller, more pliant concessionaries.

The Hamadas, as will be seen later, rose to local pre-eminence by astutely flipping their loyalty from the 'Assafs to the ascendant Sayfas, and then on to subsequent Ottoman governors once the Sayfas' star had waned. The argument can be made that, from the imperial perspective, the Shiites simply followed in a long line of peripheral tribal groupings to be elevated to local taxlordships before being disposed of again. In Tripoli these included the 'Assafs and Sayfas, as well as a number of Kurdish clans such as the emirs of al-Kura and the Mar'ab dynasty of 'Akkar; in Sidon one might mention the Ma'n and the Canpolad (Jumblatt) families, both of whom were originally Sunni Kurdish converts to Druzism, as well as the Sa'bs, a Kurdish family turned Twelver Shiite (see chapter 5) in Jabal 'Amil. Rather than seeking to ensconce purely domestic notable rulers, it appears that the Ottomans often preferred marginal, almost mercenary tribal factions as its local agents. Once these became too established and integrated into local society, their ruthless efficiency and dependence on the state became doubtful and they were apt to be replaced by newer immigrants. This thesis, if it can be substantiated for other locales and generations of Syrian feudal politics, might suggest that the Shiites' heterodox sectarianism not only posed little obstacle, but virtually

---

[18] Salibi, 'The Sayfas', 32–52; Abu-Husayn, *Provincial Leaderships*, 22–66.
[19] Istfan Duwayhi, *Tarikh al-Azmina 1095–1699*, ed. Fardinan Tawtal al-Yasu'i (Beirut: Catholic Press, 1951), 323.

recommended them to the Ottoman authorities as the ideal tax and police deputy over a largely non-Shiite, non-tribal highland population.

## Emir titles and *iltizam* tax farming

Duwayhi and other historians have interpreted these factional wars within a matrix of timeless struggle between two ancient tribal blocs, the Qays and the Yemen.[20] The well-known rivalry between these Arabian confederations determined the Umayyad Empire's expansion and eventual break-up; identification with one or the other was a factor in Middle Eastern tribal politics throughout history and may have played a role in village voting patterns as recently as the 1996 elections in Palestine.[21] Certainly the Ottomans accepted the conflict between the 'Red Flag' (the Qaysis) and the 'White Flag' (the Yemenis) as an explanation for the endless wars among local Bedouin and Druze factions, but never deliberately favoured one side over the other.[22] In any event such blocs were inherently unstable and subject to frequent realignments. Many highland tribes, in particular the Shiites, claimed no affiliations to either the Qays or the Yemen.[23]

Among the Druze the conflict was definitively resolved in the Qaysis' favour with the Shihabis' defeat of the 'Alam al-Dins at 'Ayn Dara in 1711 (only to be replaced by a new bipolar rivalry between the Jumblatt and Yazbaki factions). In Lebanist historiography this otherwise insignificant battle has come to mark the political ascendancy of the Shihabis over all Lebanese, the moment when they won the right to name emirs and shaykhs as they saw fit in their mountain principality. But was it really their prerogative to bestow such titles? Kamal Salibi has argued that the emirate was entirely an Ottoman institution, 'a fiscal agency subject to annual renewal, designed to serve Ottoman rather than Druze needs'.[24] Yet the Ottomans generally did well not to impose their local deputies too arbitrarily, and very often did choose those factions which had already established their supremacy through violence. The question of whether it was the Ottoman state or the tribal lords who ultimately had more influence on local mountain politics remains central to the appreciation of Lebanese, and Shiite Lebanese, history.

The term 'emir' (or *beğ*) can denote a tribal chief, someone traditionally chosen from among the community's most respected families to lead in times of battle and

---

[20] The most comprehensive Lebanist histories based on Safadi, Duwayhi, Shihabi and Shidyaq are Ilya Harik, *Politics and Change in a Traditional Society: Lebanon, 1711–1845* (Princeton University Press, 1968) and Yassine Soueid, *Histoire militaire des Muqâta'a-s libanais à l'époque des deux émirats*, 2 vols. (Beirut: Université Libanaise, 1985).

[21] Hathaway, *A Tale of Two Factions*, 30–6; Jean-François Legrain, 'Réalités ottomanes en Palestine d'aujourd'hui: Bethléem 1996 et 2005' in Gérard Khoury and Nadine Méouchy, eds., *États et sociétés de l'Orient arabe: En quête d'avenir 1945–2005* (Paris: Geuthner, 2007), II:375.

[22] MD 3:218; MD 5:176; MD 6:345; MD 12:243–4, 419; MD 14:136, 316; MD 16:117; MD 24:264; MD 26:44, 328; MD 40:236.

[23] 'Ali Ibrahim Darwish, *Jabal 'Amil bayna 1516–1697: Al-Hayat al-Siyasiyya wa'l-Thaqafiyya* (Beirut: Dar al-Hadi, 1993), 29–30, 87–9.

[24] Salibi, 'Lebanese Emirate', 7.

arbitrate in times of peace, as well as an army officer, a professional commander designated by a higher authority to lead troops into war or hold a territory on its behalf. The Ottomans as well as previous military regimes played on this ambiguity in order to maintain sovereignty in areas which might otherwise escape their control. In strict theory the Ottomans, like the Saljuqs and Mamluks before them, would not concede governmental or administrative powers to any native civilians but only to their own slaves and military personnel. As quasi-military units themselves, however, Bedouin, Turkmen or Kurdish tribes often represented a better means of integrating marginal territories into the state's administrative structure than enfeoffing them to non-native army officers. It is probably no coincidence, as the most recent research on the topic suggests, that the official designation of a local Bedouin chief in northern Mesopotamia as 'amir al-'Arab' over all the tribes along the desert frontier first occurred under the Saljuqs, the dynasty responsible for introducing *iqta'*-based military feudalism in the region.[25] Under the Ayyubids and the Mamluks, the emirate of the Arabs was increasingly seen as a full military governorship, its incumbent receiving an *iqta'* pension as well as tribute gifts and playing a greater role in the protection of the *hajj* and other trade routes.[26]

The Ottomans maintained and extended this strategy of co-opting tribal leaders into the military administrative hierarchy, for example awarding hereditary *beğliks* to leading Kurdish feudal families in south-east Anatolia after 1514. Perhaps the best illustration of the ambivalent status of these *beğliks* is provided by Kilis, also called the '*liva* of the Kurds' in official documents, in northern Aleppo province. In the sixteenth century Kilis was a classical military district though under the hereditary command of the Canpolad emirs. Husên Canpolad even advanced to governor of Aleppo before his nephew 'Elî joined the Celali uprisings in 1606 and the family ended up taking refuge with Fakhr al-Din ibn Ma'n in the Shuf; thereafter the *sancak* of Kilis reverted to an essentially civilian status as a tax farm under local Kurdish voivodes.[27] In the Syrian desert the Ottoman state continued to co-opt Mawali Bedouin chiefs in the *çöl beğliği* ('desert emirate'), here too blurring the distinction between native 'civilians' and its own military cadres. The Abu Rish emirs in the sixteenth century and the al-'Abbas emirs in the seventeenth and eighteenth were responsible for controlling their own and subordinate tribal confederations, but they were systematically also awarded the *sancak-beğliks* of Salamya, Deyr-Rahbe or 'Ane on the middle Euphrates.[28]

---

[25] Stefan Heidemann, *Die Renaissance der Städte in Nordsyrien und Nordmesopotamien: Städtische Entwicklung und wirtschaftliche Bedingungen in ar-Raqqa und Ḥarrān von der Zeit der beduinischen Vorherrschaft bis zu den Seldschuken* (Leiden: Brill, 2002), 271.

[26] Mustafa Hiyari, 'The Origins and Development of the Amirate of the Arabs during the Seventh/Thirteenth and Eighth/Fourteenth Centuries', *Bulletin of the School of Oriental and African Studies* 38 (1975), 509–24.

[27] Stefan Winter, 'Les Kurdes de Syrie dans les archives ottomanes (XVIIIe siècle)' in *Études Kurdes* 10 (2009), 135–9.

[28] Nejat Göyünç, 'Einige osmanisch-türkische Urkunden über die Abū Rīš, eine Šeyh-Familie der Mawālī im 16. Jahrhundert' in Holger Preißler and Heide Stein, eds., *Annäherung an das Fremde: XXVI. Deutscher Orientalistentag vom 25. bis 29.9.1995 in Leipzig* (Stuttgart: Franz Steiner, 1998), 430–4; Winter, 'The Province of Raqqa', 260–1.

All these Ottoman-era 'princes' were simply never immortalized in the founding myths of modern Syria as the Druze have been in Lebanon.

What was new about the Ottomans' use of the emiral institution was its increasingly fiscal character. The Ottomans continued to depend on tribes to police areas beyond their effective reach, to protect the *hajj* caravan or sometimes to contribute to imperial military campaigns, but with the monetarization of provincial administration in the sixteenth century tribal emirs above all had to serve, just like regular governors, as government tax agents. The principal mechanism of this service was the *iltizam* or limited-term tax farm, an Ottoman innovation by which a local notable could contract the rights to collect a predetermined amount of taxes and legal dues from a given district or other revenue source (*mukataa*) such as a customs house. As with *eyalet* governorships themselves, executive office was hereby becoming overlaid with – and indeed dependent on – economic power, the tribal leader increasingly defined by his *mültezim* or *mukataacı* status.

The Syrian coastal highlands were destined to play a special role under Ottoman rule. In Mamluk times, they had been enfeoffed like other tribal areas to local emirs, most notably the Druze Buhturids, who were charged with defending Beirut against crusader incursions, or the Turkmen 'Assafs, who were to secure the Kisrawan against restive Shiites.[29] The development of silk farming in the mountains and burgeoning cross-Mediterranean trade in the sixteenth century, however, meant that control of the coastal districts was becoming far more lucrative, and politically important, than the classical inland emirates. The Ottomans thus began to depend on *iltizam* tax farming in this region well before it became widespread in the rest of the Empire. The concomitant phenomenon of recruiting private *sekban* militias as a basis for political power, as Baki Tezcan notes in his work on Osman II's attempt to raise a new army in the provinces, first appeared among a rising class of emiral families in Syria in the sixteenth century.[30]

The earliest documented instance of a tribal leader from the coastal highlands being co-opted into the Ottoman military apparatus as an 'emir' involves the Shiite Harfush family of Baalbek. In the spring of 1568, the acting governor of Damascus was asked to prepare 1,000 archers to send in support of the imperial campaign to pacify the Yemen. They were to be led by Musa ibn Harfush, the holder of a *zeamet* appanage in the Bekaa Valley, who until then is identified only as a *mukaddem* (local headman) in the district but who would receive the *sancak* governorship of Sidon in return for his services.[31] The case in itself illustrates the shifting paradigm of military

[29] Kamal Salibi, 'The Buhturids of the Ġarb: Mediaeval Lords of Beirut and of Southern Lebanon', *Arabica* 8 (1961), 74–97; Salibi, 'Mount Lebanon under the Mamluks' in Samir Seikaly, Ramzi Baalbaki and Peter Dodd, eds., *Quest for Understanding: Arabic and Islamic Studies in Memory of Malcolm Kerr* (American University of Beirut, 1991), 15–32.

[30] Baki Tezcan, 'Searching for Osman: A Reassessment of the Deposition of the Ottoman Sultan Osman II (1618–1620)' (Princeton University doctoral thesis, 2001), 205–9; see also Abdul-Rahim Abu-Husayn, 'The *Iltizam* of Mansur Furaykh: A Case Study of *Iltizam* in Sixteenth Century Syria' in Tarif Khalidi, ed., *Land Tenure and Social Transformation in the Middle East* (American University of Beirut, 1984), 249–56.

[31] MD 7:409, 509; see also Bakhit, *The Ottoman Province of Damascus*, 175.

service in this era: only a few months later, the Sublime Porte discovered that many of the designated archers were in fact extorting campaign contributions (*bedel akçesi*) from regular *timar*-holders and ordinary subjects in the province; a stern warning (of which copies were forwarded to Ibn Harfush and several other highland feudatories including Korkmaz Ma'n) demanded that such moneys be returned or those responsible would lose their appanages.[32] In the end only some 500 archers set out from Syria, necessitating a call-up in Egypt of even 'the brothers and sons of career soldiers [*kul*] capable of handling a musket' to be sent to the Yemen instead.[33]

There is no further word on Musa Harfush's eventual participation in the Yemen campaign (which was in fact directed against the forces of the Zaydi Shiite imam), and in later years the Harfushes would be appointed *sancak-beğ*s of Homs and Tadmur rather than of Sidon. If nothing else, his being selected to lead a tribal auxiliary division in return for an official governorship in 1568, more than twenty years before the Ma'n family received their emiral title, points towards both the possibilities and the limits of Shiite enfranchisement under Ottoman rule: the progressive monetarization of provincial government and the privatization of military power in the later sixteenth century created a context in which non-Sunni tribal leaders constituted viable, even ideal, candidates for local tax and police concessions, accredited by the state and integrated into the imperial military-administrative hierarchy. Yet their success would also depend on their ability to hold sway locally, to transcend their narrow parochial bases, raise revenues and capitalize on western Syria's changing economic situation. The Harfush emirs were among the first in the region to be co-opted by the Ottoman state, but would in the long run not stand up to the competition of other local forces.

## Shiism in the Bekaa Valley

The Bekaa Valley, extending between the leeward slopes of the Lebanese coastal range and the Anti-Lebanon in the east, had been Damascus' commercial cross-roads and breadbasket since antiquity (Fig. 1). More tribal than Jabal 'Amil, it did not share to the same degree in the venerable, reclusive traditions of Shiite scholasticism. Rather, it was the ancient sepulchres and Roman-era shrines which dotted the valley that drew the devotions of its rural farming and nomad communities and structured the religious landscape. The most important of these sites was Karak Nuh, the tomb of the biblical Noah, which by the medieval period had become identified with the Shiite community and claimed a spot as a regional centre of Shiite learning. Under the Mamluks Karak Nuh served as the administrative centre of the southern Bekaa (al-Biqa' al-'Azizi). The earliest known *waqf* endowment for the shrine was established in 1331 by a Mamluk officer, Sayf al-Din Tankiz al-Husami; in 1439 the shaykh of Karak Nuh, himself a Mamluk auxiliary commander, was attacked by a mob in Damascus and killed for being a *rafidi*. The first Safavid *shaykh al-Islam* 'Abd al-'Ali and several other Iranian state

---

[32] MD 7:739.    [33] MD 7:754, 760.

Fig. 1 Northern Bekaa Valley

clerics originally hailed from Karak Nuh, but this does not seem to have been especially noted by the Ottomans. The Bedouin Hanash emirs, who controlled the Bekaa in the first decades of Ottoman rule, in accord with Husayn ibn al-Harfush and other local notables increased the Karak Nuh *waqf* endowment and confirmed the Shiite 'Alwan family as its hereditary custodians around 1528.[34] Little is known of the town thereafter; the previously mentioned *sayyid* Murtada undertook repair works on the shrine's minaret after a major earthquake in 1705.[35]

Many smaller shrines were the objects of a vaguer rural folk Islam and not necessarily identified with Shiism in the sectarian sense. The tomb of al-Nabi Ilya in the western Bekaa, which was topped with a new dome by 'Ali ibn Musa Harfush in 1590/1, was equally venerated by Shadhili sufis; the famous shrine of al-Nabi Shit (Seth) attracted the faithful from throughout the area, but the village had neither a pulpit, preacher nor imam, as 'Abd al-Ghani al-Nabulusi remarked somewhat sourly on his visit there in 1689.[36] It was not uncommon either for Muslim pastoralists to seek out Christian shrines for saintly intercession or protection, though of course the oral traditions passed down in this regard function primarily to extol the Christian faith. Other stories tell of the dreaded Harfush emirs themselves endowing one or the other local church after being saved from some

---

[34] Hasan 'Abbas Nasrallah, *Tarikh Karak Nuh* (Damascus: al-Mustashariyya al-Thaqafiyya li'l-Jumhuriyya al-Islamiyya al-Iraniyya, 1986), 18–19, 173–84.

[35] Zahir, 'Safha', 450.

[36] al-Nabulusi (d. 1731), *Al-Tuhfa al-Nabulusiyya*, 106; al-Nabulusi, 'Hullat al-Dhahab al-Abriz fi Rihlat Ba'labakk wa-Biqa' al-'Aziz' in Stefan Wild and Salah al-Din Munajjid, eds., *Zwei Reisebeschreibungen des Libanon* (Beirut: Franz Steiner, 1979), 67–8, 91.

misfortune by its patron.[37] A Thuringian traveller in the mid-eighteenth century described the 'Mutuwelli' (Shiite) villagers of the Bekaa and upper Barada Valley as being on good terms with the Druze and their women unveiled and talkative, going so far as to characterize their religious outlook as libertine.[38]

The town of Baalbek in the central Bekaa was a modest centre of Shiite learning in the Mamluk and early Ottoman periods[39] as well as the seat of the 'Alwan, Murtada and Harfush families. Its Shiite quarter was situated around a minor 'Alid shrine, the tomb of Husayn's daughter al-Sayyida Khawla. A new mosque was built by a Yunus al-Harfush near the Harfush family cemetery in 1554/5 or 1618.[40] Shiite biographical sources tell of a poetry gathering in Baalbek in 1689/90 that was attended by eleven scholars from the Bekaa and Jabal 'Amil;[41] in the 1620s, at least one local *qadi* was reputed to be Shiite.[42] While the Imami scholar Zayn al-Din ibn 'Ali 'al-Shahid al-Thani' may indeed have claimed to follow the Shafi'i legal school in order to be appointed to Baalbek's Nuriyya *madrasa* in 1545, it is unlikely that his confessional affiliation or that of the many other Shiite clerics and civil notables were a secret to anyone in town. In sum, Shiism was historically very rooted in the Bekaa but always relatively discreet, and in any case difficult to ascertain as regards many of the individual shrines, tribe members or religious figures such as the *ashraf*. It is perhaps for these reasons also that it was hardly thematized by Ottoman officials, or Damascene Sunnis like 'Abd al-Ghani al-Nabulusi, or ultimately the Harfush emirs themselves.

## The Harfush emirs of Baalbek

The Harfushes are doubtless the best-known Shiite group in Ottoman-period Lebanese history. As a result of their early rivalry with the Druze Ma'n emirs, their constant interaction with Christian communities in the Bekaa and finally their subjugation to the Shihabi emirate, the Harfushes achieved a high profile in the narrative chronicles of the day, and their rule over Baalbek and parts of the Bekaa, from obscure origins to their demise after the 1860 civil war, has been described in numerous monograph studies.[43] The following sections will trace the early history

---

[37]  Joseph Goudard (d. 1951), *La Sainte Vierge au Liban* (Paris: Feron-Vrau, 1908), 399–401, 403–4, 414, 417–19.

[38]  Stephan Schulz, 'Reise durch einen Theil von Vorderasien, Aegypten und besonders durch Syrien, vom Jahr 1752 bis 1756' in Heinrich E. G. Paulus, ed., *Sammlung der Merkwürdigsten Reisen in den Orient* (Jena: Wolfgang Stahl, 1801), VI:166–7.

[39]  See Faysal al-Atat, *al-Shu'a' fi 'Ulama' Ba'labakk wa 'l-Biqa'* (Beirut: Mu'assasat al-Nu'man, 1993).

[40]  Mikha'il Aluf, *Tarikh Ba'labakk* (Beirut: 1904), 7; al-Atat, *al-Shu'a'*, 31–2.

[41]  al-Amin, *A'yan al-Shi'a*, II:511; V:127; VI:51; VIII:11, 228, 299; IX:262–3, 379.

[42]  Mirza 'Abdallah al-Isfahani (d. c. 1718), *Riyad al-'Ulama' wa-Hiyad al-Fudala'* (Qom: Matba'at al-Khayyam, 1980), V:29; al-Atat, *al-Shu'a'*, 151.

[43]  Aluf, *Tarikh Ba'labakk*, 65–91; Sulayman Zahir (d. 1960), *Tarikh al-Shi'a al-Siyasi al-Thaqafi al-Dini* (Beirut: Mu'assasat al-A'lami li'l-Matbu'at, 2002), III:5–107; Nawfan Raja al-Hamud, *al-'Askar fi Bilad al-Sham fi'l-Qarnayn al-Sadis 'Ashar wa 'l-Sabi' 'Ashar al-Miladiyyayn* (Beirut: Dar al-Afaq al-Jadida, 1981); Abu-Husayn, *Provincial Leaderships*, 129–52; Fu'ad Khalil, *al-Harafisha: Imarat al-Musawama, 1530–1850* (Beirut: Dar al-Farabi, 1997).

of the Harfush emirs in the context of Ottoman provincial administration, and show that their deep enmeshment in local affairs, rather than the question of their heterodox religious affiliation, ultimately doomed them to a deleterious dependence on other feudal notabilities in the mid-seventeenth century and therewith to redundancy in the Ottoman administration's point of view.

Very little is known of the Harfushes' sectarian background. The Arabic term *harfush*, denoting a 'street ruffian' associated with urban trade guilds and antinomian sufism in the medieval period, provides a possible explanation for the clan's origins.[44] Family legend, in turn, traces the lineage to emir Harfush al-Khuza'i of the Mudar tribe, an 'Alid chieftain who is said to have participated in the conquest of Syria in the seventh century.[45] The story ends in 1865 when the Ottoman government ordered the last of the Harfush emirs deported to Edirne,[46] after which the only families of that name remaining in Lebanon were Maronites. In today's Syria, the Harfushes of Maqarmada village near Qardaha, whose degree of affiliation with the Baalbek emirs is not known, constitute one of the most important scholarly families of the 'Alawite community. There was at least one Imami scholar from the Bekaa by the name of Harfush in the Ottoman period: Muhammad ibn 'Ali al-Harfushi (d. 1649), a cloth-maker, grammarian and poet from Karak Nuh, was apparently persecuted for *rafd* in Damascus and then moved to Iran where he received an official state post.[47]

The Harfushes were already well established in the Bekaa on the eve of the Ottoman conquest. The late-Mamluk popular historian Ibn Tawq identifies an Ibn Harfush as *muqaddam* of the Anti-Lebanon mountain village Jubbat 'Assal as early as 1483;[48] Ibn al-Himsi and Ibn Tulun mention one as deputy (*na'ib*) of Baalbek in 1498.[49] Ibn Harfush appears in an Ottoman archival source as early as 1516, when he and several other local notables signed a letter offering their submission to Sultan Selim.[50] The Harfushes' initial relationship with their new masters seems to have been problematic, however. The governor of Syria, Canberdi al-Ghazali, executed this Ibn Harfush as a rebel in 1518, but appointed another as his deputy in Homs after

[44] W. M. Brinner, 'The Ḥarāfīsh and their "Sultan"', *Journal of the Economic and Social History of the Orient* 6 (1963), 190–215.

[45] Aluf, *Tarikh Ba'labakk*, 65; al-Amin, *A'yan al-Shi'a*, II:216–17.

[46] Başbakanlık Archives: Cevdet Dahiliye 5142.

[47] Muhibbi, *Khulasat al-Athar*, IV:49–54; Muhammad ibn Hasan al-Hurr al-'Amili (d. 1692), *Amal al-Amil fi 'Ulama' Jabal 'Amil* (Beirut: Mu'assasat al-Wafa', 1983), I:162–6; al-Amin, *A'yan al-Shi'a*, V:173; VIII:239–40; X:22–3; al-Atat, *al-Shu'a'*, 142. His son Ibrahim died in Tus in 1669/70; see al-Amin, *A'yan al-Shi'a*, II:216.

[48] Ahmad ibn Muhammad Ibn Tawq (d. 1509), *Al-Ta'liq: Yawmiyyat Shihab al-Din Ahmad Ibn Tawq: Mudhakkirat Kutibat bi-Dimashq fi Awakhir al-'Ahd al-Mamluki 885–908 h / 1380–1502 m.*, ed. Ja'far al-Muhajir (Damascus: IFÉAD, 2000), I:12, 277, 363.

[49] Ahmad ibn Muhammad Ibn al-Himsi (d. 1527/8), *Hawadith al-Zaman wa-Wafayat al-Shuyukh wa'l-Aqran*, ed. 'Umar Tadmuri (Sidon: Maktaba al-'Asriyya, 1999), II:31; Muhammad Ibn Tulun (d. 1546), *Mufakahat al-Khillan fi Hawadith al-Zaman*, ed. Muhammad Mustafa (Cairo: Dar Ihya' al-Kutub al-'Arabiyya, 1962), I:200.

[50] See Fadil Bayat, *Dirasat fi Tarikh al-'Arab fi'l-'Ahd al-'Uthmani: Ru'ya Jadida fi Daw' al-Watha'iq wa'l-Masadir al-'Uthmaniyya* (Tripoli, Libya: Dar al-Madar al-Islami, 2003), 137; Akgündüz, *Osmanlı Kanunnâmeleri*, III:213.

killing the city's *subaşı* (commissioner) during his own revolt against the Empire in 1520.[51] After the revolt the Ottomans evicted the Harfushes from the deputyship of Baalbek, which they must also have controlled until then.[52] The Maronite patriarch and historian Duwayhi mentions the 'Harfush emirate' for the first time in 1534, when a Shiite tax farmer from Mt Lebanon called Hashim al-'Ajami ('the Iranian') supposedly sought refuge with them in Baalbek but was betrayed and thrown into a well that then bore his name; the anecdote, amazing in its detail considering that Duwayhi was writing over a century and a half later, seems above all designed to insert the Harfushes into and dramatize a 'plot' to divest the 'Assaf emirs of Mt Lebanon of their tax fiefs that year.[53]

Around the middle of the century the Bekaa was assigned in appanage to the Furaykh Bedouin dynasty, a situation later Damascene chroniclers attributed to emir Mansur Furaykh being 'observant of prayers, a champion of Sunnism, and hateful of the Shiites and Druze'.[54] The Harfush clan, in contrast, were said to be 'Shiite extremists' (*ghulat fi rafd*), though the famous emir Musa al-Harfush (d. 1607) was somewhat more charitably described as 'the closest to Sunnism' among them.[55] But was religion indeed a factor in their standing with the Ottoman authorities? Timar appointment (*Ruznamçe*) records from as early as 1555 mention the Harfushes as fiefholders in Baalbek, Wadi al-'Ajam and the Golan.[56] After the Ottomans' attempt to recruit them and other highland feudalists for the Yemen campaign, they are above all cited in chancery documents for their tyranny and banditry. In 1576 'Harfuş-oğlı 'Ali', who held a tax farm on local crown reserve (*havass-ı hümayun*) lands at the time, attacked the Zabadani area in the upper Barada Valley with a force of seventy or eighty horsemen, prompting an order to the Damascus *hajj* commander to intervene on the powerless villagers' behalf.[57] Three years later, the same emir 'Ali and two brothers from Baalbek, Fakhr al-Din and Aqra', were reported to have plundered and torched several villages in the region with a force of 800 musket-armed brigands. One of the petitions for help made by the villagers provides the first concrete evidence that the Sublime Porte was apprised of the perpetrators' sectarian identity: 'In addition to constantly attacking our valley, stealing goods and property, causing harm to the folk and families and oppression and injustice by killing untold people without reason, they are Rafizis.'[58]

The Porte ordered these allegations to be investigated, but seems to have been concerned above all with reviving the villages left empty and unproductive by the

---

[51] Bakhit, *The Ottoman Province of Damascus*, 28, 175; Abu-Husayn, *Provincial Leaderships*, 130.
[52] Muhammad Ibn Tulun, *Hawadith Dimashq al-Yawmiyya: Ghadat al-Ghazw al-'Uthmani li'l-Sham 926–951 h.: Safahat Mafquda tunshir li'l-marra al-ula min Kitab Mufakahat al-Khillan fi Hawadith al-Zaman*, ed. Ahmad Ibish (Damascus: Dar al-Awa'il, 2002), 129.
[53] Duwayhi, *Tarikh*, 250–1.
[54] Muhibbi, *Khulasat al-Athar*, IV:427; see also Ghazzi, *Lutf al-Samar*, 620–1; Abu-Husayn, 'The Iltizam of Mansur Furaykh', 253.
[55] Muhibbi, *Khulasat al-Athar*, IV:432.
[56] Başbakanlık Archives: Maliyeden Müdevver (MM) 4175:32; Timar Ruznamçe (DFE.RZD) 9:7a; 38:30b. I am grateful to Alexandre Hourani for these references.
[57] MD 42:494.    [58] MD 40:227, 238.

Harfushes' depredations. Only a few months later, in early 1580, the same three perpetrators were reported to have usurped the post of *subaşı* in Baalbek, 'whose population is Sunni Muslim', and then attacked even the refugees fleeing the region; Aqraʻ, the scion of one of the most powerful Shiite families of the Bekaa, brought back the heads of eight fallen enemies and allegedly exposed them in town with the words, 'This is the punishment for those who oppose me. We make the law around here [*emr ü nehy bizümdür*]!'[59] And in fact the Ottomans seem to have had little option but to continue relying on the Shiite chiefs, all their transgressions notwithstanding, as local agents of the state. An order sent to ʻAli Harfush in 1583, apparently the first to officially address him as an 'emir', states that he had been told several times already to defend the peasants and wayfarers in the Baalbek area against Bedouin raiders and demands that he make a greater effort; an order sent to the governor of Damascus at nearly the same time warns of an impending attack against Harfuş-oğlı, 'one of the notables of Baalbek', by a group of Turkmen with Zayn al-Din ibn Baydemür, whose family had been long-standing rivals for the governorship of Baalbek.[60] In 1584 both ʻAli Harfush and ʻAbu ʻAli' Aqraʻ were accused of stirring up strife and their arrest was ordered. Abu ʻAli had the title of imperial *çavuş* (sergeant) at the time; emir ʻAli, already the superintendent (*emin*) of Baalbek, had by then also been awarded the *sancak* governorship of Tadmur in the Syrian desert.[61]

The 1585 invasion of the Shuf did not specifically target the Harfushes, but ʻAli Harfush was among the local chieftains who were subsequently deported to Istanbul for several years. During his absence the Harfush family engaged in a bitter war with Abu ʻAli Aqraʻ, who had been left in charge of Baalbek, and whom emir ʻAli put to death in 1589 after his return from exile. The conflict was not resolved, however, and the Aqraʻs again replaced the Harfushes as intendants of Baalbek the following year. ʻAli took refuge in Damascus where he was eventually imprisoned and executed on the order of the grand vizier. Abdul-Rahim Abu-Husayn, who has written extensively on the Ottoman campaign and its aftermath, surmises this must have been motivated by his Shiism and potential secret contacts with Iran rather than by 'petty local intrigues'; his son Musa, on the other hand, was allowed to succeed him in Baalbek and even received the district governorship of Homs (in the *eyalet* of Tripoli) in 1592, having gained favour with the Ottoman authorities 'at least partly by pretending Sunnism'.[62]

The argument that the Harfushes' religious bearing played a role is again undermined, however, by the fact that ʻAli Harfush himself had held the *sancak-beğlik* of Homs since at least 1585, in return for a promise to pay 100,000 florins more over four years if the province were not given to anyone else in that time.[63] Even more surprisingly, ʻAli had written to the Sublime Porte just before the

---

[59] MD 39:110, 230.
[60] MD 52:20, 32; cf. Bakhit, *The Ottoman Province of Damascus*, 175. There had been a severe drought in Tripoli and Damascus that summer; see MD 51:69, 86.
[61] MD 53:73.    [62] Abu-Husayn, *Provincial Leaderships*, 131–4.    [63] MD 61:104.

punitive campaign that year, offering to take over the tax farms of Korkmaz Ma'n and other Druze in return for a similar payment – if the province of Sidon-Beirut were reorganized and given to him as a *beğlerbeğlik!*[64] The Ottomans seem to have decided against this idea, among other reasons perhaps because 'Ali was already having trouble meeting his initial commitment of 100,000 florins, but they maintained him as governor of Homs even during his exile in Istanbul and were still willing to give him the benefit of the doubt after his return to Syria. In 1588, he petitioned successfully to have 20,000 florins that he had paid a previous governor of Damascus to not transfer the Baalbek tax farm to Aqra' applied to his overall debt.[65] Only a few weeks later, the Sublime Porte came to 'Ali's defence and issued a harsh warning to the *sancak-beğ* of Jabala, Mehmed (Mihemed) Sayfa, that attacks by his kinsmen on the Harfushes' territory would no longer be tolerated:

Claiming that 'Ali, the district governor of Homs, was the cause of that thug Hasan Sayf-oğlı's capture and death, the Sayfas are constantly assembling soldiers and attacking the *havass-ı hümayun* villages around Baalbek ... Since they are your relatives, you must have known about this affair and were thus responsible ... If they ever gather again and even think of causing harm to the people of that region, ... you will be held responsible and accountable.[66]

And in 1589, just after 'Ali Harfush had executed Aqra', the *vali* was ordered to stop 'Aqra'-oğlı's followers and some miscreants associated with them' from raiding and plundering Baalbek 'with Harfuş-oğlı as their pretext'.[67] The *Mühimme* registers unfortunately do not recount what finally made the Sublime Porte lose patience with 'Ali and order his own execution the following year,[68] but they do cast doubt on religion as having been a primary factor. Not long after his arrest the military authorities of Homs sent yet another petition to Istanbul, cheerfully announcing that the new district governor sent to replace him was 'even more rapacious and oppressive than Harfuş-oğlı' himself.[69]

## The nexus between imperial and local interests

Why did the Ottomans reinstate 'Ali's son Musa Harfush as governor of Homs as well as *emin* of Baalbek, in 1592? The Shiite emirs' situation around the turn of the seventeenth century is illustrative of the complex ties of power and mutual dependency between imperial authorities, the provincial subject population and local notable intermediaries in the reformed administrative system. In Homs 'Ali had introduced several measures in line with his mandate to raise four years' worth of back-taxes, assigning new stewards (*kethüda*) to all five quarters in town, forcing them to post a pecuniary bond (*kefale*) to ensure payment, imposing an 'investigation tax' on the families of murder victims in the district and levying new charges on silk, coffee, kilims, wool products, etc., in the bazaar. Yet when the

---

[64] MD 50:102.    [65] MD 64:15.    [66] MD 64:86.    [67] MD 66:21.    [68] MD 67:12, 41.
[69] MD 66:79.

townsmen later complained that these 'illegal innovations' (*bidatlar*) were causing Homs to become ruined and abandoned, the Sublime Porte immediately ordered an end to such 'injustice and tyranny'.[70] At the same time, a high-ranking vizier was busy tracing all the debts still owed 'Ali Harfush (including one by his old nemesis Aqra') at the time of his execution, which would be easier to seize for the fisc so long as his heir Musa was maintained in office.[71] Weakened, vulnerable and personally indebted, the Harfushes were perhaps now more than ever the ideal provincial tax collection agency.

The mixed messages coming out of Istanbul also reflect the particular concerns of certain government authorities, and warn again of the dangers of reifying the Ottoman 'state'. In 1594 the *vali* of Damascus, Murad Paşa, asked Fakhr al-Din Ma'n to capture the son of the recently executed emir Mansur ibn Furaykh; Korkmaz Furaykh attempted to flee to the Sayfas in Mt Lebanon but was finally captured and killed in the Bekaa by Musa Harfush on Ma'n's behalf.[72] But less than a year later, after the Sublime Porte received a complaint from Muhammad Furaykh that his brother Korkmaz had been murdered and robbed by 'brigands named Ma'n-oğlı, Harfuş-oğlı' and others, Murad Paşa's successor as well as the *qadi* of Damascus were ordered to restore the stolen goods to the Furaykhs, get their hands on the 'evil-doers' by any means possible and imprison them.[73] And then only a few weeks after that, this time in response to a petition by the overseer of imperial pious foundations, Musa Harfush himself received a very different writ, entreating him to expend every effort to protect the peasant villages in the Bekaa attached to the Karak Nuh *waqf*, whose population was 'fleeing from one hardship to another' and causing an untimely revenue shortfall.[74]

The Harfushes' dependence on the goodwill and protection of individual Ottoman authorities had a decisive influence on their relations with other tribal groupings in the region. Musa Harfush was initially on good terms with the Druze emir Fakhr al-Din Ma'n, whom the Porte had made *sancak-beğ* of Safad in 1590, leading later historians to posit his subordination to the nascent 'Lebanese' emirate. In fact their alliance as well as their mutual support for the government of Damascus seems to have been predicated on a strategic rivalry with the Sayfas of Tripoli, whose territorial ambitions collided with those of *vali*s and emirs alike in the neighbouring provinces. The Harfushes had been at war with part of the Sayfa family in the Bekaa, as noted, since at least 1588. Musa Harfush and Fakhr al-Din Ma'n joined forces again in 1598, apparently at the behest of the governor of Damascus, to attack Yusuf Sayfa, then governor of Tripoli, and evict him from the Kisrawan. In 1602, Musa raided the Jubbat Basharri district in Mt Lebanon, prompting a return attack by the Sayfas on Baalbek shortly after, and a year later Musa openly sided with the Damascus Janissary faction in their long-standing struggle against the Aleppo Janissaries so that they would support him over Yusuf

---

[70] MD 71:17, 299, 332.    [71] MD 71:16.
[72] Muhibbi, *Khulasat al-Athar*, IV:427–8; see also Abu-Husayn, *Provincial Leaderships*, 156–9.
[73] MD 73:461; see also MD 81:101.    [74] MD 73:369, 393.

Sayfa in the Bekaa.[75] The emirs' 'petty local intrigues' were part and parcel of the ceaseless competition for prestige and promotion within the Ottoman governing elite itself. What would catapult them to the forefront of imperial concerns in the early seventeenth century was neither the emirs' heterodoxy nor their purported independentism, but their intertwinement with a conflict of imperial scale and consequences: the Celali rebellions and 'Elî Canpolad Paşa's attempt to seize control of all Syria.

The rebellions by leading provincial governors against the central state around the turn of the seventeenth century, misleadingly assimilated to the Kızılbaş Celali revolt of the sixteenth, were the culmination of a number of interrelated crises that had begun to afflict the Empire in the post-classical age: rapid but uneven integration into the Mediterranean commercial economy; the decline of the feudal cavalry and the monetarization of administrative office, rural population pressure and the emergence of *sekban* mercenary bands; and growing competition for top-level posts among the provincial *ümera* households. In Syria, as William Griswold has demonstrated, these were further exacerbated by an incipient commercial rivalry between Tripoli and Aleppo with its new maritime outlet at Alexandretta as well as the conflict between the Damascus and Aleppo Janissaries. Thus when Aleppo's rebel strongman 'Elî Canpolad began to establish ties to Tuscany and Safavid Iran and marched south to seize Damascus and the rich coastal highlands in 1606, it was not surprising that Yusuf Sayfa of Tripoli would put himself at the forefront of Ottoman efforts to contain him, nor that the increasingly assertive Fakhr al-Din Ma'n, who no doubt shared Canpolad's thirst for greater regional autonomy, would join with him.[76]

The Harfushes, like many other local notabilities, were a good deal more equivocal about the rebellion, which probably helped preserve their position over the long run. Musa Harfush at first tried to mediate between the invading 'Elî Canpolad and the Janissaries of Damascus, while his own cousin Yunus, according to Fakhr al-Din Ma'n's biographer al-Safadi, split from him to support the rebels. Musa divested Yunus of his landholdings in the Bekaa but was then driven out himself by the combined forces of Canpolad and Ibn Ma'n, dying as a refugee in Damascus in 1607.[77] Yet after the collapse of the rebellion the Ottomans were quick to reconcile with both Fakhr al-Din and Yunus Harfush. The latter was reinstated as commissioner (*zabit*) of Baalbek – and then even had the gall to invoke 'all the tyranny and oppression caused when Canpolad-oğlı rebelled' as the cause of the region's economic ruin in a petition for tax relief he made to the Sublime Porte in 1611.[78]

The period after the Canpolad revolt indeed proved something of the Shiite emirs' heyday in western Syria. Fakhr al-Din Ma'n, despite buying himself back

[75]  Salibi, 'The Sayfas', 32; Abu-Husayn, *Provincial Leaderships*, 22–4, 135–6.
[76]  William Griswold, *The Great Anatolian Rebellion 1000–1020/1591–1611* (Berlin: Klaus Schwarz, 1983), 60–114.
[77]  Ahmad ibn Muhammad al-Khalidi al-Safadi (d. 1624/5), *Lubnan fi 'Ahd al-Amir Fakhr al-Din al-Ma'ni al-Thani*, ed. Asad Rustum and Fu'ad al-Bustani (Beirut: Lebanese University, 1969), 134.
[78]  MD 79:478.

into the good graces of several governors, continued to arouse suspicion with his independent demeanour and ascendancy over all other local factions. Driven into exile in Tuscany in 1613, the threat of him invading with European support hung over the entire region for the next years.[79] In this context Yunus Harfush soon emerged as the Ottomans' most favoured local intermediary, taking part in punitive campaigns against the Shuf in 1613 and 1614 while escaping censure when his own men robbed an imperial messenger in the Bekaa around the same time; getting the Sublime Porte to order the return of peasants who had fled the area because of the ravages caused by imperial troops; and using his influence to nominate a Damascene Janissary to a military post in Homs.[80] Most important, Ottoman backing enabled him once again to thwart his old enemies, the Sayfas and their supporters. By 1616 Yunus had been reappointed to Homs where he defeated Bedouin tribesmen allied with the Sayfas, and evicted a rebel in-law who had taken control of the Bekaa tax farms with the Sayfas' help, suing him for the revenues that he had failed to remit.[81] He was also able to demand compensation for taxes he had been paying for five years on behalf of the inhabitants of 'Aqura (in the mountains above Jubayl, but assigned to the district of Baalbek), after they had left to take up residence in Tripoli while a Sayfa was governor there. As was usual in these cases, the villagers were made to return to their old homes unless they could prove having been gone for more than ten years.[82]

Yunus Harfush's new stature, however, would inevitably bring him into conflict with the Ma'n family. Al-Safadi, our only contemporary local narrative source for this period, details how Yunus intervened with the Ottomans on their behalf, negotiating the surrender (and destruction) of some of Fakhr al-Din's fortresses but securing the reappointment of his sons to the *sancak-beğliks* of Safad and Sidon. He also married his son Ahmad to one of the Druze emir's daughters, and as the region's new feudal master soon began interfering in the nomination of officials to the Ma'ns' districts. Around 1617, Ahmad Harfush broke ground on a new mansion in Mashgara in the southern extremity of the Bekaa, ostensibly to be closer to his in-laws, but apparently also in an attempt to extend his influence into the Jabal 'Amil. The Ma'ns soon complained to Yunus that Ahmad was corresponding with and gathering all the Shiite notables of the area around him, thereby threatening the 'trust and affection' between the two families. Ahmad was made to abandon his plans but significantly did not break off his relations with the 'Amili Shiites.[83]

The Ottomans' policy of co-opting individual local notables, keeping them under personal obligation, playing them off against each other and using them to counter the influence of rival officials explains, more than their religious or supposed geo-political orientation, how even a family of Shiite emirs could emerge as the strongest

---

[79] Cf. Dror Ze'evi, *An Ottoman Century: The District of Jerusalem in the 1600s* (Albany: State University of New York Press, 1996), 20–1, 165.

[80] MD 80:51; MD 81:35, 87.

[81] MD 81:19, 20, 93, 141; see also Abu-Husayn, *Provincial Leaderships*, 139–42.    [82] MD 81:37, 87.

[83] al-Khalidi al-Safadi, *Lubnan*, 60, 66–7; see also Abu-Husayn, *Provincial Leaderships*, 142–3; Darwish, *Jabal 'Amil*, 41–5, 66–7.

faction in western Syrian feudal politics after the turbulent first decade of the seventeenth century. The same open-ended policy, however, also did not preclude the return of Fakhr al-Din ibn Ma'n from exile in 1618, allowing him to re-establish his dominance over all the other tribal factions in Damascus province and resume his rivalry with the Sayfas of Tripoli. The years following his return furthermore marked the beginning of the special relationship between the 'Duc des Druzes' and the Catholic community, whose gratitude and loyalty he earned by recruiting Maronite notables from Tripoli into his service, building churches and monasteries and inciting Maronite immigration into the Shuf, and opening the region under his control to the implantation of Latin missionaries.[84] The Harfushes, who for a while had been the primary beneficiaries of the Ottomans' administrative pragmatism, now found themselves back on difficult terrain, vying for official favour in the continuous, but in the long term fruitless, effort to maintain themselves vis-à-vis all too powerful local competitors and their backers.

## The contest with Fakhr al-Din ibn Ma'n

By 1623 the Druze emir was again so strong that, in a dispute over the district governorships of Safad, Nablus and Ajlun, he was able to rout the combined forces of the *vali* of Damascus, the Harfushes, their Janissary allies and the Sayfas, who had rallied to their side in somewhat of a regional diplomatic revolution. The *vali* himself was captured, Yunus Harfush was caught and imprisoned by Bedouin friendly to Fakhr al-Din in Salamya, and the citadel of Baalbek and other fortresses in the Bekaa were subsequently seized and razed to the ground. The 'battle of 'Anjar' has thus become one of the paroxysms of the Lebanist national narrative, a moment when the Ma'ns (with their Shihabi allies) were able to impose their order not just over all the tribal chieftaincies from northern Tripoli province to northern Palestine but also over the very strictures of Ottoman government in the region. In the nineteenth century historians of Lebanon would proclaim that Fakhr al-Din had been officially recognized as 'sultan al-barr' (ruler of the land (of Syria)) by the Ottomans.[85]

The problem is that Ottoman chancery sources for this period in general are wanting, a reflection perhaps of the crisis of central authority in the early years of the century and especially the drama surrounding the deposition and regicide of Osman II in 1622. (The Druze emir, whose power by this time was legendary even in Istanbul, was in fact invoked as both a bogeyman and as a potential ally of the sultan by contemporary observers.[86]) Fortunately, a less event-based, more long-term impression of the struggle between various local factions for control of the

---

[84] See Bernard Heyberger, *Les chrétiens du Proche-Orient au temps de la réforme catholique* (Rome: École Française, 1994), 33–4, 187–90, 194–5, 221, 274.

[85] P. M. Holt, *Egypt and the Fertile Crescent 1516–1922: A Political History* (Ithaca: Cornell University Press, 1966), Part II: 'The Ottoman Decline', 117–18; Soueid, *Histoire militaire*, 284–93. For local legends on Fakhr al-Din's siege of Baalbek see Goudard, *La Sainte Vierge au Liban*, 410.

[86] Tezcan, 'Searching for Osman', 222–3, 226–7.

Bekaa Valley before and after the battle of 'Anjar can be obtained from a recently published register of *iltizam* appointments for the province of Damascus. Covering the years 1616 to 1635, the register among other things provides documentary evidence of the Harfushes' growing marginalization as well as of the rise of the Shihabis of Wadi Taym as new contenders for government tax farms in the region. Beginning in 1618, for example, around the time of Fakhr al-Din's return from Tuscany, Yunus Harfush came under pressure to renounce the income normally due to the *emin* of Baalbek from the village of 'Aytha, after the *mufti* of Damascus (a native of 'Aytha) had petitioned for it to be set aside for himself in the supposed interest of reviving and repopulating the area. Even in later years, after the Harfushes had retaken control of the Bekaa from the Ma'ns and the *mufti* was long dead, the village remained formally excluded from their holdings.[87]

The register also sheds light on the administrative context of the *fitna* (strife) between the Harfushes and Ma'ns in 1623–4. It corroborates local chroniclers' claims that Fakhr al-Din offered to send the sultan 100,000 gold coins for the Baalbek tax concession, but casts doubt on the notion that the governor of Damascus simply 'paid no heed' to the offer or ignored the Sublime Porte's orders to instate him.[88] In fact Fakhr al-Din's offer was matched by Yunus, and the *iltizam* was reconfirmed to his son 'Ali Harfush (in whose name it had also previously been registered) by the *kadi*s of Damascus and Baalbek immediately after the battle of 'Anjar. Fakhr al-Din then carried out his promise to the grand vizier to destroy the fortresses of Baalbek and al-Labwa, which he had characterized as 'dens of thieves' in his petition for the tax farm, but in the spring of 1624 the decision to award it on the same terms to 'Ali Harfush was again upheld by the court and *divan* (government council) of Damascus.[89] Nothing in these documents suggests that Fakhr al-Din was ever granted any extraordinary authority by the Ottomans.

The Harfushes, however, soon had difficulty in living up to their commitments, and the Ma'ns wasted no time in turning this to their advantage. In another case only a few weeks later, the court took away the tax farm for the Bekaa-ı 'Aziz (southern Bekaa) and adjoining areas from 'Ali's brother Husayn Harfush, who had allegedly oppressed and ruined the land before deserting his office altogether, and gave it instead to Fakhr al-Din's son 'Ali Ma'n, the *sancak-beğ* of Safad.[90] The following summer, in 1625, Yunus Harfush was forced to explain to the same court why he still owed taxes for the two previous years, blaming the Ma'ns' 'occupation' of the Bekaa for its ruin and abandonment by the impoverished peasants.[91] The revenue from this tax farm was earmarked for the organization of the annual *hajj* caravan as well as for the sustenance of the Damascus Janissary division, and Yunus' downfall began precisely when his erstwhile allies complained they had

---

[87] Nagata Yuzo, Miura Toru and Shimizu Yasuhisa, eds., *Tax Farm Register of Damascus Province in the Seventeenth Century: Archival and Historical Studies* (Tokyo: Toyo Bunko, 2006), 23, 61, 136, 353, 355, 370. I am grateful to Tomoki Okawara for providing me with a copy of this publication.

[88] al-Khalidi al-Safadi, *Lubnan*, 139; Ghazzi, *Lutf al-Samar*, 473, 620–1; Abu-Husayn, *Provincial Leaderships*, 115, 148.

[89] Nagata et al., eds., *Tax Farm Register of Damascus*, 183.    [90] *Ibid.*, 186, 196–7.    [91] *Ibid.*, 200.

received only 'excuses and evasiveness' in lieu of money for the past year. In early 1626 the *ocak* formally petitioned for the tax farm to be transferred to 'Ali Ma'n, who, with his father's surety, had promised to increase the yearly payments, secure the financing of the *hajj*, revive the Bekaa and put an end to the Harfushes' 'oppression' once and for all.[92]

Seen in this light, the distribution of tax farms in the area seems due less to the prowess of individual emirs or the favouritism of individual *vali*s than the outcome of a relatively rational, institutional decision-making process designed to maximize government revenues and control. Inasmuch as a large proportion of the revenues from western Syria were reserved for the imperial *hajj* operation, the competition to denounce and outbid rivals for local tax contracts directly benefited what our register declares to be 'among the most important concerns of state and religion [*din ü devlet*]' in the Empire.[93] The only irony is that it was Druze and Shiite agents who would carry out this competition in the first half of the seventeenth century. Al-Safadi's continuator, Duwayhi, indicates that Yunus Harfush was executed at Fakhr al-Din's instigation in 1626; by 1633, however, the Ottomans had also lost patience with the latter's defiance and exiled him to Istanbul, where he too was executed two years later.[94] Travellers to Baalbek at the time claimed its antique citadel had been ruined by Fakhr al-Din in his war against the Harfushes; the fact that al-Nabulusi heard exactly the same explanation on his own visit to the Bekaa over fifty years later (though he noted the damage was more likely the result of an earthquake in 1201!) suggests that the legend of the emirs' great confrontation had already acquired a life and reality of its own.[95]

Starting in the summer of 1633, the Damascus *iltizam* register records the reassignation of individual tax concessions formerly held by the 'rebel' Fakhr al-Din, from Hama in the north to Safad in the south. The southern Bekaa was initially awarded to the Shihabis of Wadi Taym, the Ma'ns' closest allies, who would emerge as the most powerful faction in the region at the end of the century. Husayn Harfush, who had been ejected from the same farm a decade beforehand, took control of Baalbek and 'Anjar, but proved just as vexing this time around. The following year both the northern and southern Bekaa concessions were back in the hands of his brother 'Ali Harfush.[96] 'Ali too must have fallen foul of the authorities soon after, however, for the governor of Damascus reported an attempt on his part to retake control of Baalbek by force in 1636, apparently in concert with other tribal and *sekban* factions in the area – including, not altogether surprisingly, the now humbled Ma'ns.[97] Thereafter we have a gap of thirty years in Ottoman documents pertaining to the Harfushes; only a reference in local literature to a palace built by

---

[92]  *Ibid.*, 209–11, 260.    [93]  *Ibid.*, 139, 257.

[94]  Duwayhi, *Tarikh*, 321–3; Abu-Husayn, *Provincial Leaderships*, 125–7, 151–2.

[95]  Ramadan ibn Musa al-'Utayfi (d. 1684), 'Rihla min Dimashq al-Sham ila Tarabulus al-Sham' in Wild and Munajjid, eds., *Zwei Reisebeschreibungen*, 14; al-Nabulusi, 'Hullat al-Dhahab', 85.

[96]  Nagata *et al.*, eds., *Tax Farm Register of Damascus*, 355, 359, 370.

[97]  MD 86:74, 76; see also Duwayhi, *Tarikh*, 334; Naima Mustafa Efendi (d. 1716), *Târih-i Na'îmâ*, ed. Mehmet İpşirli (Ankara: Türk Tarih Kurumu, 2007), 839.

'Ali and Husayn's cousin 'Umar ibn Isma'il Harfush in Baalbek in 1667/8 suggests that the family, the vicissitudes of its relationship with the state notwithstanding, continued to hold some sway over the Bekaa in this period.[98] Around the same time, in August 1667, 'Ali, Husayn and 'Umar were accused of having killed and robbed two Damascene janissaries in Baalbek; five years later, according to the imperial complaints registers (*Şikayet Defterleri*) they had still not been brought to justice.[99]

## Conclusion: what emirate?

The Shiite Harfush family in many ways constituted the typical Ottoman provincial feudatory of the early modern period. Since before the conquest, their tribal cohesion and military disposition, their interrelations with similar notable families and their standing within Twelver Shiite society in the Bekaa Valley (as scholars and protectors of religious shrines) predestined them to act as local representatives of the state. The Harfushes were among the first tribal leaders to be co-opted into the imperial military apparatus as 'emirs' and, after the fiscal reforms of the later sixteenth century, the first to be awarded lump-sum tax collection contracts in combination with governor titles to secondary provinces and districts such as Homs, Tadmur and Baalbek. Like the Druze Ma'ns, who quickly surpassed them in terms of power and resources, their confessional identity was basically irrelevant in the ceaseless competition for support and contract allotments on the part of Ottoman state authorities. The inherent rivalry for local *iltizam* concessions was often grafted onto the wider competition for influence and advancement among Ottoman provincial officials, in which the Harfushes' very dependence and vulnerability could make them the ideal partners for various government actors, to serve and be disposed of again as fiscal necessities required. The Harfush emirs and their compeers were all in essence Ottoman creatures.

The story of the Harfushes thus challenges the central tenets of the Lebanist narrative, namely that the powers enjoyed by certain tribal emirs of the coastal highlands were in any way unique within the Ottoman system or translated a weakness of Ottoman provincial administration in Syria; that the Druze emirs stood for the interests of the Druze and Maronite communities and therefore, by extension, of all minority confessional groups in the area; and that the parochial and feudal alliances forged at certain times by the Ma'n family somehow constituted a unified political regime, one which lies at the core of modern Lebanon. The Harfush emirs, if one relies on the administrative sources rather than on the narrative chronicles, were no less the exponent of their particular rural society than other local taxlord dynasties of the Ottoman period.

The problem is thus not merely one of filling in the blanks, of furnishing the history of 'Ottoman Lebanon' with some details on a community that has perhaps always been a bit neglected, but of questioning the basic concepts of this

---

[98] al-Amin, *A'yan al-Shi'a*, VIII:375.    [99] Başbakanlık Archives: Şikayet Defteri (ŞD) 6:68; 8:54.

historiography. For while the Ottomans certainly recognized individual tribal notables and their families as 'emirs' (or *beğ*s) in return for their services, nothing in our sources suggests that they conceived of an 'emirate' (*beğlik*) in the abstract, that is, of a set institution of local governance in the coastal highlands that would allow us to infer the existence of a 'Druze', let alone of a 'Lebanese', polity, at this time. The history of the Harfush emirs thus begs the question: what was this 'classical system' of proto-Lebanon in which the Shiites seem always accommodated but never present? The previous chapter concluded with a caveat not to reify the Ottoman state in seeking to make sense of its 'ideology' vis-à-vis Shiism. The concrete experiences of the Harfushes and other tribal notables as Ottoman government tax farmers suggests that the prescription of terms such as 'prince' and 'Duc', of '*imara*' and even just of 'Ottoman Lebanon' to describe a provincial reality both more complex and more mundane, be subject to the same sort of caveat.

# CHAPTER 3

# Mount Lebanon under Shiite rule: the Hamada 'emirate', 1641–1685

The Shiite Hamadas of Mt Lebanon were never invested with a *sancak-beğlik*, nor were they referred to as 'emirs' in contemporary local sources. Yet for a time in the later seventeenth century, the family controlled a territory that stretched from Safita in modern-day Syria to the Futuh district in the mountains above Jubayl, south-east of Tripoli. They retained some of their tax farms until 1763, when they were evicted by the Druze emirs of Sidon, the Shihabis, and went with their affiliated clans into exile on the other side of Mt Lebanon in the Bekaa Valley. The Imami community has all but disappeared from the region of Tripoli today, and the Hamadas never became as renowned as the Harfush emirs of Baalbek or the scholar families of Jabal 'Amil. Yet the archival and literary records of their rise to power, their regular contact with the state authorities and their turbulent rapport with their local subjects and rivals mark the history of the Hamada 'emirate' as the best documented of any Shiite group in the Ottoman Empire.

The Hamadas were probably the single most important feudal power in the coastal highlands between the demise of Fakhr al-Din ibn Ma'n in 1633 and the rise of the Shihabis in 1697. Lebanese historiography, however, has been unequivocal in condemning their reign not only as repressive but also as inherently foreign and illegitimate – 'l'invasion des Métoualis [Shiites] ... très belliqueux et cruels, qui occupèrent les hautes régions, depuis Akkar jusqu'au Futûh, et, inspirant aux chrétiens une grande terreur, les refoulèrent vers la côte'.[1] '[F]anatiques, rapaces, sans foi ni loi ..., ivres de puissance et de richesses, ... les Hamadeh ... ont mis le pays des Maronites en coupe réglée et y ont commis tous les crimes possibles.'[2] Often the entire Hamada period rates but a single vituperative phrase: 'la tutelle onéreuse et tracassière de la famille des cheikhs chiites de la Biqa' septentrionale'[3] that was only brought to term by a 'national uprising'[4] in the later eighteenth century. 'The Hamadas did not recognize the

---

[1] M. Jouplain (pseudonym for Bulus Nujaym), *La question du Liban: Étude d'histoire diplomatique et de droit international* (Paris: Arthur Rousseau, 1908), 87–8.

[2] Toufic Touma, *Paysans et institutions féodales chez les Druses et les Maronites du Liban du XVIIe siècle à 1914* (1st edn 1971; Beirut: Université Libanaise, 1986), 420, 490, 636.

[3] Chevallier, *La société du Mont Liban*, 12.

[4] Philip Hitti, *Lebanon in History: From the Earliest Times to the Present* (London: Macmillan, 1957), 387.

overlordship of the Lebanese [*sic*] emirs, and their rule in north Lebanon was violent and oppressive.'[5]

The negative stereotype of the Hamadas is the legacy of an overwhelmingly Maronite narrative historiography of the period, but their contumacy and fierceness is often conveyed in Ottoman chancery documents and French consular reports as well. The purpose of the following chapters is to provide a first complete history of the Hamadas' rule in Mt Lebanon on the basis of both chronicle and documentary sources, one which tries to explain how, as state-sponsored *mukataaci*s, they could emerge as perhaps the strongest Shiite polity in the Empire, but then ultimately failed to maintain themselves within the local highland feudal order. Lebanese history has all but forgotten the violence and tyranny of the more successful of the early modern feudatories;[6] that the Hamadas' rule was uniformly defined and recorded in terms of its excesses, it will be argued, was already then a prime factor in its delegitimization and eventual elimination.

This chapter begins with the prehistory of the Shiite 'emirate' in Mt Lebanon. While Maronite historians have conventionally portrayed the Hamadas as recent intruders to the region, the first section traces the Shiite tribal presence in the Tripoli hinterland through the medieval period, and describes the Shiite-inhabited rural districts in the early sixteenth century on the basis of Ottoman tax cadastres. It can be argued that the Hamadas, whose precise origins remain obscure, were in the best position to benefit from the Ottomans' institution of *iltizam* tax farming in the region on account of their itinerancy and inherently tribal organization. Their wars with other tribal factions and their emergence as the dominant tax concessionary household in the *eyalet* of Tripoli are then examined on the basis of the classical narrative accounts. The final section presents the Ottoman archival record of the Hamadas' relations with the state authorities. While chancery documents occasionally attack them for tax truancy and excessive tyranny against their subjects, the Islamic court registers of Tripoli permit us to trace a regular, institutionalized relationship between the Shiite *mukataaci*s and the Ottoman state during the second half of the seventeenth century.

## Shiite tribalism in Mt Lebanon

Why have the Hamadas so consistently been written out of the Lebanese national narrative? Much of the explanation lies in the perception of the Shiites' ethnic and sociological origins. The myth of the Shiites' recent intrusion into a rightly Christian Mt Lebanon derives in large part from the single-volume *Tarikh al-Azmina*, compiled by the Maronite patriarch Istfan al-Duwayhi in 1699. Duwayhi first mentions a 'shaykh Hamada' in 1547, stating that he and a brother emigrated from Iran 'upon

---

[5] Kamal Salibi, *The Modern History of Lebanon* (London: Weidenfeld & Nicolson, 1965), 4.
[6] Beydoun, *Identité confessionelle*, 519.

the conquest of Tabriz', which he dates inaccurately to 1499.[7] The Hamadas' own oral tradition rejects the Iranian connection and claims they descend from the Arab Hamir tribe of Kufa, whose ancestor Hani' ibn 'Urwa ibn Mudhhij was among Husayn's supporters at Kerbela in 680 CE.[8] Already around 1700, an anonymous French diplomat reported that the Hamadas' ethnic background is disputed: 'Les uns croient qu'ils sont venus de Perse à cause qu'ils sont de la secte d'Ali. Les autres qu'ils viennent que des environs de Seide ou Sidon.'[9]

The origins question says more about the ideological stakes of Lebanese histor-iography than it provides useful information on the Shiite presence in the northern coastal highlands. In the nineteenth century, Lebanist historians embellished Duwayhi's account to present the Hamadas as natives of Bukhara and erstwhile soldiers of the Iranian shah.[10] This, along with the Persian toponym of the Shiite-inhabited 'Kisrawan', and the family ties between Safavid and Lebanese Shiite religious scholars, laid the basis for a view which became popular during the Arab literary revival (*nahda*) of the later century: namely that all Shiites are somehow Iranians.[11] As Rula Abisaab has suggested with respect to the Jabal 'Amil, the depiction of Shiism as intrinsically Persian made it possible to '[allot] specific racial roots to the sectarian communities that composed modern Lebanon so as to construe which of these could lay an "authentic" claim to the land and history of Lebanon'.[12] Not that the Hamadas' own claim to be descended from Iraqi 'Alids must be taken as objective fact. (The Druze Hamadas of Baqlin, not fortuitously, claim an ancestry in the Fatimid Ismaili homeland of North Africa.) In recent times, Lebanese Shiite historians have sought to trace the entire national community's descent from the Banu Hamdan, a pure-blood Bedouin tribe.[13]

The Hamadas' and other Syrian Shiites' primordial ethnic roots are not addressed in any administrative source and will hardly have interested sixteenth- to eighteenth-century Ottoman authorities. Their fundamental characteristic, perhaps the underlying cause of their deprecation in classical historiography, was less their racial and religious than their sociological background. Unlike Maronite rural society, which Duwayhi and other churchmen sought to edify and

---

[7] Duwayhi, *Tarikh*, 224, 258; 'Isa Iskandar al-Ma'luf (d. 1956), *Diwani al-Qatuf fi Tarikh Bani al-Ma'luf* (1st edn 1908; new edn, Damascus: Dar Hawran, 2003), 203; al-Ma'luf, *Tarikh al-Amir Fakhr al-Din al-Ma'ni al-Thani*, ed. Riyad al-Ma'luf (Beirut: Catholic Press, 1966), 70–1.

[8] al-Amin, *A'yan al-Shi'a*, II:582.

[9] Anonymous, 'Mémoire pour le Roi relatif aux Maronites, aux Druses, et aux Amédiens (entendre aux Chiites), habitants du Liban', Bibliothèque Nationale: Ms. Français 32926 fols. 93a–100a, published in Nasser Gemayel, *Les échanges culturels entre les Maronites et l'Europe: Du Collège de Rome (1584) au Collège de 'Ayn-Warqa (1789)* (Beirut: 1984), 819–20.

[10] Haydar Ahmad al-Shihabi (d. 1835), *Tarikh al-Amir Haydar Ahmad al-Shihabi, a.k.a. Al-Ghurar al-Hisan fi Akhbar Abna' al-Zaman* (Cairo: Matba'at al-Salam, 1900), 612; Tannus al-Shidyaq, *Akhbar al-A'yan fi Jabal Lubnan*, ed. Fu'ad Afram al-Bustani (Beirut: Lebanese University, 1970), 192.

[11] See H. Lammens, 'Les "Perses" du Liban et l'origine des Métoualis', *Mélanges de l'Université Saint-Joseph* 14 (1929), 23–39.

[12] Rula Abisaab, 'Shi'ite Beginnings and Scholastic Tradition in Jabal 'Amil in Lebanon', *The Muslim World* 89 (1999), 2–3.

[13] Ja'far al-Muhajir, *Al-Ta'sis li-Tarikh al-Shi'a fi Lubnan wa-Suriyya* (Beirut: Dar al-Milak, 1992), 67–89.

preserve in writing, the Shiites of Mt Lebanon were organized by tribes and still practised some form of seasonal transhumance. In one of the first serious studies on the history of north Lebanon's Shiites, Rabâh Abi-Haidar describes three 'classes' among the late Ottoman-era population: the sedentary farmer and merchant families established there since early times; the tribes (*'asha'ir*) affiliated with the Hamadas who settled in several villages forming a defensive line towards the Kisrawan and other non-Shiite regions in the fifteenth century; and migrant families noted for their learned culture who probably came from Jabal 'Amil and settled under the Hamadas' protection in the later seventeenth century.[14] Numerous semi-nomadic pastoral groups such as the Hamadas seem in fact to have entered the coastal mountains, often coming from tribal regions much further east in Anatolia or Iraq, in the wake of the Mongol invasion and until the establishment of Ottoman hegemony over the Near East. Many, including a number of well-known Kurdish clans, only assimilated slowly into local society, retaining their traditional religion, language and pastoral culture in tightly knit, endogamous communities. Their tribal order, herdsman skills and mobility made each into a natural military force, one which the Mamluk or Ottoman state authorities were eager to exploit in order to police and tax the rural highland population on their behalf. Hardy and fractious like their Anatolian counterparts, nominally Shiite in the same sense as the Kızılbaş, clans such as the Sha'irs and Hamadas, like the Harfushes, were among the most effective of these tribal/fiscal operations in the rugged, sparsely populated northern mountains. And it was their very success as agents of the Ottoman regime that has conditioned a historiographical verdict which still echoes in contemporary Lebanist discourse: '[C]ette communauté ne s'est que fort peu attachée à la terre et est restée sans lien avec la vie paysanne.'[15]

The sociological argument has been put most pithily by Kamal Salibi, who describes a perennial clash between herdsmen from Baalbek, on the one side, and the Jubbat al-Basharri district, on the other, who each year would follow the retreating snows into the mountain pastures above Tripoli: '[W]ith every spring, the goat war which had gone on in the high Lebanon since time immemorial was resumed, taking the form of a Maronite–Shiite religious conflict.'[16] Yet this reinforces a popular misconception that the Shiite tribes were only indigenous to the Bekaa Valley. The Hamadas did acquire the *iltizam* for Hermel in the northern Bekaa and ultimately found refuge there in the eighteenth century, but the presence of Shiites in Mt Lebanon, if not of the Hamada family itself, goes back far into the Middle Ages. Around the turn of the eleventh century, the Nusayri sect, which in its theology was not yet entirely distinct from what would later be considered mainstream Imami Shiism, is known to have migrated from Aleppo to the coastal mountains as far south as the Golan and northern Galilee.

---

[14] Rabâh Abi-Haidar, 'La société chiite des Bilad Jebayl à l'époque de la Mutasarrifiyya (1861–1917) d'après des documents inédits' (Sorbonne-Paris IV doctoral thesis, 1976), 86–91.

[15] Adel Ismail, *Histoire du Liban du XVIIe siècle à nos jours* (Paris: G.-P. Maisonneuve, 1955), I:25–6.

[16] Kamal Salibi, 'The Muqaddams of Bšarrī: Maronite Chieftains of the Northern Lebanon, 1382–1621', *Arabica* 15 (1968), 66.

The Druze sect, itself an offshoot of Ismaili Shiism, as well as the Maronites also moved into the coastal mountains in the eleventh century, under Fatimid rule. Until the crusader conquest of 1109, Tripoli was governed on the Fatimids' behalf by the Banu 'Ammar, a Twelver Shiite *qadi* dynasty of North African and Sicilian provenance. 'Ammarid rule is seen today as somewhat of a 'golden age' of Shiism in the region, when Tripoli was a reputed centre of Imami scholarship and commanded a large Shiite hinterland, where the district name 'Zanniyya' (or 'Danniyye' in local dialect) still recalls the 'Alid esotericism of its medieval population.[17]

The advent of mainly Turkic military regimes in the Middle East beginning in the later eleventh century has sometimes been described in terms of a 'Sunni restoration' after two centuries of Shiite ascendancy under the Fatimids, Buyids and Hamdanids. The Turkic regimes, however, had no policy of imposing socio-religious conformity (a modern anachronism) in the areas under their control. The Burid dynasty, for example, invited Ismaili Shiites to Damascus around 1120 and facilitated their implantation in the coastal mountains, mainly to win them as supporters in its struggle against the Damascene Shafi'i establishment.[18] The Ayyubids, for their part, frequently allied with the Ismaili 'assassins' against the crusaders, and probably helped settle other Shiite groups on military fiefs in the coastal highlands. Even the Mamluk sultanate of Cairo, which managed to re-establish a measure of centralized control over the Syrian lands in the later thirteenth century, recognized the local autonomy of the Ismaili emirs, extended them tax reprieves and retained their services in murdering high-level deserters who had defected to Ilkhanid Iran.[19]

Still, as the earliest of the early modern Muslim bureaucratic states, the Mamluks did introduce measures of societal and administrative consolidation that were prejudicial to the heterodox population, such as the institutionalization of four official schools of Islamic law (*madhhab*), the suppression of Zaydi Shiism in Mecca and Medina, and the promulgation of occasional rescripts against Twelvers and Nusayris in the Syrian coastlands.[20] Doubtless the best-known episode in the history of Mamluk–Shiite relations are the punitive campaigns launched against the Kisrawan district in 1292, 1300 and 1305 in an effort to bring the rebellious mountaineers under control. The Kisrawan campaigns have in fact become one of the most contested issues in Lebanese historiography, as Ahmed Beydoun has demonstrated, because of the evidence they appear to give of the region's

[17] See al-Muhajir, *Al-Ta'sis li-Tarikh al-Shi'a*, 127–47; Hashim 'Uthman, *Tarikh al-Shi'a fi Sahil Bilad al-Sham al-Shamali* (Beirut: al-A'lami, 1994), 47–80; Yahya Qasim Farhat, *Al-Shi'a fi Tarabulus: Min al-Fath al-'Arabi hatta al-Fath al-'Uthmani* (Beirut: Dar al-Milak, 1999); Qasim al-Samad, *Tarikh al-Danniyya al-Siyasi wa'l-Ijtima'i fi 'Ahd al-'Uthmani* (n.p.: Mu'assasat al-Jami'iyya, n.d.), 21–2.

[18] Jean-Michel Mouton, *Damas et sa principauté sous les Saljoukides et les Bourides 1076–1154* (Cairo: Institut Français d'Archéologie Orientale, 1994), 130–3.

[19] Charles Melville, "'Sometimes by the Sword, Sometimes by the Dagger": The Role of the Isma'ilis in Mamluk–Mongol Relations in the 8th/14th Century' in Farhad Daftary, ed., *Medieval Isma'ili History and Thought* (Cambridge University Press, 1996), 247–63.

[20] Winter, 'The Shi'ah of Syria', 155–6.

demographic composition. Whereas Maronite historians long appropriated the campaigns as an example of their community's resistance against Muslim state oppression, others have pointed to the presumed Druze and Nusayri victims as well as to an eyewitness account by the famous fundamentalist scholar Ahmad ibn Taymiyya (d. 1328) that implies the Twelver Shiites were the principal targets.[21]

Ibn Taymiyya's account, however, should above all be seen as a polemical treatise against Shiism per se, and not as historical proof that the Mamluk authorities were indeed pursuing a particular community. (His implausible claim that particular books confirming the Shiites' heresy were seized from the mountaineers during the campaign is a topos found in many such accounts.) Actually the campaigns were launched after the Kisrawanis rose up against their Druze overlords, themselves heterodox, and because they had previously captured and robbed Mamluk soldiers fleeing a Mongol attack. It was the Druze chiefs who commanded the final, devastating campaign in 1305, and only after a patently Twelver Shiite dignitary from Damascus had failed to mediate between the mountaineers and the Mamluk governor.[22] In the following years, according to another near-contemporary (Druze) observer, the state authorities 'expelled those who had stayed in the Kisrawan mountains and killed a number of their notables, [but] gave quarter to those who settled elsewhere'.[23] The Mamluks could not maintain direct pressure on the region for long, and ultimately gained more from accommodating with the local Christians and Shiites once again. The only lasting consequence of these campaigns was probably the establishment of the Turkmen 'Assaf emirs as the new paramount feudal faction in the Kisrawan, under whose patronage the Shiite Hamadas would then rise to power in the fifteenth or sixteenth century.

There are, unfortunately, no written sources from the later medieval period that might provide a more detailed picture of Mt Lebanon's society and its situation under Mamluk rule. Many historians today agree that this period saw the expansion of the Sunni community in the coastal cities and of the Druze lords in the mountains as far north as the Matn district; the Shiites remained dominant in the Kisrawan and began to move into the primarily Christian-inhabited Futuh and Jubayl districts in the fifteenth century, before being driven out of the Kisrawan by the Maronite recolonization push in the seventeenth century (see next chapter). Such inferences, however, are based mainly on the traditional oral histories of individual families, many of which in fact converted from Shiism to Maronitism over time.[24] The attempt,

---

[21] Beydoun, *Identité confessionnelle*, 83–114. Cf. Muhammad 'Ali Makki, 'La politique chi'ite au Liban du XIe au XIVe siècle', *Cahiers de l'École Supérieure des Lettres: Colloque 'Ashura'* (Beirut) 5 (1974), 41–2.

[22] See Henri Laoust, 'Remarques sur les expéditions du Kasrawan sous les premiers Mamluks', *Bulletin du Musée de Beyrouth* 4 (1940), 93–115; Salibi, 'Mount Lebanon under the Mamluks'; Winter, 'The Shi'ah of Syria', 150–4.

[23] Salih ibn Yahya (d. 1436), *Tarikh Bayrut* (Beirut: Dar al-Mashraf, 1969), 28.

[24] Ahmad Mahmud Suwaydan, *Kisrawan wa-Bilad Jubayl bayna al-Qarnayn al-Rabi' 'Ashar wa'l-Thamin 'Ashar min 'Asr al-Mamalik ila 'Asr al-Mutasarrifiya* (Beirut: Dar al-Kitab al-Hadith, 1988); 'Ali Raghib Haydar Ahmad, *Al-Muslimun al-Shi'a fi Kisrawan wa-Jubayl: Siyasiyyan, Tarikhiyyan, Ijtima'iyyan, bi'l-Watha'iq, 1842–2006* (Beirut: Dar al-Hadi, 2007), 7–8.

typically by philologists and positivist historians, to establish the true 'origins' and therewith the claims of certain tribal or sectarian groups to a particular political identity on the basis of their own oral and chronicle accounts is ultimately circular and self-defeating. The best we can infer from our sources is that the Mamluks were clearly aware of the unique challenges they faced in ruling the tribal highland region but pursued no demographic policy as such, preferring, like the Ottoman authorities after them, to turn the inherent conflicts and divisions within its highly segmented society to their own advantage.

## Ottoman tax regimes in Tripoli

Among the Ottomans' most significant acts of sovereignty in Syria (and elsewhere) after their conquest was the compilation of detailed fiscal surveys. These registers, usually referred to as the *Tahrir Defterleri*, generally recorded the taxable productivity of a given *sancak* by number of households and source of revenue. As a result they have very often been taken by *Annales*-school and local historians as providing comprehensive population statistics or unbiased data on the economic activities in the region. In fact, as the remarkable work of Margaret Venzke and others has demonstrated,[25] individual tax surveys were too limited in scope and objective to support any demographic or sociological conclusions as such. Not only could there be significant variations in the manner of tax assessment from one area to another as well as from one survey to the next, but also the very fact that these surveys concerned only particular taxpayers or social groups, types of tax liability and categories of revenue beneficiaries, suggests that *Tahrir* texts should be treated much like Ottoman chancery orders – namely as statements of authoritative claims on particular resources at particular points in time, rather than as pieces in a great edifice of imperial bookkeeping. The potential discrepancy between official tax ledgers and the reality on the ground is well summed up by the already cited Meccan traveller to Syria in 1558, who quite matter-of-factly noted the population of Homs to be '4,400 households, not including about one thousand households not appearing in the register because they don't pay any extraordinary levies'.[26]

Numerous other fiscal records exist for the *eyalet* of Tripoli, but these too must be used with caution in regard to the local tax regimes' particularities. The *jizya* capitation tax, which elsewhere can provide an indication of the Christian population's size, was generally calculated as a lump-sum (*maktu*) payment rather than on a per-household basis in the highlands of Tripoli, and was not registered in any separate accounts. The 'extraordinary' *avarız*, *nüzul* and *sürsat* levies that were assessed in cash on individual tax household-units (*avarız-hane*) were made

[25] See esp. Margaret Venzke, 'The Ottoman Tahrir Defterleri and Agricultural Productivity: The Case for Northern Syria', *Osmanlı Araştırmaları* 17 (1997), 1–13; also Heath Lowry, 'The Ottoman Tahrîr Defterleri as a Source for Social and Economic History: Pitfalls and Limitations' in Lowry, *Studies in Defterology: Ottoman Society in the Fifteenth and Sixteenth Centuries* (Istanbul: Isis Press, 1992), 3–18.
[26] Blackburn, *Journey to the Sublime Porte*, 72.

permanent starting in the later seventeenth century and thus also gave rise to a new genre of registers. Unlike in other provinces, however, Tripoli's *defter*s record no fluctuation in the assessment on the rural districts for the entirety of the seventeenth and early eighteenth centuries, and in fact the key Shiite-inhabited *mukataa*s (tax farms) do not figure at all on the lists. One of the only references to the *mukataa*s of Jubayl and Batrun occurs in a provincial accounts book from 1641, where they are included in the neighbouring *paşalık* of Damascus but with a note that they actually 'belong to' (*tabi*) Tripoli province.[27] Likewise, all the *mukataa*s of Sidon, Beirut and Safad are invariably listed under the province of Damascus in *avarız*, *sürsat* or other tax records, even long after the region technically became its own independent *eyalet* in 1660. The explanation for this is almost certainly that many revenue sources throughout the Syrian provinces were set aside for organizing the yearly *hajj* expedition, a competency of the *vali* of Damascus. The function for which these and other taxes were earmarked, rather than their territorial provenance, ultimately determined if and where they were recorded.

If nothing else, the *Tahrir* records for the *sancak* of Tripoli provide a general impression of Ottoman taxation practice in the Shiite-inhabited mountain hinterland (Map 2). The *Tahrir*s were almost all compiled in the sixteenth century, when the central bureaucracy still needed to keep precise logs of land use and productivity in order to assign individualized prebends (*timar*, *zeamet*) to imperial cavalry soldiers as well as to its provincial cadres. Later, when the rural prebend system was downgraded in favour of cash tax farming, tax parcels were no longer reassessed for each new office-holder, and fiscal surveys gradually drop from use in the seventeenth century. No registers at all appear to be extant for the Kisrawan district, which remained populated by Shiites but which formed a sub-district (*nahiye*) of Damascus and later of Sidon-Beirut rather than of Tripoli. In the registers consulted here, the Hamadas' home villages are spread over three tax districts, Jubayl country (as distinct from the town), Munaytra and the Futuh, whereby the latter two are reckoned in some *defter*s as dependencies of the first and their borders fluctuated constantly. The village Farhat, for instance, one of the Hamadas' principal residences, is alternately recorded in each of the three districts.[28] Though some villages do not appear in every register but only in those concerned with a given income type (such as *timar* or *vakıf* revenue), it can be observed that the majority of all villages listed in the Jubayl, Munaytra and Futuh districts were exclusively Christian. However, one important finding is that the villages mentioned in Rabâh Abi-Haidar's study on the Shi'a of nineteenth-century Jubayl were indeed already Muslim-inhabited in the early sixteenth,[29] and almost certainly by Shiite Muslims if one takes the villagers' predominantly 'Alid names as indicative of their confessional culture. This

[27] 'Muhasebenin irad ve masraf defteri', MM 7025:144.
[28] TD 68 (*timar* register, 1519); TD 1017 (*vakıf* register, around 1525); Tahrir Defter (TD) 421 (*mufassal* register, around 1529); TD 1107 (*mufassal* register, 1547); TD 548 (*timar* register, reign of Selim II, 1566–74); MM 842 (*hass* register, 1645/6).
[29] Abi-Haidar, 'La société chiite des Bilad Jebayl', map inset.

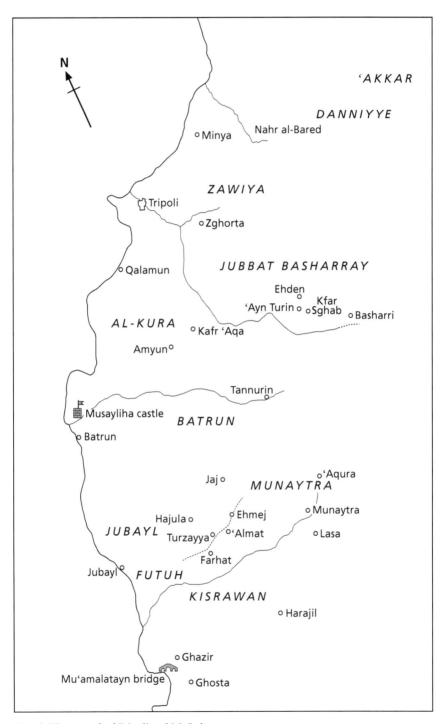

Map 2  The *sancak* of Tripoli and Mt Lebanon

conclusion would also corroborate travellers' claims that very few 'orthodox Turks', that is, Sunnis, lived among the Christian and Shiite highlanders.[30]

Two further observations may be made regarding the continuity of Mamluk and Ottoman fiscal practices in the region. After the 1516 conquest, the Ottoman state appropriated all agricultural lands as crown domain (*hass-ı hümayun*), with the exception of some private holdings (*emlak*) that were mainly set aside for pious endowments (*vakıf*).[31] In general, *hass* could either be allocated to members of the royal household as a private income reserve, or apportioned to provincial government officials and cavalry officers as *zeamet* or *timar*. In the Shiite districts, however, *hass* was very seldom reassigned. While the *nahiye*s of 'Akkar and 'Arqa in northern Lebanon were divided into hundreds of military fiefs soon after the conquest, we have only a few transient examples of Ottoman soldiers holding *timar* grants in the mountains above Jubayl. A possible explanation for this is provided by the *timar* assignment book TD 68, which establishes that the entire Futuh district, named in all subsequent Ottoman sources as the 'Fütuh-ı Beni Rehhal', was totally under the control of the Rahhal tribe well into the first decade of Ottoman rule. Almost every village is noted as 'belonging to' the unknown, possibly Shiite tribe; the only significant exceptions are a few tax collectorships or *timar*s assigned to Muhammad Sayfa, Musa Beğ Kisrawani ('Assaf?) and Shihab al-Din Kisrawani, evidently local notables from before the conquest. The Banu Rahhal are no longer designated as landlords in subsequent surveys, and some areas were infrequently assigned to Ottoman soldiers as *timar*, but most land simply became registered in the abstract as crown domain. The military-prebendal tax regime never came to predominate in the Shiite highlands as it did in other parts of Tripoli.

The second observation concerns the continuity of the Mamluk-era *vakıf* regimes in some of the Shiite and other neighbouring villages. The Ottoman conquerors were loathe to abrogate pious foundations established by their predecessors according to Islamic law, and many orders sent to Syria concern the maintenance of bequests made even by such hated figures as the last Mamluk sultan Qansuh al-Ghawri. Many rural properties in the region could also be wholly or partially committed to the upkeep of local endowments, and the Ottomans long respected these even when the beneficiaries were old notable families rather than institutions of public welfare. The village of 'Almat in the heart of Tripoli's Shiite country owed its entire tax load (2,000 *guruş* throughout the entire period) to the private family endowment of emir Qansuh al-Yahyawi, a Mamluk governor of Damascus. Hajula, also in the Futuh, paid a sizeable portion of its income tax towards the Aqbay ibn 'Abdallah family *vakıf*; its share rose from 200 *g.* upon the conquest, to 300 during Selim II's reign, to 1,600 by the mid-seventeenth century.

---

[30] Jonas Korte (d. 1747), *Reise nach dem weiland Gelobten, nun aber seit siebenzehn hundert Jahren unter dem Fluche liegenden Lande, wie auch nach Egypten, dem Berg Libanon, Syrien und Mesopotamien* (3rd edn, Halle: Johann Christian Grunert, 1751), 464–5.

[31] Various Başbakanlık records also mention *emlak* in the Tripoli highlands belonging to Fakhr al-Din ibn Ma'n and to Yusuf ibn Sayfa, though none directly in the Shiite zones.

Hajula and several other Shiite-inhabited towns including Lasa and Majdal 'Aqura also contributed moneys to the upkeep of small defensive bastions (*burc*) in the area. In the Munaytra district, several important towns supported religious institutions in the provincial capital. Up to a quarter of Majdal 'Aqura's taxes went to the Kul Hasan *medrese* in Tripoli. Again there is a steady rise in net payments from the early sixteenth century (472 g. out of a total tax burden of 2,850) to the mid-seventeenth century (2,000 g. out of 12,950), a trend visible throughout the area. Numerous other villages subsidized the Kul Hasan institution; Christian-inhabited Hadina, however, is noted in TD 1017 as insolvent on account of the ruinous oppression suffered by its population. A key pillar of this foundation was the Shiite village of Mughayra, whose taxes went not only to the Kul Hasan *medrese* but also to its *zaviye* (sufi lodge) in Tripoli city. Curiously, Mughayra's contribution to the Kul Hasan *vakıf* (which by 1645/6 had risen to a staggering 20,300 g. out of a total burden of 22,160) is noted in the final register as abrogated and reverted to the imperial reserve (*hass-ı hümayun*). The same holds true for the erstwhile Kul Hasan *vakıf* payments from Afqa, another Shiite village.

In conclusion, while the fiscal registers at our disposal are too disparate to allow for quantitative analysis, two trends affecting the Shiite districts of Tripoli province are discernible. One is the marked overall increase in tax levies by the mid-seventeenth century as seen in the last detailed *tahrir* MM 842. This may reflect either a real rise in prosperity, as the Tripoli region is gradually drawn into the overseas silk and cotton trade in this period, or the refinement of tax assessment and exaction methods at various levels of administration. The second trend is the homogenization of tax regimes. While the earliest *defter*s distinguish between revenue sources of the imperial or provincial reserve, taxes assessed by tribal prerogative, and moneys for *timar* prebends as well as private and public endowments, the last available records show the entire rural tax burden, including moneys from recently abrogated *vakıf*s, as being unified into a single, larger yearly lump-sum charge. If this analysis is accurate, and stands to comparison with other rural districts in the Syrian and Anatolian provinces, then we may see reflected in these tax records the general, long-term evolution towards more consolidated structures of authority and governance in the Ottoman provincial world. The heterogeneous, autarchic tribal leaderships that were left to dominate the rural highlands in the early modern centuries were the natural beneficiaries of these reforms.

## The rise of the Hamadas

There is no precise point when the rural districts of Tripoli province passed under the dominion of a single tribal grouping. In 1519, as indicated, the Banu Rahhal had fiscal control over almost the entire Futuh, but they disappear in the subsequent registers. For much of the sixteenth century, state-appointed tax collectors (sing. *'amil*), military *timar*-holders and *mukataacı* tax farmers existed alongside one another. The first true evidence of a regional tax collection franchise comes from TD 513, a detailed *timar* register for 1571/2, in which numerous Shiite-inhabited villages and *mezraas* (outlying farm plots) in the Futuh and Munaytra districts are recorded as dependencies (*der uhde-i*) of 'emir Mansur', the chief of the 'Assaf Turkmen. Several more towns were assigned to 'Ibrahim', most likely of the Maronite Hubaysh family that was allied with the 'Assafs. Many of the Maronite towns in the Batrun, Jubayl and Basharray (or Basharri) districts are recorded as being under the fiscal authority of the villagers themselves, but a single *mezraa* in the Jubayl district, Kafr Ruma, also fell within emir Mansur's purview.[32] The Greek Orthodox communities of the 'Qurnat al-Rum' tract are said to have had family ties and shared a certain sectarian solidarity with the area Shiites, and many families were later recruited by the Hamadas to farm and settle their lands.[33] The inclusion of a part of their district in the 'Assafs' domain suggests that their special relationship with the mountain tribesmen may in fact have predated the Hamadas' reign.

The Sunni 'Assafs are thought to have been settled in the Kisrawan by the Mamluks to act as a check on the local Shiite tribes after 1305, but there is actually very little reliable information on them up into the Ottoman period.[34] Duwayhi claims that the 'Assafs took numerous Shiite and other sectarian groups from throughout the region under their wing in the sixteenth century,[35] but this must also be understood as part of his effort to provide the 'Lebanese' emirate with a historical genealogy. The Shiite Mustarah family apparently had control of the Munaytra district as early as 1482; Hashim al-'Ajami, the shaykh of Munaytra encountered in chapter 2, later became the 'Assafs' tax agent in Jubayl while his cousin managed emir Mansur's private estates.[36] In the course of the seventeenth century, the Mustarahs and other Shiite notables would be driven out by the Hamadas and eventually take up farming in the Bekaa.[37] Muhammad 'Assaf, still according to Duwayhi, first took the Hamadas into his service after he returned from exile in Istanbul in 1585. They were invited to settle in his capital, Ghazir, as his deputies for the Jubayl district, and effectively succeeded him when he was killed without leaving any heirs in 1591.[38]

If it seems likely that the Hamadas could not have risen to prominence without some measure of support from the 'Assaf emirs in the sixteenth century, there is intriguing evidence that their roots as state authorities in the region may have run deeper than Duwayhi and subsequent historians have maintained. An anonymous, single-copy manuscript history from the late Mamluk period, conjecturally attributed by 'Umar Tadmuri to the Baalbek historian Burhan al-Din Ibrahim ibn 'Umar al-Biqa'i (d. 1480), reports that in 1471 the *qadi*s of Tripoli were ordered to pay an indemnity of 1,000 dinars to 'the heirs of Ibn Hamada', a former tax collector for the Circassian Mamluk regime in Syria. Ibn Hamada had apparently been

---

[32] TD 513:88, 115–24.    [33] Abi-Haidar, 'La société chiite', 73–4.

[34] Bakhit, *The Ottoman Province of Damascus*, 178–9.

[35] See Kamal Salibi, 'Northern Lebanon under the Dominance of Ġazīr (1517–1591)', *Arabica* 14 (1967), 144–66.

[36] Duwayhi, *Tarikh*, 244; Salibi, 'Northern Lebanon', 156.

[37] Abi-Haidar, 'La société chiite', 86–7, 159, 161.

[38] Duwayhi, *Tarikh*, 284–5; Salibi, 'Northern Lebanon', 165.

murdered during the reign of al-Zahir Khushqadam (1461–7) by the privy-counsel (*katib al-sirr*) of Cairo as part of a cover-up of his own fiscal wrongdoing.[39] Numerous notable families in the coastal highlands, as Abraham Poliak noticed, were in fact descended from Mamluk-era government officials, either from actual Mamluk emirs or from clanships co-opted by the Mamluk state.[40] If accurate, this text would suggest that the Hamadas were not after all foreign interlopers in Mt Lebanon, but part of the same phenomenon.

In any event, it is also clear that the Hamadas owed their rise to power under Ottoman rule not only to their ties with purely local actors such as the 'Assaf emirs, but also to the favour of the Ottoman authorities, specifically the governors of Tripoli. Yusuf Paşa ibn Sayfa, the Kurdish feudal lord of 'Akkar who became the first *vali* of the province in 1579, established his supremacy over the mountain hinterland when he killed the last 'Assaf emir in 1591 and married his widow so as to acquire the 'Assafs' old fiefs. The Hamadas, whom Ibn Sayfa retained as his tax deputies in the region, moved from Ghazir to Tripoli, bringing his new bride with them, and soon entered into conflict with the Shiite Mustarahs, with whom they were intermarried but who had been protégés of the 'Assaf emirs and who were now siding with the Hubaysh family. Qansuh Hamada, in a sense the founder of the Hamadas as a political faction, was felled by a stray bullet while fighting the Mustarahs in Munaytra on the Sayfas' behalf around 1592.[41]

The Hamadas, again according to Duwayhi, first became resident shaykhs of the Jubayl district in 1600, after they were sent to eliminate the village headmen of Jaj who were apparently supporting Ibn Sayfa's great nemesis Fakhr al-Din ibn Ma'n.[42] After the Druze emir's return to official grace in 1618 the Ottomans increasingly relied on him and his unmatchable *levent* army to scale back the Sayfa family's hold on Tripoli and the northern Lebanon. Within a few years, as noted in chapter 2, they had subjugated the Harfushes of Baalbek, seized control of several tax fiefs in Tripoli and driven Yusuf Sayfa from power. In 1626, the Hamadas rallied to his son and successor, Qasim ibn Sayfa, at Marqab castle further north along the coast in a bid to retake the capital. The rebels were promptly set upon by the province's new *vali*, however, and were forced to sue for their freedom.[43] After the elimination of Fakhr al-Din himself, the Hamadas became embroiled in the Sayfas' internecine wars. In 1634, they helped 'Assaf Sayfa reconquer Jubayl and Munaytra, which had been seized by 'Ali Sayfa's Druze allies in his bid for the governorship, using the opportunity to attack their old enemies, the Mustarah family. However, the Hamadas were routed by 'Ali shortly thereafter near Tripoli, allowing him to become *vali* and evict them from their

[39] Dar al-Kutub, Cairo: Ms. Tarikh 5631. Anonymous, 'Kitab fi'l-Tarikh 873–904 h.', fol. 60b–61a. I am grateful to Prof. Tadmuri for the reference to this text, and to Gasser Khalifa for procuring me a copy.

[40] A. N. Poliak, *Feudalism in Egypt, Syria, Palestine, and the Lebanon, 1250–1900* (Philadelphia: Porcupine Press, 1977).

[41] Duwayhi, *Tarikh*, 288; cf. the 1976 edn of al-Duwayhi, *Tarikh al-Azmina*, ed. Butrus Fahd (3rd imprint, Beirut: Dar Lahad Khatir, 1976), 450, 451 (hereafter Duwayhi/Fahd, *Tarikh*).

[42] Duwayhi, *Tarikh*, 295–6; cf. variant in Duwayhi/Fahd, *Tarikh*, 455.    [43] Duwayhi, *Tarikh*, 321.

fiefs.[44] Only two years later, the tide had turned again. The Ottoman government, dissatisfied with the Sayfas' ruinous mismanagement of the province, sent a new *vali* who reassigned Jubayl and Batrun to 'Ali and Ahmad, the sons of Qansuh Hamada. Realizing which side their bread was now buttered on, the Hamadas mobilized to defend the governor when he was to be removed from office only a few weeks later, but in a falling out with his other allies, namely the same Druze who had backed 'Ali Sayfa, Ahmad Hamada was killed. His brother 'Ali continued to help the Ottomans root out the last of the Sayfas until his own death around 1641.[45]

The year 1641 therefore marked both the end of the Sayfas as a political force in Tripoli, as we have seen previously, and the succession of Sirhan ibn Qansuh as head of the Hamada family. Sirhan had distinguished himself the year before in another raid against the Mustarahs in Munaytra, and he appears over the next years to have led the Hamadas in an increasingly fierce struggle to control the Jubayl and Futuh districts, and to extend his reach to other tax farms in the Maronite-dominated parts of Mt Lebanon.[46] From here on their story would be of interest to more than just local chroniclers such as Duwayhi: it is under Sirhan's leadership that the Hamadas are first encountered in the *shar'iyya* court records of Tripoli and as the 'Sirhan-oğulları' that they ultimately left their mark in Ottoman imperial historiography.

## The narrative of Shiite tyranny

If the rise of the Hamadas to pre-eminence in Tripoli's highlands is best understood in terms of the co-optation of tribal notabilities by the early modern state, they and the Shiites in general have always been presented as fundamentally alien and inimical in Maronite-oriented histories of Lebanon. In Duwayhi's chronicle as well as in popular accounts passed down from the period, the Shiites are not so much a political player in their own right as an exponent of the secular authorities' tyranny or rival Christian denominations' plotting. The discourse of Shiite aggression and iniquity, formulated in a time that saw an unprecedented expansion of the Maronite community's commercial opportunities, foreign contacts and self-awareness, became key to establishing its 'national' claim to the rural districts of the mid-Lebanon range. It would also play a critical role in the Hamadas' later fortunes as Ottoman revenue farmers.

While the Mustarahs, as we have indicated, were identified with the traditional sedentary population of Tripoli province, the Hamadas' closest pendant as a Shiite tribal lordship was the Sha'ir family. Little is known of the Sha'irs' background. Thought to have migrated from north-eastern Syria around the turn of the seventeenth century, they were most likely of Kurdish origin and became steadfast allies

---

[44] *Ibid.*, 331. See also Salibi, 'The Sayfās', 50–1; Abu-Husayn, *Provincial Leaderships*, 56–9.

[45] Duwayhi, *Tarikh*, 334–5, 336, 339; cf. slightly variant dates given in Duwayhi/Fahd, *Tarikh*, 514, 515–16, 524.

[46] Duwayhi, *Tarikh*, 338, 340.

of both the Sayfas and the Kurdish emirs of al-Kura. From their home base in the village of Tula, where they erected a palace and a mosque, the Sha'irs for many years controlled the tax farms of Batrun and occasionally Jubbat Basharray. Maronite legends about the Sha'irs' barbarity in a sense prefigure those about the Hamadas themselves:

One of them was famous for being rapacious and vicious and for preying on dangerous wild animals. They used to tie him up by day so that he could not set upon passers-by, then let him loose at night. Woe unto them who should venture near the Sha'ir palace after dark![47]

Another time the Sha'irs are said to have destroyed a small mountain hermitage and killed all the monks and their goatherds after failing to discover some promised treasure – an event to which the name of the nearby 'strangulation rock' formation supposedly still testifies.[48]

The Hamadas' expulsion of their co-religionists at some indeterminate point is also the object of considerable historical fancy. According to one account that seems to combine story elements from Duwayhi encountered earlier, it was Fakhr al-Din Ma'n who installed the Hamadas in the Sha'irs' stead because the latter were allies of Ibn Sayfa; they had to sell their famous palace to the Abi-Sa'bs (whom the Hamadas had just evicted from Jubbat Basharray) and moved up the coast to Marqab castle.[49] And another version, first collated by the Maronite historian Abu Khattar al-'Aynturini (d. 1821), reads like a page straight out of a historical novel (or more likely, inspired one):

The Hamadas played a dirty trick on them in order to be able to take their place … They brought [the Sha'irs] into misfortune by making them host them and their followers every day, once or twice, until they became poor from all the expenditure. They were left with nothing, and had to leave Tula and the Batrun region.[50]

A comical anecdote about the 'Mutawalis' in Mt Lebanon before the Hamadas tells of a whole company of Shiite retainers of the 'Assaf emir being beaten up by a young Maronite hero. The Shiites, who were known never to eat food prepared by non-believers, had mistreated his brother after he refused to build them a cooking fire one Ramadan evening. Fearing punishment after the bloodied Shiites complained to the emir, the hero bound up his hand and pretended they had thrashed him. The ruse did not fool the wise emir, however – and this is of course the point of

---

[47] Bulus Ruhana Abi-Ibrahim (d. 1893), 'Makhtut Qadim 'an 'Abrin wa-Bajja wa-Usarihima', *Awraq Lubnaniyya* 3 (1957), 237, 291.

[48] Goudard, *La Sainte Vierge au Liban*, 254.

[49] 'Abdallah Ibrahim Abi-'Abdallah, *Milaff al-Qadiyya al-Lubnaniyya min khilal Jubayl wa 'l-Batrun wa 'l-Shamal fi 'l-Tarikh: Mahd al-Mawarina wa 'l-Usar al-Ma'adiyya wa 'l-Faghaliyya wa 'l-Bajjaniyya wa 'l-Ghalbuniyya wa-Sawaha mundhu ba 'd al-Kawan hatta al-Yawm* (al-'Uqayba, Lebanon: Matba'at al-Dakkash, 1987), 166–8.

[50] Antuniyus Abu Khattar al-'Aynturini, *Mukhtasar Tarikh Jabal Lubnan* (Beirut: Dar Lahad Khatir, 1983), 58–9; see also Ma'luf, *Diwani al-Qatuf*, 232. Compare with the story of the reluctant host from Kfaryabda who is ruined by his visiting in-laws in Amin Maalouf, *Le rocher de Tanios* (Paris: Grasset, 1993), 63 ff.

the tale – who rebuked the Shiites for their boorishness and paid tribute to the Christian for his valour.[51]

By the time of the Hamadas' rise to prominence, Shiite violence was already a bit of a trope among Maronite historians, and popular tales characterizing them as 'drinkers of blood' and 'beastly tigers' abounded.[52] The first explicit reference to the Hamada family appears to occur in the manuscript chronicle of an obscure Maronite vicar, who mentions their kidnapping a daughter of the Korkmaz clan and precipitating a blood feud that ended with the latter's flight from the Futuh in 1520.[53] Duwayhi, for his part, first refers to the Hamadas in 1547, when their purportedly eponymous clan chief 'shaykh Hamada' joined a conspiracy (along with Melkite Christians) to exterminate one of the rival Maronite *muqaddam* households of the Jubbat Basharri district. He was seriously injured in the encounter and, unable to walk, he and several companions were caught and lynched by the locals.[54] Documents recently found by Sa'dun Hamada in the patriarchal archives of Bkerke suggest that the Hamadas may have sought to settle Maronite peasants on their lands as early as 1552 or 1553, but these appear to have been copied in later times and await further investigation.[55]

The closest thing in Maronite literature to a 'founding myth' of Hamada rule over Mt Lebanon concerns the killing of the Sunni headmen of Jaj. While Duwayhi, as already indicated, places the event under Yusuf Sayfa's reign, popular accounts generally connect it with the 'Assaf emirs and three semi-legendary Hamada brothers. According to one version, the emir asked the two eldest sons of 'shaykh Hamada', 'Ali Dib and Ahmad Abu Za'zu'a, to kill the headmen, the effective rulers of the Jubayl district, but they refused, arguing that their sister's marriage to one of the headmen made them in-laws. However, their younger brother, Sirhan (occasionally spelled Sirhal), went to the emir surreptitiously and agreed to the assassination in return for being named shaykh of the district. Together the brothers then ambushed and killed the headmen, thus inaugurating their reign as taxlords of Jubayl with Sirhan as their leader.[56] A more expansive version describes the Hamadas' trick of asking the people of Jaj for a goat's head to use in an upcoming wedding feast, then attacking them as they deliberated this unusual request.[57] Folk histories of Basharri indicate that Ahmad 'Abu Za'zu'a' ('the lanky' or 'convulsive') was the first Hamada invited to rule over the Maronite district in 1654. In 'Aynturini's version, he was delegated by his paternal cousin Sirhan after the inhabitants requested to be ruled by someone from the house of Hamada, and they agreed that he would govern 'as he wished' provided he safeguarded three things: the villagers' religion, their honour and their blood.[58]

---

[51] Abi-Ibrahim, 'Makhtut Qadim', 236.

[52] Salibi, 'The Muqaddams of Bšarrī', 76–7; Goudard, *La Sainte Vierge au Liban*, 335–6.

[53] Butrus Matar, private manuscript, cited in Abi-'Abdallah, *Milaff*, 210.

[54] Duwayhi, *Tarikh*, 258; Salibi, 'The Muqaddams of Bšarrī', 75–6.

[55] Hamada, *Tarikh al-Shi'a*, I:187–90.

[56] 'Aynturini, *Mukhtasar*, 58; repeated in Shidyaq, *Akhbar al-A'yan*, 192.    [57] Abi-'Abdallah, *Milaff*, 169.

[58] 'Aynturini, *Mukhtasar*, 131; also repeated in Butrus Bishara Karam, *Qala'id al-Marjan fi Tarikh Shamali Lubnan* (Beirut: n.p., 1937), 61–2.

In another variant making use of the same elements, it was Sirhan himself who was nicknamed 'Abu Za'zu'a' while governor of the Danniyye district; his sons then wrested Jubbat Basharray from the Abi-Sa'b clan, and 'Ahmad Dib Hamada Abu Za'zu'a' was commissioned by the governor of Tripoli with the aforementioned tripartite pledge of governance vis-à-vis the Christian population.[59]

From a modern perspective, it is of course not possible, or necessary, to distinguish 'the truth' about the origins of Hamada rule in Mt Lebanon from these accounts. The telling and retelling of the stories themselves would create their own reality, and later historians implicitly invoked this social contract to justify the Maronites' uprising against the Hamadas in the eighteenth century (discussed in chapter 6): 'When they realized that there would be no end to the oppression, which finally came to afflict the head of their religion after they had already forfeited their property and their blood, they raised a great uproar, and God came to their aid against [the Hamadas].'[60] The legendary tyranny of the Shiites was to become an essential part of the larger narrative of Maronite entitlement to Lebanon, a narrative which evolved in synchrony with the territorial and political expansion of the Maronite community in the early modern centuries and which therefore continues to inform national historiography to the present day.

## The Köprülü era

The reign of Sirhan ibn Hamada marks one of the most turbulent, but unfortunately also one of the most obscure periods in the history of Mt Lebanon. Duwayhi, who returned from his studies in Rome in 1656 and moved to the Qadisha Valley in Jubbat Basharri as patriarch in 1670, now takes on a near-eyewitness quality. However, it is precisely in this time that the two published versions of his chronicle, each based on a single manuscript written in Syriac, begin to diverge significantly, raising the question of both the authenticity and reliability of numerous passages in his anyhow highly partial account. Moreover, much of his information even on the region's basic political history cannot be verified with administrative sources. Owing to the long crisis of the Ottoman state during its war with Venice and the ensuing domestic military revolts, perhaps also to the loss of a large number of documents during the Ottoman retreat from Vienna in 1683, there are next to no extant chancery records dealing with Tripoli or the other Syrian provinces from the two middle decades of the seventeenth century.

Duwayhi's *History*, chiefly the 1976 Butrus Fahd edition which is the more detailed for this period, relates several clashes between the Hamadas and shifting coalitions of the 'Alam al-Dins, the Sha'irs, the emirs of al-Kura and various governors of Tripoli over the assignment and control of local tax farms in 1639, 1640, 1641, 1642, 1649 and 1651.[61] The Ottoman traveller Evliya Çelebi

---

[59]  Abi-'Abdallah, *Milaff*, 168.    [60]  'Aynturini, *Mukhtasar*, 134.
[61]  Duwayhi/Fahd, *Tarikh*, 519–20, 523–6, 533–5.

(d. ?1682), according to a little-known manuscript copy of his writings, appears to have been witness to a campaign to collect taxes from several chiefs in the area including Sirhan Hamada in 1649.[62] In 1655, a heretofore obscure *vali*, Köprülü Mehmed Paşa, set about subduing the highland factions, redistributing their *mukataa*s and taking two of the more troublesome leaders, emir Ismaʻil al-Kurdi and Saʻid ibn ʻAli Hamada, into his 'service' (detention might be more accurate) in the city, and then launching an assault on both of them when they failed to remit sufficient taxes.[63] Köprülü Mehmed, who had previous experience as governor of Tripoli as well as of Damascus, was recalled to Istanbul a few months later and would of course go on to become one of the greatest grand viziers in Ottoman history. In 1659, he dispatched a new governor to Tripoli 'with an imperial mandate against the Hamadas on account of their devastations'. The Hamadas had to flee to the Kisrawan with their families and livestock, leaving government troops to ravage their home villages in the Wadi ʻAlmat, seize their grain stores in Jubayl and award their tax concessions to their Shiite rival Qaytbay ibn al-Shaʻir and others. The following year, 'on account of the complaints sent to the Sublime Porte concerning the Shihabis and the Hamadas', Köprülü Mehmed sent his son Fazıl Ahmed Paşa to Damascus to assemble a full-scale regional punitive campaign that would ultimately target the Maʻns as well.[64] At the same time, the *sancak* of Sidon-Beirut was incorporated as its own *eyalet* separate from Tripoli and Damascus. Such a project had already been envisioned in 1613/14, probably to contain Fakhr al-Din Maʻn's ambitions in the area, but was dropped again when he went into exile.[65] Not surprisingly, most historians working from a local perspective have thus interpreted the establishment of the province in 1660 as motivated again by the Ottomans' need 'to keep Lebanon under control after the many uprisings and revolts' in this period.[66]

From an Ottoman perspective, however, factional turmoil in the highlands was hardly the main reason for reshaping the Syrian provincial administration. Fazıl Ahmed's first objective was to crush the local (*yerli*) Janissaries of Damascus and to remove several governors in the region who had rallied to the Abaza Hasan revolt in 1658, an Anatolian-based movement similar to that of the Celalis earlier and which represented by far the most serious threat to his father's vizierate.[67] Curtailing the provincial Janissaries, who were also heavily invested in the control of the Syrian hinterland, and appointing allies to governorships throughout the area

---

[62] See Halil Inalcik, 'Tax Collection, Embezzlement and Bribery in Ottoman Finances', *Turkish Studies Association Bulletin* 16 (1992), repr. in Inalcik, *Essays in Ottoman History* (Istanbul: Eren, 1998), 182.

[63] Duwayhi/Fahd, *Tarikh*, 537–8, 540. The 1951 Tawtal edition renders the latter's name as 'Saʻd'.

[64] Duwayhi/Fahd, *Tarikh*, 545–7; Mehmed Süreyya (d. 1909), *Sicill-i Osmanî*, ed. Nuri Akbayar and Seyit Ali Kahraman (Istanbul: Türkiye Ekonomik ve Toplumsal Tarih Vakfi, 1996), 1061.

[65] Abu-Husayn, 'Problems in the Ottoman Administration in Syria', 672–3; Süreyya, *Sicill-i Osmanî*, 646.

[66] Antwan ʻAbd al-Nur, *Tijarat Sayda' maʻa'l-Gharb: Min Muntasaf al-Qarn al-Sabiʻ ʻAshar ila Awakhir al-Qarn al-Thamin ʻAshar* (Beirut: Lebanese University, 1987), 37–8.

[67] Caroline Finkel, *Osman's Dream: The Story of the Ottoman Empire, 1300–1923* (New York: Basic Books, 2006), 257–62.

were key to securing the Köprülüs' position within the central apparatus. The *eyalet* of Sidon, for example, was created as a political fief for Ali Ağa Defterdar, the imperial officer sent to Damascus with Fazıl Ahmed in order to constitute a new Janissary regiment.[68] The coastal mountain districts were doubtless in need of a firm hand, but the projection of Ottoman authority in the area in 1659 perhaps more than anything served the purposes of reasserting the state's control over its own high-level functionary corps.

In any event, it is probably no coincidence that the first new chancery register to take stock of Syrian provincial affairs dates from the 'Köprülü vizierate', Fazıl Ahmed succeeding his father in that office in 1661. The register, a *Mühimme Defteri*, is among those which made their way into the archduke of Saxony's possession after the Ottoman defeat at Vienna in 1683, and has only rarely been used in modern studies.[69] Yet it contains what appears to be the earliest Ottoman references to the Hamadas: an order addressed to Korkmaz and Ahmed Ma'n in late 1660 reminds them of their outstanding tax due for the Shuf *mukataa*, and instructs them to lend their support to Fazıl Ahmed's campaign against 'the brigands Mansur and Ali Şihab-oğlı, and another named [Si]rhan'.[70] This would support Duwayhi's claim that the Shihabis fled their home district, the Wadi Taym, to take shelter with the Hamadas in Qamhaz on the edge of the Kisrawan in the winter of 1660–1; the Ma'ns, meanwhile, were also ordered to mobilize but wrote back affirming that the Shihabis and Hamadas 'had not entered their territory'.[71] Only a few weeks later, the governor of Tripoli indeed received an order from Istanbul to 'get your hands on the brigand named Sirhan no matter where he is, whether on Ma'n-oğlı's lands or in Damascus province or anywhere else'.[72]

The Porte soon realized that the Ma'ns would not deliver the expected taxes either, and by the summer of 1661 had begun to prepare a larger campaign against these 'traitors to the state'. Numerous orders to the *beğlerbeğ* of Safad, as the province of Sidon is initially referred to, criticize him for failing to collect 300 *kise* (bags of 500 silver *akçes* each) of arrears for the Shuf; the sharpest words, however, are reserved for the new *vali* of Damascus sent to replace Fazıl Ahmed, who is ordered to go into the Bekaa Valley and capture the Ma'ns as well as the Shihabis with whom they have joined, 'if your head is dear to you' ('başın sana gerek ise').[73] According to Duwayhi, the Ma'ns intended to join the others at Qamhaz; 5,000 government troops were sent and devastated the Munaytra, Futuh, Jubayl and Batrun region, torching the houses and uprooting the fruit trees of the Hamadas, Khazins, Abilama's and other leading families of the north. By the end of the year,

[68] 'Abd al-Karim Rafiq, *Bilad al-Sham wa-Misr min al-Fath al-'Uthmani ila Hamlat Nabuliyun Bunabart (1516–1798)* (Damascus: n.p., 1967), 185–94.

[69] Hans-Georg Majer, 'Fundstücke aus der vor Wien verlorenen Kanzlei Kara Mustafa Paşas (1683)' in Klaus Kreiser and Christoph Neumann, eds., *Das osmanische Reich in seinen Archivalien und Chroniken: Nejat Göyünç zu Ehren* (Istanbul: Franz Steiner, 1997), 115–22. Note that the register is mistakenly identified in his fn. 19.

[70] Sächsische Landesbibliothek/Staats- und Universitätsbibliothek, Dresden ms. Eb. 387, fol. 13b.

[71] Duwayhi/Fahd, *Tarikh*, 548.    [72] Dresden Eb. 387, fol. 28b.    [73] *Ibid.*, fols. 42a, 54a–b, 55b, 56b.

'the Ma'n-Shihabi emirate was defeated', and Korkmaz Ma'n was killed by the *vali* of Sidon the autumn after, which for Duwayhi marks the tragic end of the campaign.[74]

The newly appointed governor of Sidon (Safad) in fact received an effusive letter of praise for killing Korkmaz,[75] but further documents from the Dresden register suggest that the revolt did not end there. In the spring of 1663, separate orders were sent to the *beğlerbeğ*s of Tripoli and Safad and to the lieutenant governor of Damascus to coordinate an attack on 'Ma'n-oğlı Ahmed, his acolyte Sirhan' and various other 'mountain *mukaddem*s' and 'Druze brigands' for their sedition and, of course, their continuing failure to remit the requisite taxes. Again the Sublime Porte worried that the rebels might flee and hide on each other's territories, and admonished the provincial authorities 'not to declare "it's not my jurisdiction ..."' but to chase, capture and punish them wherever they might be found.[76] Two years later, in the spring of 1665, provincial forces from Tripoli to 'Ajlun to Gaza were being called together to launch a major regional campaign against Ahmad Ma'n and his supporters.[77]

The Hamadas' first direct experience of Ottoman authority thus occurred at a time when the Empire itself was undergoing important political changes. As governor of Tripoli, Mehmed Köprülü was apparently willing to come to some sort of accommodation with the local feudal forces, again irrespective of their confessional affiliation. As grand vizier, however, reining in the mountain 'brigands' became part of his and his son's wider effort to re-establish the centre's primacy and to consolidate their own power, and the Hamadas became caught up in an Istanbul-run police operation whose real objectives went well beyond quelling their contumacy. As such the events of 1659–65 already foreshadow the larger and more consequential punitive campaign to be analysed in the following chapter. The rivalries and intrigues among the emirs played an important part on the local level, but the reassertion of fiscal sovereignty, the creation of new jurisdictions such as the *eyalet* of Sidon and the organisation of official violence on a large scale, all of which the imperial registers begin to record anew in this period, speak above all to the resurgence of the Ottoman state under the Köprülü administration.

## The Hamadas' *iltizam* commissions

In 1690, in response to a petition sent by 'the *'ulama'*, the upright citizens, the imams, the mosque preachers and other people' of Tripoli, the governors of Tripoli and Damascus received orders from the Sublime Porte to the effect that

Sirhan and his followers have not contented themselves with getting their hands on the tax farms of Cübeyl, Betrun, Zanniye and Cübbe [Basharray] from successive *vali*s since quite some time, but have [now] also usurped the districts of Akkar, Zaviye and Kure. In addition

---

[74] Duwayhi/Fahd, *Tarikh*, 550–2.    [75] Dresden Eb. 387, fol. 89a.
[76] *Ibid.*, fols. 99b, 102a.    [77] *Ibid.*, fols. 141a–142a.

to their owing enormous tax arrears, under their rule the ... property and supplies which the local population owns outside the city have gone to ruin. And how often have they descended upon the trade and travel routes in order to kill and to plunder ... There has been no end to this sort of depravity and vice. If, in violation of custom, it is again their intent this year to seize the aforesaid tax farms of Akkar, Zaviye and Kure, whose inhabitants are Muslim, in addition to those which have long been in their hands and whose people are Druze and Christian, it is certain that the humble commoners from the rural districts will scatter and disperse on account of their oppression ... Do not give them ... tax farms inhabited by the community of Muhammad in addition to those they have held previously whose people are Druze and Christian ... Do not let them seize and oppress a single tax farm of the aforesaid, in addition to those places they have held since old, and defend the people of Islam from their usurpation and aggression.[78]

This *hüküm* is noteworthy on two counts: first, because it marks the first instance when the Ottoman administration took exception, albeit very elliptically, to the Hamadas' non-Sunni sectarian identity; and second, because the tax farms of 'Akkar and al-Zawiya had actually been under their intermittent control for decades. The official records of their tax farm commissions, not surprisingly, never made reference to their Shiism, nor for that matter to their habitual excesses and abuse of power. So did the Ottomans view the Hamadas as heretics and usurpers, or as their legitimate local agents? Whereas chancery decrees by their nature tend to highlight crises and disjunctures in the provincial administration, the court records of Tripoli depict a regular, if somewhat ambiguous, relationship between the Ottoman state and the Shiite notables during their heyday in the second half of the seventeenth century. This section focuses on Tripoli's *Şeriye* (*shar'iyya*) court registers in order to illustrate how the authorities were prepared, at least until the breakdown of this ambiguous rapport after 1685, to acknowledge and institutionalize the Hamadas' rule over Mt Lebanon by co-opting them into the accepted structures of Ottoman rural government.

The large majority of Ottoman archival documents dealing with the Hamadas concern not their well-attested though essentially infrequent rebellions, but rather their official commissions as *mukataacı* tax farmers. The earliest sets of records in this regard date from 1667–8 and are comprised in the two oldest extant registers of the Islamic court in Tripoli, copies of which are also held by the Lebanese University and the Municipality of Tripoli. Duwayhi is reticent on the Hamadas' expansion into areas beyond Jubayl and the Futuh, noting only the renewal of Hasan Dib ibn 'Ali's farm in 1649, presumably on Danniyye, and Sa'id (or Sa'd) ibn 'Ali's appointment to al-Kura in 1651 (thirty-nine years before this was denounced as a usurpation and violation of custom to the Sublime Porte).[79] It is thus all the more noteworthy that the *iltizam* contract from 1667 includes six separate districts: 'Akkar, Danniyye, Jubbat Basharray, Jubayl country, Batrun and al-Kura – virtually all of Mt Lebanon – in the Hamadas' domain.[80] The implications of this massive concession of taxation rights (a total of 120,000

---

[78] MD 100:74.    [79] Duwayhi/Fahd, *Tarikh*, 533, 535.    [80] Tripoli Islamic Court Register 1:11–12.

*esedi* silver piastres) and police jurisdiction in Tripoli's hinterland are evident.[81] Like all matters of an overtly political nature, the court proceeding in this case was composed in Turkish; only in the eighteenth century, perhaps when the local feudalists ceased to worry the imperial authorities, were the Hamadas' and other tax contracts systematically recorded in Arabic.

Moreover, the 1667 *iltizam* recognizes the corporative nature of the Hamadas' rule over the region. The contract was officially concluded between the governor of Tripoli and the aforementioned shaykh Sa'd ibn 'Ali Hamada. The latter, however, was technically only the representative (*vekil*) of the lesser known Ahmad ibn Muhammad, in whose name the tax farm was registered, probably as a means of distributing the legal liability over several members of the family. Both, in turn, are stated in the opening address to be acting on behalf of 'the most excellent of peers and paragons, *şeyh* Sirhan'. Responsibility for the protection and development of the tax fiefs and for the timely payment of the tax charge was thus assigned to Ahmad, but the guarantee (*kefale*) for the faithful execution of the *iltizam* is explicitly noted to rest with '*şeyh* Sirhan, his cousins, and all the Hamade-oğulları'.

The rest of the contract is fairly conventional and similar in its terms to others for the province. The *iltizam* was valid for a full solar year beginning in March, the first month of the Syriac-derived Ottoman fiscal calendar. Payment of 120,000 *guruş* in kind was expected in two instalments: three-quarters during the 'silk season' and the other in olive oil three months before the end of the year, that is, in December. The dues were to be collected on all lands including the governor's crown reserve (*havass-ı mirmiran*), and comprised, in addition to the regular *miri* agricultural tax, the capitation tax (*harac*), church taxes (*mal-i kenayis*) and fines for violent crimes (*cürm-i galiz*). In order to ensure the concessionary's full payment and proper conduct, the government of Tripoli also made use of another standard clause in such contracts: shaykh Sa'd and his family, as well as Ahmad's wife and children, were pledged 'to live in Tripoli city as hostages [*rehn tarikiyle*] under the … Paşa's supervision until the aforesaid charge has been fulfilled'. First complications arose the following October, when the governor died and the court had to remand the hostages into a deputy's temporary custody.[82] Disputes over family members held as bond in the capital, as will be seen shortly, would become a major factor in the breakdown of the Hamadas' relationship with the Ottoman authorities.

The nature of the Hamadas' control over northern Tripoli is further elucidated in a second set of court documents from the summer of the same year. These involve the rental of twenty villages in 'Akkar to Ahmad ibn Qansuh Hamada, for three consecutive terms or a total of nine years. While some details remain obscure, as is perhaps not untypical for debt arrangements between strongarm financiers and impoverished villagers, the contracts (this time written in Arabic) can be

---

[81] On this scale, 'revenue contracting and venal offices constituted veritable forms of governance'; Ariel Salzmann, *Toqueville in the Ottoman Empire: Rival Paths to the Modern State* (Leiden: Brill, 2004), 21.

[82] Tripoli 1:114–15.

summarized as follows: Ahmad receives title to the villages (and thus their produce) from the elders in return for paying the yearly tax charge to the government *mültezim*. In addition, he agrees to provide them with draught animals and seed, and, 'should either the sublime sultanate or the *vali* ... show mercy', pass on any tax abatement at the conclusion of the first year. Not indicated in the contract is Ahmad's cut, which may consist in a discrepancy between the villages' official tax capacity (11,820 g.) and the amount actually to be paid as *iltizam* (9,970 g.); nor the fact that the current tax farmer (who needs forward only 50 per cent of his receipts to the state anyway) is Ahmad's own brother Sirhan. The benefit to the state in this instance was Ahmad's formal undertaking to revive the twenty villages which had supposedly fallen into ruin, retrieve all the peasants who had fled and thus assure a higher remittance of taxes. While it is impossible to assess from these documents whether the project was successful, or if it mainly benefited the peasants, the government treasury, the tax farmer or his entrepreneur brother, it is interesting to observe that, in 1667, the Ottoman state regarded the Hamada family enterprise as favouring the economic development of the northern highlands.[83] The following year, Ahmad again received the concession for 'Akkar, Jubbat Basharray and, in a novel twist, for the predominantly Nusayri-inhabited district of Safita in the northern coastal mountains. Moneys to be collected included winter and summer levies, *harac* on fruit trees, a lump sum on draught animals, taxes on goats, bees and buffalo, monthly dues, festival dues, accession dues, storage and milling dues, wintering taxes for Arab and Turkmen tribes, church charges, criminal fines and the poll-tax on Christians.[84] Meanwhile, the *nahiye*s of Jubayl country (Bilad-ı Cübeyl, as opposed to the city itself) and Batrun were awarded to Sirhan's maternal cousin Dib ibn 'Asi and his own agent Mustafa ibn Nasir al-Din, with Sirhan himself again standing bond.[85]

With their tax and local government commissions stretching all the way into what is today north-western Syria, the year 1668 may well mark the greatest geographic extent of the Hamada 'emirate'. However, this inevitably also brought about tensions with the Ottoman state authorities as well as with local rivals. In 1673, according to Duwayhi, the new governor of Tripoli 'gave the Hamadas their *mukataa*s and treated them better than his predecessors, ... but they were taken with greed, stole the tax money, killed people ... and ruined the farms with their pillaging'. He thus locked Ahmad ibn Qansuh up in the citadel when he came to Tripoli to renew his *iltizam* for Jubbat Basharri the following spring and captured Muhammad ibn Hasan Dib for having paid insufficient returns on his *iltizam* for Danniyye, but left Sirhan in control of Jubayl and Batrun. In 1675, however, the governor decided to evict Sirhan and launch a major campaign against the Hamadas on account of their tax truancy. They were beaten and, after two of their shaykhs were convened to a conciliatory banquet and promptly murdered, fell burning and pillaging upon the Christian areas of Jubayl, Batrun and Basharri. In the face of a worsening situation the Sublime Porte ordered the governors of Sidon

[83] Tripoli 1:61–3.    [84] Tripoli 2/1:50, 60–2.    [85] Tripoli 2/1:76–7.

Fig. 2  Wadi 'Almat (Futuh/Bilad Jubayl)

and Damascus to step in, and by the autumn a force of 5,000 men gathered in the Bekaa were ready to attack the Hamadas as well as the Ma'ns, if they did not deliver up their Shiite allies.[86]

Good mountain sense prevailed, however. The *vali* of Sayda privately assured Ahmad Ma'n that he would not really be attacked, while he in turn disingenuously told the authorities that the Hamadas had indeed passed through his land individually, but were now gone. Also, the dispute had been over a mere 20 *kise* of silver, for which the Ma'ns would stand bond if the Hamadas' hostages were released from prison. (Another version, further embellished by the nineteenth-century historian Haydar Ahmad al-Shihabi, gives the Shihabis credit for having diverted the campaign.[87]) But the Hamadas were also intent on recovering their fiefs, and began to press the local population while the governor was away on another campaign in 1676. Upon his return, he set upon those who had supported the Hamadas and launched a devastating attack, once again with the Sha'irs' help, on their districts. All the villages of the Wadi 'Almat (Fig. 2) – Farhat, 'Almat, Mashan, Turzayya, Hasun, Ahmaj and Jaj – as well as Mughayra, Lasa, Munaytra and Afqa in the Jubbat Munaytra and others were torched, their grain supplies destroyed and Sirhan himself captured. With the death of grand vizier Köprülü Fazıl Ahmed later in the year, however, all the provincial governors in the region were replaced, and the Hamadas were once more recalled to their fiefs, and

---

[86] Duwayhi/Fahd, *Tarikh*, 559, 560–2.    [87] Cf. Duwayhi, *Tarikh*, 369–70; Shihabi, *Tarikh*, 736–7.

ordered to care for the *reaya* who had fled the savagery.[88] Court documents from 1677 indeed show that Sirhan received the *iltizam*s for Jubayl and Batrun on much the same terms as before, while his nephew Husayn ibn Ahmad was reinstated in Jubbat Basharray. Both had to send their wives to live in the capital as surety. The only noteworthy difference to earlier *iltizam* conferrals seems to be a new concern with security: Sirhan's contract explicitly makes him

responsible for the safety and protection of travellers passing anywhere between the Nahr Ibrahim and the place called Soğuk Su as well as of all other subjects, and liable for any damages and harm caused. If it becomes known and confirmed that a man has been killed wrongfully or someone robbed of something in these areas, the aforesaid shaykh Sirhan is held accountable and censurable.[89]

Similar terms were applied the following year, when Sirhan again held all three *mukataa*s (Jubayl, Batrun, Basharray) in his own right;[90] Duwayhi, for his part, indicates that the Hamadas were reconfirmed in their possessions in 1679 and/or in 1680.[91]

## The Hamadas in court

The *iltizam*s negotiated on a yearly basis at the Hanefi Islamic court of Tripoli typify the regular, institutionalized contact between the Shiite feudalists and the Ottoman state. By definition, these contracts also implicated them in a legal relationship with the rest of the population of the districts under their control, and with whom disputes or other dealings such as sales were also carried out in front of the court. The most important of these relationships was that created by the *kafala*, the pecuniary guarantee for the full payment of an *iltizam* or some other debt that could be assumed by an outside party. The *kafala* (or *daman*) exists in all schools of law, but it is only in the Hanefi school that the act of guaranteeing requires the formal consent of the lender and thus creates a binding three-way contract between, in this case, the state, the *mültezim* and the *kafil*.[92] In many of the Hamadas' early *iltizam* contracts the *kafala* appears only as a general promise on the part of the whole family to ensure its payment, besides the confinement of hostages in the citadel of Tripoli. In other cases, however, the Hamadas' *iltizam*s did involve third-party guarantors who could be called to account by the state authorities if the tax farms were not acquitted.

The district of al-Kura, for example, was initially included in Sirhan's domain, but already in 1667 the actual business of collecting its taxes was sub-farmed to the local Kurdish emirs.[93] A suit launched the following year against Ahmad ibn Isma'il al-Kurdi, friend to the Sha'ir clan and in many ways an old nemesis of the Hamadas, demonstrates the complex partnerships in which the feudatories of

---

[88]  Duwayhi/Fahd, *Tarikh*, 563–5.    [89]  Tripoli 2/2:106–7.

[90]  Tripoli 2/2:134.    [91]  Duwayhi, *Tarikh*, 373; cf. Duwayhi/Fahd, *Tarikh*, 567.

[92]  Y. Linant de Bellefonds, 'Kafāla' in *Encyclopedia of Islam*, 2nd edn (Leiden: Brill, 1978).

[93]  In 1668, the *iltizam* was awarded to a certain Şahin Ağa; see Tripoli 2/1:59.

Mt Lebanon sometimes engaged: in the spring of 1668 Sirhan, in his capacity as legal guarantor of the tax farm, claimed Ahmad still owed 1860 g. (out of a total of 22,000) for the year and sought the court's help to enforce payment 'out of fear that the defendant would disappear from Tripoli'. Ahmad retorted that the tax due had been raised 3,000 g. above what it had been originally and that he had already submitted 20,140 g. in several instalments. True, he still owed 1,860 g., but Sirhan himself had tax arrears of 15,000 g. on his own territories. He thus produced a *fatwa* from "Ali the *mufti*' which said in essence 'is it permissible for a bondsman to demand a sum back before he himself has discharged it?' The judge, ruling that Sirhan had no claim on Ahmad before the entire *iltizam* is discharged to the state, dismissed the case.[94]

The financial pressure on the Hamadas manifested itself in other aspects as well. In the summer of 1667, Mudlij al-Hamadi, the sub-*mültezim* for a single village in the district of al-Zawiya, brought two brothers to court for refusing to pay their share of taxes. Stating Aleppo as their place of origin and al-Minya as their residence, the two denied being *reaya* of, or owning property in, the village concerned. The judge, citing Mudlij's failure to prove the opposite, refused his right to levy taxes on them.[95] The Hamadas had a bit more luck with the imperial authorities. In early 1668, that is, shortly before the end of the fiscal year, a *hüküm* respectfully addressed to Sirhan and Ahmad Hamada states that while time-honoured Ottoman *kanun* law normally permits the governors' personal agents (*kethüda*) to levy customary taxes (*avaid*), these were to be suspended. The *kethüda*s were not to collect any further *avaid* in the Hamadas' domains so that the standard state agricultural tax (*miri*) would not fall short. The *miri* itself, Sirhan and Ahmad are gently reminded, was of course to be paid in full and on time.[96]

Another lawsuit from 1668 concerns the growing tax arrears of Sirhan himself, for which his bondsman, a certain Muhammad Abu 'Adhra, had been thrown in jail. The case raises several questions, especially in that prior court documents mention neither a *kafil* of that name nor an attempt to collect on the 6,000 g. debt; there is in reality no way of knowing which disputes were formally adjudicated and recorded and which were settled otherwise.[97] What appears to have brought this case before the courts was the arrival in Tripoli of a commander from the Baghdad Janissary garrison to collect. Many sources of revenue in the Empire were in fact earmarked for specific expenditures, such as the upkeep of important military installations, rather than for the treasury of the province in which they originated. The highly official nature of this case (like all those involving imperial actors it was again registered in Turkish) is most likely what impelled the local authorities to quickly settle the Janissary officer's account and release the bondsman, perhaps to recover their money directly from the Hamadas afterwards.[98]

[94] Tripoli 2/1:18–19.    [95] Tripoli 1:37–8.    [96] Tripoli 1:154.
[97] 'Adhra was the name of a notable family of Marqab, where the Hamadas may still have had ties.
[98] Tripoli 2/1:48.

Isolated disputes and even episodes of violence over the remission of taxes do not seem to have poisoned the Hamadas' overall solid working rapport with the Ottomans. Though leading figures such as Sirhan and Ahmad generally did not risk appearing in the provincial capital in person, they maintained regular and perhaps even cordial relations with the state authorities through their agents at the *shar'iyya* tribunal. Not only the yearly *iltizam* conferrals but, as we have seen, rental contracts with villagers and lawsuits against business associates or delinquent taxpayers were adjudicated by the state-appointed Hanefi judge or notary. Recent scholarship on the social practices of Ottoman law has begun to emphasize the many ways in which supposedly marginal actors such as women, slaves and non-Muslims made use of the courts. A few examples of the Hamadas' voluntary recourse to Sunni Islamic judicature, which we propose to present here in closing, also help illustrate the Shiites' integration in wider Ottoman society.

Two transaction deeds from 1668 record the sale of important properties by members of the extended clan to local Christians. These documents, potentially a reflection of the financial straits in which the Hamadas were finding themselves, provide some rare albeit elliptical clues as to the material life of the Shiite notables in the seventeenth century. The first concerns a house in Tripoli sold by Baz ibn Qaytbay ibn Hamada to 'the deacon's son Rizqallah'. The property, priced at 150 g. with all its amenities, was located in the privileged Christian quarter of Hajjarin al-Nasara and bounded on the south, east and north by that of a certain emir Muhammad. Baz ibn Qaytbay himself had purchased this apparently well-appointed estate only two years previously from his own maternal aunt,[99] when the Hamada family as a whole was enjoying greater liquidity. The second deed involves Muhammad ibn Hasan Dib al-Hamadi's sale of a sizeable rural estate in the district of al-Zawiya to a local inhabitant. The property, which Muhammad had legally purchased from his father and which was again valued at 150 g., included 'everything the principal owns in the village Basba'al in mulberry trees, olives, grapevines, houses and non-irrigable [*salikh*] lands'.[100]

If we reach ahead a few decades, a deed from July 1716 documents Husayn ibn Hamada's sale, with his brother-in-law's approval, of properties bequeathed to his wife by a previous husband. These included shares of several gardens in 'Akkar, houses in Tripoli and parts of a buffalo herd grazed at Safita, for a total of 90 g.[101] A lawsuit from July 1729 refers to a small Hamada estate located on Arwad Island off the coast of Tartus. In this instance, Mustafa ibn 'Ali Hamada 'al-Arwadi' tried to evict a native of nearby Marqab from the house, described as dilapidated but situated on the seashore and adjoined by the local garrison commander's kitchen garden. He had acquired possession from his own father twelve years before, long before the current occupant. The respondent testified that he had indeed purchased it only eight months previously from Hamada senior for 8 g. and some wheat, and then restored it at his own cost to render it inhabitable. Unable, after a ten-day recess, to provide evidence of his ownership, Mustafa Hamada was ordered to

---

[99] Tripoli 2/1:21.    [100] Tripoli 2/1:33.    [101] Tripoli 4/1:13.

cease and desist from harassing the Marqabi in his title as lawful proprietor.[102] In June 1731, the court notarized an agent's sale of properties belonging to Haydar ibn Zayd Hamada, including an unidentified ruined orchard garden, a ruined palace situated on the same grounds and two wood-roofed houses, for 150 g.[103]

Members of the Hamada family also stepped before the Ottoman *kadı* in other matters. In a further instalment of the Hamadas' love/hate saga with the Kurdish emirs of al-Kura, 'Abd al-Salam ibn Isma'il Hamada took emir Isma'il ibn Ahmad to court in July 1724, claiming to have paid a dowry of 200 g. for the hand of his daughter Zlêxa seven years earlier. The emir acknowledged neither the betrothal nor the payment, and upon being interrogated herself, 'Zlêxa answered that she did not know a thing about any of this, that she does not consent to marry, that she would not accept him and that she will not leave her village.' 'Abd al-Salam Hamada's agent was asked to present proof of payment, but retorted that they sought the girl's hand and not a refund. To the *kadı*, this was sufficient to invalidate the suit: a lawful engagement would have spelled out a promise to the girl that she cannot be forced to marry against her will, this being the consent of the Hanefi jurists.[104] And finally, in a complex inheritance case from September 1745, Muhammad ibn 'Ali Hamada was appointed legal guardian of his deceased brother Ahmad's minor-aged daughter Khadija, and authorized to dispose of her heritage in order to provide for her maintenance.[105] The property, jointly controlled by Khadija and her father's widow Halima, consisted of an apartment and a large storage vault in the Tripoli harbour quarter. With the judge's permission for dissolving the estate, the warehouse was assessed to constitute the minor's prescribed three-quarters share and, subtractions being made for the deceased's debts, sold on her behalf for 70 g.[106]

## Conclusion: the fragile consensus

From their home district in the Wadi 'Almat on the low ridges of Mt Lebanon, from where they could easily dominate the coastal villages or flee into the higher mountains when necessary, and where ruins of Ottoman-era houses are visible to the present day, the Hamadas commanded over a vast part of Tripoli's rural hinterland and constituted the most important, but perhaps also the most feared and reviled feudal faction of what was to become northern Lebanon. Their life on the literal and figurative edges of Ottoman Lebanese society is vividly conjured up by the French diplomat D'Arvieux, who encountered a group of Hamada riders at the Qanubin monastery, seat of the Maronite patriarchate, around 1660:

[N]ous vîmes arriver une vingtaine de soldats armés de bons mousquets. Leur figure nous fit peur. C'étaient des gens secs, halés, maigres, décharnés, les yeux bordés de noir, presque nus. Ils entrèrent d'un air féroce dans le parvis sans saluer personne. Ils nous regardèrent attentivement un assez long temps sans rien dire. Il est certain qu'ils nous auraient bien embarrassés, si nous les avions rencontrés dans ces sentiers étroits, où le moindre faux pas

---

[102] Tripoli 5:53.    [103] Tripoli 6:12.    [104] Tripoli 4/2:35.    [105] Tripoli 8:293.    [106] Tripoli 8:295–6.

qu'aurait fait un cheval, l'aurait précipité avec son cavalier dans des lieux où on aurait eu peine à trouver les plus grosses parties de leurs corps: car quoique nous fussions tous bien armés, ces gens accoutumés à grimper les montagnes commes des chèvres sauvages, auraient eu bon marché de nous s'il avait fallu en venir aux mains.

... [L]es sujets de ce prince [Serhhan ben Hhameidié] ... sonts des corps de bronze; il y avait plus de deux mois qu'ils avaient abandonné leurs villages et leurs maisons, et qu'ils s'étaient retirés sur la cime des rochers, où ils couchaient exposés à toutes les injures de l'air sans en être incommodés. Ce sont des gens d'une force et d'une santé inaltérables, souffrants sans peine les plus grandes fatigues, d'une grande sobriété et d'un courage sans égal. Les janissaires les plus braves et les plus aguérris ne leur feraient pas faire un pas en arrière. Ils se servent du mousquet et du sabre, avec une force et une adresse merveilleuse.

Lorsque la poudre leur manque, ils en font eux-mêmes. Pour cet effet, chacun d'eux porte dans un petit sac du soufre et du salpêtre. Ils font promptement du charbon avec du bois de saule. Ils le pilent avec un bâton dans un creux de rocher, et y mettent la dose nécessaire de soufre et de salpêtre, et font ainsi leur poudre qui est très bonne.

Ils n'étaient venus à Cannobin, que pour sçavoir des nouvelles du patriarche de la part de leur prince, et lui offrir leurs services en cas de besoin.

Leur arrivée nous avait d'abord donné de l'inquiétude, nous avions pris nos armes, on se reconnut, on se parla, on nous fit déjeûner et boire ensemble, et nous reconnûmes que c'étaient de fort bonnes gens.[107]

The Hamadas' reign over Mt Lebanon in the seventeenth century indeed presents somewhat of a paradox. On the one hand, the 'Sirhan-oğulları' were the ultimate outsiders in the Ottoman provincial world. As insubordinate tribalists and Shiite sectarians, they embodied a marginal culture which neither the central state authorities (beginning with the Mamluks) nor Maronite notables (beginning with

---

[107]  Laurent d'Arvieux (d. 1702), *Mémoires*, ed. Antoine Abedelnour (Beirut: Dar Lahad Khatir, 1982), 189–90.

We saw arrive some twenty soldiers armed with good muskets. Their appearance frightened us. They were lean, tan, gaunt, emaciated, their eyes outlined in black, almost naked. They entered the portico with a fierce air, greeting no one, and looked at us closely for quite a while without saying anything. It is certain that they would have greatly troubled us had we encountered them on one of those narrow paths where the slightest misstep a horse makes would throw it together with its rider down to where it could be hard to find even the biggest body parts. For even though we were all well armed, these people, who are accustomed to scaling the mountains like wild goats, would have had easy prey with us had it come to a fight.

... The followers of this prince [Sirhan ibn Hamada] ... are iron men; they had quit their villages and houses over two months ago and withdrawn to the mountain peaks, where they sleep exposed to all the climate's hardships without inconvenience. These are people of inalterable health and force, bearing the greatest exertions with ease, of great sobriety and unequalled courage. The bravest and toughest Janissaries would not make them step back. They wield the musket and the sabre with marvellous force and address.

When they are out of gunpowder, they make some themselves. For this each one of them carries a small bag of sulphur and saltpetre. They quickly make coal from willow wood, crush it in a rock hollow with a stick, and put in the necessary amount of sulphur and saltpetre, thus making their powder which is very good.

They only came to Cannobin to ask news of the patriarch on the part of their prince, and to offer him their services if he needed.

Their arrival had worried us at first, we had taken our weapons, we acknowledged one another, we talked, we were given to eat and drink together, and we realized that they were good honest people.

Duwayhi) saw as belonging in their vision of local society. Yet at the same time, Shiite pastoral nomads had dominated the Syrian coastal range since the high Middle Ages, and the Hamada confederacy's martial, endogamous sociology in effect predestined them to act as an inter-regional taxation and police deputy once the Ottoman administration abandoned military appanages in favour of *iltizam* farming in the agrarian hinterland. The Shiites and other heterodox highlanders were merely typical of the many peripheral groups that circumscribed and gave form to the societal diversity that characterized the early modern Ottoman Empire.

This tension between deviance and conformity, as we have attempted to show here, defined the history of the Hamadas' relationship with the Ottoman state officials in the second half of the seventeenth century. The governors of the western *eyalet*s of Syria embarked on numerous missions to bring the Shiites to heal when their tax payments were in arrears or their subjects unduly oppressed. However, the archival records of their *iltizam* appointments suggest also that the state appreciated the Hamada enterprise precisely for the order and authority it was able to impose on much of Tripoli, relying on them to police, tax and even develop the region economically on its behalf, irrespective of their sectarian identity. Whereas the literary narratives of Lebanon's history have tended to interpret its feudal regime only in terms of Druze-Maronite sovereignty, the success of the Shiite Hamada 'emirate' provides a striking illustration of the ambiguous consensus of power between the early modern disciplining state and its more deviant constituencies. The Ottomans had no illusions as to the Hamadas' heresy, violence and tax-cheating, yet with rare exceptions they were unable or simply unwilling to invest themselves in replacing an institution which, in the larger scheme of things, functioned passably well.

This consensus, always fragile at best, was not to survive the tumultuous decade-and-a-half of political and social crisis that was precipitated by the Empire's catastrophic 1683 Vienna campaign. In Mt Lebanon, as signalled in a Tripoli *shar'iyya* court affidavit from October 1685, long-simmering tensions between the state authorities and the Hamadas, and more specifically a dispute over their Kurdish subcontractor's tax arrears in al-Kura, finally came to a boil:

His brother Muhammad was placed as a hostage in Tripoli city as surety for the said amount. Three days ago, while this Muhammad was at the city gate with the guards assigned to him, Sirhan-oğlı [Husayn]'s armed henchmen … came, pulled swords on the guards, took Muhammad and fled. They are hiding with *şeyh* Husayn and the entirety of state moneys from their commissions is lost.[108]

This was to be the opening shot of a more fundamental challenge to the state authority on the Shiites' part, one that ended in the unprecedentedly destructive punitive campaign of 1693–4. This conflict and its origins in the long-term structural tensions and strains that befell Ottoman provincial society in the late seventeenth century are the subject of the next chapter.

---

[108] Tripoli 3:5.

# CHAPTER 4

# The reshaping of authority: the Shiites and the state in crisis, 1685–1699

The Hamadas' reign over Mt Lebanon in the later seventeenth century epitomized the Ottoman state's regularization and co-optation of parochial forms of self-government in the provincial periphery. The imperial administration was not only prepared to ignore their socio-religious deviance, but actively promoted the Hamadas and similar tribal groups as its taxation and police deputies over extensive, otherwise inaccessible hinterland areas. This concord between local Shiite notables and the state began to unravel during the critical period of external crisis and domestic reform that characterized the last decades of the century. The Hamadas' attack on Tripoli in September 1685 to liberate the guarantors of their *iltizam* contracts heralded almost fifteen years of punitive expeditions, counter-raids and generalized instability in Tripoli and beyond. The Hamadas entered this conflict as the most powerful taxlord dynasty of the *eyalet* if not the entire Syrian coastlands; the massive Ottoman military campaign of 1693–4 left them physically broken and politically dependent on the paramount Druze emirs of Sidon and, increasingly, their Maronite subalterns. This revolt is detailed not just in several local chronicles but in a large extant corpus of Ottoman chancery decrees and in at least three imperial histories, making it the single best-documented episode in the history of Ottoman Shiism.

The interest of the Shiites' rebellion, this chapter argues, goes beyond the narrative significance of its events, in that it bespeaks several *longue-durée* ruptures in the domestic, regional and imperial governance of the western coastal highlands. On the most local level, the heirs and allies of Sirhan ibn Hamada became drawn into a protracted blood-feud against their Maronite neighbours which elicited official intervention. Though the Hamadas regained their tax collector concessions for some time afterwards, the crisis denoted a long-term decline vis-à-vis the French-subsidized Maronite lay notability, in particular the Khazin family of the Kisrawan, and its efforts to colonize, develop and control the fertile northern highlands. The Ottoman state authority, which long recognized the Hamadas as its premier medium of fiscal exploitation in the area, henceforth began to engage the Maronite leaders and their self-appointed feudal protectors, the Druze emirs of the southern Shuf range, to assume increased responsibilities for the government of rural Tripoli.

The question of changing jurisdictions also applies to the regionally rooted civilian gubernatorial households that were starting to supplant the older military service elite in the Ottoman provincial hierarchy. Seen from the bureaucratic perspective, the great punitive campaign against the Hamadas was as much a motor of inter-Ottoman competition as of local feudal rivalries. Finally, the wealth of chancery documentation for this conflict demands that it be situated within the larger context of imperial politics. The central administration's intense new concern with the heretics in the Syrian hinterland, it will be argued, proceeded not from a revived anti-Shiite religious impulse but from an Empire-wide drive to quell wartime rural banditry and settle the semi-nomadic tribes of the rural interior. In this light, the Hamadas' conflict with authority in the period 1685–99 appears as much the result of the Ottoman state's march towards administrative rationalization, bureaucratic modernization and societal discipline as of the Shiites' actual contumacy.

## The Shiite rebellion

In the late summer of 1685, an imperial order issued in Edirne in response to a complaint made by the governor of Tripoli relates that Sirhan Hamada (possibly the grandson of the more famous chief of the same name, whose date of death is unknown) had remitted no taxes for the Jubayl and Batrun districts for the previous year and only five sacks of silver for the current. He had then absconded to Damascene lands to seek the help of Ahmad Ma'n, who was therefore summoned 'not to protect' him (*sahib çıkmayub*) but to ensure, along with the *kadı* and the deputy governor of that province, that the arrears be paid in full.[1] In the course of the year the Hamadas had also killed the emir of al-Kura and replaced him with someone of their choosing, and generally permitted their followers to pillage in the highlands, apparently without the state intervening; Duwayhi, for his part, reports that they murdered a shaykh of the 'Akkar district as well as a nephew of the *paşa* and, together with the Harfushes, attacked villages in the Kisrawan before descending on Tripoli in the autumn to 'extricate their hostages from the citadel by the sword'.[2] He goes on to describe how Ahmad Ma'n led a vast punitive expedition on the state's behalf which laid waste to the Hamadas' districts, but then took pity on them and declined to take over their *iltizam*s for himself. However, in this instance again Duwayhi's dates are off and his references are to an earlier governor, raising the possibility that he has either collated events from a previous campaign, or that the Hamadas in fact descended on Tripoli on more than one occasion to liberate their hostages.

In any event, a court deposition from May 1686 recounts an extraordinary encounter, following weeks of violence and bloodshed in the highlands, between Sirhan Hamada and an Ottoman representative in a village near Tripoli:

---

[1] Tripoli 3:165.    [2] Tripoli 3:5; Duwayhi/Fahd, *Tarikh*, 572–3.

Two months before the date of this writing, as the honourable Paşa was delegated to the Bedouin war and headed towards Raqqa, the aforesaid Sirhan had his people and kin and the thugs affiliated with them fall upon the righteous believers. They killed several men and destroyed houses in the districts of Hısnü'l-Ekrad and Zanniye [Danniyye] in order to terrorize and intimidate the subjects, and stole and plundered their property, supplies and livestock, tormenting and afflicting a great many folks. All the people of Zanniye have fled and are dispersed and the state tax moneys are lost. Moreover, they came with 5 to 600 archers and wiped out the silkworm and thread of I'al, a village belonging to the Harameyn foundation in Zanniye. The men of the environs have disappeared and the silk-growing subjects have scattered …

The ex-Janissary officer İbrahim Çavuş Ağa was appointed and sent to meet with Sirhan in the said village. Asked 'what is your aim in oppressing and tormenting the righteous believers?' he answered, 'I have the power to improve or to waste, to build or to destroy your land. If, between now and the afternoon prayer, the Paşa's lieutenant … does not release our hostages from the citadel and send them safe and sound, I will kill people in every direction. I will wreak havoc and destruction from the county of Hısnü'l-Ekrad to the citadel of Jubayl; I will ruin the silk crop, obliterate the state taxes, and not care about the sultan's reproof or punishment!'[3]

The court then deliberated and gave in to Sirhan's demands in the interest of protecting the rural populace's livelihood. Almost incredibly, we see the *iltizam*s for Jubayl and Batrun reconfirmed to the Hamadas a week later.[4] Papers filed soon thereafter, all noted to bear their chiefs' personal signatures and stamps, again contained first-person pledges of faithful discharge (also of the Jubbat Basharray and Danniyye contracts) and formal undertakings to pay the arrears from the two previous years.[5] An imperial *Şikayet* order to Ahmad Ma'n at exactly the same moment, paradoxically, lists Sirhan, his son Husayn and his nephews 'Umar, Muhammad, Nasir and Hasan as perpetrators of vice and corruption and demands their surrender to the governor of Tripoli for punishment.[6] The provincial author-ities' failure to execute these orders and indeed their unprecedented appeasement policy marks perhaps the pinnacle of the Hamadas' power in the region.

This arrangement notwithstanding, the Hamadas still had grievances against their local enemies, and killed the head of the Ra'd family in Danniyye and others before twelve of their own followers were caught and impaled later in the year.[7] The main reason for the renewed violence, however, seems to have been their growing ties with the Harfush emirs of Baalbek. We last referred to the Harfushes in the 1630s, as they struggled with the Ma'ns and, increasingly, the Shihabis, for control of the Bekaa farms. While they were generally able to maintain their position, they also fell victim to the sort of internecine disputes that had weakened them at the beginning of the century: in 1671, according to Duwayhi, 'emir 'Ali ibn al-Harfush sought the aid of the (Damascene) authorities [*dawlat al-basha*] and defeated his cousins 'Ammar, Shadid and Yunus, plundered their goods, burnt their houses and seized control of Baalbek country'.[8] Several years later the whole family was on the defensive as Faris Shihabi took the 1680 tax concession for

---

[3] Tripoli 3:64–5.    [4] Tripoli 3:69–70.    [5] Tripoli 3:129–30.    [6] ŞD 10:29.
[7] Duwayhi/Fahd, *Tarikh*, 574.    [8] *Ibid.*, 557; cf. Duwayhi, *Tarikh*, 366.

Baalbek and proceeded to drive out the Harfushes with 2,000 horsemen; the Shiite folk tradition has preserved the memory of the Shihabis' and their Druze supporters' oppression in the region.[9] The now paramount Harfush emir 'Umar (or 'Ammar) thus called on the Hamadas for help for perhaps the first time. The united Shiite forces were able to kill Faris and fifty of his men in a night-time raid on their camp near Yunin, but then reached a settlement through the Ma'ns' intercession which left the Harfushes in control of Baalbek and indemnified the Shihabis for their leader's death.[10] Again the Harfushes seem to have become divided among themselves, however, for 'Umar is noted to have died in 1683 while in exile in the Shiite village of Turzayya in Mt Lebanon, where he had gone anew to seek the Hamadas' protection, while his cousin Shadid was returned as *mültezim* of the Baalbek district.[11]

Already in 1685, however, another tax farmer complained to the Sublime Porte that the 'Rafizi brigands who had settled in Baalbek' were once again making revenue collection very difficult.[12] Then the following year, Shadid apparently thought to capitalize on the governor's absence to attack Ra's Baalbek in the northern Bekaa and burn its fortress. Yet this proved to be a mistake, and he fled to take refuge with the Hamadas when he found himself confronted by a new coalition of government troops and local forces led by the Ra'ds, the Sha'irs and of course the Shihabis. The coalition pursued him across Mt Lebanon and proceeded to ravage his host Husayn Sirhan's lands, along with the tomb of 'Umar Harfush in Turzayya, before the Hamada–Harfush forces could mount an ambush and slaughter forty-five of their number. The soldiers and the Druze, Bedouin and Turkmen with them all fled in defeat, leaving first the governor and then 'opportunists' to devastate the city of Jubayl and its citadel.[13]

This account (for which we must turn again to the 1951 edition of Duwayhi as the other terminates at this time) is one of the few concerning the Harfushes and Hamadas to have found wider reception in the secondary literature.[14] It is moreover one that is corroborated by the Tripoli court records: an imperial order addressed to the governor of Sidon in December 1686 recounts that

Sirhan's son Hüseyin, who sowed vice and malice and obliterated the state tax receipts owed by Sirhan, was ordered captured and imprisoned together with his cousins Ahmed-oğlı Hüseyin and Şedid and the thugs Sa'd-oğlı Ömer and Mehmed Kansuh in a noble ferman addressed to the past and current governor of Sidon and to Ma'n-oğlı Ahmed. Furthermore, an august ferman was reiterated and directed to the governor of Tripoli, Ali Paşa, concerning the brigand called Harfuş-oğlı Şedid who lives in the Baalbek district. After the said

---

[9] al-Amin, *A'yan al-Shi'a*, VII:334–6; VIII:386.
[10] Duwayhi/Fahd, *Tarikh*, 568–9; Anonymous, *Tarikh al-Umara' al-Shihabiyyin bi-Qalam Ahad Umara'ihim min Wadi Taym*, ed. Salim Hasan Hashshi (Beirut: al-Mudiriyya al-'Amma li'l-Athar, 1971), 77, 80–1.
[11] Duwayhi/Fahd, *Tarikh*, 571.    [12] Başbakanlık Archives: Ali Emiri IV. Mehmed 2948.
[13] Duwayhi, *Tarikh*, 377.
[14] Muhammad Kurd 'Ali (d. 1953), *Khitat al-Sham* (Damascus: Maktabat al-Nuri, 1983), II:263–4; al-Amin, *A'yan al-Shi'a*, VII:334–5.

governor moved against Harfus-oğlı in accordance with the noble order, the brigand Sirhan protected him, taking all his effects and family and hiding them. Since they would not forswear tormenting and afflicting the Baalbek and Tripoli regions, it became necessary to attack Sirhan.[15]

But perhaps more importantly, the *hüküm* elaborates on the Druze emir's role, which is curiously occulted by Duwayhi, and suggests that the rebellion was more calamitous than his account allows:

A day before [the Harfushes and Hamadas] reached the villages where they ensconce themselves in the Jubayl mountains, they hid the entirety of their families, goods and effects in villages of the Kisrawan, on the border of Jubayl, in Ma'n-oğlı's lands, and sought refuge with Ma'n-oğlı. In order to protect their families, they became violent in their rebellion. Their men split into groups and caused no end of damage and spoliation in the Tripoli area, and utterly tormented and injured the righteous believers. In addition to completely desolating and ruining the Jubayl, Batrun, Jubbat Basharray and Zanniye districts, they have attempted to wipe out and obliterate the state tax receipts of all the other districts. All the notables of Tripoli came to and petitioned Ali Paşa. He went to the Jubayl citadel on the border to inquire about and spy on the brigands' situation.

After spies had verified that 'Sirhan's grandsons Sirhan and İsmail, their mothers, all the brigands' families and the people of Jubayl and Batrun in general' remained ensconced in the villages of the Kisrawan, the authorities of Tripoli devised a new stratagem which seems to have won the Sublime Porte's approval: blame the *vali* of Sidon. Inasmuch as the latter was under orders to ensure the collection of all state taxes under his jurisdiction, the decree coolly informs İsmail Paşa that he would also be held liable for the financial shortfalls occasioned in Tripoli by the Shiites now hiding in his province. Little is known of the rebellion's actual conclusion, but just three months later, in March 1687, the Hamadas were once again awarded the *iltizam*s for Jubbat Basharray and Danniyye;[16] the Harfushes were still being accused of withholding tax moneys and squeezing villagers in the northern Bekaa a year later.[17]

## The Khazins and the Maronite 'recolonization' of the Kisrawan

The Tripoli court registers for the next decades are unfortunately no longer extant, but the Hamadas are reported to have obtained the tax contracts for the entire Tripolitan hinterland (Jubayl, Batrun, al-Kura, Jubbat Basharri and Danniyye) as late as March 1692 and 1693.[18] Nevertheless, the quasi-civil war of 1685–6 established several precedents which were to play a decisive role in later years. For one, the authorities began more deliberately to promote the Hamadas' local enemies. The Ra'd family was given the Danniyye *mukataa* in 1686 and then without interruption from 1693 onward;[19] the Dandashes were rewarded for their

---

[15] Tripoli 3:185.    [16] Tripoli 3:149.    [17] ŞD 11:174.    [18] Duwayhi, *Tarikh*, 378, 379.
[19] They were only driven out by the Egyptians in 1831; see al-Samad, *Tarikh al-Danniyya*, 30–1.

participation in the anti-Harfush coalition with the tax concession for Hermel and 'Akkar. The Sha'irs, the Shiite family whom the Hamadas had driven from Batrun a half-century earlier, returned to power there and undertook, together with their long-standing Kurdish partners, to seize Jubayl on the state's behalf in 1694, while Baalbek and other fiefs were assigned to one of the governor's military retainers.[20] The Hamadas, who had once enjoyed the state's favour precisely for their tractable, mercenary quality, now found themselves confronted, at the height of their power in the late seventeenth century, with a new generation of ambitious feudal lords in the ceaseless competition for government tax farms.

Perhaps the Hamadas' most formidable new challengers, however, were not the feudal factions of Mt Lebanon but the Khazins, an upstart Maronite family whom Fakhr al-Din Ma'n had for all intents and purposes made hereditary tax farmers of the Kisrawan district north-east of Beirut in 1617 and who would serve for generations as the Druze emirs' Christian adjutants. The Khazins, in turn, began to invest their growing wealth and prestige in the protection of the Jesuits and other Latin missionary orders in the Levant. When France decided to name a vice-consul to Beirut in 1658, the choice fell on Abu Nawfal al-Khazin (d. 1679), who was by then thought of as the 'Prince des Maronites' and who had been knighted by the pope. Professional merchant-diplomats such as the Chevalier D'Arvieux – the author of the not unsympathetic portrayal of the Hamadas quoted on pp. 85–6 – bitterly resented this appointment, describing 'ce prince de théâtre' as a 'paysan grossier' who did more harm than good to France's commercial interests and standing with the Ottomans.[21] The twin backing of France and the Ma'n emirs, however, enabled the Khazins to establish their primacy within the Maronite community, even to some extent to the detriment of the patriarchate. By 1695, when the Khazins spearheaded the foundation of a new monastic order, the 'Lebanese Order of St Antoine', the economic and political centre of the community had largely shifted from Jubbat Basharri in Mt Lebanon to the Kisrawan.[22]

The Kisrawan Shiites' main dealings with the Khazins in these years concerned the 'sale' of villages or agricultural lands under their control (technically sultanic property) to use for establishing new monasteries and settler colonies. Maronite historians have characterized this buyout of areas previously dominated by the tribalists as the 'recolonization' of an ancestral homeland and a 'restoration' of its supposedly ancient churches, a narrative which dovetailed nicely with that of Shiite despoliation and illegitimacy examined above. The connection between the Shiites' tyranny and the influx of Maronite settlers under the Khazins' stewardship is brought out by the Maronite pastor Jirjis Zughayb (d. 1729), whose writings have been published as 'The Christians' Return to the Kisrawan Heights'. Zughayb, for example, relates the story of an attack by the local 'Mutawalis' on

---

[20] Duwayhi, *Tarikh*, 379–80.   [21] D'Arvieux, *Mémoires*, 150–3.

[22] René Ristelhueber, *Traditions françaises au Liban* (Paris: Librairie Félix Alcan, 1918), 131–46; Richard van Leeuwen, *Notables and Clergy in Mount Lebanon: The Khazin Sheikhs and the Maronite Church (1736–1840)* (Leiden: Brill, 1994), 81–5, 101–7; see also Salibi, *A House of Many Mansions*, 104–6.

some Ottoman tax collectors and a subsequent punitive campaign which left their village Harajil in ruins and forced many of them to flee to the Bekaa. After the campaign, Abu Nadir al-Khazin (d. 1647), whom the Shiites had previously scorned and abused, would

come to them to help them and give them money, and they would give him pieces of land for a cloak, or a gun, or a *waqiyya* of gunpowder, and on this basis they would sign deeds for him. Three years later, after some mediation with the authorities, the people of Harajil were allowed to return to their houses and live as before ... When they returned, each took possession of his house and his property, and so shaykh Abu Nadir's purchases were no longer valid and he gained nothing at all from what he had bought. The shaykh began to loan them money again to rebuild their houses and bought from them a second time, writing out deeds that were signed by both Christians and Mutawalis. The Mutawalis remained tenants on the lands the shaykh bought from them. Later shaykh Abu Nawfal al-Khazin came and bought even more than in Abu Nadir's day. He came to be respected and esteemed by the Mutawalis.[23]

The Shiites nevertheless continued to make life very difficult for the new settlers,

until the shaykh, taking some men with him, rode to the shaykhs of the Druze and told them what the Mutawalis were doing. The shaykhs of the Druze supported him and gave him full authority to act. They also informed the government of everything the Mutawalis had done to the Muslims and Christians, and how they intended to lay hands upon the property of the people. Officers sent by the government started to seize some of the Mutawalis, tie their hands to their backs and take them to prison. They would take some every two or three days, until the others kept quiet and stayed at home.[24]

It is perhaps in the context of the Shiites' retreat in the Kisrawan that the Hamadas were drawn more actively into a conflict with the Khazins and thus began to come to the attention of Maronite chroniclers of the period. Their assault on the Kisrawan during the 1685 rebellion, for example, is vividly evoked by Shayban al-Khazin, who relates how the villagers of 'Ashqut had devised a plan for a small party to hide by the roadside and give a fox-cry when the Hamadas passed so as to alert the others. That night, however, their courage failed them and they could not utter a sound, leaving the Hamadas free to devastate the town.[25] In the autumn of 1691, the inhabitants of Ghosta just above Jounieh managed to kill Ahmad (Abu Musa) Za'rur, one of the last remaining Shiite notables of the Kisrawan. The nineteenth-century historian Mansur al-Hattuni, citing an older oral tradition, relates that the Khazins arranged the killing in order to put an end to his infamous tyranny, then sent the gunman to Wadi Taym for three years to

---

[23] Jirjis Zughayb, *'Awdat al-Nasara ila Jurud Kisrawan*, ed. Bulus Qara'li (Beirut: Jarrus Bars, 1963), 15; quote modified from the English translation by Haifa Mikhael Malouf-Limam, 'A Troubled Period in the History of Kisrawan from an Original Lebanese Manuscript', *Arab Historical Review for Ottoman Studies* 11–12 (1995), 153.

[24] Zughayb, *'Awdat al-Nasara*, 16–17; quote modified from Malouf-Limam, 'A Troubled Period', 154.

[25] Retold in Mansur al-Hattuni, *Nubdha Tarikhiyya fi'l-Muqata'a al-Kisrawaniyya*, ed. Nazir 'Abbud (n.p.: Dar Nazir 'Abbud, [1986]), 90.

protect him from the Shiites' revenge.[26] The Za'rur and 'Awjan families affiliated with the Hamadas in fact began a merciless war against the Khazins and their supporters, as related, mostly in Lebanese patois, by the Maronite cleric 'Awn Kamil ibn Nujaym (d. 1696):

They came to the Kisrawan and pillaged all of the supplies, hunted the Kisrawanis on their land and reprieved no one they caught. There were herds, supplies and other things on the Kisrawanis' lands and they took it all. They went and caught [n.] when he was in Tripoli and killed him, then turned to the Patriarch in Qanubin monastery and mistreated and harmed him, and they hunted the Kisrawanis in the Baalbek region and everywhere their reach extended. Their only dealing with Christians would be to kill them.[27]

It is of course difficult to assess to what degree these accounts reflect actual historical events. Numerous Maronites trace their origins to an epic flight from the Shiite-dominated north to the Kisrawan in this period,[28] but communal violence, murders involving a Muslim arch-enemy or the search for new havens are in fact topological themes in many family foundation myths.[29] For the Khazins, at any rate, evoking the 'plight of the Christians' under the Hamadas was the primary means to stimulate the Europeans' imagination and secure their material aid for establishing the mountain monasteries which perfectly symbolized the idea of an Oriental refuge against Muslim tyranny. Towards the end of the century, the government of the 'très chrétien' Louis XIV began providing the Khazins with cash as well as diplomatic help in order to purchase the tax concessions of the areas they were seizing and colonizing; by 1697, Husn al-Khazin (d. 1707), who at one point had entertained hopes of an audience before the king, had furthermore lobbied successfully to be upgraded from vice- to full consul of Beirut.[30] The senior French consul at Sidon (at whose expense this change occurred), on the other hand, adamantly dismissed the Khazins' reasons for constantly seeking France's favours and 'protection':

La nation maronite est tiranisée aujourd'huy comme elle l'a été depuis environ cinquante ans … [L]es pachas depuis ce tems-là jusqu'aujourd'huy, qui ont commandé à Tripoly, ont ordinairement arrenté ce pais aux Amédéens [Hamadas], de qui les Maronites du Mont-Liban prétendent être tiranisés. C'est pour cette raison qu'ils leur font payer les droits ordinaires que doivent les terres qui leur arrentent et des maisons qu'ils ont en propriété. Ils paient ces droits tout de même que font les Turcs du païs. Mais ils ne souffrent pas plus

---

[26]  Ibid., 92–3. See also al-Ma'luf, Diwani al-Qatuf, 231–2.

[27]  'Awn Kamil ibn Nujaym, 'Nubdha min Tarikh Lubnan fi'l-Qarn al-Sabi' 'Ashar', al-Mashriq 25 (1927), 815.

[28]  Goudard, La Sainte Vierge au Liban, 138, 171, 173, 209.

[29]  Heyberger, Les chrétiens du Proche-Orient, 27; Sabine Mohasseb-Saliba, 'Monastères doubles, familles, propriétés et pouvoirs au Mont Liban: L'itinéraire du couvent maronite de Mar Challita Mouqbès (XVIIème–XIXème siècles)' (Université de Provence Aix-Marseille I doctoral thesis, 2006), 40–1.

[30]  'Lettre du Roi au Magnifique Seigneur Nassif, Prince des Maronites' and 'Lettres Patentes du Roi, en Faveur de l'emir Hassun Casen, Maronite', reproduced in Jean De La Roque (d. 1745), Voyage de Syrie et du Mont-Liban, ed. Jean Raymond (Beirut: Dar Lahad Khater, 1981), 210–12; Ristelhueber, Traditions françaises, 147–53.

qu'eux de ce côte-là. Mais je puis dire ... qu'ils naissent avec les plaintes à leurs bouches, car pour bien à leurs aises qu'ils soient, ils ont toujours quelque chose à dire là-dessus, et surtout aux gens qui ne les connaissent point et qui les écoutent, et desquels ils peuvent attraper quelque chose.[31]

Unfortunately for the Hamadas, not only Versailles but also the Sublime Porte, as it turns out, would be quite inclined to listen to allegations of tyranny and abuse in the highlands in this period.

## The expansion of the Druze emirate

The second and equally significant consequence of the Shiite rebellion was the growing presence of the Druze emir in Tripoli *eyalet* politics. The Ma'ns of the Shuf mountain in Sidon had long been on good terms with the Hamadas, and stood by them again in the 1685–6 struggle and indeed through much of the later Ottoman punitive operations. One of the reasons this episode remains relatively obscure in Lebanese historiography, Professor Abu-Husayn has suggested, is that the author-patriarch Istfan Duwayhi sought to hide his Druze patron's own rather equivocal stance vis-à-vis the state authority during the insurgence.[32] The Ottomans had of course called on the help of feudal parties from outside the province in many past conflicts, for example in 1598 and 1616 to subdue the Sayfas, but it can be argued that only in the decade-long battle against the Shiites in the late seventeenth century were the Ma'ns and then the Shihabis systematically given the responsibility for controlling their northern compeers. If this perception is borne out, it could entail a substantial revision of the standard historical narrative of Druze rule extending over two Ottoman *eyalet*s: the all-encompassing 'Lebanese emirate' not only did not incarnate the ancient idea of a trans-confessional mountain principality, but on the contrary originated precisely in a Köprülü-era Ottoman government plan to quell the Shiites' influence in the northern hinterland.

Ahmad Ma'n's first test in this regard came in February 1691, when he received a direct order to join yet another campaign against the Harfush emirs. According to identical *hüküm*s sent to the governors of Damascus, Tripoli and the *sancak* of 'Ajlun, 'the gangster known as Harfuş-oğlı Şedid together with the Shiite heretics [Revafız] from around Baalbek attacked and pillaged the town and are constantly

---

[31] Archives Nationales, Paris: Affaires Étrangères [AE] B/I (Seyde) 1017:321a–b; see also Hamada, *Tarikh al-Shi'a*, II:209–23, 268–72.

The Maronite nation is as tyrannized today as it has been for about fifty years ... Since that time and until today, the pashas who governed Tripoli have ordinarily rented this land to the Hamadas, by whom the Maronites of Mt Lebanon claim to be tyrannized. It is for this reason that they make them pay the normal dues on the lands they rent them and the houses they own. They pay these dues exactly like the Turks of the country. They do not suffer more than them in this respect. But I can say ... that they are born with a complaint on their lips, for no matter how well off they are, they always have something more to add, especially to people who do not know them well and listen to them, and from whom they can gain something.

[32] Abdul-Rahim Abu-Husayn, 'The Unknown Career of Ahmad Ma'n (1667–1697)', *Archivum Ottomanicum* 17 (1999), 241–7.

bent on killing people, ravishing Muslims and committing vice and brigandage'.[33] The narrative sources reveal nothing about what precipitated this new outburst on the Harfushes' part. Some vital context is provided, however, by a single entry in an imperial *Şikayet* register the following month. The complainant 'Mehmed' had held the Baalbek *mukataa* for the three previous years before Shadid Harfush acquired the rights to the town of Baalbek and certain farms and villages, and seized the entire tax levy and produce that had accrued by that time, namely 24,000 *guruş* and three *kantar*s of raw silk thread. What is important for our purposes is less the fact that Tripoli's magistrates were charged to recover this sum than the identity of Shadid's business partners, who were withholding 10,000 g. of the Baalbek dues: Husayn ibn Sirhan, his son Isma'il, 'Isa ibn Ahmad, Hasan ibn Husayn Dib Hamada and two Damascene Janissary officers.[34]

The Sublime Porte knew all too well that the savvy Ahmad Ma'n could not be relied on in a matter which evidently involved much more than the 'brigandage' of some 'Shiite heretics from around Baalbek', and the order addressed to him warns sinisterly against abetting the Harfushes and their associates:

Beware ... if it comes to my royal attention that you are accommodating and hiding just one of these criminals with you, the crushing punishment and the concatenation of sovereign fury that your forefathers [i.e. Fakhr al-Din, Korkmaz] incurred will happen to you as well![35]

The 'Sirhan-oğulları İsmail and İsa' received copies of the same ominous *hüküm*. Shadid Harfush was not apprehended, however, and in November of the same year (1691) the governor of Damascus was urged a second time to go fight the 'Revafız' in the Bekaa.[36]

In the meantime, the Sublime Porte had another concern to bring to the Shuf emir's attention. We have already seen that the governor of Tripoli once received instructions not to award the Hamadas the *iltizam*s for 'Akkar, al-Zawiya and al-Kura on the specious grounds that these districts were Sunni-inhabited.[37] In November 1691, the governor as well as Ahmad Ma'n were forwarded a complaint from 'the inhabitants of the Kura and Danniye districts' that, for a few years now, 'the Rafizi Kızılbaş thugs have sown corruption with the help of four or five locals, and gradually seized control of the region'.[38] The following March, the Porte tried to assemble the first truly inter-provincial punitive campaign against the Shiites, ordering the governors of Tripoli, Damascus and Sidon-Beirut, the *kadı*s and *molla*s under their authority, Ahmad Ma'n, and the district governors of Homs and Safad 'to capture and punish according to law the Shiite heretic brigands living in the mountains of Tripoli'.[39] There is no indication in the chronicles that such a police action did then take place; the Hamadas, as stated, reacquired their usual tax farms from the *vali* that spring and the next.

Nevertheless, the state's increasingly fundamental criticism of the Shiites' role in the feudal politics of Tripoli, its application of the legal category 'Kızılbaş' to

---

[33] MD 100:137, 140.    [34] ŞD 15:113.    [35] MD 100:139.    [36] MD 102:78.    [37] See pp. 77–8.
[38] MD 102:67.    [39] MD 102:180, 181.

the Hamadas for the first time and the growing involvement of Ahmad Ma'n in the province beg explanation. Despite the rhetoric of heresy vs Islam now being deployed, our chronicle sources suggest that it was in fact renewed tensions between the Shiites and the Maronites in the Kisrawan that once again led the Porte to pay close attention to the area. In October 1692, the governor of Damascus was warned that 'the Rafizi Sirhan-oğlı Hüseyin and his sons' had collected the *miri* taxes and other surcharges from most of the villages in Jubayl, Batrun, Kura, Danniyye, Jubbat Basharray and 'Akkar, but had failed to remit any of it to the state (Fig. 3).[40] The following month, according to Ibn Nujaym, the Za'rurs murdered a Christian notable at Harajil, whereupon 'the cry of the Kisrawan fell upon them', that is, gunshots and yells reverberated around the mountain gorges in the traditional call to arms. Led by the Khazins, the Maronite villagers set out and ravaged Husayn Sirhan's lands across the border in the Futuh, killing and plundering and threatening further vengeance. When the Khazins and Ahmad Ma'n were asked to join a government punitive campaign against the Hamadas three months later, 1,000 volunteers from the Kisrawan reported for duty.[41] By February 1693, the Porte had indeed decided to respond with a more efficacious operation against the Shiites. What is interesting is that the unusually vituperative orders sent to the governor of Damascus (of which an original is extant in the Başbakanlık), his colleagues and Ahmad Ma'n also make no mention of the fact that the Hamadas had served the state as *mukataacı*s in the region for over forty years:

The Kızılbaş sect that appeared in the Tripoli region and settled in difficult, rocky country has usurped the state tax farms of the area and swallowed the income legally due to the treasury of Islamdom ... These brigands neither follow the holy law nor submit to the governors, whence their perfidy regarding the state taxes is as bad as their tyranny and oppression of the humble commoners. Their existence is the reason for the ruin of the land ... Correspond with [the other governors] and agree on a precise and consensual time based on your judgement ... and attack the aforesaid faction in the mountains where they live. Arrest all these brigands and give them the punishment they deserve by law.[42]

From this moment on, the rebellion became important enough to capture the attention not just of local chroniclers but of Ottoman imperial historians as well. The chancery bureaucrat Defterdar Sarı Mehmed (d. 1717), who seems to have had access to the relevant *Mühimme* documents, provides a highly idealized account of the warfare, which in the pen of the *vakanüvis* (court historiographer) Mehmed Raşid Efendi (d. 1735) would subsequently become the official state version of the great anti-Shiite campaign:

A memorandum arrived ... stating that by the grace of God on High the thread of their association was snapped. Many of them fell prey to the sword, and of their chiefs, Hüseyin Sirhan-oğlı, his cousins Hasan and İsa, and numerous accursed ones like them, became fodder for the blade of force and destruction. Ma'n-oğlı, their accessory, as well as those

---

[40] Başbakanlık Archives: Ali Emiri II. Ahmed 477.    [41] Ibn Nujaym, 'Nubdha', 816–17.
[42] Ali Emiri II. Ahmed 392; see also MD 104:155.

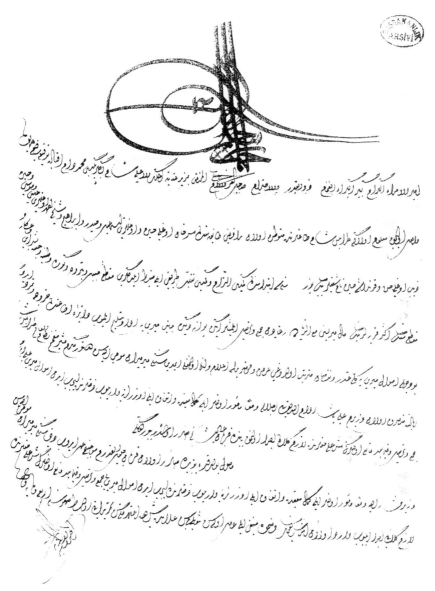

Fig. 3 Ottoman ferman against the Hamadas. Başbakanlık Archives: Ali Emiri II. Ahmed 477, dated late October 1692.

brigands spared of the sword, went the way of seeking quarter and swore off the wickedness and insubordination which had been their habit until now.[43]

The local chronicles tell a more sobering story: the Ottoman and assorted feudal forces devastated the Shiites' home districts, burning their houses, abducting their

[43] Mehmed Efendi Raşid, *Tarih* (Istanbul: n.p., 1865/6), II:194–5; cf. Defterdar Sarı Mehmed Paşa, *Zübde-i Vekayiât: Tahlil ve Metin (1066–1116/1656–1704)*, ed. Abdülkadir Özcan (Ankara: Türk Tarih Kurumu, 1995), 429–30.

women and stealing their livestock. Of the men and their families, some 150 perished not in battle but in heavy snows, as they tried to escape with the help of Shadid Harfush over the wintry mountain passes and into the Bekaa. The note-worthy disagreement among these sources concerns the role of the Ma'ns' Christian deputies: Duwayhi claims that the Khazins had a change of heart and now prevented the wholesale slaughter of the surviving Shiites, leading the govern-ment army away and claiming they had no permission from the emir to leave the *eyalet* of Tripoli.[44] Ibn Nujaym, on the other hand, indicates that 'the Khazins received great fortunes and benefits' from the jubilant governor of Tripoli, 'who invested and conferred them with numerous gifts and pledged his support'. In the late summer, Husayn ibn Sirhan and several cousins happened upon a company of Kisrawanis who had just repulsed a raid by the *paşa*'s mercenaries. Mistaking them for friends he identified himself ('It's me, Husayn! Recognize me!'), but instead they set upon and killed him and his companions. Only in the next year could Ahmad Ma'n effect a reconciliation between the Hamadas and the Khazins.[45]

As the Hamadas' rebellion began to have ramifications beyond Mt Lebanon, in the Shiite-inhabited Bekaa and Kisrawan districts in the neighbouring provinces of Damascus and Sidon, it became an increasing source of concern for imperial administrators (and historians) and naturally began to implicate more and more authorities from outside Tripoli. Ahmad Ma'n's emerging role as arbiter between the local factions, however, also marks a more fundamental bid to extend his influence, especially among the region's Maronite community; to concretize the Druze 'emirate', as it were, in this time of wider political change. For the moment, his equivocal, mediating stance between the Shiite rebels and the Ottoman state would incur the authorities' wrath, and the 1694 imperial campaign was directed against him as much as the Hamadas. Partially as a result of this drawn-out crisis, however, it would then be the Ottomans themselves who, for want of a better alternative, would endorse and support the expansion of the Druze emirs' control over the northern highlands.

### The imperial punitive campaign

The initial campaign against the Shiites was not completed as expeditiously as the Ottoman state chronicles suggest. As late as October 1693, the Damascene scholar and traveller 'Abd al-Ghani al-Nabulusi reported from Tripoli that governor Ali Paşa remained in the field, 'battling the pertinacious heretics, the Hamada faction'.[46] The Hamadas were indeed regrouping, and in the spring launched a deadly attack against the Kurdish emirs who had taken over the Jubayl and Batrun fiefs.[47] At almost the same time, however, an important change occured which was

---

[44] Duwayhi, *Tarikh*, 379.    [45] Ibn Nujaym, 'Nubdha', 617–18.

[46] 'Abd al-Ghani al-Nabulusi, *al-Haqiqa wa 'l-Mujaz fi Rihla Bilad al-Sham wa-Misr wa 'l-Hijaz*, ed. Riyad 'Abd al-Hamid Murad (Damascus: Dar al-Ma'rifa, 1989), 202, 226.

[47] Ibn Nujaym, 'Nubdha', 818; Duwayhi, *Tarikh*, 380.

to have a decisive impact on the Hamadas' struggle for the next years: Ali Paşa was summoned to Istanbul, in April, and made grand vizier. In this capacity, he immediately set about organizing a massive new campaign, directing his successor in Tripoli, Arslan Paşa, his colleagues from Aleppo, Damascus and Sidon, the district governors of Kilis, Hama, Homs, Lajjun and Gaza, feudal contingents from Aleppo, Salamya, Dayr al-Zor/Rahba, Jabala and Baalbek, and finally the chief inspector (*müfettiş*) of the Anatolian army to coordinate and to annihilate the Shiites and Ahmad Ma'n once and for all time.[48] When, according to the court historian Raşid, the

Sirhan-oğulları faction ... heard and learnt that [Arslan Paşa] and these 20,000 men had reached the places known as Baalbek and the plain of the southern Bekaa, fear and dread befell their insides ... They fled into the surroundings and environs ... and the many good-for-nothings who were caught received the punishment they deserved. So these regions were cleaned, as was required, of their filth and villainy.[49]

But why was the new grand vizier willing to commit so many men and resources to 'cleaning' the Syrian hinterland, when he himself was now camped at Edirne, preparing the far more crucial Danube campaign that would set out (but fail) to retake the fortress of Peterwardein from the Habsburgs that summer?[50] One key factor was the shift of focus to Ahmad Ma'n, whom the Sublime Porte had explicitly requested to assume more responsibility in the region. The imperial orders now issued by Ali Paşa place the blame for his failure to eliminate the Hamadas while governor of Tripoli squarely on the Druze emir's shoulders:

It was learnt that Ma'n-oğlı Ahmed, who is based in the mountains of Sidon-Beirut, is not minding his own affairs but is supporting the accursed Kızılbaş ... who live in the mountains of Tripoli and all the other villains in the area, and these brigands are constantly wrecking villages and oppressing Muslims in the Tripoli highlands ... It is clear and evident that so long as that wellhead of depravity and tyranny, the aforesaid Ma'n-oğlı, has not been punished, the evil and sedition of the accursed corrupters will not be repulsed.[51]

Ali Paşa's personal bitterness towards the Druze emir comes to light most clearly in our third Ottoman narrative source. The author of the single-manuscript *Tevarih-i Sultan Süleyman* remains anonymous, but from his lengthy first-hand account of the Hungarian campaign it is evident that he was a close associate of the grand vizier.[52] Accordingly, the *Tevarih* version of the Tripoli campaign, unlike Raşid's and Sarı Mehmed's idealized summaries, is a thoroughly subjective account from Ali Paşa's viewpoint. The focus is on the 1693 operation which Ali led personally: After he was appointed *vali* of Tripoli, Ali went up into 'the Sirhan mountains'

---

[48] MD 105:5–11.    [49] Raşid, *Tarih*, II:225–6; Sarı Mehmed, *Zübde*, 484–5.
[50] Silahdar Fındıklılı Mehmed Ağa (d. 1723/4), *Silahdar Tarihi* (Istanbul: Orhaniye Press, 1928), II:742–6; Raşid, *Tarih*, II:256.
[51] MD 105:10–11.
[52] *Anonim Osmanlı Tarihi (1099–1116/1688–1704)*, ed. Abdülkadir Özcan (Ankara: Türk Tarih Kurumu, 2000), xvi–xvii, 55 ff.

(literally, the mountains of the wolf) to look into the inhabitants' state of affairs, and found out for himself that:

> Some, evidently a plentiful group, are their [i.e. Kızılbaş] followers. Resisting them is difficult. It was reluctantly decided to turn them a blind eye ... But others indicated that they are weary of the tyranny of their rule though unable to do anything about it. If Ma'n-oğlı were to stand aside, it would be easy to repulse the Sirhanids.[53]

Ali Paşa thereupon wrote to Ahmad Ma'n in the hope of convincing him, as a previous governor of Tripoli had tried and failed to do in 1685, to take over the Hamadas' tax farms. The Druze emir feigned submission and even supplicated the Paşa to 'do justice' and avenge 'the numerous men of our tribes' whom the 'Sirhan-oğulları killed unwarranted', perhaps a reference to the Kisrawani victims of the recent Shiite–Maronite vendetta. The anonymous history says nothing further of his failure to support the governor, only that Ali, as grand vizier, once more turned his attention to 'that leaven of villainy, Ma'n-oğlı, and their other acolytes and riff-raff' and mounted a final effort to annihilate the rebels.[54]

Paradoxically, it is in the very context of Ahmad Ma'n's fall from grace that the concept of a single Druze 'emirate' is evoked for the first time in Ottoman documents. Already in 1689, the Sublime Porte had addressed him honorifically as 'the repository of the emirate' ('cenab-ı imaret-mab') while trying to elicit his contribution to the Empire's 'jihad' in the Balkans.[55] In a rare mention of his subsequent insurgence, Duwayhi then indicates that his seven tax farms in Sidon were rescinded and given to his Druze arch-rival, Musa 'Alam al-Din, in 1694.[56] An order sent to the provincial authorities throughout the region, however, also requires his cession of 'the beğlik', which is explicitly tied to the four (Druze-inhabited) mountain districts Shuf, Jurd, Matn and Gharb, but not the three (Shiite and Christian) districts of Kisrawan, Marj 'Ayun (Jizzin) and Iqlim Kharnub.[57] The order goes on to award Musa 'Alam al-Din, who was already recognized as an emir in the tribal sense, the rank of sancakbeğ of Safad, making him only the third local feudatory (after the Harfush emirs of Homs and Fakhr al-Din Ma'n in Safad) to formally hold an Ottoman military district governorship. While the 'beğlik' is of course not characterized anywhere as being 'Druze', the campaign targeting its incumbent was actually serving to systematize the rule of a single feudal faction over multiple tax districts in the highland region.

The 'Alam al-Dins' fortunes were to be short-lived. In March 1695, Ahmad Ma'n incited a revolt in his former territories that forced Musa to flee to Sidon. The French consul there reported that Ahmad Ma'n had initially taken refuge with the Bedouins near Damascus, but continued to enjoy such popularity in the region that his replacement lived in constant danger of assassination.[58] At first, the Sublime Porte promised yet another expedition to wipe out Ahmad Ma'n and his Shiite

---

[53] Ibid., 95.    [54] Ibid., 96.    [55] MD 98:77.    [56] Duwayhi, Tarikh, 380–1.
[57] MD 105:9. MD 105:6 appears to be a draft of the same hüküm.
[58] AE B/I 1017 (Seyde), fol. 84a.

allies, and advised Musa to conciliate his subjects with tax abatements.[59] By then, however, the ageing sultan Ahmed II had died, occasioning Ali Paşa's dismissal from the grand vizierate in May. The governor of Sidon, always eager to win powerful and generous friends, paid an accession gift in the Ma'nids' name and persuaded the Porte that the tax farm revenues would surely increase if they were henceforth left in their possession. By August 1695, the new administration in Istanbul had resigned itself to the inevitable, and issued Ahmad Ma'n a writ of forgiveness – on the condition that

he remain occupied with his own affairs; serve in loyalty and uprightness, not patronize the Kızılbaş, the heretical Shiite brigands and other corrupters in and around Tripoli, not harm the villages and wayfarers in the environs, pay the yearly remittance from the Şuf, Kisrevan and the associated tax farms of which he has taken hold, in its entirety, to the *vali*s, and proscribe and repulse the heretical Shiites and other brigands of the region.[60]

As to the 'Kızılbaş and heretical Shiites' themselves, Ibn Nujaym relates that the entire district of Tripoli hunted after the Hamadas through the autumn of 1694; several of them met their ends in the jails of Sidon, 'from the narrowness of their confinement', captured while fleeing south to shelter with their co-religionists in Jabal 'Amil. 'All this', Ibn Nujaym concludes, 'happened to the Hamadas in a single year on account of Ali Paşa.'[61] The Hamadas would not recover as quickly as the Ma'ns, though already in the following year they engaged in another skirmish against the Sha'irs in their old fief of Batrun.[62] By February 1696, they or their followers succeeded anew in attracting the Sublime Porte's attention: the 'accursed Kızılbaş' were, apparently with reinforcements from Jabal 'Amil, terrorizing wayfarers and peasants in the 'Sirhan mountains' of Tripoli, only this time they are explicitly described in the *Mühimme*s as 'subjects of Ma'n-oğlı's government'.[63] Consequently, the Druze emir himself received a stern warning to interdict their activities in the north:

You are bound and obliged to the defence and protection of the people of your country and to the control and disciplining of this sort of brigands. The harm inflicted on the poor and the weak through their evil and wickedness is attributable to your disregard and negligence![64]

The Hamadas' reign over rural Mt Lebanon, as will be seen in chapter 6, did not really end with the punitive campaign of 1693–4. While we have no documentary evidence for when precisely they were reappointed as government tax concessionaries, Duwayhi reports in the last pages of his chronicle that Bashir al-Shihabi, who inherited the Druze emirate with the Ottomans' blessing after the death of Ahmad Ma'n, 'interceded with the governor on the Hamadas' behalf so that they returned to their homelands' in 1698, and 'bonded their administration against any despoliation and grievance'.[65] The responsibility given to the Shuf emirs for controlling the Shiite *mültezim*s of Tripoli province must therefore be seen as the most

[59] MD 106:22–4.    [60] MD 106:239.    [61] Ibn Nujaym, 'Nubdha', 818–19.    [62] *Ibid.*, 820.
[63] MD 108:81.    [64] MD 108:259.    [65] Duwayhi, *Tarikh*, 383–4.

fundamental consequence of their fifteen-year challenge to Ottoman authority. As early as September 1685, the Sublime Porte had offered the Hamadas' fiefs to Ahmad Ma'n, knowing him to enjoy the trust and support of the local Maronite population and hoping he might deliver more tax moneys than the unpopular Shiite agents had been able. In the subsequent years of violence, the state demanded the paramount emirs' military aid against the rebels, going so far, under the vindictive Ali Paşa, to turn its weapons against Ahmad Ma'n himself when he tried to stay aloof from the war. Yet it could not do without the emiral institution as such, and made controlling the northern Shiites the precondition for rehabilitating Ma'n in 1696. This de facto cross-border jurisdiction was further consolidated with the Shihabi emirs, who, having effectuated the Hamadas' restoration in 1698, assumed the legal bond (*kefalet*) for the faithful discharge of their *iltizam* commissions. On the local level, the consequences of the long struggle between the Shiite tax farmers and the Ottoman authorities were therefore doubly momentous: the recognition of the Druze 'emirate' of the Shuf; and its acquisition of a direct political and financial stake in the feudal affairs of the *eyalet* of Tripoli.

## Changing paradigms of provincial administration

The consolidation of jurisdictions was also an important factor in the campaign from the Ottoman provincial administrative point of view. We have already seen that the Khazins allegedly refused to pursue the Hamadas into the Bekaa Valley in the winter of 1693, claiming that they had no authorization to cross the Damascus/ Tripoli boundary. The Sublime Porte did worry about rebels escaping to other territories: campaign preparations in 1694 included orders to the governors of Tripoli and Sidon to 'have the harbours on these coasts and elsewhere watched, as is required, and seize and punish canonically any of these thugs who arrive intending to flee by boat', and a similar *hüküm* was sent to the *beğ* of the desert *sancak* Dayr al-Zor and Rahba, telling him to capture and extradite to Tripoli any of Ibn Ma'n's 'Kızılbaş followers' who might come his way.[66] The problem of jurisdictions is also raised by the nineteenth-century historian Haydar Ahmad al-Shihabi, who asserts that the northern Bekaa was attached to Tripoli in 1692 to enable the governor to apprehend Hamada rebels attempting to flee there.[67] This claim (which belies the Khazins' supposed apprehensions about crossing provincial borders) can in fact be corroborated, and nuanced, with recourse to the *Şikayet* registers. An entry from April/May 1694 recalls that Ali Paşa wrote to the Sublime Porte while still governor of Tripoli, asking for (and receiving) permission to take the lucrative Baalbek *mukataa* away from Damascus and annex it to his province, 'in order to prevent and repulse attacks on the poor subjects by the Rafızı brigands

---

[66] MD 105:8–9, 14, 18. Parts of the following sections have appeared in Stefan Winter, 'Shiite Emirs and Ottoman Authorities: The Campaign against the Hamadas of Mt Lebanon, 1693–1694', *Archivum Ottomanicum* 18 (2000), 209–45.

[67] Shihabi, *Tarikh*, 743.

who have taken over the Tripoli area'.[68] What the document does not mention, of course, is the identity of the Baalbek *mukataa*'s tenants at the time, namely the Shiite Harfush emirs. For Ali Paşa, it seems, the advantages of territorial aggrandizement must have outweighed the bother of having to deal with even more 'Rafizi brigands' now.

It is therefore useful to consider the events of 1693–4 from the perspectives of competing government authorities as well. The anti-Shiite campaign was not Ali Paşa's private initiative, but the varying degrees in which Ottoman officials could choose to implement imperial directives is suggestive of fundamental differences of interest and, it may be argued, of a changing paradigm of Ottoman provincial administration in this period. The decrees promulgated under Ali Paşa's grand vizierate, while not openly critical of his predecessors, pin his reputation on his past successes in battling the Kızılbaş enemy:

> Despite the *vali*s' circumspection, perseverance and attention, the elimination and extirpation of these godforsaken ones did not come to pass. With their banditry continuing unabated, my most honourable commander, my proudest marshal [etc., etc.] Ali Paşa was assigned ... last year to uproot and extirpate them, and with the help of God on High, most became fodder to the blade of death and destruction. Those who were spared of the sword found neither repose nor the force to sow corruption anew.[69]

His lead role in the (albeit rather dubious) victory against the Hamadas in 1693 is also emphasized by the court historiographers Raşid and Sarı Mehmed, and of course in the Berlin anonymous history:

> Camp was pitched near Tripoli and an army assembled, and with foresight and wise counsel, they set out into the Sirhan mountains ... Glory be to God on High, the authors of sedition and insurrection were destroyed by the army of righteousness, the heaven-succoured host. Those arrogant impious rebels' impure bodies became smeared with the blood of justice.

Previous *vali*s of Tripoli, in contrast, 'had deemed fit, perhaps even with happy hearts' to leave the Hamadas the tax farms which they had seized illegally.[70]

Why would these other ex-governors have been less zealous in persecuting the Shiite brigands? An answer is suggested by comparing their professional career paths and ambitions with those of someone like Ali Paşa. The governor of Damascus, when the first inter-regional campaign was called against the Hamadas in 1692, was Gürcü Mehmed Paşa. A career soldier, Mehmed was already famous in his native Georgia before entering the Ottomans' service. In Damascus he mainly distinguished himself by quelling a Janissary revolt, and later married into the royal family.[71] The second governor who received orders to fight the Hamadas in March 1692 but neglected to do so was Kavanos Ahmed Paşa of Sidon. Originally from Russia, Ahmed was captured as a child and reared in the Inner Court (*Enderun*) of the Ottoman palace. He held several important

---

[68] ŞD 17:129.    [69] MD 105:5, 10–11, 15, 16.    [70] *Anonim Osmanlı Tarihi*, 95.
[71] Süreyya, *Sicill-i Osmanî*, 1064.

*beğlerbeğlik*s besides Sidon, married into the Köprülü vizier family, and worked his way higher to become *nişancı*, deputy vizier and, in 1703, grand vizier.[72]

The key figure assigned to fight the Hamadas in 1692 was of course the *paşa* of Tripoli, Bozoklu Mustafa Paşa. Mustafa was again a product of the Inner Court and graduated as the sultan's ceremonial sword-bearer before becoming grand admiral of the Empire. Appointed to Damascus in 1688/9, he proved ineffective against the Janissaries but succeeded all the same in marrying into the Ottoman royal household.[73] He was dismissed from Damascus in favour of Gürcü Mehmed and was demoted to Tripoli, but was soon rehabilitated and, 'in deference to his former rights, and being one of the [grand vizier]'s fellow palace servants', was named imperial campaign deputy in the summer of 1692.[74] It is by no means clear that he ever went to Tripoli personally in the interim, for the Arab chronicles consistently identify the governor in this period as 'Mehmed'. Whoever was in charge in Tripoli, the Hamadas were reconfirmed in their *iltizam* commissions in 1692, and Mustafa's marching orders against them, as well as against the Harfushes of Baalbek and rebellious Nusayris in Latakia,[75] all went unheeded. This caused him no harm, for he was promoted grand vizier in March 1693. Unfortunately his court connections could not preserve him from palace intrigues, and he was ejected and imprisoned a year later for dereliction of duty (supposedly spending too much time hunting). The intercession of his princess wife, however, secured him another reprieve and an appointment to Sidon, where he continued to blissfully ignore imperial orders against the area's Shiites, exerting himself only, as indicated above, to effect the beneficent Druze emir's rehabilitation in 1695.

Though speculative, we may posit here a circle of 'classical' Ottoman soldier-bureaucrats who shared in the same upbringing, career outlooks and style of management. As foreign converts and/or products of the Inner Court, Bozoklu Mustafa, Gürcü Mehmed and Kavanos Ahmed had no local power bases of their own but depended entirely on court favour and professional *esprit de corps* on their pilgrimage up the stations of state authority. Occupying a key *beğlerbeğlik* such as Damascus could be a springboard to higher office in the *asitane*, the imperial centre. Active intervention in the domestic affairs of second-rank provinces, for example chasing Shiite swashbucklers through the Syrian hinterland, was not high on their list of priorities.

Not so for the likes of Ali Paşa. Ali was a native of Dimotika, a hub of the old Turkish aristocracy in Thrace. He became a secretary and rose through the ranks of the civil bureaucracy, twice holding the post of chief *defterdar*.[76] As a freeborn Muslim, neither bearing arms nor marrying into the House of Osman were viable career options. Rather, Ali became a typical example of the reform-era statesman who attained office on the basis of his fiscal administrative capabilities. The governorship of Tripoli was, astoundingly, the first and only provincial posting of Ali's career, and served as his stepping stone to the grand vizierate in April 1694.

---

[72] *Ibid.*, 213–14.    [73] *Ibid.*, 1190–1.    [74] Raşid, *Tarih*, II:189.    [75] MD 100:140; MD 102:61.
[76] Süreyya, *Sicill-i Osmanî*, 294–5.

To Ali, authority in Tripoli bore a completely different meaning and possibility than to Bozoklu Mustafa. Soon after his appointment, as we have seen, he used the long-simmering Shiite disturbance to press for the annexation of the Bekaa tax district to his own dominion. Irrespective of the real need to quiet the Hamadas, Ali Paşa's singular preoccupation with extirpating rebels, to the point of confronting the powerful Druze emir of Sidon province, also denotes his ulterior motive of establishing a reputation for severity and military verve. His fervour in campaigning into the autumn of 1693 and his ongoing attention to the Hamadas after becoming grand vizier in April 1694 go in the same direction.

Above all, Ali had to build himself a supporting party to offset his lack of local notability or palace affiliation. One method, while still governor of Tripoli, was to place personal retainers and lesser tribal chiefs such as the al-Kura Kurds and the Sha'irs in the tax offices wrested from the Hamadas. More important, however, was his strategic partnership with the Mataracı-oğlu (Ibn al-Mataraji) household of Latakia. The Mataracı ('campaign gourd carrier') family's history is obscure, though an imperial order concerning the inheritance of Mataracı Ali, a Janissary who died in Latakia around 1666, suggests a possible origin.[77] The Mataracıs ruled the town with an iron fist and various sources suggest that Arslan Mehmed Mataracı-oğlu was selected as governor of Tripoli in 1694 precisely in order to continue Ali Paşa's crusade.[78] Arslan himself had no experience whatsoever when he became *beğlerbeği* of Tripoli; Haydar al-Shihabi may have been conveying a widespread if inaccurate impression when he characterized him as "Ali's *mamluk*'.[79] Arslan was said to be proficient in Islamic jurisprudence,[80] and perhaps shared with Ali Paşa a personal disdain for the heterodox Muslims with whom they were intimately familiar in western Syria. His brother Kaplan, who had succeeded their father in Latakia, was made *vali* of Sidon in return for his services and later alternated with Arslan as pilgrimage commander; Arslan was appointed to Damascus, then returned once more to Tripoli, 'having no equal in keeping the Arabs under discipline'.[81] Thus if the Mataracıs came to form one of the principal ruling households in reform-period Syria,[82] it was largely thanks to their alliance with the neophyte grand vizier. Conversely when Ali Paşa, from the distance of his Balkan command post in 1694, was issuing decrees which bound all of Syria from Kilis to Gaza to Arslan's leadership in a great regional military enterprise, this was as much a political end in itself as a quest to tame the sons of Sirhan.

While civilians such as Ali Paşa and the Mataracı-oğlus had a greater stake in the anti-Shiite campaign than their slave-soldier colleagues, it is precisely the latters' military skills that they lacked. As early as June 1694, the Sublime Porte advised Arslan Paşa to turn to Tursun Mehmed Paşa, *müfettiş* (inspector) of the central and left wings of the Anatolian army, 'should you notice yourself to be short in means

[77] ŞD 4:149.
[78] Ibn Nujaym, 'Nubdha', 818; Nabulusi, *al-Haqiqa*, 181–2; Süreyya, *Sicill-i Osmanî*, 324.
[79] Shihabi, *Tarikh*, 743.    [80] Nabulusi, *al-Tuhfa al-Nabulusiyya*, 87.
[81] Süreyya, *Sicill-i Osmanî*, 324; Raşid, *Tarih*, II:479.
[82] Karl Barbir, *Ottoman Rule in Damascus, 1708–1758* (Princeton University Press, 1980), 62–3.

and lacking the power' to complete the mission; Tursun Mehmed for his part received instructions to complete his troop mobilization for the upcoming campaign in Europe, but also to 'keep an eye on the said governor' and his faltering military venture in Tripoli.[83] However, the professional commander does not seem to have shared the grand vizier's enthusiasm for waging war in Mt Lebanon. In November, the chancery upbraided Arslan for not confirming Tursun's arrival to take charge: 'News from you has been expected and anticipated but to this moment there still has not been any sign or indication from you. You are guilty of negligence and carelessness!'[84] Unsure of the campaign's situation, the Sublime Porte now began to reissue orders to all the authorities of Syria, chiding them for their inaction and ordering them to coordinate with Tursun.[85] A *hüküm* to the governor of Damascus implores him to join the campaign himself rather than merely sending his *kethüda*; another to Sidon seems, from our vantage point, almost tragically oblivious to the identity of the new *vali* – Bozoklu Mustafa – and his abysmal record in hunting rebels.[86] When combined with the Arab chronicles' reports of only limited fighting, it becomes clear that Ali Paşa's great anti-Shiite campaign simply fizzled away by the late autumn. In December, a final angry *hüküm* went out to its leaders. Tursun Mehmed, having been given the rank of *vali* of Aleppo in the meantime, is now also accused of negligence for not reporting more progress. He is admonished one last time to finish the job, turn authority back over to Arslan and return to his original post in Anatolia, so that he may prepare the next imperial campaign which was to set out for Hungary that spring.[87]

Plans made in April 1695 for a renewed operation to 'wipe the entirety of the Shiite heretics and depraved brigands off the face of the earth'[88] were abandoned after Ali Paşa was removed from the grand vizierate the following month. Among its proposed commanders, İsmail Paşa of Damascus was retired from active duty – and went on to defect to the Safavids in 1701;[89] Bozoklu Mustafa was promoted again to the governorship of Damascus before finally returning home to the *asitane*, in 1697, to serve two more terms as deputy grand vizier. The Mataracı-oğlu household, for its part, was allowed to monopolize the top provincial posts until Arslan's death in 1704, their reign in many ways prefiguring that of the 'Azm dynasty which would dominate Syrian politics in the eighteenth century. The campaign against the Hamadas must thus also be seen in the light of the general, long-term shift from the classical, socially disinterested military service elite to a more engaged, locally rooted civilian notable (*ayan*) class of provincial office-holders. This process was of course not unilinear or solely motivated by such local rebellions. However, the events of 1693–4 in Mt Lebanon can, on a microhistorical level, be said to encapsulate a fundamental, *longue-durée* change in the Ottoman Empire's governing structures in this time.

---

[83] MD 105:10–11. On Tursun Mehmed, see Süreyya, *Sicill-i Osmanî*, 1639–40.
[84] MD 105:15; ŞD 17:559.    [85] MD 105:14, 16, 17–18.    [86] MD 105:17; MD 105:14.
[87] MD 105:35.    [88] MD 106:22–3.    [89] Süreyya, *Sicill-i Osmanî*, 832.

## Shiism and Ottoman tribal control

The crisis between the Hamadas and the Ottoman authorities in the closing years of the seventeenth century bespeaks a growing conflict with local rivals, a changing regional economic context and a shifting paradigm of provincial administration. Nevertheless, a military operation on the scale of the 1693–4 campaign cannot be fully explained without also locating it inside the larger context of imperial policy-making in this period. Imperial considerations did not predestine the action taken against the Syrian Shiites, but they did set the parameters within which such action was conceivable then and remains intelligible today. The final section of this chapter re-examines the chancery documentation to show that the appeal to a religious ethic served only to frame the more mundane, if equally ideological, socio-economic concerns at the heart of the campaign. The last great 'Kızılbaş' war in Ottoman history, we argue, ensued from the early modern Empire's programme of brigand control, mercenary demobilization and tribal settlement rather than from a renewed anti-Shiite impulse.

The Hamadas' purported irreligion headlines the edicts sent to the provincial authorities in 1693–4: they are decried as either '*Revafiz*', a term generically applied to Twelver Shiites, or as 'Kızılbaş brigands', and the preambles of the orders issued towards the end of the campaign almost invariably refer to them as 'accursed Kızılbaş whose destruction is an incumbent religious duty'. The anonymous Berlin history further tries to confessionalize the Hamadas' rebelliousness by explaining that 'the Revafiz sect considers it their duty to battle and fight the people of Islam'.[90] Their victims, in contrast, are the *reaya*, that is, the Ottoman sultan's 'flock', who are sometimes also characterized as obedient '*Müslimin*', despite the fact that most will have been Maronite Christians. And a noteworthy phrase included in the more detailed of the May/June 1694 *hüküm*s affirms that 'Ali Paşa ... was appointed to uproot and eliminate them on the basis of my imperial command, promulgated last year as per a noble *fetva*.'[91]

Abu-Husayn has taken these documents as proof that the Hamadas were Kızılbaş of eastern Anatolian provenance and thus 'a clan whose loyalty went to the Shiite Safavids of Persia, the traditional enemies of the Sunnite Ottomans', and therefore 'seized the opportunity' of the Ottomans' disastrous military involvement on the Hungarian front to 'stage their rebellion'.[92] Yet nothing indicates that the Ottomans in fact connected the Hamadas with Iran, and no formal legal opinion has ever surfaced with regard to them or any other Shiite community in Syria. The reference in these texts is rather to the still valid ruling of Ebu's-Suud against the Kızılbaş in general, and it fulfilled the same function as in the sixteenth century: the application of the legal category 'heterodox outlaw' to the Hamadas (and Harfushes) rather than an appraisal of their ethnic background or political loyalties.

---

[90] *Anonim Osmanlı Tarihi*, 95.    [91] MD 105:5, 6, 9, 10.
[92] Abu-Husayn, 'Unknown Career', 244; Abu-Husayn, *The View from Istanbul*, 9–10, 106, 144.

Relations with Iran can safely be excluded as a factor in the treatment of Ottoman Shiites in the late seventeenth century. The two empires, which had not made war in over half a century, now enjoyed the perhaps friendliest ties in their history. A regular exchange of ambassadors had begun after the death of Murad IV in 1640; in the 1690s the Safavid shah was instrumental in restoring Ottoman sovereignty over Basra following its seizure by the Musha'sha' Arabs.[93] The export of Iranian silk through Izmir and Aleppo peaked in the decades around the turn of the century[94] and Ottoman diplomatic manuals attest to the cordial relations between the two courts in this time. Around 1689, an embassy announcing the accession of Sultan Süleyman was extremely well received in Isfahan and Kelb Ali Khan, the governor of Ganja, was sent back with it to convey the shah's congratulations. The Ottoman chronicler Silahdar Mehmed (d. 1723/4) later felt obliged to characterize him as 'a biting-mutt scoundrel of an unshaven Kızılbaş heretic pimp', but evidently the imperial court did not feel that way then. After a long trip across Anatolia (by which time Ahmed II had succeeded Süleyman), Kelb Ali was allowed to proceed to Edirne where he was lodged in a serail and wined and dined by the grand vizier. In late February 1692, just days before the first inter-regional mobilization was ordered against the Hamadas, the *khan* was admitted to the sultan's presence to offer his letters and precious gifts ('one elephant, five racehorses unique to Iran, forty-five Persian camels', etc.) which he had brought with him.[95]

Moreover, where Ottoman documents cite individual Shiites such as Sirhan Hamada or Shadid Harfush by name, the labels 'Revafiz' and 'Kızılbaş' are conspicuously not applied to them personally but only to their 'followers'. The *Mühimme*s also consistently avoided mention of the Druze emirs' religious identity; a telling example of the chancery's tact in this regard is the omission, in otherwise identical documents issued to the civic authorities of Tripoli and to Ahmad Ma'n in 1692, of the references to 'heretical' Shiites in the latter.[96] The Ottomans were only too well aware of the Lebanese feudalists' sectarian affiliations, but had little interest in delegitimizing individuals on whom they had relied as local proxies in the past and would have to continue to do so in the future. While the Hamadas were stripped of their Sunni-inhabited fiefs in the summer of 1690, as we have seen, the imperial *hüküm*s neither explicitly condemn them as heretics nor divest them of their other landholdings. The insistence on their 'Kızılbaş' and 'Revafiz' identity in later decrees invokes a legal justification for killing Shiite troublemakers but also underscores the gravity of the crime that really concerned the Ottoman administration: '*eşkıyalık*', that is, 'brigandage' or simply 'tyranny' in the wider sense. The very fact that the Shiites were identified with brigandage

[93] 'Abbas Isma'il Sabbagh, *Tarikh al-'Alaqat al-'Uthmaniyya al-Iraniyya* (Beirut: Dar al-Nafa'is, 1999), 166–71, 196–7.

[94] Rudolph Matthee, *The Politics of Trade in Safavid Iran: Silk for Silver, 1600–1730* (Cambridge University Press, 1999), 223–5.

[95] *Silahdar Tarihi*, II:620–2; Raşid, *Tarih*, II:182.    [96] MD 102:180–1.

suggests that their challenge to authority was understood as a social or fiscal, but not a confessional, problem.

The problem of rural-based banditry was of course endemic to many early modern states. With regard to the Ottoman Empire, it has even been argued that the genius of its consolidation consisted in its willingness to co-opt outlaws into, rather than shut them out from, patterns of state patronage.[97] However, as with administrative and military organization in general, the changing financial and military needs of the Empire radically transformed provincial brigandage over the course of the seventeenth century as well. By giving tribesmen and landless peasants firearms to serve in large irregular infantries, the Ottomans themselves contributed to the rise of mercenary gangs that virtually ruled Anatolia when the regular soldiery was away on campaign. At the same time, as we have seen, these so-called Saruca and Sekban companies formed the backbone of the notable households that came to dominate provincial politics. Istanbul occasionally attempted to check their influence by sending special recruiters-cum-brigand fighters (müfettiş) such as Tursun Mehmed to Anatolia as well as by a more innovative technique: nefir-i 'amm, or the general conscription of the non-military subject population. First used during the Celali revolts around the beginning of the century, civilian militiamen (il erleri) would hereby be recruited by the town or village notables and then registered by the kadı for armed service against local bandit groups or overly rapacious governors – striking testimony to the devolution of power in the Empire.[98]

In the war after the second siege of Vienna civilian draftees were even used on the battle front, but the nefir-i 'amm served above all to thwart the rebellion of Yeğen Osman Paşa and his 'Türedi' ('rabble') Anatolian Sekban companies in 1688–9.[99] Given the real danger posed to the state by Yeğen Osman and his army, it is significant that the Sublime Porte chose to label the Hamadas too as 'Türidi brigands'[100] in 1691 and call a nefir-i 'amm once the focus of the punitive operation had shifted to Ahmad Ma'n. Chancery decrees from the spring of 1694 order the mobilization of all provincial forces 'not assigned to the imperial campaign' plus the private household armies of the region's governors, but also, 'by way of a general conscription, the civilian militiamen capable of war and battle, and sufficient men from the provinces of Tripoli, Sidon-Beirut, Damascus and Aleppo, as well as those il erleri under their government able to bear arms'.[101] The Shiite rebellion will hardly have precipitated a levée en masse throughout Syria; in November, at any rate, Istanbul had to issue new orders to deploy the local (yerlü)

[97] Karen Barkey, *Bandits and Bureaucrats: The Ottoman Route to State Centralization* (Ithaca: Cornell University Press, 1994), esp. p. 176.

[98] See Halil Inalcik, 'Military and Fiscal Transformation in the Ottoman Empire, 1600–1700', *Archivum Ottomanicum* 6 (1980), 304–11; repr. in *Studies in Ottoman Social and Economic History* (London: Variorum, 1985).

[99] *Silahdar Tarihi*, II:357–63, 402–4, 409–18; Raşid, *Tarih*, II:39–40, 73–6; Inalcik, 'Military and Fiscal Transformation', 299–302; Finkel, *Osman's Dream*, 300–4.

[100] MD 102:67.    [101] MD 105:5–7, 10–11.

Damascene Janissary division as well.[102] Still, the formal delegation of *reaya*-class subjects to combat even minor rebels, when this job would have been left to professional *askeri*s and their retainer households only a few years – or, specifically in this case, a few months – before, is again symptomatic of more fundamental, long-term shifts in the nature of the state's relationship to its subjects. In a sense, the use of *nefir-i 'amm* and *il erleri* to police rural districts prefigured the spread of *derbend* foundations in the eighteenth century, whereby entire communities were settled at isolated but strategically important communications links to help territorialize the Ottoman state's control of its far-flung lands.[103] The Hamadas fell victim in 1693–4 not so much to ancient religious antipathies as to a changing imperial administrative vision.

This change is perhaps best exemplified by the institution of an imperial *iskan siyaseti*, or tribal settlement policy, in the late seventeenth century. Throughout history, state-building particularly in the Middle East – with its vast steppes and deserts – has depended in large measure on a sovereign's ability to incorporate and, where possible, sedentarize the pastoral nomadic populace. In the Ottoman Empire, this pursuit took many forms, from promoting settlement around dervish cloisters on the European military frontier in early times, to the forced deportation (*sürgün*) of entire tribes to newly conquered lands in the sixteenth century, to the investiture of clan chiefs with land titles in the nineteenth. The protracted struggle with the Habsburg Reich now brought a special urgency to tribal control as well. Years of war-induced mercenary brigandage aggravated the Empire's already dire financial straits, while both were compounded by substantial territorial losses in the Balkans that set off a wave of refugees towards Anatolia. It is against this backdrop that the Ottomans introduced, as Cengiz Orhonlu has suggested, a distinctive programme for tribal settlement and taxation in the years 1691–6.[104] By combining fiscal incentives with land grants designed to disperse larger confederations, the Sublime Porte hoped to revive marginal farmlands and abandoned villages in areas such as Raqqa and eastern Anatolia and to ease the tribesmen's pressure on the tax-paying settled agricultural population. As far as the initiative and time-frame proposed by Orhonlu are accurate, *iskan siyaseti* provides the most useful paradigm for understanding the Empire's quest to discipline the Hamadas in 1693–4.

The discourse in the 1694 decrees against the 'Kızılbaş' cloaks the rather instrumentalist vector of earlier orders. As we have seen, the Hamadas were originally denounced for annexing Sunni-inhabited areas to their tax collectorship, whereby the Sublime Porte's chief concern was that 'the humble commoners from the rural districts will scatter and disperse on account of their oppression'. This

---

[102] MD 105:17–18.

[103] Cengiz Orhonlu, *Osmanlı İmparatorluğu'nda Derbend Teşkilatı* (2nd edn, Istanbul: Eren, 1990); Yusuf Halaçoğlu, *XVIII. Yüzyılda Osmanlı İmparatorluğu'nun İskan Siyaseti ve Aşiretlerin Yerleştirilmesi* (Ankara: Türk Tarih Kurumu, 1988), 94–108.

[104] Cengiz Orhonlu, *Osmanlı İmparatorluğu'nda Aşiretlerin İskani* (Istanbul: Eren, 1987), comprising *Osmanlı İmparatorluğu'nda Aşiretleri İskan Teşebbüsü (1691–1696)*, published in 1963, and 'Osmanlı İmparatorluğu'nda Aşiretlerin İskanı' in *Türk Kültürü Araştırmaları* 15 (1976).

solicitude for the taxable *reaya*'s welfare characterizes the different orders from the winter of 1691/2 as well:

The Kızılbaş ... came to the district of Kura, killed eleven of its men, transgressed on their properties and goods, seized their crops, leaving their folk and families hungry and abject ...

The Rafizi brigands living in the Tripoli mountains have been invading the surroundings of Tripoli for a few years, stealing the buffalo, oxen and other livestock of the impoverished *reaya*, killing people, plundering property and sowing corruption and sedition ...

In addition to usurping the state tax farms in these regions and eating up and swallowing the receipts which are legally due to the treasury of Islam, their tyranny and oppression of the impoverished *reaya* has exceeded all bounds. These are unable to preserve their folk and families or guard and dispose as they wish their property, supplies, beasts, livestock, farms and fruit trees.

The real issue, however, was the damage ultimately being caused to the state purse:

The impoverished *reaya* are unable to pay the *miri* tax and most have left their homes and quit the land. The fate of those who stay is worsening, for they do not have the resources and ability to pay the *miri* ...

The aforesaid brigands neither observe the holy law nor obey the *valis*. In the measure that they refuse to pay the *miri* and oppress and tyrannize the impoverished *reaya*, their presence in these regions is the cause for the start and perdurance of upheaval and the reason for the [ruin] of the land. It is necessary to repulse their tyranny and oppression of the impoverished *reaya* as well as their excuses and sluggishness concerning the *miri* tax, and eliminate their presence from these regions.[105]

The Sublime Porte generally did not stipulate what should be done with captured *eşkıya*. The decrees from 1693–4 carry several variations of 'take them all and give them the punishment which they deserve by law', which essentially meant to execute them.[106] However, the earlier *hüküm*s suggest a higher degree of flexibility. One which we have already cited in other contexts quotes the notables of Tripoli complaining, 'it is certain that all the *reaya* will disperse and scatter if, besides a few of the aforesaid brigands being taken and imprisoned in the Tripoli citadel, they are not also "punished"/executed'.[107] The Tripoli authorities commenced the final part of the 1694 campaign by killing the hostages detained as surety for the Hamadas' *iltizam*s,[108] which suggests that they had still hoped for a peaceable solution until then. Two decrees from late 1691, one against the Hamadas and the other against Nusayri bandits in the Latakia region, stipulate exiling individuals who do not deserve execution, their names to be registered in the chief account books.[109]

The radical solutions that Ottoman-Islamic law demanded for dealing with 'Kızılbaş' found little echo in the pragmatism of the Empire's provincial administration. The rule of heterodox tribalists in the desert and mountain periphery may have contradicted Ebu's-Suud's precepts, but it was an actively supported

---

[105] MD 102:67, 180–1; MD 104:155.    [106] Imber, 'Persecution', 270–2.    [107] MD 102:180.
[108] Ibn Nujaym, 'Nubdha', 818.    [109] MD 102:61.

component of Ottoman rural governance in Syria. The local Shiites became as much a part of the Empire's ambitious social engineering as any other tribal constituency. As the February 1691 order to the *valis* of Tripoli and Damascus concerning Shadid Harfush makes clear, they were in effect subject to Ottoman *iskan siyaseti* despite a religious identity which technically should have earmarked them for elimination:

Propose to and convince the Revafız living in the villages in the mountain passes near Baalbek ... to surrender these brigands to the people of the [afflicted] villages, and to leave the high mountains themselves and collectively descend to the [Bekaa] plain, settle and mind their own affairs ... For those who evict the aforesaid brigand from their homes and leave the ... high mountains, descend to the plain and keep to their own affairs, so much the better. As for those who aid the brigands and hinder their surrender, and who continue to inflict evil and villainy on the Muslims, their blood can be shed legally; punish them.[110]

The Porte's offer to the 'Revafız' still stood ten months later, after a first campaign to capture Shadid had failed.[111]

Not surprisingly the Ottomans also sought to extract the maximum advantage from the military operations themselves. The official objective of the campaign as told to the notables of Tripoli in 1694 was still 'to render the country prosperous and to better the conditions of the faithful', but in fact Arslan and Tursun Paşas received precise instructions on confiscating, if necessary on pain of torture, the defeated tribalists' possessions for the benefit of the state:

Seize all the mobile and stationary goods that are to be found; their cash, effects, beasts, livestock and all of their property and stores, whatever there is, for the tax registry, the accountancy and the fisc. In addition to this, investigate and discover the money buried and hidden in the places where they live or camp ... and in [other] sites you might think of and suspect, by whatever means necessary, [interrogating] the captured men and those people who know. Dig up the suspected places. Widen the search and efforts and have it found. Seize it for the fisc, and report to and appraise my august throne with a register.[112]

The Hamadas and other Shiites of Syria may theoretically have been 'accursed Kızılbaş whose elimination is an incumbent religious duty', but relocating, taxing, settling or expropriating them was better still.

## Conclusion: a new era?

The fragile consensus, the paradox of Shiite rule under Ottoman sovereignty in Mt Lebanon, was seriously called into question by a series of distinct but interrelated transformations that began to affect Syrian provincial society and the Empire at large towards the end of the seventeenth century. On the local level, the Hamadas' dominance was increasingly challenged by the Maronite Christian community as it evolved into the Ma'ns' main commercial and political ally in this period. The Maronites' colonization of formerly Shiite-inhabited districts (Fig. 4), spearheaded

---

[110] MD 100:137, 140.    [111] MD 102:78.    [112] MD 105:7, 8, 16, 18.

Fig. 4 Sayyidat al-Haqla church, Kisrawan. Fresco said to depict a Shiite woman with a sick child praying to the Virgin Mary.

by the Khazin family and underwritten by Catholic Europe, thus coincided with and in fact defined the emergence of the 'Druze emirate' as a regional locus of power. The more effective, efficient government of the Ma'ns and especially the Shihabis who succeeded them in 1697 ultimately answered to the new logic of Ottoman fiscalism and would thus serve as the Empire's premier instrument of control in the coastal highlands. Over time, the Druze–Maronite condominium would establish a political and narrative title to all 'Lebanon' in which the Shi'a was left little room.

This consolidation of local jurisdictions was mirrored on the provincial administrative level. Starting with the Köprülü reforms, the government of Syria increasingly came under the control of regionally rooted civilian notable households. The punitive expedition of 1693–4 also marked a shift in power from the largely absentee, socially unengaged military service elite to professional tax extraction regimes (and their allies in the imperial capital), which dominate later Syrian history. Finally, the Hamadas and Harfushes suffered from the Empire's redoubled efforts to deepen its territorial *mainmise* and satisfy the ever greater financial needs to compete against the modern European powers. By promoting an armed citizenry and instituting imperial tribal settlement policies, the central government progressively encroached on the space of the traditionally free-wheeling, semi-nomadic desert and mountain clans. The same characteristics which had recommended the Shiites as classical tax concessionaries (tribalism, segregation, mercenariness) also made them prime candidates for the state's social engineering projects at the turn of the modern era.

The political and judicial rhetoric against the 'Kızılbaş' notwithstanding, the Hamadas and Harfushes were above all the victims of rationalization and *sozialdisziplinierung* (societal disciplining), long-term historical processes that were in fact typical of early modern state formation throughout the region. This is not to say that their sectarian identity was irrelevant to their increasing marginalization. France's protection of the Maronites, the Druze emirs' choice of local partners, the civilian governors' quest to eradicate heterodox rebels in Tripoli and the reinvocation of Ebu's-Suud's definitions of illegal heresy all played to the special disadvantage of the Shiites in this time. The underlying causes of these processes, however, went far deeper than the particular social and economic crises which hit the Ottoman Empire between 1685 and 1699, and would thus continue to profoundly shape the Lebanese Shiites' fate in the century to come.

# CHAPTER 5

# Jabal 'Amil in the Ottoman period: the origins of 'south Lebanon', 1666–1781

Jabal 'Amil, the traditional name for the less elevated but still rugged, remote extension of the Syrian coastal range lying to the south-east of Sidon, is home to the oldest and most illustrious Twelver Shiite community in the region. Since at least the Middle Ages its large population of *ashraf* and Shiite scholar families has made it a high place of Imami learning, piety and asceticism; the migration of many of its *mujtahid*s to institutionalize Shiism in Iran in the sixteenth century would consecrate the "Amili' identity as one of distinction within the Shiite universe. During the Ottoman period this identity was fuelled by poverty and isolation, by the perceived hostility of the Ottoman state and of local neighbours, but also by pride in its scholars and its independent feudal lords. This golden age of autonomy would end in the late eighteenth century, with the increasing dominance of the Shihabi emirate and, particularly important in the Shiite collective memory, the appointment of Cezzar 'the butcher' Ahmed Paşa as governor of Sidon in 1775. Henceforth the history of Jabal 'Amil would be one of bloodshed and dispossession, of loss of identity and finally marginalization, in what is today referred to, sometimes dismissively and euphemistically, as no more than 'the South'.

The historiography of the Shiites of Jabal 'Amil in the early modern period, however, presents some particular problems. Compared with Mt Lebanon or the Bekaa, where Christian ecclesiarchs were there to chronicle the *gestes* of their Druze patrons from the beginning of Ottoman rule, the feudal lordships of Jabal 'Amil dwelt in relative obscurity until the eighteenth century. Traditional Shiite biographical literature, on the other hand, focused almost entirely on great scholars whose lives and careers appear as if removed from the secular world. As a result, native historians of Jabal 'Amil, as Fouad Ajami writes, have given the time before Cezzar Ahmed 'the nostalgic glow that agrarian populations give, in retrospect, to some imagined age of bliss and plenty':

The people of Jabal 'Amil lived in dignity and prosperity even during times of war and catastrophes. No taxes overwhelmed them; no rulers oppressed them and plundered their wealth ... After storms blew over they devoted themselves to their agricultural work, to exploiting their land the way they wanted to without taxes, without fees, and without monopoly. Their own rulers were merciful toward them. If a Shiite travelled to some other place beyond his land, he travelled proud of his heritage, with none daring to challenge or

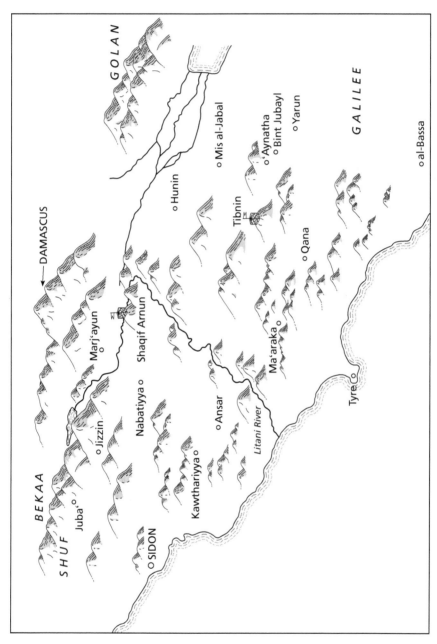

Map 3  Jabal ʿAmil

belittle him. Peace reigned among the *zu 'ama* (the leaders) and they were united. Each *za 'im* (leader) was free in his own territory, governing it, protecting its borders, preserving it. No authority was higher than that of the *za 'im*, and no guardian, except the authority of the *'ulama '*.[1]

The aim of this chapter is to reconsider the history of Jabal 'Amil (Map 3) from the perspective of the nominal state authority. As elsewhere in Syria, the image conveyed in state administrative documents is of course just as ideal, suggesting regular taxation, efficient justice and constant order, in contrast to the serene oblivion and/or the murder, mayhem, pillage and plunder often conveyed in narrative literature. The Ottomans' principal challenge in the area, it appears, was not controlling the rural Shiite populace but curbing the ambitious Ma'n and Shihabi families as well as a new sort of regional commercial potentate in the eighteenth century, the Galilee-based cotton baron Zahir al-'Umar. If the Shiite *zu 'ama* of Jabal 'Amil lagged far behind the Hamadas or Harfushes in importance, this chapter will argue, it was by exploiting a growing political rivalry between the Shihabi emirate and Zahir al-'Umar that they were able to maintain a high degree of autonomy locally until late in the century. Yet in the end, our Ottoman documents are eloquent above all by their silence: in the course of the eighteenth century the chancery appears to have lost all touch with the region, essentially abandoning its interest and authority to the Druze–Maronite condominium that would eventually incorporate Jabal 'Amil as the southern periphery of 'the Lebanon'. The Shiites' last great exploits, such as the occupation of Sidon by shaykh Nasif Nassar in 1771, and their growing submission to the Shihabi emirs were barely registered by the Ottomans; it is perhaps metaphoric of the Empire's overall loss of knowledge/ power that French consular correspondence replaces Ottoman documentation as the premier source for the history of the area as the century progresses.

## Sidon and Safad under Ottoman rule

Jabal 'Amil was usually divided between two governorships in the Ottoman period. The northern districts formed part of the *sancak* of Sidon-Beirut, whose hinterland was initially dominated by the Bedouin Hanash emirs and later by the Druze chieftains of the Shuf and Gharb mountains. Compared with Mt Lebanon and the Bekaa Valley there is actually very little documentation on the area in the sixteenth century; the new Ottoman administration, as Bakhit and Abu-Husayn have shown, was above all concerned with preventing the local sale of firearms and putting down endless Druze revolts prior to the major punitive campaign of 1585.[2] The *sancak* of Safad, which comprised the southern districts of Jabal 'Amil and

---

[1]  Fouad Ajami, *The Vanished Imam: Musa al Sadr and the Shia of Lebanon* (Ithaca: Cornell University Press, 1986), 52–3, with citation from Al Safa, *Tarikh Jabal 'Amil*, 104.

[2]  Bakhit, *The Ottoman Province of Damascus*, 16–17, 204; Abu-Husayn, 'Problems in the Ottoman Administration in Syria', 665–7; Abu-Husayn, *The View from Istanbul*, 11–23; Inalcık, 'Tax Collection', 181–2.

belonged, like Sidon-Beirut, to the *eyalet* of Damascus, was no easier to control. After meeting more resistance here during the conquest than perhaps anywhere else in Syria, the Ottomans had to contend with coastal piracy, smuggling and Bedouin rebellions for much of the sixteenth century.[3] The Shiite-inhabited district of Shaqif Arnun, site of the ancient crusader fortress of Beaufort, was one of several in the province which the Ottomans tried repeatedly to revive and rede-velop through the distribution of *timar* grants; in 1577 the Sublime Porte also attempted to settle peasants around the *derbend* (pass) of Naqura, 'a haunt of robbers and brigands', which marked (then as now) Safad's border with Sidon-Beirut's jurisdiction.[4] Being divided between two *sancak*s, one dominated by the Druze and the other by the Bedouins, may have hindered the development of a stronger, more unified autonomous leadership in Jabal 'Amil; ultimately, however, it also saved the local population from complete absorption into the burgeoning Shihabi emirate in the eighteenth century.

As elsewhere in the Empire, administrative units such as *sancak*s, *eyalet*s and tax farms were not precisely delimited but could be reorganized according to the government's needs or the assignee's personal importance. We have already seen that the Ottomans briefly contemplated turning Sidon-Beirut into a *beğlerbeğlik* under 'Ali Harfush in 1585; starting in 1590 Fakhr al-Din Ma'n and his sons held Safad and then Sidon-Beirut for many years as *sancak-beğ*s. The two were brought together as a single province during Fakhr al-Din's exile in 1614–15, but the final establishment of the *beğlerbeğlik* or *eyalet*, which was initially named for Safad and later for Sidon, only occurred in 1660 in the context of the Köprülü viziers' restoration of central authority over the state bureaucracy. Even then, the province remained subordinate to Damascus in many regards. Because most of Sidon's revenues were earmarked for the *hajj* caravan or other expenses related to the governorship of Damascus, its accounts were frequently included among the latter's and the *vali* of Damascus could cross the border to collect taxes or enforce the law. In the eighteenth century this hierarchy of authority was reflected in the fact that Sidon was often assigned to a junior member of the 'Azm dynasty governing in Damascus.

Even after Fakhr al-Din's downfall in 1633 the province of Sidon continued to be marked by his time in power. Tax documents record the *emlak-ı İbn-i Ma'n*, the 'properties of Ibn Ma'n', as a separate category of taxable landholdings (akin to the *emlak-ı İbn-i Seyfa* in Tripoli), and many public buildings in the area were thought to have been founded by the great emir himself. This could occasion conflict, when tenants such as the French merchants of Sidon or sufis living in a small *khan* in Beirut claimed to be exempt from paying regular rent to their respective *waqf* foundations.[5] A large-scale study of Ottoman tax cadastres notes that the northern

---

[3] Heyd, *Ottoman Documents on Palestine*, 80–1, 83–5, 88, 111–13; Bakhit, *The Ottoman Province of Damascus*, 13, 196–7, 207; MD 26:328; MD 36:302; MD 42:274, 483.

[4] MD 12:46–7; MD 14:872–3; MD 31:123; MD 33:159; Heyd, *Ottoman Documents on Palestine*, 100.

[5] Başbakanlık Archives: Başmuhasebe Kalemi/Sayda ve Beyrut Mukataası (D.BŞM.SBM) 1:61; 2:12–13; 4:29.

portion of the *sancak* of Safad on both sides of the Litani River saw a significant increase in its population density between the late sixteenth and the early nineteenth centuries, suggesting that it also benefited economically from the influx of Christian settlers that began under the Ma'n emirs and continued under the Shihabis.[6]

Little is known of the Shiite-inhabited tax farms in the area. Those for which *iltizam* records are extant (Shaqif, Bishara, Shumar) seem to have been under the control of Fakhr al-Din and his son 'Ali, the *sancak-beğ* of Sidon and Safad, in the first part of the seventeenth century.[7] As early as 1615, however, one of the Shihabi emirs is already noted as guarantor (*kefil*) of moneys owed by a local shaykh of the Bishara tax farm.[8] In 1633 these and other fiefs previously held by the Ma'ns were all transferred to the Shihabis, who had begun to extend their influence beyond the Wadi Taym (*sancak* of Damascus) by overbidding for concessions in the Bekaa and as far away as Nablus.[9] The farms constituting Jabal 'Amil, as will be seen, passed under the control of local Shiite notables sometime in the second half of the century, but would remain under pressure from the Ma'ns and the Shihabis for years to come.

## Shiism in Jabal 'Amil

Starting with Muhammad ibn Makki 'al-Shahid al-Awwal', a well-known Shiite scholar from Jizzin martyred in 1384, the local history of Jabal 'Amil has been viewed mainly through the lens of its *'ulama'*, through their theological and legal treatises, the accounts of their travels in search of knowledge and the biographies of their families. Lebanese Shiite historians who began to draw on these sources in the early twentieth century in an effort to discover their community's past have therefore tended to emphasize the religious aspects of life in Jabal 'Amil, the roles of individual scholars and their networks extending all the way to Iran, and the self-containment of the Shi'a under Ottoman rule. In the vast, if somewhat self-referential modern literature, Jabal 'Amil is made to be the site of a sustained intellectual and literary 'movement' in the early modern period, with 'schools' of Shiite higher learning in countless villages and rich private libraries (only later destroyed by Cezzar), a closed society cut off from the world around it.[10]

Yet if 'Amili scholars became famous above all by moving to Safavid Iran in the sixteenth century, Shiite biographical sources also tell of immigration to Jabal

---

[6] Wolf-Dieter Hütteroth and Kamal Abdulfattah, *Historical Geography of Palestine, Transjordan and Southern Syria in the Late Sixteenth Century* (Erlangen: Palm und Enke, 1977), 62.

[7] Nagata *et al.*, eds., *Tax Farm Register of Damascus*, 56, 139, 296.

[8] MD 81:100.

[9] Nagata *et al.*, eds., *Tax Farm Register of Damascus*, 63, 66, 102, 127, 184, 190, 213, 355, 358, 369.

[10] See especially Ahmad Rida with Shakib Arslan, 'Al-Matawila aw al-Shi'a fi Jabal 'Amil', *al-'Irfan* 2 (1910), 237–42, 286–9, 330–7, 381–92, 444–50; Muhsin al-Amin, *Khitat Jabal 'Amil* (new edn, Beirut: Dar al-Muhibba al-Bayda', 2002); Ibrahim Beydoun *et al.*, *Safahat min Tarikh Jabal 'Amil* (Beirut: Dar al-Farabi, 1979); Muhammad Kazim Makki, *al-Haraka al-Fikriyya wa 'l-Adabiyya fi Jabal 'Amil* (Beirut: Dar al-Andalus, 1982).

'Amil from outside the Empire, as well as of frequent exchanges with Twelver communities in Jubayl, Damascus, Iraq, Mecca and Yemen throughout the Ottoman period.[11] Closer to home, one member of the illustrious Hurr al-'Amili family is reported to have served in the *shari'a* court of Juba' village in 1676; another apparently had connections with the Ottoman authorities in Sidon and is described as a friend of governor Osman Paşa in the 1720s.[12] The religious practices of ordinary villagers are, by their nature, only rarely attested in written sources, but shrine worship and other popular devotions evidently flourished under Ottoman dominion too. Among the oldest mosques in the region is that reportedly built by the 'Ali al-Saghirs in Hunin (now in northern Israel) in 1752/3, while several others date from the 1760s.[13] The shrine of Khidr in 'Aynatha (near Bint Jubayl) was extensively restored during Sultan Süleyman's reign,[14] and a shaykh from the same village rebuilt the larger Sham' sanctuary on the coastal plain near Tyre around 1688.[15] A glance at a sixteenth-century Ottoman *Tapu* cadastre for Sidon shows that many villages were initially under the fiscal responsibility of the inhabitants themselves, with the incomes from ancillary farms (*mezraa*) frequently being reserved for family *vakıf*s or the upkeep of small local sanctuaries such as that of *Hazret* Shu'ayb al-Nabi in Shaqif.[16]

Like in Mt Lebanon or the Bekaa, many rural shrines were shared by several confessional communities. Perhaps the most famous example in the region was a sanctuary just beyond Beirut that was dedicated to Khidr (Turkish: Hızır), a pre-Islamic water and fertility saint venerated by various Muslim denominations and identified by Syrian Orthodox Christians with St George, the patron saint of the coastal littoral. An entry in a unique finance (*Ahkam*) register preserved in Dresden claims that the site had been a mosque in ancient times, before 'the infidels seized it and turned it into a church. It became a mosque one or two more times until the infidels again made it a church.' It was reconsecrated as a mosque in 1633/4, immediately after Fakhr al-Din Ma'n's capture, but was then again converted into a church 'through the support of Ma'n-oğlı Mülhem and the custodian's brother Hasan'. Following a complaint by the city's Sunni religious notables, the Sublime Porte decided to remove the shrine from the sphere of popular religion altogether and declared it to be a congregational mosque where Friday prayers were henceforth to be held.[17] The French diplomat D'Arvieux relates that St George, according to both Christian and Muslim lore, thereupon visited an early death upon the governor of Sidon responsible for the conversion.[18]

---

[11] al-Amin, *A'yan al-Shi'a*, II:217–18, 464, 569; V:187; VI:137–8, 264, 275; VII:159–62, 165, 166, 315, 377, 378, 428–9; VIII:176, 235, 289–90, 333–8; IX:59–60, 167–71, 272–3, 420, 431–2; X:11, 52–5, 126, 318.

[12] *Ibid.*, X:288; VIII:16.

[13] Ibrahim Al Sulayman, *Buldan Jabal 'Amil: Qila'uhu wa-Madarisuhu wa-Jusuruhu wa-Murujuhu wa-Matahinuhu wa-Jibaluhu wa-Mashahiduhu* (Beirut: al-Da'ira, 1995), 438, 580–3.

[14] al-Amin, *A'yan al-Shi'a*, VIII:160.    [15] *Ibid.*, V:467–8; VI:192.    [16] TD 559:66, 258.

[17] Sächsische Landesbibliothek/Staats- und Universitätsbibliothek, Dresden: Ms. Eb. 358, fol. 96a.

[18] D'Arvieux, *Mémoires*, 159–61.

In Jabal 'Amil itself several Christian sites are again identified with Shiite founders: a stone church in the small Maronite village of Darbessin (Dayr Bassim), according to local legend, was built by shaykh Husayn Mansur of the Munkar family around the middle of the eighteenth century (it is actually older) after he had burned the wooden one fighting the Ottoman authorities; two of his children had then choked to death before he swore to the Virgin Mary to rebuild her house, going so far as to threaten the *paşa* of Sidon when he demanded to see an imperial firman for the church. The church was known for its healing qualities – as was, incidentally, an older Muslim shrine in the same village.[19] A sanctuary dedicated to Mary inside the grotto of Mantara was also revered by Druze, Shiite and Sunni shepherds from the area who brought their flocks there to be blessed; it had, according to one account, first been 'rediscovered' by a Shiite farmer.[20] Such stories of course function primarily in the popular Maronite tradition to 'prove' the power of *setna* (Our Lady) Mary, but they can also be seen to accompany and make sense of important socio-political changes. Maronite immigration to regions under Druze control began to affect Jabal 'Amil in the seventeenth century, where numerous peasant families settled on Shiite lands before troubles with the 'Métoualis' caused them to seek Cezzar's protection later in the eighteenth century. Much like in the Kisrawan, the 'restoration' of churches and the appropriation of traditions surrounding older holy sites were a key ideological component of the Maronite community's expansion in this time. From a religious standpoint, the Shiites of Jabal 'Amil were, in reality, anything except isolated from the world around them.

## Retreat in the northern mukataas

The paucity of documentary sources on the Jabal 'Amil Shiites' indigenous leaderships is partially indicative of the fact that they gave the Ottoman state a lot fewer headaches than the Hamadas or Harfushes; their history really only comes to light through their increasingly futile bid to resist the Ma'n and Shihabi emirs' domination. In the northern part of the Jabal, the rule of Shiite feudal families is barely attested before the second half of the seventeenth century, when the entire *sancak* (viz *eyalet*) of Sidon-Beirut had been apportioned as *iltizam*. The mountain district of Jizzin had been an important Shiite centre in the Middle Ages and was later supposedly under the authority of a local *muqaddam* household related to the 'Ali al-Saghir clan. By the eighteenth century, however, Maronite colonists brought in by the Ma'ns and Jumblatts (Canpolats) had largely displaced the Shiite population before starting to move into the Iqlim al-Tuffah and Shumar as well. Some Shiites did remain in the district (and, like the local Druze, venerated the Marian shrine at Bisri); Jizzin's mosque was torn down only in 1885. The *muqaddam*s, however, had early been reduced to poverty and do not figure in any sources of the Ottoman period.[21]

---

[19] Goudard, *La Sainte Vierge au Liban*, 50–1.    [20] *Ibid.*, 55, 58.

[21] *Ibid.*, 85–7, 92–3; al-Amin, *A 'yan al-Shi'a*, X:288; al-Amin, *Khitat*, 228–9; 'Ali al-Zayn, *Li'l-Bahth 'an Tarikhina fi Lubnan* (Beirut: 1973), 255–6, 328.

Of the principal Shiite feudatories in this time, the Munkar family of Juba',
hometown of the illustrious Hurr al-'Amili and Zayn al-Din al-Shahid *'ulama'*
dynasties, had apparently been notable religious scholars themselves before
accepting the Ottoman tax concession (at least in subcontract from the Ma'ns)
for the Shumar district.[22] The Munkars are first mentioned in the narrative literature
in 1613, when Fakhr al-Din Ma'n ransacked their homes in Kawthariyya after
villagers in the area complained to him of their oppression; the following year, the
governor of Damascus in turn appointed Nasir al-Din and 'Ali Munkar, who were
considered to be the pre-eminent Shiite shaykhs of the district, to lead a punitive
raid against the Ma'ns at Bisri. In 1617 the Munkars and other Shiites pledged their
support to the new *sancak-beğ* of Safad who had arrived to replace the exiled
Ma'nid emir, and later the same year they responded enthusiastically to Ahmad
Harfush's already cited attempt to establish a palace in the southern Bekaa, before
the Ma'ns enjoined the senior Harfush emir not to trespass on their sphere of
influence.[23] Fakhr al-Din seized Nasir al-Din Munkar immediately after returning
from exile in 1618, releasing him only after Yunus Harfush provided a caution for
his good conduct, but then proceeded to ravage the lands and seize the crops of the
Munkars, 'Ali al-Saghirs and others a few months later when they again fled to the
Harfushes in order to avoid paying their tax arrears. The minor Shiite chieftains of
the area were evidently keen to find allies against the ever more dominant Ma'ns,
and took the fateful decision several years later to shelter the rival Druze emir, 'Ali
'Alam al-Din, during a bitter inter-Druze power struggle in the Shuf. Mulham
Ma'n responded to this by attacking the Munkars' capital Ansar in the Shumar
district in 1638, leaving scores of Shiite villagers dead.[24]

The other major *zu 'ama* family of the north, the Sa'bs, were based in the castle of
Shaqif Arnun near Nabatiyya and had a markedly different background: like
several of the mountain taxlord dynasties particularly in Tripoli, the Sa'bs were
of Kurdish tribal origin, and never really integrated into the traditional scholarly
networks of Jabal 'Amil.[25] An Ottoman *timar* register indicates that Shaqif was
assigned to Ahmad Abu Sa'b, probably the family's progenitor, as early as 1571.[26]
In 1582 the Sublime Porte complained that this Ahmad Abu Sa'b owed twenty-one
loads of gold for 'some *mukataas* in the province of Safad that are always in
rebellion', which had been sold to him three years earlier. He had now joined the
rebel Korkmaz Ma'n and was helping to lay waste to the entire region.[27] At the

---

[22] al-Amin, *A'yan al-Shi'a*, III:174 (on Ahmad ibn Mansur al-Munkari, d. 1748); VII:315 (on
Sulayman al-Munkari, d. 1734/5); al-Amin, *Khitat*, 208, 222–5.

[23] al-Khalidi al-Safadi, *Lubnan*, 16, 36–7, 60, 66–7; Duwayhi, *Tarikh*, 310; see also al-Zayn, *Li'l-Bahth*, 255.

[24] al-Khalidi al-Safadi, *Lubnan*, 70–2; Duwayhi, *Tarikh*, 337; al-Amin, *Khitat*, 209; Rida, 'al-Matawila',
286; Darwish, *Jabal 'Amil*, 41, 44–5, 66–7; Abu-Husayn, *Provincial Leaderships*, 103–7.

[25] al-Amin, *A'yan al-Shi'a*, VII:331; VIII:349; Sulayman Zahir (d. 1960), *Qala'at al-Shaqif*, ed.
'Abdallah Sulayman Zahir (Beirut: al-Dar al-Islamiyya, 2002), 38.

[26] Başbakanlık Archives: Timar Ruznamçe (DFE.RZD) 38:62b. I am grateful to Alexandre Hourani for
this reference.

[27] MD 47:43.

height of their power the Ma'ns acquired the tax farm and occupied the castle of Shaqif itself; it was partially dismantled after their eclipse in 1615,[28] but reverted to the Sa'bs at some later point. The Sa'bs are believed to have fought what serves in essence as the founding myth of Shiite autonomy in Jabal 'Amil: the 1666 'battle of Nabatiyya'. The source for this event, a chronicle written by the late-Ottoman 'Amili historian 'Ali al-Subayti, remains unpublished but was repeatedly cited in al-'Irfan, a journal founded in 1909 in order to foster the Shiite community's cultural awakening in Lebanon. According to Subayti's account, Ahmad Ma'n attempted to seize Nabatiyya after the *Matawila* (Shiites) 'declared their independence' from him, but suffered a serious military defeat at the hands of the local shaykhs. The following year, the Shiites routed a second force sent against them by the *vali* of Sidon.[29]

Whatever their factual content, the stories of these and other battles carried in al-'Irfan were meant to underline the autonomy, but also the internal cohesion and unity, of Jabal 'Amil in historic times. The 'Amilis' constant preparedness to fight their hostile neighbours is exemplified by the tale of a mid-eighteenth-century shepherd from Tyre, who, shooting at animals one night, led the adjoining villages to fear an imminent attack. Throughout the night, the Shiites' *sawt*, the gunshot alarm, rang 'from Juba' on the slope of Mt Lebanon to al-Bassa on the border of Acre. It was not yet dawn when thousands had responded and assembled with their horses ready for war.'[30] For historians such as Al Safa these accounts give proof of the Shiites' perseverance in maintaining their independence from the 'Lebanese' emirs; in contrast 'Ali al-Zayn, whose *Li'l-Bahth 'an Tarikhina* (1973) constituted the first serious critical revision of Shiite history in Lebanon, has already questioned whether the Ma'ns and Shihabis ever possessed any formal suzerainty over Jabal 'Amil against which the Shiites needed to rebel.[31]

There are very few archival sources on Jabal 'Amil in the second half of the seventeenth century, but some *iltizam* contracts for the northern tax farms in 1699 are fortunately preserved in the oldest extant volume of records at the Sunni Islamic court in Sidon. These provide an important glimpse of the Shihabis' influence in the area shortly after their accession to the Druze emirate. Not surprisingly, the Shihabis are seen to have inherited the Ma'ns' still partially Shiite-inhabited tax district of Jizzin.[32] More surprising is the fact that Kaplan Paşa (brother of the Hamadas' nemesis Arslan Paşa of Tripoli) also awarded the *iltizam* for Shaqif and the Iqlim al-Tuffah to Bashir Shihabi in 1699.[33] The two Shiite *zu'ama* families in this instance seem to have been reduced to sharing a single tax concession: Muhammad ibn Nasir al-Din Munkar was initially allotted the Iqlim Shumar, one of the family's two traditional fiefs, but received a new *şartname* (contract)

---

[28] Abu-Husayn, *Provincial Leaderships*, 33, 88, 91–2, 95, 99.

[29] Rida, 'al-Matawila', 287; 'Ali al-Subayti, 'Jabal 'Amil fi Qarnayn', al-'Irfan 5 (1914), 21; Sulayman Zahir, '(Asma') Qura Jabal 'Amil', al-'Irfan 8 (1922), 657; see also Al Safa, *Tarikh*, 113; Soueid, *Histoire militaire*, 332–3.

[30] Rida, 'al-Matawila', 287.    [31] Al Safa, *Tarikh*, 108–14; al-Zayn, *Li'l-Bahth*, 317–18.

[32] Sunni Islamic Court of Sidon, Register 1:10.    [33] Sidon 1:8–9.

for only half its dues after the court recognized that the other part 'has passed into the care of Sulayman ibn shaykh Sa'b'.[34] The Munkars and Sa'bs continue to appear in the narrative sources of the eighteenth century; the Shaqif and Shumar *mukataa*s, however, are then very often mentioned along with the larger Bilad Bishara concession.

## The 'Ali al-Saghirs of the Bilad Bishara

The best-known Shiite taxlordship in Jabal 'Amil was that of the 'Ali al-Saghirs, who controlled the four cantons south of the Litani River (Hunin, Ma'araka, Qana, Tibnin) collectively known as the *Bilad Bishara* for much of the seventeenth and eighteenth centuries. The 'Lands of Bishara' were possibly named for an officer of the Ayyubid sultan Salah al-Din, under whom the coastal highlands were first apportioned as military appanages (*iqta'*) in the Middle Ages, although Mamluk sources also suggest that the 'Banu Bishara' may have been a Shiite tribe of the area.[35] The Ottoman regime, as already stated, was not overly concerned by the local Shiite population; one of the first orders explicitly against the 'Druze and Revafiz who are not of the four [orthodox] *mezhebs*' in Safad in 1582 dealt as usual with brigandage and weapons stock-piling rather than religion or politics.[36] In the sixteenth century the Bishara lands appear to have been dominated by the Shiite Sudun family of Qana, whom local historiography traces to a Circassian officer of the Mamluk sultanate in Cairo, and by the Al Shukr *sayyid* family of 'Aynatha. The house of 'Ali al-Saghir first appears (along with the Munkars and Shukrs) as a local opponent of the Ma'nids in 1617.[37] According to 'Amili tradition, 'Ali and Husayn al-Saghir, reputed descendants of a leading Shiite tribe from the past, went on to eliminate the rival Suduns and Shukrs in 1639 and 1649 respectively, and therewith established a single-family Shiite reign over the entire southern Jabal 'Amil that would last until the tyrannical rule of Cezzar Ahmed Paşa in the eighteenth century.[38]

'Ali and Husayn al-Saghir are first mentioned in Ottoman chancery documents in 1654, when they were blamed for a shortfall in taxes from some estates under their control around Tyre which were destined for the purchase of soap for a *waqf* foundation in Damascus.[39] The family fell into disarray not long thereafter, when Husayn and his son Hasan died within a year of each other, in 1655 and 1656, and the governor of the newly formed *eyalet* of Sidon inaugurated his reign in 1661 by launching a war against the Shiite feudalists. 'Ali al-Saghir and several of his sons were killed in subsequent fighting, with the last son dying suddenly in 1679/80.[40]

[34] Sidon 1:28.    [35] Poliak, *Feudalism*, 12–13.    [36] MD 46:358.
[37] al-Khalidi al-Safadi, *Lubnan*, 60; Duwayhi, *Tarikh*, 310.
[38] al-Amin, *A'yan al-Shi'a*, III:44; IV:21; VII:404; X:79, 182–5; Al Safa, *Tarikh*, 36–41; Zahir, 'Asma' Qura', 434, 438, 527; Soueid, *Histoire militaire*, 36–8; Darwish, *Jabal 'Amil*, 43, 58; al-Zayn, *Li'l-Bahth*, 263–97.
[39] ŞD 3:121.
[40] al-Amin, *A'yan al-Shi'a*, III:44, 53; V:56; VI:119; VIII:290; Shihabi, *Tarikh*, 733, 739; Rafiq, *Bilad al-Sham*, 190–6; Soueid, *Histoire militaire*, 331–2.

There seem to have followed some years of crisis in the Bishara lands, during which leadership was exercised by lesser notables such as the Zayn scholar family of Bint Jubayl, who for instance had to fend off a major Palestinian incursion in 1683/4.[41] The Shihabis in turn launched a devastating raid into the Bilad Bishara in 1693.[42]

Yet unlike the Shiite *zu'ama* of the northern Jabal 'Amil, who were hard-pressed to withstand the Shuf and Wadi Taym emirs, the 'Ali al-Saghirs were ensconced enough in the southern districts to constitute one of the region's ineluctable pivots of feudal power in their own right. Al-Zayn, noting that they were not subject to the Ma'ns' revenge after Fakhr al-Din's return to power, has suggested that they may have owed their continuing supremacy over Jabal 'Amil to a silent understanding with the paramount Druze emirs.[43] In any event it is probably no coincidence that 'Ali's son Mushrif, who emerged as the new clan chief towards the end of the century, was sought out by the Hamadas as they fled from the carnage in Mt Lebanon in 1694. The Ottomans initially ordered the *vali* of Sidon to prevent 'the Kızılbaş thugs subject to Ma'n-oğlı's government' from crossing back into Tripoli, and in 1696 warned the Druze emir himself that the Hamadas were once more causing trouble 'either with your support and backing or with that of *şeyh* Müşrif, the refuge of villainy for the Kızılbaş thugs living near the Sidon tax farms'.[44] The southern Lebanese folk tradition as well recalls Mushrif as a particularly powerful shaykh, ascribing him a veritable 'capital city' (Mazra'at Mushrif) on the coast north of Tyre. The site long contained vestiges of a palace and mosque built by him around 1697, though legend has it the mosque was never used because he was seen as such an ungodly tyrant.[45]

If the 'Ali al-Saghirs were able to turn feudal politics in the region to their advantage, using their ties with the Harfushes and Hamadas and, not least, the Ma'ns' own rather ambiguous rapport with the Ottoman state to preserve some measure of autonomy in Jabal 'Amil in the seventeenth century, this would prove progressively more difficult under the Shihabis. We have already seen that Bashir Shihabi intervened with Arslan Paşa of Tripoli to have the Hamadas reinstated in their tax farms under his caution in 1698. The same year, however, he also came to Kaplan Paşa's aid after Mushrif 'Ali al-Saghir had supposedly 'killed some government men and planned a revolt' in the *Bilad Bishara*. With a force of 8,000 men Bashir was able to arrest Mushrif, his brother Muhammad and a companion and deliver them to the *vali*. The companion was immediately impaled while the 'Ali al-Saghirs were imprisoned; Bashir, according to Duwayhi, was entrusted with 'the government of the province of Sidon from the Safad area to the Mu'amalatayn bridge [the border with Tripoli]. He came to enjoy immense favour, not only with the honourable Qablan Basha but also with his brother.'[46]

---

[41]  al-Zayn, *Li'l-Bahth*, 320–92.
[42]  Shihabi, *Tarikh*, 743.    [43]  al-Zayn, *Li'l-Bahth*, 264–5, 288.    [44]  MD 108:81, 259.
[45]  al-Amin, *Khitat*, 293; al-Amin, *A'yan al-Shi'a*, X:125–6; Al Sulayman, *Buldan*, 403–6. These and other myths surrounding Mushrif have been debunked by 'Ali al-Zayn in 'Adwa' 'ala Tarikh al-Iqta'iyya al-'Amiliyya', *Awraq Lubnaniyya* 3 (1957), 420–7, 463–72. See also his *Li'l-Bahth*, 366–8, 389–93.
[46]  Duwayhi, *Tarikh*, 383.

## The struggle against Shihabi hegemony

The history of the Shihabi emirate still awaits a thorough study on the basis of Ottoman sources. Originally from Shahba in southern Syria, the Shihabi family was well established in the Wadi al-Taym (today's south-eastern Lebanon) by the time of the Ottoman conquest. We have seen that they were among the Harfushes' leading competitors in the Bekaa in the seventeenth century and inherited many of the Ma'ns' tax farms in the area, in addition to expanding southward into Jabal 'Amil and beyond. Though Sunnis, the Shihabis were related to the Ma'ns by marriage, and the Ottoman authorities pushed for the Shuf and Kisrawan concession and the status of pre-eminence among the Druze to be attributed to the under-age emir Haydar Shihabi, 'the exemplar of the tribes and the clans', when Ahmad Ma'n died without male issue in 1697.[47] As a result of inner family conflicts, however, authority was first exercised by his uncle Bashir, who together with Mansur Shihabi can be seen to have held the Safad and Marj'ayun tax farms as well as the rights to certain other dues including from Bishara and Shaqif in 1699.[48] After Bashir's death (by poisoning, according to family history) in 1706, the Ottomans were again quick to invest Haydar as their local intermediary, persistently addressing him as 'Ma'n-oğlı Mir Hayderü'ş-Şihabi'[49] in order to stress his filiation with the increasingly real, if still not formally recognized, 'Druze' emirate.

In Lebanist historiography, the accession of the Shihabis (and their supremacy over the other Druze clans after the battle of 'Ayn Dara in 1711) marks another step in the establishment of a single local sovereignty over northern and southern Lebanon. Despite the continual setbacks attested in the narrative literature, however, the Shiites of Jabal 'Amil were not divested of their lands that easily. The Sa'bs and Munkars, as indicated, retained at least one of the northern tax farms in 1699; the *iltizam* for the Bilad Bishara was made out to a previously unattested 'Ali Hajj Ahmad, probably a scion of the 'Ali al-Saghir clan, the same year.[50] Mushrif appears to have died in prison around 1702 while 'Ali Mansur al-Munkar was captured and killed at about the same time.[51] This may help explain an extraordinary chancery order from 1705, in which 'Ali Hajj Ahmad, Ahmad Nassar, Mikha'il ibn 'Ali Mansur al-Munkar, Sulayman Sa'b and others are named as former tenants of the Bishara tax farm who had recently been expelled for 'rebelliousness'. They had then fled to the Qantara (Qunaytra) district in the Golan, where they had formed an army and proceeded to raid dozens of villages back in the Bilad Bishara. So much destruction had been wrought that 'not one *reaya* remained in the villages and the entire region was abandoned'; the *vali*s of Sidon-Beirut and Damascus were told to submit an inventory of all the stolen goods and stop the perpetrators.[52] The following year, the Sublime Porte again became concerned that 'the Kızılbaş in the Sidon-Beirut mountains' might come to

---

[47] MD 110:195.    [48] Sidon 1:6–7.    [49] MD 115:194, 589–91; MD 130:118–19.    [50] Sidon 1:5.
[51] Subayti, 'Jabal 'Amil', 21; al-Zayn, *Li'l-Bahth*, 402.
[52] ŞD 40:675 (volume also classified as MD 114/1).

the Hamadas' aid during a punitive campaign in Tripoli and gave orders 'to block and tie up all the trails and passages' between the two provinces.[53]

The 'Ali al-Saghirs were nonetheless back in possession of the Bilad Bishara in 1707, when they and the Sa'bs and Munkars were crushed by the Shihabis in a vicious battle just outside Nabatiyya. According to the family history of Haydar Ahmad al-Shihabi (d. 1835), of which the second book replaces Duwayhi as our principal narrative source for this period, the Shiites had been seeking revenge against the Shihabis but their ranks were 'torn to pieces' in less than an hour; the survivors sought refuge in the town, where a great number were pursued and massacred. Afterwards the Bilad Bishara were given to emir Haydar's deputy Mahmud Abu Harmush – whose oppression and insubordination eventually led to the intra-Druze confrontation at 'Ayn Dara. In 1712 Qasim al-Shihabi acquired the *iltizam* and, according even to the family history, 'wrought numerous injustices' on the Bilad Bishara. Haydar in turn fought the Shiites again at al-Qurayya in 1718/19.[54] The 'Amili historical tradition, for its part, also remembers Haydar for having killed one Shiite religious scholar and wrongly imprisoned another during his reign.[55]

However, tax documents suggest that the Bishara, Shaqif and Shumar fiefs continued to be in the hands of local shaykhs in 1710 and in 1714,[56] and it is precisely in this period that French consular dispatches from Sidon begin to give evidence of the Shiites' importance and relative autonomy in the area. The 'Chek des Metualis' was noted to pay the substantial sum of 85 sacks of silver (compare with the Druze emir's 150 sacks for the Shuf and Kisrawan) for the Bishara *iltizam* in 1717, which now included the plain of Tyre.[57] The shaykhs of Bishara, at least as far as the French were concerned, also had sufficient leverage with the authorities when it came to dealing with foreigners. In 1713, for example, they went straight to the governor of Damascus for help after Tuscan corsairs attacked an Ottoman vessel anchored under their protection in the port of Tyre. The *paşa*, invoking a treaty which banned such acts inside coastal waters, used their complaint to demand heavy restitutions from the French. In another incident only a few weeks later, Maltese pirates kidnapped a child from a beach between Tyre and Acre, again prompting the locals to seek official help: 'Le Pere de cette petite fille avec les Cheiks de Becharé sont accourus a Seyde et y ont beaucoup pleuré devant Ibrahim Pacha menaceants de saisir a leur péage toute les françois qui y passeront.' The consul was prevailed upon to intervene and ransom the girl at the *vali*'s expense.[58]

The French *'nation'* at Sidon had numerous direct dealings with the Shiite shaykhs, from whom they purchased cotton, wheat and gall nuts (for use in dyeing). Individual merchants were occasionally also accused of posting the

[53] ŞD 40:722, 723.
[54] Haydar Ahmad al-Shihabi, *Lubnan fi 'Ahd al-Umara' al-Shihabiyyin*, ed. Asad Rustum and Fu'ad al-Bustani (Beirut: Lebanese University, 1969), 8–10, 16–17; Soueid, *Histoire militaire*, 372–6.
[55] al-Amin, *A'yan al-Shi'a*, VIII:16; see also al-Zayn, *Li'l-Bahth*, 374–6, 394–7, 402–3.
[56] D.BŞM.SBM 2:22; MD 120:101.    [57] AE B/I 1020 (Seyde), fol. 137b.
[58] AE B/I 1019 (Seyde), fols. 182a, 185a–b, 195b–196a.

legal guarantee (*kefalet*) on the local shaykhs' tax farms in order to secure the rights to the cotton harvest in advance. The consuls sought to prohibit this 'dangerous business' (which stoked competition among the merchants) on the pretext that the shaykhs had so much power that it could prove difficult to make them honour the agreements.[59] The hinterland of Sidon and Tyre was generally seen as a lawless country where criminals would flee to seek refuge with the Shiites. In 1741 the tax farmer of Tyre arrested and held the captains of several French vessels in order to force the release of a friend who had been jailed for his debts; in other instances, however, the French extended credit or exchanged gifts with the Shiite shaykhs after successfully mediating between them and the Ottoman authorities.[60]

Their independent dealings with the French and the Ottomans, however, did not spare the Shiites from mounting pressure from the Shihabi emirs. In 1730 Haydar conducted a major raid on Shaqif, Shumar and the Bilad Bishara in which, according to a local monk reporting the event to his superior, forty Shiites were killed and hundreds taken into captivity.[61] After Haydar's death in 1732 his son Mulham launched an attack on the 'Ali al-Saghirs – supposedly because they had celebrated by colouring their horses' tails with henna. Mulham first took care to secure the tax rights to the Bilad Bishara from the *vali* of Sidon, As'ad Paşa al-'Azm, then joined forces with Salman Sa'b of Shaqif. Together they defeated the Bishara forces at Yarun, capturing Nassar ibn 'Ali al-Saghir and chasing his brothers cross-country all the way to Qunaytra; Salman Sa'b was awarded the Bishara tax farm while the 'Ali al-Saghirs had to appear humbly before the emir to ransom Nassar. The Sa'bs' alliance with the Shihabis is probably also the reason why Haydar al-Faris 'fled to Druze country' several years later to seek shelter with emir Mulham when his brother Ahmad, the taxlord of Shaqif at the time, was killed by the governor of Sidon.[62]

In 1743, however, Mulham committed the greatest slaughter seen in Jabal 'Amil up to that point. According to H. A. al-Shihabi, the campaign was ordered by the *vali* of Sidon after the Sa'bs and Munkars had failed to remit their taxes and began to encroach on the Iqlim al-Tuffah, which was then under Mulham's control. Some Shiite notables went to the *vali* and placated him with gifts and promises of loyalty, but the emir refused to accept any deal made without his knowledge and proceeded to annihilate 'the entirety of the Shiite parties' in a cataclysmic battle outside the village of Ansar: 'The earth shook from the noise ... and the Mutawalis' army broke under his attack ... The Lebanese [*sic*] pursued and plundered them, killing the majority of them.' Some fled into Ansar but the village itself was torched and

---

[59] AE B/I 1022 (Seyde), fols. 184a–b, 288a–b, 314a–315a; AE B/I 1023 (Seyde), fols. 30a–32a, 47b–49a, 227a; AE B/I 1025 (Seyde), fols. 71b–72a, 118a–120b, 122a–125a, 308a; AE B/I 1026 (Seyde), p. 554; AE B/I 1029 (Seyde), fols. 160a, 377b–378b, 392a–394b, 412a–b, 420a–b.

[60] AE B/I 1025 (Seyde), fols. 132a–133b, 278a–280a; AE B/I 1026 (Seyde), pp. 201–2, 358, 370, 580; AE B/I 1028 (Seyde), unnumbered fol., 2 December 1751.

[61] Letter from al-Labudi to Iskandar, 15 January 1731, in Butrus Fahd, *Tarikh al-Rahbaniyya al-Lubnaniyya: Bi-Far'ayha al-Halabi wa'l-Lubnani, 1693–1742* (Jounieh, Lebanon: Matba'at al-Karim, 1963–9), I:336.

[62] Shihabi, *Lubnan*, 29, 31; Soueid, *Histoire militaire*, 388–9; al-Amin, *A'yan al-Shi'a*, III:60.

the inhabitants put to the sword. The contemporary Greek Orthodox chronicler Mikha'il Burayk reported 1,500 Shiite dead – while the Christian families of Ansar were spared by a miracle of the Virgin Mary. The following year, the Shiites were able to inflict a serious defeat on the emir's Druze forces at Marj'ayun, but were held off from an incursion into the Shuf by the governor of Sidon.[63]

The Ottoman *vali*s were of course not uniformly on the side of the Shihabi emirs, and indeed had many clashes with them over the remission of taxes and such matters in the course of the eighteenth century. However, the growing tendency of the central government to rule through local intermediaries, to abandon authority to provincial *ayan* dynasties such as the 'Azms and to tribal potentates in the rural periphery, only served to reinforce the Shihabis' control in the region. If the state had formerly asserted itself in inaccessible, unruly hinterland areas by intervening in local conflicts and playing different factions off one another, its increasingly disengaged, hands-off approach favoured the preservation and consolidation of existing power relations. This policy is well summarized in an imperial *hüküm* from 1754, when the chancery noted with misgiving that the Bishara, Shumar and Shaqif fiefs in Sidon-Beirut were vacant because the previous tax farmers had thrown in the towel and refused to renew their *iltizam* commissions. No matter how much he tried, the governor of Sidon had informed Istanbul, 'whether with kindness, goodwill and coaxing, or with threats, warnings and severity', he was unable to 'engage those who had for so long contracted the *iltizam*s each year'. The Sublime Porte, dismissing 'their inane excuses for their failure to assume the *iltizam*s, and their desire for a reduction of the *iltizam* fee', ordered the governor not to yield a single *akçe* but 'to bring the previous tax farmers and … assign them the *iltizam*s no matter what'. Their accounts would be examined in the coming year by As'ad Paşa al-'Azm, who was now the governor of Damascus, and under the supervision of Mulham Shihabi, and any amount levied in excess would be returned to the peasants of the land. Further disciplinary action was threatened, if the veteran Shiite tax farmers of Jabal 'Amil still refused to serve as specified.[64]

## Nasif Nassar and Zahir al-'Umar

From about the middle of the eighteenth century onward there appeared a new factor which was to have a major impact on the Shiites of Jabal 'Amil and their struggle for autonomy: the rise of the Galilean taxlord and rebel governor Zahir al-'Umar (d. 1775). The story of Zahir, the leader of a local Bedouin confederation who acquired the tax farm of Tiberias, gained monopoly control of the entire cotton production of the north Palestinian hinterland and rebuilt the dilapidated port of Acre into the centre of an eastern Mediterranean mercantile empire before being

---

[63] Shihabi, *Lubnan*, 29, 31–2, 34; Mikha'il Burayk (d. after 1782), *Tarikh al-Sham, 1720–1782*, ed. Ahmad Ghassan Sabanu (Damascus: Dar Qutayba, 1982), 55–6; Subayti, 'Jabal 'Amil', 21–2; al-Zayn, *Li'l-Bahth*, 434–6.

[64] MD 156:77.

brought back to heel by the Ottomans, is one of the foremost examples of *ayan* rule in the eighteenth century. However, this also put him into direct competition with the Shihabis, whose commercial venture rivalled his own and with whom the effective border ran straight through the cotton-rich Jabal 'Amil. The leeway this great rivalry afforded the Shiite feudalists, before the Ottoman state stepped in and reasserted control in the person of Cezzar Ahmed Paşa, prevented the area's complete integration into the Shihabi sphere of influence and thus played a key role in preserving its distinct political character within Lebanon down into modern times.

The Shiites' relationship with Zahir al-'Umar did not necessarily begin on the best of terms. As early as 1721, the shaykhs of Bishara appear to have joined the governor of Damascus in an expedition against the rising power in Safad;[65] the Sunni Damascene chronicler Ahmad al-Budayri, for his part, connects the Druze–Shiite slaughter of 1743 with their participation in a larger Ottoman campaign against Zahir (rather than a merely 'Lebanese' affair) and in which the Shiites (under Nassar 'Ali al-Saghir) again sided with the government.[66] However, when an all-out war erupted between them and the Shihabis in 1750, it was Zahir's forces who helped the Shiites stand their ground. As always, the conflict is subject to highly divergent accounts: Shihabi claims that the Munkar shaykhs were encroaching on the Jizzin district and had killed two of the Jumblatts' men – a dispute which the 'Amili tradition, in turn, relates to a long-standing feud between neighbouring villages, one in the Shuf and the other in Jizzin, originally over a stolen donkey. In any event, Mulham Shihabi sacked the town of Juba' and massacred hundreds of its inhabitants, many of whom had apparently sought refuge in a nearby religious shrine. He then proceeded to ravage the Shaqif, Tuffah and Bishara districts, and it is likely at this point that the Shiites, possibly under the leadership of Zahir al-Nassar, sought Zahir al-'Umar's help and defeated the Shihabis near Marj'ayun.[67] Whatever the precise sequence of events, the alliance between the Shiites and the 'Umar clan in the 'great Mutawali-Druze war' is also corroborated by the Damascene chronicler Budayri.[68]

The Shiites' growing self-assurance in the following years is reflected in the French diplomatic correspondence as well. According to the consul of Sidon, Zahir al-'Umar's example was inspiring 'un nombre de petits cheks de la secte d'Aly, qui habittent les campagnes … de faire les tirans & les rebelles'[69] and demand ever higher prices for their produce or services. The French merchants' most eminent Shiite interlocutor was shaykh Kaplan (Qablan) Hasan (d. 1785), the tax farmer and effective governor of Tyre. Kaplan was in regular contact with the French about the building of storehouses for their commercial stock or the protection of

---

[65] Shihabi, *Lubnan*, 17; 'Abbud al-Sabbagh (eighteenth century), *al-Rawd al-Zahir fi Tarikh al-Zahir* (Irbid: Mu'assasat Hamada, 1999), 25–30; Rida, 'Matawila', 287–8.

[66] Ahmad al-Budayri al-Hallaq (d. after 1762), *Hawadith Dimashq al-Yawmiyya, 1741–1762* (2nd edn, Damascus: Dar Sa'd al-Din, 1997), 114–16.

[67] Shihabi, *Lubnan*, 41, 43; al-Zayn, *Li'l-Bahth*, 440–53.    [68] Budayri, *Hawadith*, 201–2.

[69] AE B/I 1030 (Seyde), fol. 207a.

Fig. 5  Peninsula of Tyre, early twentieth century

their ships in Tyre (Fig. 5), but in 1756 he threatened to break with them and 'faire toute sorte de mal à toute votre nation', even against the orders of his superiors, after pirates flying the flag of Monaco had seized men, women and children in a brazen attack on the harbour district. The case, which the French considered particularly awkward 'car ces cheks ... sont presque tous des rebelles qui se moquent des pachas, & même du grand seigneur', was resolved only after Zahir al-ʻUmar was prevailed upon to calm his Shiite colleague.[70] Just six months later, however, the French consul complained again that Kaplan was flouting the 'noble Capitulations' (France's putative commercial advantages in the Ottoman Empire) and his own government's authority by demanding compensation for the return of goods from a boat that had sunk off the coast of Tyre. Particularly galling this time was the fact that Kaplan had impounded the merchandise until the consul sought an official answer from the French minister of state to his request.[71]

By far the most powerful Shiite shaykh in this period, however, was Nasif Nassar. Nasif seems to have inherited the leadership of the 'Ali al-Saghir clan in 1749/50 after his brother Zahir Nassar, according to one account, died falling from the roof of a palace he had just built.[72] The French first refer to Nasif, 'un jeune

[70] AE B/I 1029 (Seyde), fols. 22a–b, 25a, 160a; AE B/I 1030 (Seyde), fol. 201b; AE B/I 1031 (Seyde), unnumbered fols., 9 May, 11 May, 20 August 1756.
[71] AE B/I 1031 (Seyde), unnumbered fols., 20 February, 22 February, 22 March, 7 April, 20 April, 5 May, 21 May, 27 June 1757; AE B/I 1032 (Seyde), fols. 162a–163a; see also Abdul-Karim Rafeq, *The Province of Damascus, 1723–1783* (Beirut: Khayats, 1966), 246, 260–1, 303.
[72] al-Amin, *Aʻyan al-Shiʻa*, VII:404.

homme de très mauvaise foi', in 1755, when he apparently not only refused to honour an agreement his late brother had contracted for the sale of wheat but also sought to reopen all the family's past accounts with the merchant in question, failing which he would arrest all the French who passed through his territory and bar them from using the port of Tyre. The consul at one point asked the governor of Sidon to intervene but was told he had no power whatsoever over the shaykhs; in fact, the governor hoped the French might transmit their complaint to Istanbul so that the Sublime Porte 'open its eyes' and restore order in the province! Despite Zahir al-'Umar's offer to mediate, the case continued to drag on for nearly a decade, and ended only after the death of the merchant when the French and Shiites went before the Islamic tribunal in Sidon to effect a settlement between the two estates.[73] In 1767, the French recognized Nasif as the 'grand chek des Mutualis' and felt obliged to present him with a gold watch, after he had come to Sidon to give the consul a horse ('which wasn't worth its feed') and pay his respects to the *nation*.[74]

Nasif Nassar is also the hero of a unique eyewitness account of Jabal 'Amil's history in the eighteenth century. First published in the pages of *al-'Irfan*, the chronicle of Haydar Rida al-Rukayni (d. 1784) is particularly valuable in that it presents a far less monolithic picture of 'the Shiites' than contemporary Ottoman, French or even 'Lebanese' sources. Thus the years of Nasif's rise to power were marked by numerous battles not only against Bedouin and Druze enemies but also between and within the Shiite clans. In 1757, for example, after Haydar Faris' nephew 'Isa had been captured in Shaqif, Nasif's brother Mahmud raided the Sa'bs' district of Shumar; the assault on the Sa'bs was followed up by Husayn Mansur of the Munkars a few years later in the Tuffah, while Nasif, supported by his uncles Kaplan and 'Abbas Muhammad, hit Shaqif and Shumar a second time. Nasif's other brother Hamza, on the other hand, had only just before besieged their cousin Wakid in Sham' in a major family flare-up; and in 1765 the Munkar chieftain 'Abbas al-'Ali together with 'Ali Mansur attempted to seize the family castle at Mis al-Jabal before he had his goats and other livestock stolen in a raid by Abu Hamd of the 'Ali al-Saghirs, but got his revenge by nabbing Kaplan (who was at the same time a cousin of his) and imprisoning him in the castle of Marun the following summer ...[75]

Given such a state of affairs, it was only natural that Nasif Nassar and the others would also be drawn into the continuous feuding between Zahir al-'Umar and his rebel sons in northern Palestine in these years. Nasif and 'Abbas intervened on

---

[73] AE B/I 1030 (Seyde), fols. 192b–193b, 201a–b, 207b–208a, 221a–223b, 238a–c, 239a–240b, 242b–244a, 245a, 280a–281b, 281Xa–b, 284a–b, 285a–286a, 349a–b, 360a–b; AE B/I 1032 (Seyde), fols. 17b, 86a–b, 98a–b, 115a–b, 182b–183a, 195a–196b, 198a–207a, 382a–385a, 387a–388b, 405a–410b.

[74] AE B/I 1033 (Seyde), fols. 207b, 275b–279b, 281a–b.

[75] Haydar Rida al-Rukayni, *Jabal 'Amil fi Qarn, 1163 h.–1247 h.*, ed. Hasan Muhammad Salih (Beirut: Dar al-Jihan, 1998), 27, 28, 33, 37, 40, 43. See also MD 162:93 and Sidon 2:2 regarding the Shiites' tax farm appointments in this time.

Zahir's behalf as early as 1754, the same year that Zahir complained the French had incited another Shiite (probably Kaplan) to write to the governor of Damascus in support of his son 'Ali.[76] Kaplan did join 'Ali in a major incursion into Marj'ayun in 1765, while Nasif and 'Abbas, backed by government soldiers, crushed 'Ali's forces only shortly after.[77] All the shaykhs of Bishara, the Tuffah and Shaqif, however, seem to have supported Zahir's other son Osman against Zahir, and against 'Ali, the following year.[78] These hostilities culminated in Zahir's capture of the villages al-Bassa and Yarun in the southern Jabal 'Amil, and a major battle against Nasif himself in late 1766.

However, like the Zaydanis (Zahir al-'Umar's clan), the Shiites also remained under constant pressure from the governors of Sidon and the Druze.[79] As Amnon Cohen has argued (in a study which still sets the standard in the field of Ottoman-Arab provincial history), their 'lust for power' never prevented Zahir's sons from putting aside their differences and rallying around him whenever they were truly threatened from the outside,[80] and it was not surprising that Nasif would ultimately ally with his more powerful neighbour against their common enemies too. The precise outcome of their confrontation in 1766 is disputed: there followed at least two more battles and local legend tells of Nasif's sons being kidnapped and held for ransom in Acre, while the French describe Nasif as Zahir's 'principal adversaire' as late as September 1767.[81] Both Rukayni and Zahir's biographer Mikha'il Sabbagh (d. 1816), however, suggest that a peace treaty was then signed which effectively placed Nasif and the Shiites of Jabal 'Amil under Zahir's overlordship.[82] In concrete terms, as the French traveller Volney indicated a few years later, this meant that Zahir assumed the legal bond (*kefalet*) on their tax farms, making him, rather than the Shihabi emirs, the Shiites' principal intermediary and guarantor vis-à-vis the Ottoman state.[83]

Rukayni confirms that Nasif acted as something of Zahir's right-hand man in the next years, accompanying him on punitive campaigns as far away as Nablus on several occasions.[84] The defining moment of the Shiites' alliance with Zahir, however, was the result of political events with implications far beyond the borders

---

[76] Rukayni, *Jabal 'Amil*, 29; AE B/I 1030 (Seyde), fol. 55a–b.

[77] MD 164:138; Rukayni, *Jabal 'Amil*, 42.

[78] Rukayni, *Jabal 'Amil*, 45–7; AE B/I 1033 (Seyde), fol. 131a–b.

[79] Rawfa'il ibn Yusuf Karama (d. 1800), *Hawadith Lubnan wa-Suriya: Min sanat 1745 ila sanat 1800*, ed. Basilus Qattan (n.p.: Jarrus Pars, n.d.), 10; Rukayni, *Jabal 'Amil*, 28, 35, 43, 44, 49; Budayri, *Hawadith*, 183, 199; al-Zayn, *Li'l-Bahth*, 458–61.

[80] Amnon Cohen, *Palestine in the 18th Century* (Jerusalem: Magnes Press, 1973), 83–8.

[81] Rukayni, *Jabal 'Amil*, 48, 51–2; AE B/I 1033 (Seyde), fol. 320a–b.

[82] Rukayni, *Jabal 'Amil*, 52–3; Mikha'il Nikula al-Sabbagh, *Tarikh al-Shaykh Zahir al-'Umar al-Zaydani Hakim 'Akka wa-Bilad Safad*, ed. Qustantin al-Basha (Harisa, Lebanon: Matba'at al-Muqaddas Bulus, 1935), 39–41; see also Ahmad Hasan Joudah, *Revolt in Palestine in the Eighteenth Century: The Era of Shaykh Zahir al-'Umar* (Princeton: Kingston Press, 1987), 26–7; Thomas Philipp, *Acre: The Rise and Fall of a Palestinian City, 1730–1831* (New York: Columbia University Press, 2001), 36–8.

[83] C. F. Volney (d. 1820), *Travels through Egypt and Syria in the Years 1783, 1784, and 1785* (New York: Evert Duyckinck, 1798), II:62.

[84] Rukayni, *Jabal 'Amil*, 56, 57, 60, 66, 68, 72.

of Syria: in 1770, as the Ottoman Empire was involved in a disastrous war with Russia that would end four years later with the humiliating treaty of Küçük Kaynarca, the Mamluk strongman of Egypt, Ali Beğ, rose in revolt and sent his lieutenant Muhammad Abu'l-Dhahab to seize control of Syria. This provided Zahir and the Shiites with an unprecedented opportunity to free themselves of the grasp of the 'Azms, who were once again in control of both Damascus and Sidon, as well as of the Shihabis, who were once more rallying to the 'Azms' side. In the summer of 1771 Nasif and the Shiites participated in the Egyptian forces' first siege of Damascus, then joined Zahir to defeat Osman Paşa in a battle on Lake Tiberias that has since been mythologized in local historiography and poetry (but is unaccounted for in Ottoman sources). The government forces, which included two viziers sent specially from Anatolia, were so badly routed that most died drowning when they tried to save themselves by jumping in the lake.[85] Eight weeks later, Zahir and the Shiites crushed the Druze in another battle so devastating as to drive al-Shihabi to new heights of rhetorical flourish ('There had never been such a terrible defeat, and many died from exhaustion. Some lost their minds, and many threw away their weapons and clothes. It was said that some hung their clothes in the trees and just stood there waiting for someone to come kill them').[86] After so much struggle the road was now open for Nasif and the Shiites to descend upon Sidon, on 23 October 1771, and seize the capital of the *eyalet* itself.

The Shiites' occupation of Sidon as allies of Zahir al-'Umar probably marks the apex of their power in the Ottoman period. The French, who had been anticipating this coup for months, early received Nasif's assurances that their interests would be safeguarded and continued to trade in Sidon under the Shiites' protection;[87] the following summer, in a battle mentioned even in Cevdet Paşa's Tanzimat-era *History* of the Ottoman Empire, some 10,000 Shiite and Egyptian troops fought off a siege by Druze and government forces after Yusuf Shihabi had undertaken to reconquer the area on the state's behalf.[88] Over the next years, the French consuls would report, not without a certain amount of admiration, of the Shiites' role in this 'révolution en Syrie', of Zahir convening an 'assemblée générale de tous les cheïks mutualis' and of his ability to mobilize up to 6,000 Shiite fighters, and of the 'grande sécurité' they succeeded in imposing on the whole region.[89]

[85] *Ibid.*, 58–62; Burayk, *Tarikh al-Sham*, 106; Sabbagh, *Tarikh al-Shaykh Zahir*, 100–2; Shihabi, *Lubnan*, 79, 87–9; Sabbagh, *al-Rawd al-Zahir*, 67–9; AE B/I 1035 (Seyde), fols. 94a–95b; al-Zayn, *Li'l-Bahth*, 509–18.

[86] Shihabi, *Lubnan*, 91; Karama, *Hawadith Lubnan*, 39; Rukayni, *Jabal 'Amil*, 64; Volney, *Travels*, II:71; Al Safa, *Tarikh*, 125–32; al-Zayn, *Li'l-Bahth*, 519–46; Soueid, *Histoire militaire*, 451–6.

[87] AE B/I 1035 (Seyde), fols. 15b, 23b, 45b–46b, 56a, 63b, 64b, 70b–71a, 115a–b, 121a–b, 128b–130a.

[88] Rukayni, *Jabal 'Amil*, 66; Karama, *Hawadith Lubnan*, 40; Sabbagh, *Tarikh al-Shaykh Zahir*, 113; Sabbagh, *al-Rawd al-Zahir*, 75; Shihabi, *Lubnan*, 92–4, 97; Ahmed Cevdet Paşa (d. 1895), *Tarih-i Cevdet* (Istanbul: Matbaa-i Osmaniye, 1891/2), I:334–5; al-Zayn, *Li'l-Bahth*, 563–91; Soueid, *Histoire militaire*, 431–48.

[89] AE B/I 1035 (Seyde), fols. 202a–b, 214a–b, 219b, 222b, 223a–b, 226b, 227a, 232a, 236b–237a, 253b–254a, 240b–241a, 255a, 257a–b, 271b–272a; AE B/I 1036 (Seyde), fols. 6a–b, 40b, 80b, 222a, 320a–b.

Ils sont braves et leurs premier succès, ainsy que l'habitude, ou ils sont de commander depuis un an, leur donne une confiance, qui vaudroit elle seule de la bravoure. Ce ne sont cependant que des paysans armés, qui ne peuvent pas abandonner leurs terres pour long-temps. Vaisseux autrefois et subjugués par les Druses, ils les meprisent aujourd'huy à un point inconcevable.[90]

## The forging of Lebanese history

The Shiites' relationship with the Druze emirate at this critical juncture in the late eighteenth century also provides us with a unique case study in the workings (and, as it were, outright fabrications) of Lebanist historiography. French consular reports from the time of the Egyptian occupation provide numerous, in their own way subjective, accounts of Druze–Shiite hostilities, but it is surprising to find that these have frequently been sanitized or distorted in Adel Ismail's *Documents diplomatiques et consulaires*, the largest published collection of primary sources on Lebanon's history.[91] Like any compilation of documents this one is of course highly selective; the main criteria for the editor, a former diplomat and later Lebanon's permanent delegate to the United Nations Educational, Scientific and Cultural Organization (UNESCO), as well as for the project's coordinator, Lebanon's then Director of Antiquities, *émir* Maurice Chéhab, seem to have been presenting texts which bolster the image of the Shihabi emirs as the natural rulers of historic Lebanon. To this end, numerous documents from the consular correspondence volumes (which are kept today at the Archives Nationales in Paris) were either left out, or, even more problematically, were abridged surreptitiously, their paragraphs rearranged and punctuation added or deleted, and all indication of their original location and pagination omitted.

In some cases the changes are cosmetic; in others, however, the editor has taken it upon himself to expunge whole phrases, including condescending remarks about the local population or references likely to be seen as confessionalist, such as to the forced conversion of Christians or regarding the Druzes' purported irreligion.[92] In fairness the Shiites too have profited from deletions, for example where the French characterized them as bandits, 'people of bad faith', 'hateful of Turks, Christians and all mankind', or excessively cruel towards victims of their brigandage.[93] For the most part, however, Ismail has sought to preserve the reputation of the Druze

---

[90] AE B/I 1035 (Seyde), fol. 227b.

They are brave, and their first victories, as well as the authority they have now had for a year, have given them a confidence that itself amounts to valour. Yet they are no more than armed peasants, who cannot leave their land for long. Formerly vassals to and oppressed by the Druze, they now look down upon them to an unimaginable degree.

[91] Adel Ismail, ed., *Documents diplomatiques et consulaires relatifs à l'histoire du Liban* (Beirut: Éditions des Œuvres politiques et historiques, 1975–99).

[92] Compare, e.g., Ismail, *Documents*, II:211, 252, 268, with AE B/I 1035 (Seyde), fols. 202b, 254a, 323a, respectively.

[93] Compare Ismail, *Documents*, II:196, 222, 253, 385, 386 with AE B/I 1035 (Seyde), fols. 114b, 223a, 255a; AE B/I 1039 (Seyde), fols. 113b, 113Xb, respectively.

emirs, in one instance excising all the unfavourable qualifiers from a consul's assessment of their military prospects: 'Les Druses devenus timides par les défaites [honteuses] qu'ils ont essuyées, [plus accoutumés à assassiner qu'à se battre,] ignorant surtout l'art des sièges, [et manquant de courage qui dans ce pays pourroit y suppléer,] ne prendraient jamais eux seuls, la ville de Baruth ...'[94] The most egregiously biased example of such editing concerns precisely their war against the Shiites in 1771. Here Ismail omits several documents which mention the Druze ravaging Shiite villages, deletes a reference to the killing of peasants in another and then doctors the account of a confrontation between them to make the Shiites, rather than the Druze, appear as the more violent. Compare the text arrangement in the *Documents diplomatiques et consulaires*:

Le hasard fit malheureusement que l'avant-garde de l'armée du Prince rencontra une partie de quelques cavaliers muthualis. Elle luy tomba dessus.

Faisant feu et le sabre à la main, ces cavaliers se deffendirent, mais la supériorité du nombre les força à plier pour attendre la jonction du chek.

with the original:

Le hasard fit malheureusement que l'avant-garde de l'armée du Prince rencontra une partie de quelques cavaliers muthualis. Elle luy tomba dessus faisant feu et le sabre à la main. Ces cavaliers se deffendirent, mais la supériorité du nombre les força à plier pour attendre la jonction des cheks.

After the shaykhs arrive and rout the Druze, Ismail drops another full sentence describing the latters' disorderly retreat and 'mauvais cômandement', to finally end with a tiny sleight relieving the Shihabi emir of some of the opprobrium: 'L'Emir, se voyant si mal secondé et abandonné, ménagea la retraite [in the original: sa retraite] et les Muthualis furent maîtres du champ de bataille.'[95]

In later years, the Druze and Shiites of course appear together as the victims of Cezzar Ahmed's atrocities. But here again, Ismail excludes those documents which mainly concern the Shiites, and elsewhere removes individual paragraphs dealing with their execution or the display of their severed heads in Sidon, their suffering presumably being less relevant to the history of Lebanon than that of the Christians and Druze.[96] Many other such examples may yet be found. In the end, it is as if the author, having already concluded in his 1955 monograph that the Shiite

---

[94] Compare Ismail, *Documents*, II:293 with AE B/I 1036 (Seyde), fols. 101b–102a.

[95] Compare Ismail, *Documents*, II:195–6 with AE B/I 1035 (Seyde), fols. 113b–114a.

As luck would unfortunately have it, the advance guard of the Prince's army encountered a party of several Mutawali horsemen. They [the advance guard] attacked them.

Shooting and wielding their swords, these horsemen defended themselves, but the numerical superiority forced them to retreat and await the arrival of the shaykh.

As luck would unfortunately have it, the advance guard of the Prince's army encountered a party of several Mutawali horsemen. They attacked them, shooting and wielding their swords. These horsemen defended themselves, but the numerical superiority forced them to retreat and await the arrival of the shaykhs.

[96] Compare Ismail, *Documents*, II:421 with AE B/I 1040 (Seyde), fols. 232b–233a.

community 'was not very attached to the land and had no link with peasant life' in Lebanon (cited on p. 61), then proceeded to tailor the evidence to back it up.

## Cezzar and the Shiites

The war with Russia occupied all of the Empire's resources and explains why Syrian affairs figure so little in administrative documents of the time, but in 1774 the Sublime Porte was ready to turn its attention back to the Arab provinces. Initially it confirmed both Muhammad Abu'l-Dhahab and Zahir al-'Umar in their possessions, so long as they remitted the taxes that had by then accrued, but then used the one against the other in order to regain control of the region. In 1775, abandoned by his erstwhile Egyptian friends, his traitorous son 'Ali and finally even his Shiite allies, Zahir was killed defending Acre. Cezzar Ahmed, a Bosnian adventurer who had made his name slaughtering Bedouin in Egypt and had most recently been in the service of the 'Azms and Shihabis, was awarded the *eyalet* of Sidon; he and his proxies would rule it with an iron fist until his death in 1804. The Shiite tradition recalls this period as one of unmitigated horror, marked by the extermination of Jabal 'Amil's indigenous feudal lords, the burning of its libraries and the end of its autonomy.[97]

It is thus tempting to explain the repression of the local Shiite population in the late eighteenth century above all in terms of the reassertion of Ottoman state power. The image of Cezzar as a particularly ruthless Ottoman despot is indeed shared by other narratives as well, his killing of Yusuf Shihabi (in 1791) and his oppression of both Christians and Druze making him one of the principal foils for modern Lebanese history. A close look at the sources, however, suggests that the local dynamics of the changeover from Zahir to Cezzar were more complex than the simple Egyptian–Ottoman dichotomy. For one, the Shiites' relationship with their Egyptian 'liberators' had begun to sour almost as soon as the latter were in control of the region. In early 1773 Nasif flatly refused Ali Beğ's request for help to put down a rebellion against his authority in Cairo, and many Shiites began to desert his and Zahir al-'Umar's forces when their siege of Beirut proved more difficult than expected.[98] Instead the Shiites quietly began to mend their fences with the Druze, first with the Jumblatts and finally with the Shihabis themselves, their mutual need for peace beginning to outweigh the advantages each had hoped to gain with Egyptian or Ottoman backing. In September Nasif led a Shiite force into the Bekaa Valley in support of Yusuf Shihabi, the mere appearance of which supposedly caused Osman Paşa's men to flee in terror and result in one of the most embarrassing Ottoman defeats of the entire encounter.[99] A few weeks later

---

[97] Al Safa, *Tarikh*, 135–40; 'Ali al-Zayn, *Fusul min Tarikh al-Shi'a fi Lubnan* (Beirut: Dar al-Kalima, 1979), 37–78.

[98] AE B/I 1036 (Seyde), fol. 250a–b.

[99] AE B/I 1036 (Seyde), fols. 252a, 259a–260a, 267b, 271a–b; Rukayni, *Jabal 'Amil*, 70; Karama, *Hawadith Lubnan*, 43; Shihabi, *Lubnan*, 103–4; Cevdet, *Tarih*, I:338.

the Shihabis convened a reconciliatory meeting with Zahir and the Shiites at Dayr al-Qamar, where 'les emirs témoignèrent aussi beaucoup d'affection aux cheiks muthualis'.[100]

Rukayni as well as H. A. al-Shihabi are remarkably reticent on these events; over the next months the Shiites appear to have stayed away from further confrontations and resumed their role of trying to mediate between Zahir and his querulous sons, as well as negotiating a peace with the Ottoman *serasker* (expeditionary commander) in the Bilad Bishara.[101] Just when Zahir seemed at the height of his power, however, his one-time partner Abu'l-Dhahab returned from Egypt to oust him at the Ottomans' behest. The Shiite shaykhs very nervously came to meet Abu'l-Dhahab at Acre in June 1775 but were finally reconfirmed in their posses-sions – perhaps a sign of their increasing irrelevance to the conflict. In any event, they did not hesitate either to turn on his deputy in Sidon when he was killed soon after, and finally on Zahir and some of his former collaborators, whom they arrested in order to reingratiate themselves with the Ottoman authorities.[102]

Given their more than equivocal stance in the final stages of the rebellion, it is perhaps not surprising that the Shiites would initially have a rather accommodative relationship with Cezzar himself. Upon his appointment to the governorship of Sidon, Cezzar apparently hoped the French might induce the Shiite shaykhs of the area to pay their respects to him, especially since they had been balking at paying the new taxes the state was asking of them;[103] during his first visit to Tyre in the spring of 1776 he made a point of staying with one of the principal Shiite notables there, and in the course of the summer he was joined by Nasif's cavalry as he set out to finally eliminate Zahir's son 'Ali.[104] In the autumn an agreement was worked out on the payment of the Shiites' taxes through the mediation of shaykh Kaplan, 'le seul des metualis qui ait toujours su cultiver les bonnes graces de la Porte', giving cause to the Ottoman grand admiral who had been sent to the region to complain of Cezzar's excessive indulgence towards the former rebels.[105]

The Shiites' honeymoon with Cezzar naturally had an effect on their recent reconciliation with the Shihabi emirs. The Druze were as divided among them-selves as the other clans of the region, and the Shiite shaykhs now allied with Cezzar lost no time in backing different factions among the sons of 'Ali Jumblatt and within the Shihabi dynasty itself. Cezzar fostered and exploited these rifts so as to strengthen his own authority in the coastal hinterland, sending the Shiites to fight various Bedouin, Druze and Turkmen groups and receiving Nasif's aid against his real enemy, the 'Azm governor of Damascus, in 1780.[106] The following year Nasif

---

[100] AE B/I 1036 (Seyde), fols. 257b, 261a–262b; see also Anonymous, *Tarikh al-Umara'*, 126.
[101] AE B/I 1036 (Seyde), fols. 291a–292a, 294b.
[102] Rukayni, *Jabal 'Amil*, 74–5; AE B/I 1037 (Seyde), fols. 55b, 88a, 94b, 131b; Sabbagh, *al-Rawd al-Zahir*, 96, 100, 104.
[103] AE B/I 1037 (Seyde), fols. 142a–b, 175a–b.
[104] Rukayni, *Jabal 'Amil*, 79–81; Sabbagh, *Tarikh al-Shaykh Zahir*, 179–80.
[105] AE B/I 1037 (Seyde), fols. 237a–238a, 244a; MD 173:253.
[106] Shihabi, *Lubnan*, 116; Rukayni, *Jabal 'Amil*, 80, 84, 89, 91; Karama, *Hawadith Lubnan*, 63; AE B/I 1039 (Seyde), fol. 28b; MD 175:351; see also Philipp, *Acre*, 61–8.

joined forces with Cezzar in order to restore Yusuf Shihabi to power in the Shuf, after the latter had been evicted by his brothers; the inhabitants of the Shuf, at least according to Rukayni, were so terrified of the Shiites that Yusuf himself wrote to Nasif supplicating him to withdraw. Nasif maintained that he was acting on official state orders, but nonetheless wrote to Cezzar so that he showed mercy to the rebel Druze.[107] As late as May 1781, Nasif and Yusuf were again fighting the governor of Damascus and his own Druze allies on Cezzar's behalf.[108]

The Shiites' favourable circumstances were not to last, however. Less than five months later, the French consul could report that:

Le Pacha après avoir subjugué les Druses, et avoir remis en place le grand emir Youssef qui avoit été chassé, il a resté quelque tems tranquile. Il y a quelques jours, qu'il est tombé sur les Mutualis, qui habitent les montagnes qui sont sur Sour ... Le premier jour Nassif le principal des cheks (princes) Mutualis, ayant voulu empecher les troupes du pacha d'entrer dans son pais, au premier combat qu'il a eû, ce chek a été tué.[109]

The death of Nasif Nassar and some 470 other 'brigands' in a three-hour battle against Cezzar's forces near Yarun on 24 September 1781 ('the fifth day of 'Id al-Fitr') for all purposes marks the end of the relative autonomy the Shiites of Jabal 'Amil had enjoyed until then. The remaining shaykhs were driven out of their castles and, after making a joint stand at Shaqif Arnun, fled to take shelter with the Harfushes in Baalbek; untold riches and the defenders' women were said to have been seized and brought to Sidon as slaves while the castles were all razed to the ground.[110] Cezzar apparently sent a series of reports to the Sublime Porte which provided several key details on his annihilation of the 'Kızılbaş', including that Nasif's son 'Aqid led a desperate last attempt against his army in the Bekaa in mid-October, but had to flee after this too failed. By the end of the year, the Sublime Porte had addressed Cezzar a rhapsodic letter of praise for the 'plenteous effort and service produced ... in the necessary display of zeal and perceptiveness in accord-ance with the buried treasure of your uprightness-concealing heart' (in essence thanking him for the hundreds of Shiite heads taken as trophies) and assuring him of the state's unending support as he continued to 'preserve the righteous from their evil and corruption and clean the land of the filth of their existence'.[111]

---

[107] Rukayni, *Jabal 'Amil*, 94–6; Anonymous, *Tarikh al-Umara'*, 141–2; Soueid, *Histoire militaire*, 471–3.

[108] Rukayni, *Jabal 'Amil*, 97–8.

[109] AE B/I 1039 (Seyde), fols. 120b–121a.

The pasha, having subjugated the Druze and reinstated the great emir Youssef who had been evicted, stayed quiet for some time. A few days ago, he fell upon the Mutawalis who live in the mountains above Tyre ... The first day, Nasif, the leading Mutawali shaykh (prince), wanting to prevent the pasha's troops from entering his country, was killed during the first battle.

[110] Rukayni, *Jabal 'Amil*, 99–100; Karama, *Hawadith Lubnan*, 68; Burayk, *Tarikh al-Sham*, 121; Hananiyya al-Munayyir (d. 1823), *al-Durr al-Marsuf fi Tarikh al-Shuf*, ed. Ighnatiyus Sarkis (Beirut: Jarrus Bars, n.d. [1984]), 35–6; see especially also Cohen, *Palestine*, 100–2.

[111] MD 179:172–3.

Fig. 6  Tibnin castle ruins (1997)

The 'Amili tradition of course supports this bleak assessment of the Shiites' fortunes after 1781, recalling how the land now fell prey to enemies, how its once powerful shaykhs died in exile as far away as Iraq, or were reduced to poverty and humiliation at home.[112] For all that, however, one may question whether Cezzar's reign really did bring about such a fundamental change in the Shiite community's situation. Subayti, for one, indicates that Cezzar had actually been intervening against Nasif on behalf of the shaykh of Hunin, and not intending to subjugate the entire Jabal;[113] the French consul reporting the capture of Shaqif insists that its occupants were well treated after their surrender, and that their flight to Baalbek was in fact coordinated with Cezzar in order to make the besieging soldiers think there was nothing left to plunder. The French also state that some of the defenders were given appanages in the area in order to support themselves after their defeat, and elsewhere suggest that the local populace may in fact have felt less oppressed by 'ce nouveau genre de gouvernement que par leurs cheks qui les devoroient'.[114] Above all, Cezzar's turn in power ultimately brought about little change in the Shiites' difficult rapport with the Shihabi emirate. Rukayni and the French concur that it was the Druze who took the lead in bringing Shiite captives to Cezzar in Sidon, while Ismail Shihabi took protection money and taxes from the survivors.[115] In 1783 the 'Ali al-Saghirs and others who had fled abroad returned to aid Yusuf Shihabi in a renewed clash with Cezzar, and were thus able to recover

[112] Rukayni, *Jabal 'Amil*, 100–3; al-Amin, *A'yan al-Shi'a*, X:182–5.
[113] See Zahir, *Qala'at al-Shaqif*, 79.    [114] AE B/I 1039 (Seyde), fols. 114a–b; 238a–241a.
[115] AE B/I 1039 (Seyde), fol. 113Xa; Rukayni, *Jabal 'Amil*, 100.

their home castle of Tibnin (Fig. 6). Only two years later, however, after Yusuf had once more got Cezzar's help to oust his cousin Ismail, he again turned on his allies and sent the 'Ali al-Saghirs to Acre where they were promptly executed.[116]

In the final analysis, Cezzar does not appear to have acted much differently towards the Shiites than other *valis* before him. Disregarding the unusual crisis occasioned by the war with Russia, the Egyptian occupation and Zahir al-'Umar's seizure of power between 1770 and 1775, Ottoman policy in the hinterland of Sidon and elsewhere was designed to maintain a dynamic, even violent equilibrium among the local factions with a view to maximizing the authorities' ability to intervene, arbitrate and tax. Thomas Philipp has indicated the necessity of breaking through the historiographical clichés associated with the 'butcher', many of which were in fact products of western observers or local historians of the subsequent period seeking to construct a particular picture of his tyranny.[117] Compared with the brief, liberating period of Zahir's rebellion, Cezzar's long reign as governor of Sidon and later Damascus did provide many occasions for the harsh reassertion of state power over the Shiites as well as other highland feudalists. The collective memory of his personal cruelty, however, should not skew the fact that Cezzar above all represented a return to the normal mode of Ottoman *ayan* rule in the eighteenth century.

## Conclusion: a golden age?

What, then, changed for the Shiites of Jabal 'Amil between 1666 and 1781? From the battle of Nabatiyya to the killing of Nasif Nassar, historians such as Rukayni, Subayti and Al Safa have laid out a narrative of Jabal 'Amil's history in which a golden age of vigour and freedom that peaked under Zahir al-'Umar is opposed to the descent into poverty and marginality that began with Cezzar Ahmed. This narrative melds easily into that of Lebanism, in which the Ottoman state and its tyranny also serve as a mere backdrop to the more noteworthy actions of the 'Lebanese emirate' that begins to take concrete form in this time. Marxist historian Mas'ud Dahir, for his part, has preferred to see the violence and oppression as class-based, and suggested that the 'Amilis' constant 'uprisings' (*intifadat*) be seen as the first manifestation of popular resistance to the increasing centralization of economic and political power in the hands of Lebanon's unified feudal regime.[118] In either reading, however, the eighteenth century remains largely idealized, providing the epitome of the pre-modern Ruritania on which modern political identities in Lebanon are built.

The crossing of local with Ottoman and French sources suggests a different reading. Much like in Mt Lebanon and the Bekaa, there seems to be a clear progression from the time when Shiite *mukataacis* are fully integrated in their

---

[116] Shihabi, *Lubnan*, 137, 141; Rukayni, *Jabal 'Amil*, 107, 111.    [117] Philipp, *Acre*, 48–61.

[118] Mas'ud Dahir, *Al-Intifadat al-Lubnaniyya didd al-Nizam al-Muqata'aji* (Beirut: Dar al-Farabi, 1988), 39–46.

own right in the provincial administrative apparatus, in the seventeenth century, to their increasing dependence on, and finally subjugation to, bigger players such as Zahir and the Shihabis in the eighteenth. Ottoman tax records in the decades before and after the founding of the *eyalet* of Sidon make regular reference to Shiite notable families such as the Sa'bs, Munkars and especially the 'Ali al-Saghirs as local tax agents; even after the crisis of the late seventeenth century in which the 'Ali al-Saghirs were fingered as accomplices of the Hamadas, they and the other shaykhs continued to enjoy a high level of autonomy and regular, institutionalized contacts with both the Ottoman authorities and French consular officials. The replacement of the Ma'ns with the Shihabis as the paramount leaders of the Druze, however, also heralded a new phase of Maronite colonization and Druze military pressure in Jabal 'Amil. From 1750 onward the Shiites thus began to solicit the support of Zahir al-'Umar as he extended his economic and political control over the north Palestinian hinterland, going so far as to help him and his Egyptian allies seize control of Sidon during their great wartime rebellion against the Ottoman state in 1771.

The cleavages between and among the Shiites, the Zaydanis, the Druze and various state authorities were at times so intense, and the tactical alliances across these lines so volatile, that none can be said to have consistently acted as a coherent political group. The Shiite occupation of Sidon nevertheless constitutes a turning point in the entire community's fate. The exceptional circumstances provided by the Russian-backed Egyptian invasion of Syria briefly permitted the Shiites under Nasif al-Nassar to triumph over the 'Azm governors, who as the region's leading *ayan* dynasty had most consistently sought to circumscribe the Shiite feudalists'

Fig. 7  Shaqif Arnun castle ruins (2000)

power, and to defeat the paramount Shihabi emirs, who had consistently been trying to expand into the Jabal 'Amil (and had thus developed a general pattern, numerous exceptions notwithstanding, of collaborating with the 'Azms against the Shiites in the eighteenth century). But it is the Ottoman and Druze backlash against this 'revolution' that would most affect the Shiites' long-term prospects, a backlash they perhaps helped bring upon themselves through their precipitate involvement with allies from outside the region whose reliability was by the very nature of that conflict uncertain. With the end of the Egyptian presence and the elimination of Zahir, the Shiites were confronted with the re-establishment of Ottoman state authority in the person of Cezzar Ahmed Paşa. This, we suggested, was in itself not as critical as is sometimes claimed, but left the 'Amili Shiites as a whole exposed and more dependent than ever on the Shihabi emirate.

The reality of the changing power ratio between the Shihabi emirs, who in the course of the century changed religion to match that of their Maronite subjects, and lesser feudal notables such as the Shiite *zu'ama*, is often obscured in the historicized mythologies of a common struggle against Ottoman tyranny or of blissful confessional coexistence. For most of the eighteenth century, political upheaval, the decline of central state authority, the relative neutrality of France and crises such as the Egyptian intervention were indeed sufficient to maintain the classical, generally quite violent equilibrium between competing highland factions in Sidon's hinterland (Fig. 7). In the nineteenth century, however, little would remain of this questionable golden age to stand in the way of the Shihabis' unifying vision for the whole of 'Lebanon'.

# CHAPTER 6

# From dependence to redundancy: the decline of Shiite rule in Tripoli and the Bekaa, 1699–1788

'The age of the *ayan*' is how Ottomanist historiography has come to view the eighteenth century, as local civilian notables, rural magnates and resident governor dynasties assumed the reins of an increasingly decentralized, privatized provincial administrative apparatus. The reforms adopted in this time, many of which had been made necessary or were accelerated by the debilitating war involving the Empire at the close of the seventeenth century, had important consequences in the Syrian provinces: the establishment of the Mataracı and then the 'Azm families as governors of multiple *eyalet*s; the awarding of lifetime tax farms (*malikane*) in peripheral districts such as Kilis or the Qusayr (and perhaps most notably to Zahir al-'Umar in Acre at the height of his power); and the institution of tribal settlement projects (*iskan*) designed to reduce banditry and raise productivity in borderland areas such as the province of Raqqa or in the coastal highlands.[1] The reforms thus also had major, though sometimes contradictory repercussions for the Shiite populations of the region. If the leading Shiite *mukataaci*s of Mt Lebanon and the Bekaa Valley initially benefited from the slackening of central control to regain nearly complete autonomy, after their long rebellion against the authorities, the concentration of economic and political power in the hands of new regional dynasts such as the Shihabi emirs would reduce them to dependence and finally lead to their replacement, towards the end of the century, as local intermediaries of the state. The Ottoman 'ancien régime' of the eighteenth century did not in itself predestine the Shiites' failure, but established a context in which traditional feudal lords such as the Hamadas and Harfushes could in the end not stand against their better-connected and more liberal competitors.

There is of course no precise moment when the system of Shiite tribal self-rule ceased to function in the northern highland region. The Harfushes retained their fiscal authority, though not their title of *sancak-beğ*, for much of the eighteenth and well into the nineteenth century. The price for their continuing role, however, was a

---

[1] See Bruce McGowan, 'The Age of the *Ayan*s, 1699–1812' in Halil Inalcik and Donald Quataert, eds., *An Economic and Social History of the Ottoman Empire, 1300–1914* (Cambridge University Press, 1994), 637–758; Ariel Salzmann, 'An Ancien Régime Revisited: "Privatization" and Political Economy in the Eighteenth-Century Ottoman Empire', *Politics & Society* 21 (1993), 393–423; Barbir, *Ottoman Rule*.

near-total subordination to the Shihabi household, which as late as 1680 had been no more than an equal rival for the northern Bekaa tax concessions but which now had to intervene repeatedly with the state authorities on the Harfushes' behalf. By the mid-eighteenth century, this chapter will argue, the Ottomans recognized the Harfush emirs as the primary representatives of the Twelver Shiite community in Syria in their capacity as subalterns of the Shihabis. The Hamadas, for their part, kept their tax fiefs for another two generations after being rehabilitated under the auspices of the Shihabi emirate in 1698. In some ways this period marked the apex of Shiite tribal power in Mt Lebanon, as the Hamadas became unassailable in their function as taxlords and arrantly dominated the local Maronite peasantry and clergy. Yet at the same time, their inability to forge new partnerships with an upstart Maronite commercial and monastic 'bourgeoisie' left them alienated from an important segment of their subject population, which thus began to turn to the Druze emirate of Sidon as its principal protector and guarantor of communal development. By 1763, Yusuf al-Shihabi had rallied to the idea of evicting the Hamadas from their farms, and lent his weight to a series of Maronite revolts which would bring about the definitive end of Shiite rule in Tripoli over the next decade and disperse much of the Shiite population of Mt Lebanon.

After their move to the Bekaa the Hamadas would participate (together with the Harfushes) in an insurrection against Egyptian rule in 1840, and from their base in Hermel the family indeed remained active in Lebanese politics well into the republican era. The eclipse of their distinctive, semi-autonomous rule under Ottoman sovereignty, however, must ultimately be seen against the wider background of imperial administrative reform and state modernization in the eighteenth century. As such the story of their marginalization not only reflects that of the Lebanese Shiite community in general, but also helps illustrate the profound transformation of provincial society in Syria as a whole in this time.

## The Voyvodalık of the Bekaa

The paradigmatic shift in Ottoman provincial administration in the eighteenth century is reflected in a change in the official designation of the government of the Harfush emirs in Baalbek: from the time of their restoration as local police and tax concessionaries they are no longer referred to as *subaşı* or *emin*, nor recognized as *sancak-beğ* of Tadmur or Homs, but are consistently named in chancery documents as *voyvoda* (voivode) of Baalbek or the Bekaa Valley. The Slavic term *voyvoda*, literally 'warlord', had long been in use in the Balkan provinces to designate local feudal lords in the service of the Ottoman state. In the eighteenth century, however, it also gained currency throughout the Asian provinces, where it could simply indicate a *sancak*-level governor (e.g. Diyarbekir; Hama) but where it appears to have been used especially in tribal-dominated districts (Kilis; Saruc) or for large nomad confederations (Yeni İl Turkmen; Reşwan Kurds). These voivodes, like their Slavic counterparts, were generally of the native population and not 'Osmanlıs' in the strict sense. The recategorization of the Bekaa as a *voyvodalık* suggests that the state would continue to recognize the Harfushes here as uncontested tribal masters, but no longer regarded them as integrated in the imperial military hierarchy.

The decentralization and privatization of certain administrative structures did not necessarily mean a decline of state sovereignty – particularly not in an area such as the Bekaa, which remained the chief granary of the province of Damascus (and thus of the imperial *hajj* enterprise) and which was covered in *vakıf* land. Fiscal documents from 1695 (also the year *malikane* tax farming was introduced in the Empire), for example, detail Ottoman efforts to assign individual concessions in the valley, including Shiite strongholds such as Ra's Baalbek and Hermel, to local notables who would defend them against renewed sedition on the Harfushes' part.[2] In 1699, Feyzullah Efendi, the vastly influential *şeyhü'l-İslam* who would be assassinated in the 'Edirne incident' of 1703, transformed the Baalbek district into a giant fiscal estate to benefit four imperial colleges under his direction. The ostensible aim of this investment, which still awaits a thorough study, was to revive the region following the recent tribal and mercenary upheaval, but already a contemporary Damascene observer implied that another aim was to strengthen the state's grip on the Shiite-inhabited villages from which Shadid Harfush had just been evicted.[3]

In any case, the Harfushes appear to have been back in control of Baalbek by 1702, when local accounts indicate that a Christian shaykh of 'Aqura in Mt Lebanon entered emir Husayn's service as *yazıcı*, or secretary, on account of his Turkish skills.[4] In 1711, French consular reports suggest, Husayn gave shelter to Haydar Shihabi and then supplied 2,500 troops to help him wipe out his Druze rivals at 'Ayn Dara and establish himself as sole emir of the Shuf – a contribution curiously not addressed in H. A. al-Shihabi or any other chronicles of the period.[5] If this put him at loggerheads with the governor of Damascus, who was supporting the rival Shihabi emir, it did nothing to compromise his standing with the imperial authorities: As the *voyvoda* of Baalbek 'on behalf of the former *şeyhü'l-İslam* Feyzullah Efendi', Husayn traded large amounts of grain, silk and cash through an agent in Damascus in order to send payments on to Istanbul. Upon his death in 1712 (at the agent's house in Damascus, according to Ottoman reports; in a popular uprising in a Baalbek garden, according to a local history), the outstanding charges were imputed to his agent rather than to his heirs, who were apparently able to produce receipts.[6] His cousin Isma'il bought himself back into the good graces of

[2] MM 9879:90–1, 464–5.
[3] Muhammad ibn Kannan al-Salihi (d. 1740/1), *Yawmiyyat Shamiyya: Min 1111 hatta 1153h – 1699 hatta 1740 m*, ed. Akram Hasan al-'Ulabi (Damascus: Dar al-Tabba', n.d.), 21. Deeds (*temlikname*) for the estate are recorded in the Staatsbibliothek Preußischer Kulturbesitz, Berlin: Ms. Or. quart. 1827, fols. 91b–116b.
[4] 'Aynturini, *Mukhtasar*, 64; see also Ma'luf, *Diwani al-Qatuf*, 286; al-Amin, *A'yan al-Shi'a*, VI:265.
[5] AE B/I 1018 (Seyde), 932–3.
[6] MD 120:168; MD 122:78; cf. Aluf, *Tarikh Ba'labakk*, 75. The year 1724 cited here is erroneous.

the *vali* of Damascus with a substantial gift of horses, mules and other goods, and was reconfirmed as tax farmer of Baalbek later the same year.[7]

The few sources available depict Isma'il's reign as a period of relative calm. In 1719, according to another local chronicler, he personally attended to the *hajj* caravan with a unit of 200 camels and as many musket-bearing guards.[8] Three years later, the Sublime Porte noted that his namesake Isma'il Hamada had rebelled by refusing to renew his tax lease on Jubayl, and 'roused up most of its subjects and sent them to the land belonging to the Kızılbaş known as İsmail Harfuş in the Baalbek district'. The order, however, demanded only that the imperial accounts (*ahkam*) be checked to see where these subjects should be taxed, and assigned no particular blame to the Harfush emir.[9] Around the same time, the Harfushes are also said to have forged an alliance with the Zughaybs, another (partially) Shiite clan that had recently emigrated from Iraq, to help protect the peasants of the northern Bekaa against increasingly frequent Bedouin incursions in the area.[10]

The Sublime Porte continued to view tribal control as the most urgent concern of rural government, and we find one imperial *hüküm* (from July 1729) addressed to emir Isma'il himself, courteously asking that he apply himself in ridding the area of the Arab, Kurdish and Turkmen bandits whose depredations had caused the religious notables of Baalbek to lodge an official complaint in Istanbul. This may have been a particularly sensitive situation for Isma'il, to infer from similar orders sent to the authorities in Damascus, Sidon and Tripoli, for the key perpetrator in the most recent attack appears to have been his kinsman: the previous month, a certain 'emir Ali' had ambushed a caravan of forty camels and mules bringing merchandise from Damascus in the mountain pass at Zabadani, imprisoning the traders and muleteers in the nearby village of Madaya, whose mayor was obviously colluding with him. The incident had been reported to the governor of Sidon, who together with the two other governors was more severely criticized than Isma'il himself for their inattention to security in the region.[11]

Only a few months later, however, Isma'il himself drew serious rebuke for having too magnanimously received members of a (most likely Shiite) gang that had been terrorizing the Beirut area and had been ordered to be deported to Cyprus:

After these bandits fled to Baalbek, [an] imperial envoy also came to Baalbek and found them there. When he showed you the imperial order and asked for them, you displayed crudeness, saying 'They have sought refuge under my protection' and did not deliver them to the envoy, sending him back empty-handed. You are answerable [for this] and reproved. Now this time, when this imperial order arrives, surrender them to the envoy ... and don't patronize and host bandits fleeing from Damascus or Sidon or Beirut or Tripoli or Hama or Homs![12]

---

[7] Ibn Kannan, *Yawmiyyat*, 194.
[8] Muhammad al-Makki (d. after 1722), *Tarikh Hims*, ed. 'Umar Najib al-'Umar (Damascus: IFÉAD, 1987), 238.
[9] MD 130:415.    [10] al-Amin, *A'yan al-Shi'a*, VI:151–2.
[11] MD 135:372, 392.    [12] MD 136:24.

Perhaps it was this episode that launched emir Isma'il on a more confrontational course with the Ottoman authorities and would eventually drive him into the arms of the Shihabis. In February 1731, to be sure, a sharecropping contract preserved in the Islamic court records of Damascus cites him in the respectable situation of renting the town of al-Labwa in the northern Bekaa for three years from its lifetime (*malikane*) tax farmer.[13] Just two years later, however, the governor of Sidon received word that Isma'il had absconded with his entire family and more than thirty sacks of money from the Baalbek *iltizam*, first crossing into Sidon to take refuge with 'the Druze emir Mülhem' and then returning to ravage the Bekaa with his and with Isma'il Hamada's help.[14] Shihabi backing must have proved efficacious, however, for Isma'il Harfush was back as voivode of Baalbek in the autumn of 1734, even if his days were numbered. In a *hüküm* to Damascus, the Sublime Porte now cited the rapine and injustices committed under his rule as the reason for the desolation of the Baalbek region, and demanded his head. An indication of how seriously the state viewed his misconduct is that for the first time in years, it is characterized as 'arising from his being of the Rafizi *mezheb*'. A parallel order to the governor of Tripoli, where the Sublime Porte feared Isma'il might attempt to flee, goes even further: again describing the Harfush emir as a Shiite heretic, it invokes 'the noble *fetva* given in respect to this sort of people' – a reference once again to the sixteenth-century juridical opinions of Ebu's-Suud Efendi in regards to executing individuals identified as Rafizis and Kızılbaş.[15] Five months later, a local chronicler could indeed report that the *paşa* had succeeded in killing Isma'il after lulling him into security and arranging a meeting with him; his possessions were subsequently ordered confiscated by the state.[16]

A contemporary Arab traveller to the region reported that the Harfushes were quelled in the year 1737,[17] but this cannot have been very consequential because the Sublime Porte noted that Isma'il's sons Husayn and Haydar and their men had 'robbed' the *şeyhü'l-Islam* endowment village of Hashmash the same year and later seized eighty sacks of wheat, forty-five of barley and another thirty of seed, which the *kadı* of Damascus had registered as the reason for the Bekaa's shortfall in tax receipts. Only at the end of 1744, after repeated orders to recuperate the stolen goods had gone unheeded, did the Porte finally order the Baalbek concession to be awarded to someone other than the Harfushes.[18] But on the ground, this was complicated by the inevitable internecine rivalry between the two brothers, in which the Shihabi emir sided with Husayn while Haydar was supported by the governor of Damascus. Upon the governor's departure on *hajj* in 1745, Mulham Shihabi was able to send his army into the Bekaa to remove Haydar and install

[13] Markaz al-Watha'iq al-Tarikhiyya, Damascus: Damascus Islamic Court Records 40:286. I am grateful to Brigitte Marino for this reference.

[14] MD 139:88–9; Cevdet Dahiliye 2805.    [15] MD 140:226, 311.

[16] Ibn Kannan, *Yawmiyyat*, 461; Cevdet Maliye 7539.

[17] Ahmad ibn Salih al-Adhami al-Tarabulusi (d. 1746), 'Rihla ila Halab wa'l-Sham', ed. 'Abd al-Qadir al-Maghribi, *Majallat al-Majma' al-'Ilmi al-'Arabi* 7 (1927), 349.

[18] MD 150:230; MD 151:41–2.

Husayn by force; virtually the same scenario was played out a second time in 1749.[19] The now permanent struggle between the Harfush brothers effectively ensured that one of them would always be in power in Baalbek – though at the pleasure of more important regional players whose proxies they had now become in a larger political conflict.

## The 'Kızılbaş Mukataa' of Mt Lebanon

The 1693–4 punitive campaign against the Hamadas, which involved thousands of troops from as far away as Kilis and Gaza, propelled the governor of Tripoli to the grand vizierate, ruined the Futuh district and led to the dispersal and death of hundreds of Shiites in the snows of Mt Lebanon, ultimately achieved very little. Already in 1696, as we have seen, the Sublime Porte complained that the 'Rafizi brigands' were beginning to move back into the area from Jabal 'Amil; two years later, the Hamadas were reinstated in the Jubayl and Batrun tax farms through the intercession of Bashir Shihabi. In 1706, after the Hamadas not only defaulted on their taxes but also robbed a caravan heading from Sidon to Aleppo, killing three men and making off with the cargo of silk, the governor of Tripoli intoned a familiar, plaintive refrain: 'So long as they are not struck and punished, it is clear that the state income will be lost and the people and tax farms ruined.'[20]

Much like with the *voyvodalık* of the Bekaa, the Ottoman state in the early decades of the eighteenth century had neither hope nor intention of controlling the tribal hinterland of Tripoli directly. The result of decentralization, this section argues, was that the area under Hamada rule began to appear as a nearly hermetic outlaw republic in the government imagination. The French vice-consul of Tripoli in 1705 remarked that the *vali*s had no revenues from Mt Lebanon other than what the Hamadas felt like giving him: 'ils en chassent les agas et les soldats et commandent en souverains sur les X.tiens'.[21] To contemporaries it was evident that Ottoman jurisdiction did not extend into the Shiites' mountain realm, which was originally defined in the *iltizam* contracts as extending from the Nahr Ibrahim, the southern limit of the Futuh heights, to 'the place called Soğuk Su' (i.e. the Nahr al-Bared) north of Tripoli, and later 'from the defile of Musayliha to the Mu'amalatayn bridge'.[22] In 1686, as we have seen, Sirhan could threaten to desolate the entire region from Hisn al-Akrad to Jubayl; in 1740, to cite another case, the Sublime Porte complained that 'İsmail [Hamade], known as the Kızılbaş *şeyh*' was forever providing bandits a haven from the law. Orders had been sent throughout the region to apprehend and extradite some criminals who had escaped from Tripoli, yet Isma'il gave them shelter for several days before permitting them to escape once more.[23] All the roads in the district, the senior consul at Sidon

---

[19] Shihabi, *Lubnan*, 35, 38.    [20] ŞD 40:722.
[21] AE B/I 1114 (Tripoli), fol. 116a.    [22] Tripoli 2/2:106, 134; Tripoli 12:145–6.
[23] MD 147:84; Cevdet Dahiliye 10864.

reported to the French ambassador in Istanbul in May 1742, were 'infestés par les Amediens'.[24]

Musayliha castle (Fig. 8) in the narrow valley just north of Batrun and the citadel of Jubayl were perceived as the border posts guarding the hostile Shiite principality. The company of Ottoman *mustahfizan* troops based in Musayliha complained repeatedly that they were not receiving all the allocations they were due from the tax farms of Hama, even though their castle lay 'on the border with the Kızılbaş';[25] an entry in the Tripoli court records in 1750 notes the appointment of a new *bölükbaşı* (commander) to the '*mustahfizan* defending the tower and bridge house at Musayliha' whose main duty consisted in 'protecting wayfarers passing the said spot on the road to Sidon and Egypt from the Kızılbaş brigands'.[26] The crusader-era citadel of Jubayl marked the southern limit of Shiite control and had a similar guard-post function. In 1731, for example, the Hamadas' *iltizam* contracts were negotiated in the citadel, as presumably neither the shaykhs nor the Tripoli court officials would venture across the de facto border.[27] Later the sessions were sometimes held in Kafr 'Aqa village in al-Kura or 'on the banks of the Badhidh River at the border of these districts', an area held by the Kurdish emirs who were on reasonably good terms with the Hamadas, and which perhaps served as a sort of neutral ground between the state and them.[28]

Within these territorial limits, the Shiites' lawlessness was, quite literally, legendary. The Maronite folk tradition, as we have seen in chapter four, remembers the Hamadas as the cruellest of all feudal lords, and as the only ones who would violate the peasant women. A French vice-consul at Tripoli in 1726 reported that the Hamadas had a strong 'inclination' to commit robbery, 'ensorte que quand on est obligé de passer sur leur terres, il faut estre tellement accompagné qu'on soit en état de pouvoir leur resister'.[29] Sometimes it seems as if their iniquity served as a bit of a legal trope, for instance in 1713 when the *qadi* of Tripoli denounced an obscure former deputy *naqib al-ashraf* for 'always interfering, uniting with the depraved Kızılbaş, inciting them, and constantly pushing them to kill and rob the *reaya* and other righteous believers'. The deputy defended himself against these accusations in an official complaint to the Sublime Porte but was nonetheless imprisoned in the island fortress of Arwad and later Raqqa for his supposed crimes.[30] In a lawsuit over a stolen black mule ('present here at court') in 1731, the court accepted the original (Christian) owner's testimony that it had been taken in a recent raid by the Hamadas and illegally sold (to a Muslim dignitary) in the Bekaa Valley, and thus ordered its restitution.[31]

The degree of the Hamada fiefdom's removal from Ottoman jurisdiction is reflected in a 1710 *mukataa* register for the province of Tripoli, where the Jubayl, Batrun and Basharri tax farms are listed as being assigned, 'since the

[24] AE B/I 84 (Alep), fol. 98b.
[25] Markaz al-Watha'iq, Damascus: Hama Islamic Court Records 42:212, 392.
[26] Tripoli 11:88.     [27] Tripoli 6:6–7.     [28] Tripoli 8:172; 12:144–7; 15:32, 98–9.
[29] AE B/I 1116 (Tripoli), fol. 92a.     [30] MD 121:1.     [31] Tripoli 6:75.

Fig. 8  Musayliha castle

days of their forefathers', to 'şeyh İsmail Hamade the Kızılbaş' and his brother and cousin, with 'Ma'n-oğlı Hayder Şihabi' posting the *kefalet*. Due to a revolt by Haydar Shihabi that year, however, the payments had fallen into arrears; Isma'il had taken to oppressing the poor villagers and 'does not listen to reason when he is urged to'. Only a few pages later, the same register indicates that nobody had taken out the contract on the taxes for the town of Jubayl since all of the inhabitants had fled the Shiites' depredations and no revenues could be expected. The governor, deeming the fortress of Jubayl to be 'essential for protecting the land and sea routes', had therefore supplemented its Janissary guard with twenty of his own men.[32] Not many of these were still alive a year later, however, when a second *mukataa* register appraised Istanbul of the deteriorating situation in Tripoli:

[Şeyh İsmail] continues his highway robbery and despoiling travellers of their goods. One day, in a moment of the occupants' inadvertence, he conquered the citadel of Cübeyl lying on the passage between Tripoli to Beirut. Castle-warden Yusuf and fifteen Muslims fell martyr. Our *kethüda* was dispatched to repulse their harm and villainy and take the tax farm in charge for the year 1123, but the said faction persisted in its atrocities and drove all the inhabitants with their beasts and livestock into the Kisrevan Mountain. They themselves took refuge and hid in inaccessible caves and canyons at the summits of this same mountain, and blocked in the inhabitants and prevented them from returning.[33]

The French vice-consul provides a slightly different account of this new confrontation with the state: Isma'il had indeed descended upon Jubayl 'and cut the commanding officer and twelve or thirteen of his soldiers to pieces', but only after the *kethüda* had laid waste to the Hamadas' houses and 70,000 of their mulberry trees. The rationale behind this campaign and rumours that the *vali* himself would take the field against the Shiites were received with scorn on the vice-consul's part:

S'il est bien conseillé il n'en fera rien, car il seroit batu. Si son [*kethüda*] lorsqu'il avoit pres de 4000 hommes s'étoit ataché a les detruire au lieu de couper des arbres il en seroit venû a bout et auroit conservé [100,000] Écus de rente par an.[34]

The spectre of a new war against the 'Amediens qui sont Turcs rebelles au G[rand] Seigneur' had first been raised in the spring of 1709 and the latest uprising had ensued from a skirmish with the *paşa*'s retainers the following summer, rather than in coordination with the Shihabis.[35] Haydar's victory over his Druze rivals at 'Ayn Dara in 1711, which Lebanist historiography celebrates as a defining moment in the development of a unified national regime, ultimately had little to do with feudal affairs outside of Sidon, but in strengthening his grip on the Druze emirate it did allow him to pursue a more interventionist policy in 'protecting' the Hamadas and other allies in the north. The French consul of Sidon now confirmed in 1714 that 'l'Emir est leur caution au Pacha de Tripoly' and actually spent very little time in the province of Sidon;[36] in 1717 he stepped in to avert a major clan war in Tripoli after the governor had conspired with the Ra'd shaykhs of Danniyye, the Kurdish emirs of al-Kura and the Mar'abis of the 'Akkar to assassinate 'Isa Hamada. According to the Maronite abbot Aghustin Zinda (d. after 1738), 'Isa had both been withholding taxes and trying to seize control of the 'Akkar when he was lured

---

[32] MM 3347:4, 7.     [33] MM 3348:3, 6.

[34] AE B/I 1114 (Tripoli), fols. 359b–360a.

  He would be well advised not to do anything, for he will be beaten. If his [*kethüda*], while he had 4000 men, would have moved to destroy them instead of cutting their trees, he would have prevailed and would have preserved [100,000] piastres of income per year.

[35] AE B/I 1114 (Tripoli), fols. 262a–b, 289a.

[36] AE B/I 1019 (Seyde), fol. 288a.

to a mountain monastery to negotiate a power-sharing agreement with the Mar'abis. Instead, he, a son and several Shiite and Maronite supporters were killed in a night-time attack on the monastery, while the survivors were taken to Tripoli and executed, and their heads sent to Istanbul. With Haydar's moderation, however, the local Maronite notables quickly agreed on the succession of 'Isa's son Isma'il as their taxlord, thus forestalling further instability and possible state military intervention in the highlands.[37] French diplomats, at first concerned over the negative impact a wider conflict might have on trade, soon noted with satisfaction that

cet événement est cause d'un trouble qui finira bientôt, car le Pacha de Tripoly ne fait de grands préparatifs de guerre que pour obliger Ismain, autre p[rinci]pal Chek des Amediens [Hamadas] ... d'en venir a un traitté de paix sous la caution de l'Emir des Druses dépendant du Gouvernement de Seyde et chés lequel ledt. Chek Ismaïn s'est refugié parce que ces rebelles sont tous d'accord pour leur propre conservation.[38]

By consistently posting the *kefalet* on the Hamadas' tax farms the next years, Haydar Shihabi did not necessarily put an end to the violence but managed to impose himself as the Ottomans' chief intermediary in the Tripoli highlands. In 1720, he stopped the *vali* from launching a renewed war against the 'Kızılbaş faction' after the latter had sent two expeditions per year for the previous three years and had still not been able to collect their taxes. Reinstated yet again with the Shihabis' help, the Hamadas waited for the government forces to depart on *cerde*, the annual pilgrimage relief campaign, then attacked and pillaged the Danniyye district. After the governor's son laid siege to them for twenty days in Batrun, the Hamadas resorted to the act of disobedience which the shaykhs of Jabal 'Amil used to great effect some years later: they refused to renew their *iltizam* commissions altogether for the next year, meaning that no taxes would be remitted at all for the area. Orders for a new campaign to bring 'these bandits clambering on the rock ledges of rebellion' back down to 'the main-street of submission' went out in the spring of 1721 to Tripoli, Damascus, Sidon and of course to emir Haydar himself.[39]

Much like the Ma'ns before them, however, the Shihabis sought to win the Hamadas' loyalty by giving them cover whenever they were being pursued by government forces. In the spring of 1727, for example, the Sublime Porte again found that 'the Bani Hamada brigands have forever been trying to lay hands on the

---

[37] Aghustin Zinda, *Al-Tarikh al-Lubnani (1714–1728)*, ed. Juzif Qizzi (Kaslik, Lebanon: Jami'at al-Ruh al-Muqaddas, 1988), 19–21; see also Faruq Hublus, *Tarikh 'Akkar al-Idari wa 'l-Ijtima 'i wa 'l-Iqtisadi 1700–1914* (Beirut: Dar al-Da'ira, 1987), 24–9, 284–8.

[38] AE B/I 1020 (Seyde), fols. 140b–141a.

...this event is causing a disturbance which will end soon, because the pasha of Tripoli is only making great preparations for war in order to force Ismain, the other leading [Hamada] shaykh, to reach a peace treaty under the bond of the Druze emirs of the province of Sidon, with whom the said shaykh Ismaïn has sought refuge, because all these rebels are in agreement over their own preservation.

[39] MD 130:117–19.

Jubayl, Batrun and Jubbat Basharri fiefs'. As a result of a punitive operation 'near the border to the place called Kisrawan in Sidon', which interestingly is characterized here as 'their native country [*yurdları*]', they had 'crossed into Sidon lands and started to ensconce themselves in the villages of the Kisrawan'.[40] The complicity of the Shihabis, who had undisputed authority over the Kisrawan as well as rural Sidon, is not directly alluded to, but 'Hamade-oğlı Kızılbaş İsmail' was back in power just two years later, when the Sublime Porte thought it likely he would again capitalize on the governor's departure on *cerde* to resume his sedition and therefore ordered the lieutenant commanders of Tripoli and Latakia to mobilize pre-emptively.[41]

In light of Haydar Shihabi's continuing support, simply rescinding Isma'il the Kızılbaş's tax franchise was just not a viable option for the Ottoman state. The apparent incongruence of its stance on Shiite tax farmers is well brought out in a report made by the governor of Tripoli to the Sublime Porte around this time, and which speaks to the inroads that decentralized or privatized rule was enabling *ayan* such as the Shihabis to make in the region:

> The Kızılbaş *mukataa* in its entirety constitutes one of the tax farms attached to Tripoli, and each year the ... governors have given it in *iltizam* to İsmail Hamade, one of its inhabitants, with Ma'n-oğlı Mir Hayder's guarantee, on the assumption that the people from the surrounding villages are then safe from having their properties stolen and plundered.[42]

The Ottoman authorities were to be very disappointed in this assumption, and the Shihabis would have to intervene frequently to assume the Hamadas' tax debts, restore them to their farms, or dissuade them from further revolts. In letting the Shihabis take more and more responsibility for them, however, the Hamadas were also opening the door to their more active participation in the local politics of Mt Lebanon.

## The Hamadas and the Maronite Church

As tax farmers of Jubayl, Batrun and the Jubbat Basharri, the Hamadas were the secular lords of the greater part of the Maronite population of Mt Lebanon as well as of the central institutions of the Maronite Church. The monastery of Qanubin, the seat of the Maronite patriarchate lying deep in the Qadisha Valley in the mountains of Jubbat al-Basharri, classical Maronite strongholds such as Ehden, Zghorta and Tannurin, and of course the many new priories and settlements that began to dot the northern highlands in this period were located on Hamada lands and paid their worldly taxes to the Shiite *mukataacıs*. The contemporary chronicler Zughayb recounts how Maronite settlers begged the Shiites' permission to rebuild an ancient church in Harajil, accepted the non-religious name (Sayyidat Lawza) and the layout they chose for it, and then got a parcel of land as well as a helping hand from them.[43]

[40] MD 134:86.    [41] MD 135:387.    [42] MD 130:415.
[43] Zughayb, *'Awdat al-Nasara*, 18–21; Malouf-Limam, 'A troubled period', 156–8.

This alone undercuts the old notion that the Empire's non-Muslim communities (*millet*s) were systematically left under their own fiscal and juridical authority; it also explains why the Hamadas regularly intervened or were drawn into profane and even ecclesiastic disputes within the Maronite community itself.

The most notable example of the Hamadas' involvement in Church affairs is their role in the election of several patriarchs at the beginning of the eighteenth century. The story begins in the autumn of 1703, when 'Isa Hamada and his retainers rode to Qanubin in order to collect an advance on the year's tax payment, as ordered by the *paşa* of Tripoli. But the venerable old patriarch Istfan Duwayhi refused, 'ce qui fut cause qu'il[s] le maltraitterent par plusieurs soufflets, et quantité de coups de bâtons' or, according to another version, caused him to be 'outragé et frappé au visage a coups de pentoufles par le Cheik Aysse'. The Khazins thereupon came with 600–700 men to take the patriarch away to the Kisrawan, while Bashir Shihabi worked to avert a full-scale Shiite–Maronite clan war. When Duwayhi died just days after returning to Qanubin early the next year, the Khazins insisted on holding elections for a new patriarch under their auspices in the Kisrawan to ensure that no bishop would pay the Hamadas for their backing 'et ce faire elire par force, ce qui est arrivé autres fois'.[44] These fears were not entirely unfounded, for no sooner had the new patriarch returned to Qanubin to take office than he too died, whereupon his nephew bribed the Hamadas 300 piastres to be elected in his stead before the Khazins could reappear on the scene. The French vice-consul at Tripoli reporting these events was well aware that 'ces infideles qui sont Gouverneurs et Maistres du Liban sont à Canobin et disposent des suffrages des habitants qui s'entendent avec eux'. But ultimately he was even more concerned by the Khazins' influence over the Maronite clergy, and therefore demanded they always hold the election at Qanubin 'où leur suffrages sont plus libres qu'au Castrevan'.[45]

In the end the Hamadas were persuaded to evacuate the monastery, and the Khazins to let their bishops come freely, each in hopes of increasing their candidate's chances of being elected. Vice-consul Poullard, who would later go on to become full consul at Sidon and later at Cairo, repeatedly congratulated himself for having bettered the Maronites' lot by impressing France's love for the patriarchate on the Shiites. In his greatest coup, he even prevailed upon shaykh 'Isa to provide a guard of honour at the lavish induction ceremony for the new patriarch in 1705 – as described in an expense account he submitted some years later to the royal marine intendancy for his personal reimbursement.[46] While later historians have used this episode to exemplify the 'Métoualis'' oppression of the Maronites, some of the contemporary French reports stand out for their sober if not downright sympathetic portrayal of the Hamadas. In 1710, the new vice-consul described 'Isa as a sprightly old fellow who loves the French; France's missionaries, the shaykh had assured him, would enjoy every convenience so long as his kin ruled Mt

---

[44] AE B/I 1017 (Seyde), fols. 407a–b, 467a; AE B/I 1114 (Tripoli), fols. 34a–b, 136a.

[45] AE B/I 1114 (Tripoli), fols. 123a–b (leaves misbound), 126b.

[46] AE B/I 1114 (Tripoli), fols. 116a–b, 136 a–b; see also Ristelhueber, *Traditions françaises*, 203–19.

Lebanon.[47] Barely a year later, this vice-consul had to intercede with the *vali* to ensure the safety of a local Carmelite monastery, where he feared the Hamadas might flee in the course of the latest punitive campaign. Despite attaining the requested 'bouïardy' (*buyurıldı*; gubernatorial order) the vice-consul in his official report heaped aspersions not on the refractory Shiites, but on the governor's wargaming which he predicted would end in total defeat.[48] Another time, the vice-consul intervened with the Hamadas themselves to reopen the Mar Sarkis monastery, after a friar from Franche-Comté had nearly caused a revolt by shooting a local Maronite peasant dead. As secular lords of the district the Hamadas were able to demand even more compensation than the victim's family.[49]

The most blatant case of the Shiites' embroilment in Maronite politics is the twisted scandal which involved patriarch Ya'qub ('Jacques') 'Awwad and which finally contributed to the assassination of 'Isa Hamada in 1717. 'Awwad, who had in essence been the vice-consul's choice for patriarch, was summarily deposed and defrocked by the Kisrawan bishops in 1710 for crimes both shocking and unimaginable: 'inceste avec sa propre soeur, êt une niece, sodomie, bestialité, êt homicides en la personne d'un de ses Religieux qui l'avois surpris in flagranti delicto avec sa soeur'. He was placed under arrest in a local monastery, for fear that his example 'n'attirât plusieurs de ses parents au mahomedisme', and that he 'ne récourut à la protection du chek des amediens'.[50] The French diplomats received strict instructions to remain neutral in the conflict, even as the opposing parties tried to draw them into it. For example, they were asked to help recover a large sum of money which 'Awwad had left with some monks of the Lebanese Order to hide from his Khazin-backed rivals. But 'Isa Hamada had found where the money was hidden, and assured the vice-consul that 'non seulement le G. Seigneur avec toute sa puissance, mais encore Mahomet ny Aly de la secte dont il est ne luy feroient pas rendre cette somme'. In fact the vice-consul had no intention of intervening against the Shiites, he advised the hapless Maronites, for shaykh 'Isa had learnt of the hiding place, and got the deposit receipt for the money, from none other than the patriarch's own nephew.[51]

By late 1712 the pope had ordered 'Awwad's reinstatement as patriarch, a decision which the French anticipated would be very difficult to enact vis-à-vis the Khazins and the agitated local community. 'Awwad returned to Mt Lebanon in early February 1714, studiously avoiding the Kisrawan and going instead to Jubayl to pay his respects to Isma'il Hamada, and from there to the Jubbat Basharri where he was honoured and fêted at 'Isa's mansion.[52] The Khazins were incensed over this snub, all the more so when the Hamadas reinstalled 'Awwad in Qanubin and

[47]  AE B/I 1114 (Tripoli), fols. 282b–283a, 285b.
[48]  AE B/I 1114 (Tripoli), fols. 348a–b, 354a–b, 359b–360a.
[49]  See Stefan Winter, 'Un lys dans des épines: Maronites et Chiites au Mont Liban, 1698–1763', *Arabica* 51 (2004), 490–1.
[50]  AE B/I 1114 (Tripoli), fol. 285b.
[51]  AE B/I 1114 (Tripoli), fol. 289a–b; Fahd, *Tarikh al-Rahbaniyya*, I:78–9; 'Aynturini, *Mukhtasar*, 150.
[52]  AE B/I 1019 (Seyde), fols. 136a, 274a–b, 288a; see also Fahd, *Tarikh al-Rahbaniyya*, III:264–7.

'comencérent à obliger les Maronites du mont Liban leurs sujets à reconnoistre leur Patriarche de gré ou de force'. Clercs loyal to the Khazins therefore 'si sono intrapresi un opera diabolica', to quote 'Awwad himself, and entered into open rebellion against the pope's decree. While the Jesuits, the Shiites and the French strove to have it enforced, an Aleppine Lebanese-Order monk was commissioned to get the governor's help to evict the patriarch anew. The governor in turn hired the Mar'abi shaykhs of 'Akkar to mount an assault on Qanubin with 200 men in early 1714, an act of unprecedented heavy-handedness which, though ultimately thwarted by bad weather, the vice-consul attributed to the Khazins' vehement refusal to see the Hamadas' candidate supersede their own.[53] Three years later, it was precisely this coalition of the governor's and the Mar'abis' forces that succeeded in killing shaykh 'Isa – a martyr, in the end, for the sake (among other contributing factors) of Catholic legitimacy in Mt Lebanon!

## The Lebanese Order

The Maronite abbot Aghustin Zinda, a member of the Aleppine branch of the Lebanese Order, also cites several 'divine reasons' for 'Isa Hamada's death, including his theft of money which 'Awwad had deposited with the monks (which 'Isa used for his son Ibrahim's nuptials, resulting in the birth of a crippled child and Ibrahim's own death shortly thereafter), and his extortion and general ruin of the entire region. In 1716, moreover, 'Isa attempted to confiscate some money which a Jesuit postulant had left with a French merchant in Tripoli and which was apparently also destined for the Lebanese Order. When this failed, he ransacked the church of Zghorta, seized its liturgical instruments, imprisoned the bishop, several curates and the Jesuit's whole family, reportedly threatening to have the men beaten to death, the women and girls raped, and the boys circumcised and sold as slaves. The French vice-consul quickly gave in to 'Isa's demands and had the amount paid out to him – leading to wild recriminations within the *nation* over the fact that the Jesuit had been asking for his money back for five years before 'Isa got wind of it.[54]

Shiite misrule, we remarked in chapter 4, was a key part of the narrative of Maronite entitlement to the Kisrawan and Mt Lebanon, integral to the 'recolonization' drive through which the Khazins established themselves as secular leaders of the community in the late seventeenth and early eighteenth centuries and thus a veritable *raison d'être* for the Lebanese Order of St Antoine. As early as 1706 and 1707, Maronite documents refer to the foundation of new priories 'outside the despotic Hamadas' lands' in the Kisrawan and Shuf;[55] in 1720, the monks suggested to the Apostolic See that French moneys be used to purchase the tax

[53] AE B/I 1019 (Seyde), fols. 274a–275a, 305a–b; AE B/I 1114 (Tripoli), fols. 456a–462b.
[54] Zinda, *al-Tarikh al-Lubnani*, 15–18; AE B/I 1115 (Tripoli), fols. 3a–4a, 5a–10b, 41a–49a, 50a, 53a–54a. The postulant, a former archbishop of Ehden, had been a key figure in the drive to depose patriarch 'Awwad; see Heyberger, *Les chrétiens du Proche-Orient*, 417–18, 463.
[55] Fahd, *Tarikh al-Rahbaniyya*, I:85–6, II:31; III:251.

concessions in the Shihabis' name and 'liberate north Lebanon from the Hamadas' oppression'.[56] In 1725, to cite another example, the Hamadas attacked a Khazin shaykh who had come to visit the patriarch, demanding he cede control of the 'Akkar district which they claimed was theirs by right of inheritance. The monks of Quzhayya, according to this account, drove off the assailants, giving way to a renewed war between the Hamadas and the Khazins.[57] Numerous later sources relating to the Order reiterate the Druze–Maronite condominium's role in

the revival of the lands of Jubayl and Batrun, and the reassurance of its people who had fled it because of the Shiites' tyranny and their ruining the lands. What pain and hardships and toil and misery did the friars endure for the sake of building these monasteries and reviving these ruined properties, and defending them from the depredations of the Shiites who had no sympathy for them in these works.[58]

In reality, some of these documents offer a much more nuanced picture of the Hamadas' relationship with the Lebanese monks. 'Isa himself is recorded to have rented lands in 'Akkar to the Order in 1713;[59] other properties were sold or even given in trust to Maronite priories such as Dayr Kafifan and exempted from taxation.[60] Isma'il Hamada was a much respected acquaintance of the Order's superior Tuma al-Labudi (who once narrowly prevented several Shiites travelling with him from lynching a group of rival monks for him), and helped reinstate a disgraced metropolitan at his request in 1735.[61] Countless documents in the patriarchal archives at Bkerke and from individual communities, only a part of which have been discovered thus far, refer to land sales or grants by the Hamadas around the middle of the century.[62] In 1754, Haydar and Husayn Hamada issued the local ('Baladi' or 'Jabali') branch of the Order patents which gave them exclusive control of the most important monasteries of Jubbat al-Basharri.[63] In Batrun, Isma'il's brother Ibrahim supervised the bequest of the garden village of Hub, described as an 'earthly paradise', as a tax-exempt foundation. The land apparently fell into ruin after the donor's death when some relatives, backed by the Khazins, challenged the will. Ibrahim of his own initiative then invited the friars to return and revive the land which was theirs by right, thus effectively embarrassing the Khazins into giving their consent also.[64] The Hamadas' patronage of the Baladi

---

[56] Butrus al-Tayyah, 'Risala Tuhaddithu Thawra fi Tarikh Lubnan', *Awraq Lubnaniyya* 8 (1957), 364.

[57] Fahd, *Tarikh al-Rahbaniyya*, I:81–2; see also Mohasseb-Saliba, 'Monastères doubles', 486–7.

[58] Luwis Bulaybil, *Tarikh al-Rahbaniyya al-Lubnaniyya al-Maruniyya*, 3 vols. (Cairo, 1924), II:276–8; see also citations in Fahd, *Tarikh al-Rahbaniyya*, I:87, IV:352; Yusuf Daghir, private manuscript quoted in Sharbal Daghir, *Tannurin fi'l-Hiqba al-'Uthmaniyya: Hajar, Bashar, 'Amir wa-Dat[h]ir* (Beirut: al-Firat, 2006), 26.

[59] Fahd, *Tarikh al-Rahbaniyya*, II:489.

[60] Abi-'Abdallah, *Milaff*, 121–2, 228. Dayr Kafifan also received lands belonging to 'Umar Hamada after the family's eviction from Mt Lebanon.

[61] Correspondence in Fahd, *Tarikh al-Rahbaniyya*, II:118–19, 349–50; Mohasseb-Saliba, 'Monastères doubles', 127.

[62] E.g. www.mountlebanon.org/deed.html; Hamada, *Tarikh al-Shi'a*, II:246–52, 266–7.

[63] Bulaybil, *Tarikh al-Rahbaniyya*, II:156; see also Fahd, *Tarikh al-Rahbaniyya*, IV:211–12.

[64] Bulaybil, *Tarikh al-Rahbaniyya*, II:276–7; Fahd, *Tarikh al-Rahbaniyya*, III:133–4.

branch is evident right up until the end of their rule: just prior to an October 1763 synod at which the Lebanese Order was, in principle, sworn to eternal indivisibility, Sulayman Hamada paid tribute to a separate meeting of Baladi monks by taking away the Mar Antuniyus monastery from the Aleppine branch and giving control to them.[65]

It would thus seem that Shiite 'oppression' was very much a question of perspective. The historical accounts that have established the Hamadas' reputation in this regard arose largely out of their struggle with the Khazins, in which 'protecting' the patriarch was always at stake, as well as from intra-Maronite conflicts over certain monasteries and other properties. In particular, the scission of the Lebanese Order, beginning in 1754, into the mutually antagonistic Aleppine and Baladi branches, which reflected a profound conflict between local and Latin Church influences in the Maronite community and whose importance in Lebanon's history probably remains underestimated, will also have coloured the way the Hamadas were recalled in later ecclesiastic sources. For the Shihabis, as Bernard Heyberger has shown, reaffirming Rome's central authority and strengthening the hand of the local bishops vis-à-vis the more diffuse power of the Aleppine monks and the patriarchate may have been a means of consolidating their own secular rule over the Maronite community in this time.[66] The Hamadas' sometimes ambiguous rapport with various local actors and institutions of the Maronite Church, of which much more can doubtless still be learnt from monastic archives in Lebanon and abroad, must be seen as part of the wider evolution of *ayan* rule in northern Lebanon in the eighteenth century rather than as proof of their perpetual malice.

## The inversion of power

If the Hamadas were frequently drawn into intra-Maronite disputes, the opposite was also true: beginning in the early decades of the eighteenth century we have more and more evidence of conflicts within the Hamada clan itself, in which rival groups of Christian supporters came to play a role. After 'Isa's murder in 1717, his sons and nephews initially disputed his succession in Jubbat Basharri, before dividing the district into six sub-fiefs.[67] Then in late 1720, Isma'il sent letters to the government in Tripoli stating the reason for his refusal to renew his concession on Jubayl and Batrun: 'I will not take the *mukataa*s this year. I have fallen out with my family and relatives.'[68] While this estrangement may have been a bit contrived, Zinda tells of a more serious feud in 1728 between 'Isa's sons Isma'il and Ibrahim and their cousins in Jubbat Basharri, who had the backing of the local monks as well as of the patriarch. What followed was a generalized war between the Jubayl/Batrun and Basharri branches (with the Harfushes reportedly also drawn in at one point) in which the other's monasteries were targeted; in one particular outrage a

---

[65] Bulaybil, *Tarikh al-Rahbaniyya*, II:264–5; Fahd, *Tarikh al-Rahbaniyya*, IV:336–7.
[66] Bernard Heyberger, *Hindiyya: Mystique et criminelle (1720–1798)* (Paris: Aubier, 2001), 269–70.
[67] Zinda, *al-Tarikh al-Lubnani*, 22–3.     [68] MD 130:117, 118.

Hamada shaykh apparently went so far, after getting the door slammed in his face when he came to kill an enemy friar at Quzhayya, as to beat up the monastery donkey tied up outside.[69] In 1738, renewed strife between Isma'il and his cousins in Basharri caused one group of local monks to try and destroy the others' priories. Isma'il was subsequently able to take control of the district, and was reconciled with some of his cousins but not with others.[70]

But it is in the business of tax farming that the Hamadas' involvement with, and finally dependence on, their Christian subjects become most evident. Already in 1726, the Hamadas convened a large assembly of village shaykhs under their authority to discuss how to respond to a massive increase in the tax payment bond demanded by the *vali*. In the end, the majority decided not to provide the guarantee on the Hamadas' concession but rather to quit the region for a few years, so that it would go to ruin and the increase would have to be rescinded.[71] The Hamadas' *iltizam* contracts, which are extant again from 1731 onward, indeed point to the changing nature of their relationship with their agents and guarantors. In general, the terms of payment, including the amounts to be remitted, are the same as in the earlier contracts discussed in chapter 3. The most significant difference in the newer series appears to be the systematic inclusion of one or several independent bondsmen (*kafil*) rather than the vague mention of a collective guarantee for the *iltizam* on the part of the family. In 1738, the Hamadas initially placed a security hostage in residence with the Kurdish emirs of al-Kura, but the latter were ordered to surrender him to Tripoli in the course of the summer, and thereafter posted a cash guarantee on their friends' tax farm.[72] The Hamadas' increasingly strained relationship with the state authorities in this period is also reflected in the fact that they no longer came down to the capital to renew their commissions every year, but were now almost always represented by an officially accredited agent (*wakil*) at court. With time, these *kafil*s and *wakil*s would emerge as powerful new partners in the Hamadas' tax farming enterprise.

Most of the Hamadas' *iltizam*s in the eighteenth century were guaranteed by a whole team of village shaykhs from the district concerned. These shaykhs, who came from between three (as in the case of Batrun) and eighteen (Jubayl country) different villages, are named individually in the contract and thus ensured the distribution of the tax farmers' fiscal liability over the entire local population. The Hermel farm in the northern Bekaa was occasionally underwritten by İki Kapulı Süleyman Ağa, a janissary commander from Homs and himself the tax farmer of Hisn al-Akrad. In 1751, however, the contract was sworn in front of an Orthodox cleric acting as the Muslim *qadi*'s deputy, and not subject to a specific *kefalet*. Of all the Hamadas' *iltizam*s, only Batrun was regularly co-guaranteed by a Muslim

[69] Zinda, *al-Tarikh al-Lubnani*, 226; correspondence in Fahd, *Tarikh al-Rahbaniyya*, I:167.
[70] Fahd, *Tarikh al-Rahbaniyya*, II:248, 449.
[71] Zinda, *al-Tarikh al-Lubnani*, 65–6; Fahd, *Tarikh al-Rahbaniyya*, III:62–3.
[72] Tripoli 7:101, 130.

(probably Shiite) village shaykh; almost all the other *kafil*s were, like the vast majority of the highland population, Maronite Christians.[73]

The infighting within the Hamada family is reflected in the *iltizam* contracts for the Jubbat al-Basharri, which beginning in 1748 was parcelled out to as many as five different brothers.[74] What is interesting about these partial contracts, unlike those for Jubayl and Batrun which were sometimes shared amicably between two or three brothers of the southern branch, is that they were generally underwritten by the same village shaykhs who were already representing them as their *wakil*s in court, and that it is stipulated these guarantors would 'mutually bond each other' for the payment of the *iltizam* as well as for the tax farmer's good conduct. From 1752 onward, this formula is encountered in virtually all of the Hamadas' tax contracts, including those where the *kefalet* was provided by a whole group of village shaykhs.[75] While this may reflect a semantic shift more than a legal innovation, it indicates that the responsibility that was once assigned collectively to the entire Hamada family for the discharge of their tax farms is, around the middle of the eighteenth century, being transferred to the subject population of each individual district.

In any event, it is precisely the village shaykhs named in our documents – Jirjis Bulus al-Duwayhi of Ehden, Ilyas Abu Yusuf of Kafr Sghab, and 'Isa Musa al-Khuri and Yuhanna Dahir of Basharri, according to the Maronite chronicler 'Aynturini – who then led the revolt against the Hamadas in Jubbat al-Basharri in 1759.[76] For the next two years these shaykhs exercised the tax farm themselves, then ceded it to the Ra'd family. The Ra'ds, who had kicked the Hamadas out of Danniyye two decades earlier, had in fact provided the guarantee on their *iltizam* for Jubbat Basharri in 1759.[77] In the Jubayl and Batrun fiefs, where the Hamadas would be driven out four years later (see below), the *kefalet* was provided by the sons of Yusuf Dahdah, the Maronite shaykh of al-'Aqura who had joined the Hamadas after serving as the Harfushes' *yazıcı* in Baalbek at the beginning of the century. The Dahdahs were granted numerous properties in the region but were forced to sell these when the Hamadas defaulted on their payment, causing them to turn on their erstwhile patrons and lobby for the farms to be awarded to the Shihabis instead. Thereafter they administered the Jubayl and Batrun farms as *mutawalli* (trustee) on the Shihabis' behalf.[78] The Shihabis, as we have seen, had frequently guaranteed the Hamadas' commissions in the past; in 1749 Mulham posted the *kefalet* on their combined tax debt for Basharri, Jubayl and Batrun, then took over the farms temporarily four years later as they began to enter into conflict with the local Maronite shaykhs.[79] Thus when the Shihabis, the Maronite lay aristocracy and other local notables finally joined forces in 1763 to replace the Shiite *mukataacı*s altogether, it was really after decades of experience as their

---

[73] Tripoli 6:6–7; 7:5–7, 10, 45–7, 287, 290; 8:170–2, 329; 9:139–40; 10:47; 12:34, 144–6.
[74] Tripoli 10:25–7; 12:153–6; 14:294–8.
[75] Tripoli 12:146–7, 178; 14:375–6; 15:32–3, 98–9; 17:17–19; 21:29.
[76] 'Aynturini, *Mukhtasar*, 132–5.    [77] Tripoli 15:194, 210; al-Samad, *Tarikh al-Danniyya*, 29–35.
[78] 'Aynturini, *Mukhtasar*, 65; Hattuni, *Nubdha Tarikhiyya*, 99, 153–4.    [79] Tripoli 10:262; 13:146–7.

agents, guardians and warrantors vis-à-vis the Ottoman authorities. Much like in Jabal 'Amil, where *ayan* such as Zahir al-'Umar and even some foreign merchants were providing guarantees on local tax farms in order to acquire a vested interest in them, the Hamadas in the second half of the eighteenth century had given their partners and creditors both the reasons and the means to intervene and implant a more judicious, fiscally beneficial form of governance in Mt Lebanon.

## The Shihabi emirate's Shiite subsidiary in Baalbek

The reign of the Harfushes, and in particular the struggle for power that ensued between Haydar and Husayn after the death of their father in 1735, was largely seen as disastrous for the Bekaa region. We have already referred to their ravages of the *şeyhü'l-İslam* village of Hashmash. Then around 1745, according to the Greek Catholic (Melkite) chronicler Karama, Husayn took sides in a local dispute and killed a shaykh of Ra's Baalbek, leading the patriarch to place an interdict on the priests who had denounced him. The same year, Husayn imprisoned the local metropolitan to force him to come up with the surety for his *iltizam* concession, so that the latter had to go collecting alms at Homs and quit the region soon afterwards to move to Beirut with his family. Later, Haydar's henchmen seized and beheaded a vicar associated with Husayn, after he had refused to save himself by apostatizing.[80] 'Noble orders were promulgated time and again to eliminate their vice and let right be done,' but in 1746 'the thug called Harfuşi İsmail-oğlı mir Hüseyin of the abominable extremist [*ghulat*] Shiites' committed the greatest outrage against Ottoman society imaginable: for reasons not explicitly stated, but 'in insubordination to the holy law and the royal decrees, and openly displaying the signs of heresy', Husayn had been badgering the *mufti* of Baalbek to devise legal rulings favourable to himself, and when this failed, had him hanged. This ad hoc execution of a Muslim religious dignitary (and the expropriation of his belongings) caused an outcry throughout Syria, with various provincial officials now writing to Istanbul to complain of the Harfushes' tyranny and transgressions. In response, the Sublime Porte could only reiterate its earlier orders: 'From now on, do not assign the Baalbek *mukataa* to this thug Hüseyin ... nor to any relatives or family or followers of his reprehensible lineage ... Give it to someone just.'[81]

In the end these noble intentions only went so far as to reassign the tax farm to Haydar. The Ottomans mounted a campaign to catch Husayn and bring him to justice, but soon had to admit that his whereabouts were unknown. By the fall of 1747 they had their answer: he had of course sought refuge with Mulham Shihabi. Worse, with the latter's backing, he had 'gathered three or four hundred bandits and attacked a caravan going from Damascus to Beirut, stealing 100 bags of goods. Furthermore, he ruined the villages around Baalbek and burned their provisions, then attacked wayfarers around Baalbek.'[82] There was, however, little the state was

---

[80] Karama, *Hawadith Lubnan*, 8–9, 10, 12.    [81] MD 152:170–1, 245, 256.
[82] MD 153:69, 120; see also Budayri, *Hawadith*, 138.

willing or able to do. The Shihabis themselves were threatening to wrest control of the Bekaa Valley from the 'Azm governors of Damascus at this time, while Husayn was reputed to enjoy the protection of the *kızlar ağası*, the imperial chief black eunuch, who, as overseer of the royal family's pious foundations, had a disproportionate say in the administration of the Bekaa.[83] It is in this context that the Sublime Porte issued Husayn a rather improbable writ of forgiveness just two months later:

The ex-*mültezim* of the Baalbek tax-fief, Harfuş-oğlı (may his power be augmented), sent a petition to my noble threshold, pointing out that as tax farmer of the said district, he always paid and submitted the *miri* tax to the venerable officials on time and with interest, received its quittances, and never undertook anything against the holy law. Then the sons of the deceased *müfti* of Baalbek, Yahya Efendi, accused him of murder and petitioned for the return of their belongings … [An officer] was sent who attacked [Husayn] and robbed and plundered all his goods and effects and all that he owned, and he had to go into exile. Today, he and his folk and family stand humbled and perplexed, deserving of compassion and benevolence. His crime is forgiven and he is to be burdened no longer.[84]

The bits about Husayn 'of the abominable extremist Shiites' whose iniquity 'comes from being of the Rafızi *mezheb*' were evidently forgotten. Two years later, as indicated, Mulham had once again installed his protégé in Baalbek; when some English archaeologists came to tour the area in 1751 Husayn received them respectfully, 'declaring himself the Sultan's slave'.[85]

The conflict between the Harfush brothers indeed came to a head around this time, with Haydar terrorizing the entire region in his bid to retake power. In the spring of 1751, Husayn was attacked and killed by gunmen as he left the town mosque. Haydar thereby resumed control and, according to the Damascene chronicler Budayri, immediately set upon the *mufti* of Baalbek once more, burning him and a brother to death and destroying their house and vineyards.[86] Yet this does not seem to have had any consequences, since the Shihabis now extended their protection to the surviving Harfush in order to maintain influence in the Bekaa. In 1755, the Sublime Porte issued Haydar a stern warning after all three *vali*s of the Syrian region had written to accuse him of constantly attacking and despoiling the villages he was supposed to be safeguarding: 'Your thirst and addiction for this sort of illegal and unacceptable tyranny and oppression has caused the fire of my royal fury to be ignited!' But the order also makes clear that powerful individuals were interceding for him, and that he would thus be left in office on the condition that he 'wake from his slumber of remissness', repent and engage to protect the humble commoners.[87] The following year, Haydar was even given the *mukataa* for Hermel in the province of Tripoli, almost certainly with the Shihabis' blessing, after it had been taken away from the Hamadas.[88]

---

[83] Robert Wood (d. 1771), *The Ruins of Balbec, otherwise Heliopolis in Coelosyria* (London: n.p., 1757), 3.
[84] MD 153:169.     [85] Wood, *The Ruins of Balbec*, 3–4.
[86] Budayri, *Hawadith*, 207, 210.     [87] MD 157:195; see also Budayri, *Hawadith*, 232.
[88] Tripoli 14:236.

Much like in Mt Lebanon and Jabal 'Amil, the Shiites' exercise of government in Baalbek as well as their supposed excesses must be considered in light of the conflicts and rivalries inside the Ottoman ruling apparatus, between regional *ayan* households and of course within the local Christian community. In 1754, for example, Haydar had seven Greek Orthodox notables arrested and tortured, but only because someone had wrongly accused them of defying a metropolitan who had just been elected with Haydar's support. The metropolitan himself then intervened to get them released, excommunicated the informant – and rejected Haydar's call to reinstate him until he showed true repentance.[89] Like the Hamadas, the Harfush emirs were involved on more than one occasion in the selection of Church officials and the running of local monasteries.[90] Tradition holds that many Christians quit the Baalbek region in the eighteenth century for the newer, more secure town of Zahle on account of the Harfushes' oppression and rapacity, but more critical studies have questioned this interpretation, pointing out that the Harfushes were closely allied to the Orthodox Ma'luf family of Zahle (where indeed Mustafa Harfush took refuge some years later) and showing that depredations from various quarters as well as Zahle's growing commercial attractiveness accounted for Baalbek's decline in the eighteenth century.[91] What repression there was did not always target the Christian community per se. The Shiite 'Usayran family, for example, is also said to have left Baalbek in this period to avoid expropriation by the Harfushes, establishing itself as one of the premier commercial households of Sidon and later even serving as consuls of Iran.[92]

If the Harfushes' rule in Baalbek had many points in common with that of the Hamadas in Mt Lebanon, there were also some important differences that help explain why they would outlast the 'Kızılbaş *mukataa*' by a good century and only fall victim to Ottoman centralization policies in the Tanzimat era. Essentially, the Shihabi emirate's reach did not extend into the Bekaa the same way that it unfolded over the northern Lebanon. While the Shihabis had been contenders for tax farms in the area since before their accession to the Druze emirate, the fact that the Bekaa was generally included in the *eyalet* (and *sancak*) of Damascus and contained, particularly in the eighteenth century, a large proportion of lands assigned to imperial *vakıf* foundations, meant that their power was more circumscribed here than in either Sidon or Tripoli. Moreover, with a population that was predominantly Shiite and Greek Orthodox, neither the defence of the Maronite community nor France's political interests were much of a factor here. The Shihabis were thus quite happy to maintain their influence, and carry out their struggle against the Damascus government, through the intermediary of an obstreperous but vulnerable local client. In 1760, the holders of a *malikane* on the Baalbek tax concession for which Haydar was *mültezim* complained that he had not paid anything for three

[89] Karama, *Hawadith Lubnan*, 18.
[90] *Ibid.*, 52–3; Goudard, *La Sainte Vierge au Liban*, 399.
[91] Alixa Naff, 'A Social History of Zahle, a Principal Market Town in Nineteenth-Century Lebanon' (UCLA doctoral thesis, 1972), 72–86, 519.
[92] al-Amin, *A'yan al-Shi'a*, II:497–8; VI:349; personal communication by Khatme Osseiran-Hanna.

years, in addition to all the harm he was causing the people, instead keeping the money to share with his five brothers and a nephew. Orders to arrest him had been sent to the governor of Tripoli, but as he had departed on *cerde* the orders had also been forwarded to the governors of Sidon and Damascus as well as to the Shihabi emirs of the Shuf.[93] Once again this had little effect, however, and a similar complaint sent by the comptroller of imperial *vakıf*s to the sultan the following year may serve to summarize the legacy of Harfushid rule in the Bekaa in the eighteenth century:

Twelve years ago, Hüseyin, the son of the boorish and heretical emir İsmail Harfuş who had been executed under wrath thirty years prior, became voivode of Baalbek by some means. In addition to oppressing and afflicting the commonalty, this Hüseyin committed all sorts of transgressions (even though the aforesaid *vakıf*s were in every respect free, safe and exempt, and only the trustees were empowered to collect while the voivodes traditionally did not interfere), causing all the money for the *vakıf* to be short and deficient ... Ten years ago, Hüseyin's brother Hayder, he too a Kızılbaş, appeared and killed Hüseyin, and became voivode by some heavy-handed means in his stead. Through his tyranny and oppression he has dispersed the righteous believers, in particular the Sunnis, and takes heed of no one. Even more insubordinate than his brother, he coveted and seized the entire *vakıf* for himself and, with the worst of trouble, would give only a half or a third of the money to the trustees, but for three years now he has not paid a thing. Inasmuch as the trustee's deputy cannot collect by himself, it is evident that this will cause God's *vakıf* to go to great ruin and come to nought, and your noble attention is humbly sought and implored.[94]

The pattern of Harfushid oppression, Ottoman reproof and Shihabi intervention could and did continue for many more years. The story may conveniently be interrupted in the 1760s, when the Harfushes became entangled in the process of the Hamadas' extirpation from Mt Lebanon: in July 1762, the emirs of the Shuf were informed that Haydar had joined his 'Kızılbaş' colleagues while the governor of Tripoli was again away on the *cerde*, and had attacked Jubbat Basharri, where they killed several men and women, enslaving their children; two years later, he once more went after his usual nemesis and killed the *mufti*'s cousin in Baalbek.[95] In 1767, Haydar seized a Catholic monastery in Ra's Baalbek after a Shiite family complained that the friars had converted their daughter and sent her off to Rome, where (according to Karama) she died 'in the odour of sanctity'.[96] Bashir Shihabi had to intercede to win the release of a friar whom Haydar had caught and tortured with hot iron, and it is indeed at this time that he seems to have lost his overlords' favour. Later that summer, when the Hamadas were driven out of Jubayl they fled to Baalbek to take shelter with Haydar, but they were pursued by Yusuf Shihabi and they had to flee together to Hermel in the north. Haydar was ousted from the *voyvodalık* and went to seek refuge in Jabal 'Amil.[97] In the autumn, Osman Paşa of

---

[93] MD 161:381–2, 386.    [94] Cevdet Evkaf 9176.
[95] MD 162:413–14; Tripoli 17:145, 146; Cevdet Askeriye 44227; MD 164:182.
[96] Karama, *Hawadith Lubnan*, 34–5.
[97] *Ibid.*, 35–6; Rukayni, *Jabal 'Amil*, 50–1; AE B/I 1033 (Seyde), fol. 321a.

Damascus wrote to his brother, the *vali* of Sidon, asking that 'our friend' Yusuf Shihabi seize Haydar so that he might be brought to trial and made to pay his outstanding tax debts. This does not seem to have occurred, however, perhaps because Nasif Nassar personally intervened with Yusuf on Haydar's behalf.[98] At any rate, the altercation did nothing to change the underlying fact of the Harfushes' vassalage to the Shihabi emirs, for Yusuf merely had Haydar's younger brother Muhammad installed as voivode of Baalbek in his stead. The imperial authorities, for their part, once again acquiesced in the choice.[99]

## The 'national uprising'

The events which would later be called a Lebanese 'national uprising' against the Hamadas[100] extended over a full decade in the later eighteenth century, and marked only the culmination of the long process of marginalization of the region's Shiites. In 1759, as we have seen, the Hamadas' own agents and bondsmen rose in revolt and seized control of the Jubbat Basharri, the heartland of the Maronite community which the Hamadas had held in concession intermittently since the mid-seventeenth century. The governor of Tripoli, according to 'Aynturini, was so pleased with the resulting increase in tax remittances and security in the district that he provided the Maronite leaders with gunpowder and ammunition and issued them a *buyuruldı* that they might keep everything they took from the Shiites they killed.[101] Of course the Hamadas did not go quietly: in the autumn of 1761 the French consul reported that 'la guerre qu'on pousse à outrance dans le Mont Liban' was still preventing him from pursuing his botanical research in the area; 'Les paysans chretiens autorisés de la Porte ont dépossedé du Gouvernement les Methu-Aly, qui de leur côté tâchent d'y rentrer à main armée, mais jusqu'à présent ils n'ont pas pû y parvenir.'[102] The Hamadas were joined by the Harfushes the following spring in the already-cited attack on Jubbat Basharri, where they killed several shaykhs (including those of the Sakr and Geagea families), took prisoners back to the Bekaa and 'stole everything, down to the pastry bowls'. The Ra'ds of Danniyye, whom the *vali* had delegated to defend the Maronites, helped repulse a second and even greater attack a month later, while a large force of feudal contingents from throughout the region fought the Hamadas and devastated the Jubayl highlands towards the end of the year.[103]

It is in response to this violence that the Shihabis got involved in earnest and agreed with the Ottoman authorities on the final destruction of Shiite rule in the area. This can be considered on several levels: like the Maronite shaykhs and the Ra'ds, the Shihabis had in the past acquired vested interests in the rural tax farms of Tripoli by posting the payment bond, and probably came to view the expulsion of the unruly Hamadas as a necessary measure to ensure their continuing financial

---

[98] AE B/I 1033 (Seyde), fol. 371b.   [99] Cevdet Dahiliye 901.
[100] Hitti, *Lebanon in History*, 387; see also chapter 3.   [101] 'Aynturini, *Mukhtasar*, 134–5.
[102] AE B/I 1120 (Tripoli), fol. 77b.   [103] 'Aynturini, *Mukhtasar*, 135–6.

viability. On another level, the takeover of the northern farms marked an important step in the consolidation of the Shihabi dynasty as such. After Mulham's death in 1754 there ensued another power struggle within the family until his son Mansur was recognized as emir in both Beirut and the Shuf. Mansur's nephew Yusuf, however, continued to rally resistance against him, and was naturally supported in this by the governor of Damascus, who in turn recommended Yusuf to his son, the governor of Tripoli.[104] As a result, Yusuf was awarded the Jubayl, Batrun and Jubbat Basharri fiefs as early as March 1763, before Mansur abdicated and left him in sole possession of the emirate in 1771. What is remarkable about the *iltizam* contracts preserved in Tripoli, however, is that these were already negotiated in the Shihabis' capital Dayr al-Qamar in the Shuf in 1763, suggesting that the degree of Yusuf's conflict with the rest of the family then may in fact have been largely overstated.[105]

And finally, the formal establishment of Shihabi rule over Mt Lebanon sealed the 'Druze' emirate's amalgamation with the Maronite community, whose confession the dynasty had by and large already adopted by this time. 'Aynturini asserts that the shaykhs of Jubbat Basharri solicited emir Mansur Shihabi's support even before Yusuf was awarded the tax farms in the area;[106] H. A. al-Shihabi, for his part, recounts that

the people of the Jubayl region were inclined towards Yusuf, and he got the better of its masters, the Hamadas. He had a war with and fought them for days ... until he weakened and defeated them. Sometimes he would vanquish them violently by the sword, and sometimes he would beguile them with gifts and kindness. He also reduced them by stirring strife among them. It was not long before he ruined most of them and humbled the others, so that they could no longer seek power. He was helped in this by the people of the said districts.[107]

The few documentary sources available seem to confirm that the 'uprising' was neither linear nor its outcome entirely predictable. Most notably, a report by the French consul on Yusuf in May 1764 indicates that several Shiites 'qui s'attendent a avoir des sous fermes de ces cantons se sont joint a luy',[108] suggesting that the Hamadas may initially even have welcomed him as an intermediary with the Ottoman authorities, much as the Shiites of Jabal 'Amil did with Zahir al-'Umar. In 1767, however, the Hamadas had to seek refuge in Baalbek when Yusuf drove them out of Jubayl, apparently the only incident of the period, as we have seen, to find an echo in Ottoman chancery sources. Two years later, he again attacked a group of Hamadas, so that they actually went to seek the help of the governor of Tripoli; the government forces, however, were badly routed.[109] What H. A. al-Shihabi does not say is that it was apparently the *vali* who was angry over Yusuf's refusal to remit extraordinary taxes that year, and thus 'fit proposer sous main au methu-aly' to retake possession of their old fiefs. Yusuf, according to the French

---

[104] Shihabi, *Lubnan*, 62; Soueid, *Histoire militaire*, 405–8.    [105] Tripoli 17:214, 215.
[106] 'Aynturini, *Mukhtasar*, 136–7.    [107] Shihabi, *Lubnan*, 62.    [108] AE B/I 1120 (Tripoli), fol. 295a.
[109] Shihabi, *Lubnan*, 80.

consul, declared that he would be happy to cede the concession if he were reimbursed for all that he had invested in it, then sent 300 men to seize the village of Amyun on the approach to Tripoli. Only when the ragged band of mainly Nusayri peasants the governor had managed to assemble failed to dislodge the Shihabis' superior forces did Osman Paşa of Damascus write to his son to stop this nonsense, leaving Yusuf in undisputed mastery of the region.[110]

The end for the Hamadas came in 1771, when they made a last-ditch effort to throw off Shihabi suzerainty after Yusuf returned to Beirut to assume the reins of the emirate. Shihabi family history tells that the Hamadas attacked an uncle whom Yusuf had left behind in Jubayl, and were then crushed by his *kethüda* Saʻd al-Khuri, the Maronites of Jubbat Basharri and a force of Maghribi troops belonging to his new partner Cezzar Ahmed in a devastating final battle at Qalamun, near Tripoli. In a report sent to his head office in Aleppo, the French consul in fact specifies that the Shiites were encouraged to revolt by the governor and emir Mansur. After their defeat, forty Hamada families sought to take refuge in Tripoli, but were 'for the most part robbed by the local Janissaries and their women raped in the city's surroundings, where these soldiers had been sent ... to facilitate [their] entry. Our pasha did what he could to return these poor wretches their goods, but his authority is rather weak here.'[111] The following year Yusuf himself returned north to subjugate the Raʻds and punish the Kurdish emirs of al-Kura, whom he suspected of having tried to help the fleeing Shiites.[112]

To what extent were the events of 1759–71 a 'national' uprising? The expansion of Shihabi rule beyond the *eyalet* of Sidon marks the true inception of the political regime that would in the nineteenth century be known as Lebanon. This cumulation of powers in the hands of the Shihabis is reflected first and foremost in the *iltizam* contracts for Tripoli province: whereas the Hamadas' tax concessions had been marked by a growing diversity of individual holders, court agents and guarantors, beginning in 1763 and for the rest of the century the districts were uniformly awarded to the Shihabi emir and without bond from the local population.[113] The primary beneficiary of these changes, other than direct agents of the Shihabis such as the Dahdahs, was the Maronite religious community. Many of the landed properties and other belongings the Hamadas had left behind in Jubayl were donated by the Shihabis to the Lebanese Order of monks, which could now begin to restore and revive the many monasteries and villages that had supposedly been abandoned because of the Shiites.[114] Popular legend still connects numerous

[110] AE B/I 1121 (Tripoli), fols. 19a–22b; see also ʻAynturini, *Mukhtasar*, 68–9.
[111] AE B/I 92 (Alep), fol. 118a–b.
[112] Shihabi, *Lubnan*, 94–6; Anonymous, *Tarikh al-Umaraʻ*, 119–21; ʻAynturini, *Mukhtasar*, 69–71, 137; Cevdet, *Tarih*, I:336; Soueid, *Histoire militaire*, 461–3.
[113] Tripoli 17:214–15; 18/1:38–41; 18/2:45–8; 20/1:77–80; 20/3:146–9; 21:202–3, 205; 22:29–31, 142–3, 165–6; 23:11–13; 26/1:83–6.
[114] Bulaybil, *Tarikh al-Rahbaniyya*, I:401, II:273–8; Fahd, *Tarikh al-Rahbaniyya*, II:490–1, IV:352; Hattuni, *Nubdha Tarikhiyya*, 154–62.

Marian shrines in the northern highlands with Shiite founders or miracles worked on Shiite devotees, but also credits Her for the Shiites' elimination: 'le plus grand geste de Notre-Dame ... fut la deliverance du joug des Métoualis, de ces brigands dont nous connaissons déjà les exploits ... La Vierge n'aime pas les Métoualis; elle nous en a débarrassés.'[115] The Hamadas' ejection from Mt Lebanon remains a veritable watershed in the Maronite collective memory, the dividing line between a past defined by Muslim and Turkish oppression and a future of freedom and self-determination. It is ultimately not surprising that it has become a central paradigm of Lebanese national history per se.

## The Shiites under Shihabi rule

The perennial conflict within the Harfush family, harmful as it may have been for the population of the Bekaa as well as for the imperial purse, provided an arena for the Shihabis' rivalry with the Ottoman governors and thus continued unabated. After Haydar Harfush was replaced in the *voyvodalık* by his brother Muhammad, their other brother Mustafa raided the vicinity of Baalbek in 1769, killing and plundering; two years later, Karama reports that the friars of Sayyidat al-Ra's had to flee their monastery while the Harfushes were again battling it out, and only returned once the Shiites had agreed on which one of them would rule.[116] But despite all the instability, the family's position as such was unassailable: the same year, the French consul of Sidon noted that Yusuf Shihabi was greatly incensed because the *vali* of Damascus had dared to attack the 'chek des Muthualis sous sa protection qui gouverne la ville de Balbec', and threatened to withdraw his support in the battle against Zahir al-'Umar and the Egyptians.[117]

It was likely Haydar Harfush who returned to power at this time, for when he died in 1774, H. A. al-Shihabi indicates that he was replaced as 'ruler of the Baalbek region' by his brother Mustafa. Haydar's son Darwish thereupon went to Yusuf Shihabi to complain that he should rightfully succeed his father, however, and then went to Zahir al-'Umar when he was rebuffed. In the end Zahir and Yusuf decided among themselves that rule over the Bekaa would be split between Harfush uncle and nephew.[118] This, in turn, was contested by the governor of Damascus, who expulsed Mustafa and reinstated Muhammad just two years later. Muhammad is noted to have intervened, along with his brother 'Ali, in a dispute among Orthodox friars over control of a local monastery in 1776, but he too came under pressure the following year when the new governor of Sidon, Cezzar Ahmed Paşa, sent a deputy to Baalbek to seize some racehorses which Muhammad had left

[115] Goudard, *La Sainte Vierge au Liban*, 192, 198, 217–18, 232–9, 245, 260–1, 282–6, 335–40.
[116] Rukayni, *Jabal 'Amil*, 56; Karama, *Hawadith Lubnan*, 39.
[117] AE B/I 1035 (Seyde), fol. 46b.
[118] Shihabi, *Lubnan*, 106.

in the care of the famous 'Alwani family of *sayyids*.[119] It appears that the Sublime Porte was ready to augment Cezzar's authority throughout the region in an attempt to reassert firm central control after the long war with Russia. An imperial order issued to Muhammad in early 1779 observes that 'it has not been possible to give the *iltizam* for the aforesaid *mukataa* to anyone other than the Harfuş-oğlus' and reminds him that responsibility for collecting on their debt had been transferred to Cezzar after the *vali* of Damascus proved unable for four (or five) years to obtain the full amount from Mustafa Harfush. Inasmuch as an important part of these moneys was earmarked for the Damascene Janissary garrison, Cezzar was no longer to accept any of their standard excuses.[120]

Muhammad was in fact dismissed later that year and went to live, just like the brother he had helped evict from the *voyvodalık* a few years earlier, in Jabal 'Amil. After conferring with Nasif Nassar and aided by his cavalry, he attempted to return to Baalbek in early 1781, but this does not seem to have been successful as he left again soon afterwards to meet with Yusuf Shihabi in Dayr al-Qamar.[121] Over the next months, in any event, it was Mustafa Harfush who fought with his brother Ahmad and the *vali* of Damascus for control of the Bekaa, causing the people of Zahle to flee for their lives on more than one occasion. In 1782 Muhammad even had a falling-out with Yusuf Shihabi, and was imprisoned in Damascus when he came to seek the governor's support, but won release by paying a ransom and delivering one of his more vicious comrades to the executioner. All this did not affect his basic standing: later the same year, he was able to arrange with Yusuf Shihabi and the governor for shaykh Kaplan, one of many Shiites from Jabal 'Amil to have fled to the Bekaa after Nasif Nassar's death, to be awarded the tax farm for Ra's Baalbek and Hermel.[122]

This cycle could of course continue indefinitely. Towards the end of 1782 Muhammad finally got help from Yusuf Shihabi to wrest control of Baalbek back from Mustafa, who fled to Homs to assemble forces to retake the city anew. Muhammad thereupon moved to Sidon for good, seeking shelter with Yusuf Shihabi, according to one version, or with Cezzar Ahmed, according to another.[123] Two years later, the governor of Damascus, apparently backed by Cezzar, resolved to take more decisive action against the Harfushes and sent an army into the Bekaa to arrest Mustafa together with five of his brothers. Three of them were hanged while the other three were imprisoned in Damascus in order to put an end to their tyranny over the region; shaykh Kaplan too lost his post but was well received, along with Nasif Nassar's son 'Aqid, by the governor.[124] Cezzar took control of the

---

[119]  Karama, *Hawadith Lubnan*, 48, 52–3; Munayyir, *al-Durr al-Marsuf*, 25; Rukayni, *Jabal 'Amil*, 82.
[120]  Cevdet Maliye 7110. The crisis may have been accentuated by the fact that 1188 (1774/5) was a 'siviş' year, a year not figuring in the Ottoman fiscal calendar to periodically correct for the discrepancy with the shorter Islamic lunar year.
[121]  Rukayni, *Jabal 'Amil*, 87, 92; Munayyir, *al-Durr al-Marsuf*, 35.
[122]  Karama, *Hawadith Lubnan*, 66–70, 74.
[123]  Shihabi, *Lubnan*, 134; Karama, *Hawadith Lubnan*, 74.
[124]  Karama, *Hawadith Lubnan*, 80–1; Rukayni, *Jabal 'Amil*, 107–8, 111.

Bekaa and was even appointed to the governorship of Damascus for one year, but a new generation of Harfushes was already preparing to assume the old mantle: in 1787, Mustafa's son Jahjah routed the deputy governor of Baalbek while the *vali* was away on *hajj* and retook possession of the family palace. The *vali* appointed to Damascus the following year immediately threatened Jahjah with action, causing him to wreak havoc on Baalbek and the countryside and finally ensconce himself in a nearby village, begging the Shihabis for help. The governor sent Jahjah's cousin Kanj (Genç) Muhammad ('Muhammad jr') with a company of soldiers and some Maghribi mercenaries to take over Baalbek and capture Jahjah, but just as they were about to attack, the Shihabis arrived. When Jahjah heard this,

his resolve, which had been on the verge of evaporating, was strengthened. He and his men began a barrage of fire, screaming 'Here's to you, emir Yusuf Shihabi!' When the state forces saw the mountain army come upon them from behind, and emir Jahjah's men from the front, they thought the mountain army was great in number, and fear befell their insides. They turned on their heels and fled back to Baalbek … When the paşa heard what had happened in the area he was upset at the ineffectiveness of his orders … He was forced to write to emir Yusuf … so that emir Jahjah paid an indemnity of 1,000 *gurush* and some buffalo, and returned to rule the country of Baalbek as before.[125]

By 1788, in other words, the Shiites of Lebanon had become little more than subalterns in a larger struggle opposing different Shihabi emirs or the Shihabis and the governors of Sidon and Damascus. We have already seen that Cezzar spent much of the decade tightening his grip on the province of Sidon and Jabal 'Amil, and it is also in the context of his consolidation of power over the whole region that we last encounter the Hamadas. In 1779 Cezzar seized on a local dispute in Tripoli and actually helped the remaining Hamadas defeat the feudal lords of 'Akkar, who were being backed by the governor of the province.[126] In 1788, however, the Hamadas who were still in the area sided with Yusuf Shihabi in his struggle against Cezzar and he who would become the most powerful ruler in Lebanon's history, emir Bashir II. Abandoned by his erstwhile supporters (including Jahjah Harfush) in the south, Yusuf made one last stand with the help of the Hamadas and other local factions in the mountains above Jubayl before ceding to Cezzar and Bashir.[127] Thereafter the northern Shiites apparently cease to play any role in the fortunes of Lebanon.

The Wadi 'Almat and other parts of Jubayl and the Kisrawan are of course still partially inhabited by Shiites today, and documentary evidence suggests that the Hamadas retained some of their properties in the region in the nineteenth century.[128] Most of the Shiite clans, however, and eventually the Hamadas themselves, found refuge on the arid slopes of the northern Bekaa and in Hermel or Baalbek following their defeat in 1771. The Nasir al-Din tribe, which traces its origins to Bazyun in the Futuh, practises seasonal nomadism to this day in the remote Jubab

[125] Karama, *Hawadith Lubnan*, 103, 105–7; see also Munayyir, *al-Durr al-Marsuf*, 57, 59–61.
[126] Rukayni, *Jabal 'Amil*, 87.    [127] Shihabi, *Lubnan*, 145, 148.    [128] Daghir, *Tannurin*, 97.

Fig. 9  Ruins in Jubab al-Humr (Bekaa Valley)

al-Humr on the eastern flank of Mt Lebanon (Fig. 9); in a sense they constitute the last living remnants of the Ottoman-era confederation.[129]

## Conclusion: the logic of Lebanon

The reform of Ottoman provincial administration in the eighteenth century was the root cause for the long-term decline of Shiite rule in Mt Lebanon and the Bekaa. Up until the crisis of the Ottoman state in the last years of the seventeenth century, which played itself out in the region through a massive punitive operation against the Shiites and other highland feudalists, families such as the Hamadas and Harfushes were equal if not privileged contenders for government tax collection concessions and might even hold rank in the military-administrative hierarchy. With the growing privatization of provincial government office and the decentralization of Ottoman state authority in the eighteenth century, however, the entire edifice of tax farming became increasingly dependent on regionally based civilian governor dynasties such as the 'Azms, on the one hand, and powerful local feudal families such as the Shihabi emirs, on the other. As the Ottomans' designated intermediary in the coastal highlands, the 'Druze' emirs played a key role in

---

[129] Michel Salamé, 'Une tribu chiite des montagnes de Hermel (Liban): Les Nacer ed-Dine', *Revue de Géographie de Lyon* 32 (1957), 117–26; cf. Ghassan Fawzi Taha, *Shi'at Lubnan: Al-'Ashira, al-Hizb, al-Dawla (Ba'labakk-al-Hirmil Namudhajan)* (Beirut: Ma'had al-Ma'arif al-Hikmiyya, 2006), 21–34.

restoring and maintaining the Hamadas and Harfushes in power in the eighteenth century, but at the price of a protection that would become ever more compromising for the Shiites.

This protection could take several forms, from providing mutual haven and support during internecine struggles or conflict with government forces, to interceding with the state authorities to effect a reconciliation or reinstatement as tax concessionaries. The most tangible expression of this relationship, however, was the *kefalet* or security guarantee which the Shihabis or their allies began to post especially on the Hamadas' tax farms in Mt Lebanon. In shouldering more and more of the responsibility for the northern tax districts, the Shihabis and, increasingly, the shaykhs of the local Maronite population acquired a direct stake in the Hamadas' exercise of government. The Hamadas' relations with the Maronites were of course complex, determined not only by the collection (or extortion) of taxes but also by their patronage of certain individuals and institutions of the Maronite Church. Yet it is precisely in this period that a new Maronite lay elite, led by families such as the Khazins, Khuris and Shidyaqs, backed by France and the Lebanese Order and supported by the Shihabi emirs, began to assert a claim to Mt Lebanon in the name of their sectarian community, much as had previously happened in the Kisrawan. By the second half of the eighteenth century, a Shihabi takeover of the northern *mukataa*s corresponded as much to the Maronites' quest for more autonomy as to the Ottoman authorities' desire for more revenue; the Hamadas would henceforth be recalled, in local histories and folklore as much as in the imperial discourse, as nothing more than an aberration in the natural order of things.

The incorporation of the Bekaa into the Shihabis' sphere of influence occurred less directly and over a longer period of time but was in the end no less effective. In light of the district's importance to the government of Damascus and the imperial *vakf* administration, and with neither the Maronite community's political future nor France's interests immediately at stake, the Shihabis were willing to support one or the other Harfush emir against his rivals and use him against the Ottoman authorities, rather than attempt to assume full control. This policy of co-optation closely tied the Harfushes' fate to that of the Shihabi emirate, and explains why the Harfushes are much more accounted for in modern Lebanist historiography than other leading Shiite families. It also had profound consequences for the Shiite community which extend into present times and must be left for another discussion: whether the fact that the Bekaa had by the nineteenth century lost all semblance of an organic, locally grounded leadership akin to the *zu'ama* of Jabal 'Amil made it that much more of a likely venue for the rise of foreign-inspired, ideological mass movements such as Communism, Nasserism and the Hezbollah in the modern era.

Either way, the end of the Harfushes' independence and the elimination of the Hamadas from Mt Lebanon close the long chapter of Shiite feudal autonomy under Ottoman imperial rule. The formal extension of the Shihabi emirate over the north of Lebanon in the late eighteenth century, and with it the national history of Lebanon as such, must be seen as a product of the Shiites' defeat.

# Conclusion

The written record of Lebanon's Shi'a under Ottoman rule presents a twofold paradox. Where imperial documents and chronicles identify Shiites as such, they are labelled as Revafiz and Kızılbaş, legally assimilated to heresy and rhetorically excluded from Ottoman society. And yet these same sources also make clear to what extent leading Shiite families were in fact co-opted by the early modern Ottoman state, integrated into the provincial administration and assigned wide-ranging fiscal and police powers in the area. Similarly, Arabic-language sources almost universally condemn the Shiites as particularly lawless and inimical to local society, as religious and social pariahs and ultimately as alien to 'Lebanon'. And yet the narrative of Lebanese nationhood is predicated on the universal embrace of Ma'nid and Shihabi rule, as if the rise of the Druze emirate somehow also benefited those who were its main victims. The Shiites' place in both Ottoman and Lebanese history remains unresolved: their sectarian identity did not prevent their success within the nominally Sunni context of imperial rule, but in the end it conditioned their failure within the nominally non- or pan-confessional feudal system of modern Lebanon.

The present study has aimed at resolving some of these contradictions by examining the 'rise and fall' of the Hamadas, Harfushes and other Shiite families from a long-term, Ottoman administrative perspective. Its main findings can be summarized as follows. Classical thinkers such as Ebu's-Suud Efendi did establish a legal framework for religious persecution which remained in effect until the Tanzimat reforms, but how and when different state actors in Istanbul and the provinces chose to invoke these terms depended on the requirements and possibilities of local government. Shiite rule over Mt Lebanon, the Bekaa and Jabal 'Amil was essentially an Ottoman innovation of the later sixteenth century, when the Ottomans began to assign tax farming contracts to local tribal leaders rather than attempting to impose direct control over remote and unruly hinterland areas. The Harfushes of Baalbek received the *iltizam* concession for the Bekaa as well as a rank in the provincial military hierarchy (the district governorship of Homs or Tadmur) in recognition of their long-standing position of dominance within local Shiite society; the threat posed by the Druze Ma'n emirs and the Harfushes' very vulnerability made them one of the Ottomans' most sought-after local intermediaries in the early seventeenth century. In the province of Tripoli, the Hamada family of the Wadi 'Almat came to prominence around the same time as lieutenants of the Sayfa dynasty, before being charged, on account of their endogenous tribal organization and ruthless efficiency, with multiple tax collection assignments in the Shiite- and Christian-dominated hinterland of Mt Lebanon. While Maronite historians even then tended to demonize the 'Mutawalis' as interlopers and portray the Druze as the only rightful 'princes' of their country, the crossing of imperial, provincial and foreign diplomatic sources suggests that the Hamadas and Harfushes were in every way quintessential of Ottoman rural government in the pre-modern era.

The ambiguous rapport between the Shiite feudatories, the local population and the state authorities began to break down in the final decade-and-a-half of the seventeenth century, we argued, due to the prolonged crisis and ensuing reform attempts occasioned by the Empire's disastrous war in southern Europe, as well as the increasingly effective complaints of the Maronite notables of Mt Lebanon about the Hamadas' misrule. As part of an Empire-wide effort to clamp down on mercenary brigandage, settle tribes and revive desperately needed sources of revenue, the Sublime Porte embarked on a far-reaching discipline-and-punish initiative in these years which was reflected in a major punitive campaign into Mt Lebanon in 1693–4. The campaign, vigorously pursued by a new class of civilian governor households, did not actually eliminate the rule of local Shiite notables, but subjected them for all intents and purposes to the Druze emirs of Sidon, marking the first time a single feudal authority was extended over all that would be seen as the 'Lebanese emirate' by the end of the eighteenth century.

Meanwhile, the privatization of Ottoman provincial rule and the concentration of power in the hands of local *ayan* dynasties such as the Shihabis, on the one hand, and France's diplomatic and financial backing, on the other, enabled new Maronite entrepreneurs such as the Khazins and the Lebanese Order of monks to colonize and develop agricultural lands in the Kisrawan and Mt Lebanon and assume an ever greater role in the Shiites' tax concessions. In the course of the eighteenth century the Hamadas became increasingly dependent on the Druze emirs' political protection as well as on their own subjects' financial guarantees for their tax farms, and in the process came to be seen as ever more of an obstacle on the Maronites' path to self-determination. Having outlived their usefulness to both local society and the Ottoman state, the Hamadas were easily driven from power and exiled from Mt Lebanon once the Shihabis had converted to Maronitism and were ready to expand into the north in the 1760s.

The Shiites of Jabal 'Amil in the *eyalet* of Sidon came under similar pressure from the Druze–Maronite condominium in the eighteenth century, particularly after the Ottoman state all but abandoned sovereignty in the area to the 'Azm governors and their Shihabi supporters. Thanks to their relative isolation and good commercial contacts with the French, families such as the 'Ali al-Saghirs were able to maintain their position as tax farmers and even gain control of the port of Tyre in the mid-eighteenth century, but ultimately had to seek the backing of the rebel governor of Acre, Zahir al-'Umar, against the 'Lebanese' emirs. The Shiites' occupation of Sidon in 1771 as part of a wider revolt against Ottoman rule marked the pinnacle of their autonomous power, but the restoration of Ottoman control under Cezzar Ahmed Paşa only a few years later left the community devastated and more subject than ever to the Druze emirs. The Harfushes, on the other hand, were able to maintain their hold on the Bekaa Valley into the next century precisely by subordinating themselves to the Shihabis. Despite (or rather on account of) their constant internecine rivalries and conflict with the state authorities, the Harfushes served as a local dependency of the Shihabi emirate and would thus be remembered more than any other Shiite group as a constituent of the 'classical system' of Lebanese rule. By the last quarter of the eighteenth century, the decentralization of Ottoman provincial authority, the rise of a modern secular elite among the Christians and the Shihabi dynasty's consolidation of power in Sidon, Tripoli and the Bekaa had essentially made the more traditional, *mukataa*-based rule of families such as the Hamadas, the Harfushes and the *zu'ama* of Jabal 'Amil anachronistic and redundant.

The late 1780s thus seem an appropriate moment to end our study of Lebanon's Shiites in the early modern period. On the local level, the year 1788 marks the accession of Bashir II to the Shihabi emirate. Despite his initial difficulties in overcoming resistance within the dynasty and his dependence on Cezzar, Bashir would succeed, by the end of the century, in imposing a unified administrative and legal system throughout the highlands of Sidon and Tripoli under his control. Henceforth the history of the Shiite community cannot be divorced from the growing reality of a properly Lebanese sovereignty in the region. For the Ottoman Empire, the following year marks the accession of Sultan Selim III, and the cautious beginnings of reform. While the modernizing policies inherent in the Nizam-ı Cedid ('New Order') were not to come to full fruition before the Tanzimat, the creation of a new treasury in 1793 and the rollback of tax farming by provincial *ayan* heralded the end of what can be considered as the Ottoman 'ancien régime'.[1] The nineteenth-century reform era – characterized, from a historian's perspective, by a significantly larger and very different documentary basis than that available for the present study – would also see the Shiites of Lebanon subjected to new paradigms of state centralization, integration and control. Finally, the start of the French revolution in 1789 (in addition to causing an interruption in the consular reports that were also an important source for this study) points towards a changing international context. The West's growing economic and military power over the Middle East, epitomized by Bonaparte's invasion of Egypt and campaign to Syria in 1798 (in which the Shiites of Jabal 'Amil initially provided support to the French) stood in direct relationship to the weakening of Ottoman sovereignty and the emergence of new political entities, such as the *kaimmakamiye* and later the *vilayet* of Mt Lebanon. Nationalist ideology, meanwhile, would provide historians of the nineteenth century with new tools and cultural references for interpreting this evolution. The story of the Shiites of

---

[1] Salzmann, 'An Ancien Régime Revisited'.

Lebanon in the modern era entails many departures from the classical modules of Ottoman rule; it must be left for another study.

## The triumph of Lebanism

The transformation of Lebanese provincial society between the Ottoman conquest and the end of the eighteenth century produced both winners and losers. Yet historians of modern Lebanon have laboured in acknowledging this fact, preferring to subsume the diversity of experiences under a unified and largely teleological narrative of emerging nationhood. The 'erosion of the regional distribution of the religious communities', to quote only one of the more authoritative works on Arab history in the Ottoman period, 'contributed to the development of a sense of Lebanese nationality, rooted in a common soil and transcending confessional differences'.[2] Countless studies have indeed sought to show that religious identities played no role in the apportionment of feudal powers in Lebanon, that the different communities and especially their elites subscribed to the same language of hierarchy and coexistence, that 'the emirate' was an organic (and unique) representation of local society as a whole vis-à-vis the Ottoman Empire. But the idea that the 'erosion' of an older order, the expansion of some at the expense of others, nevertheless serves the greater interest of all – a proposition that unfortunately continues to inform historical writing on colonialism in the Middle East in general – is intellectually untenable. The discussion of Lebanon under Ottoman rule has often been geared today to denying the historical basis of confessionalism as a political system. Yet the fact that some of the main characters in this history are systematically written out of the narrative in the process undermines the very aims this discussion is meant to achieve.

To 'have already forgotten' the divisive tragedies of the past, it has been said, is key to the construction of a common national genealogy in the present.[3] Forgetting, however, is not the same as obfuscating what happened in the first place. A serious reappraisal of the Ottoman parameters of Lebanese history, not just the use of certain archival sources but also a conscious effort to inscribe the local politics of notables, religious heterodoxy, tribalism and tax farming into the larger matrices of imperial rule is the first step in coming to a better, more integrated understanding of Lebanese society and Shiism in the early modern period. Mas'ud Dahir took the lead in proposing an unreservedly class-based reading of the historic roots of confessionalism at the height of the civil war;[4] a new generation of Maronite historians today has begun to question the 'diabolic image' of the Shiites in the received myths of Lebanese exceptionalism and work to bring them back into the narrative.[5] Yet the task remains formidable. Twenty years since the end of the war,

---

[2] Holt, *Egypt and the Fertile Crescent*, 122.
[3] Benedict Anderson, *Imagined Communities: Reflections on the Origin and Spread of Nationalism* (new edn, New York: Verso, 2006), 199–201.
[4] Mas'ud Dahir, *Al-Judhur al-Tarikhiyya li 'l-Mas'ala al-Ta'ifyya al-Lubnaniyya, 1697–1861* (Beirut: Ma'had al-Inma' al-'Arabi, 1981).
[5] Daghir, *Tannurin*, 120–1; Mohasseb-Saliba, 'Monastères doubles', 613–15.

Ahmed Beydoun and Kamal Salibi's ground-breaking critiques of the confessionalist premises of Lebanese national historiography continue for the most part to be ignored. The spate of popular and journalistic histories that have appeared in recent years, many no doubt motivated by the renewed political uncertainty, but also a good number of academic works are once more insisting on the immovable truths of Lebanism, of perpetual persecution and of the mountain refuge, of Ottoman oppression and of the classical system of local rule. But as long as Ottoman documentation is disregarded in favour of narrative chronicles, as long as the likes of Tannus Shidyaq are treated as a historical authority on the seventeenth and eighteenth centuries rather than as an ideologue of the nineteenth, this history will remain deficient and, in the eyes of a growing number of Lebanese, implausible. The individual stories of the Hamadas, the Harfushes and the *zu'ama* of Jabal 'Amil, more than just being important unto themselves, can open a new window on the history of Lebanon as a whole, and perhaps play a part in coming to a new consensus over its meaning.

# Bibliography

## Archival materials

### Unpublished

Damascus, Markaz al-Watha'iq al-Tarikhiyya

    Damascus Islamic Court register 40.
    Hama Islamic Court register 42.

Dresden, Sächsische Landesbibliothek

    Eb. 358 (Ahkam Defteri); Eb. 387 (Mühimme Defteri).

Istanbul, Başbakanlık Osmanlı Arşivi

    Ali Emiri II. Ahmed 392, 477; IV. Mehmed 2948; II. Mustafa 7607.
    Başmuhasebe Kalemi/Sayda ve Beyrut Mukataası (D.BŞM.SBM) 1–4.
    Cevdet Askeriye 44227.
    Cevdet Dahiliye 901, 2805, 5142, 10864, 12818, 12876.
    Cevdet Evkaf 9176, 14884, 20088, 22285, 23416, 26009, 27935, 32176.
    Cevdet Maliye 1802, 7110, 7441, 7539, 12639, 16167.
    Maliyeden Müdevver [MM] 842, 2787, 2993, 3135, 3300, 3347, 3348, 3423, 3971, 4175,
        4409, 4418, 6640, 7025, 9480, 9833, 9835, 9862, 9879, 10146, 10155, 10215, 16189.
    Mühimme Defterleri [MD] 1–180.
    Mühimme Zeyli Defterleri 1–16.
    Şikayet Defterleri [ŞD] 1–30, 40, 50, 60.
    Tahrir Defterleri [TD] 68, 169, 421, 513, 548, 559, 767, 1017, 1107.

Paris, Archives Nationales – Affaires Étrangères [AE]

    Consular series B/I (Alep) 84, 92.
    Consular series B/I (Seyde) 1017–41.
    Consular series B/I (Tripoli) 1114–24.

Sidon, Sunni Shar'iyya Court [Sidon]

    Registers 1–2.

Tripoli, Shar'iyya Court (Qasr al-Nawfal) [Tripoli]

Registers 1–28.

**Published**

Akgündüz, Ahmed, ed. *Osmanlı Kanunnâmeleri ve Hukukî Tahlilleri*, 9 vols. (Istanbul: FEY Vakfı/Osmanlı Araştırmaları Vakfı, 1990–6).

Düzdağ, M. Ertuğrul, ed. *Şeyhülislâm Ebussu'ûd Efendi'nin Fetvalarına göre Kanunî Devrinde Osmanlı Hayatı: Fetâvâ-yı Ebussu'ûd Efendî* (Istanbul: Şûle Yayınları, 1998).

Heyd, Uriel. *Ottoman Documents on Palestine, 1552–1615: A Study of the Firman according to the Mühimme Defteri* (Oxford: Clarendon Press, 1960).

Ismail, Adel, ed. *Documents diplomatiques et consulaires relatifs à l'histoire du Liban* (Beirut: Éditions des Œuvres politiques et historiques, 1975–99).

Nagata, Yuzo, Miura Toru and Shimizu Yasuhisa, eds. *Tax Farm Register of Damascus Province in the Seventeenth Century: Archival and Historical Studies* (Tokyo: Toyo Bunko, 2006).

Öz, Baki, ed. *Alevilik ile ilgili Osmanlı Belgeleri* (Istanbul: Can Yayınları, 1995).

Refik, Ahmet. *Onaltıncı Asirda Râfizîlik ve Bektaşîlik*, new edn by Mehmet Yaman (Istanbul: Ufuk Matbaası, 1994).

Şener, Cemal, ed. *Osmanlı Belgelerinde Aleviler-Bektaşiler* (Istanbul: Karacaahmet Sultan Derneği, 2002).

Şener, Cemal and Ahmet Hezarfen, eds. *Osmanlı Arşivi'nde Mühimme ve İrade Defterlerinde Aleviler-Bektaşiler* (Istanbul: Karacaahmet Sultan Derneği, 2002).

Tadmuri, 'Umar, Fridrik Maqtu' and Nikula Ziyada, eds. *Watha'iq al-Mahkama al-Shar'iyya bi-Tarabulus: al-Sijill al-Awwal 1077–1078 h / 1666–1667 m* (Tripoli: Lebanese University, 1982).

## Contemporary literary sources

**Unpublished**

Anonymous. *Kitab fi'l-Tarikh 873–904 h*. Dar al-Kutub, Cairo: Tarikh 5631.

Anonymous. *Risale der Redd-i Revafız*. Süleymaniye Kütüphanesi, Istanbul: Serez 1451.

al-Ghurabi, Husayn. *Al-Radd 'ala al-Shi'a*. Staatsbibliothek Preußischer Kulturbesitz, Berlin: Or. 2132.

al-Kurani, Yusuf ibn Muhammad. *Al-Yamaniyyat al-Maslula 'ala 'l-Rawafid al-Makhdhula*. Bibliothèque Nationale (Richelieu), Paris: Ms. Arabe 1462.

**Published**

al-Adhami al-Tarabulusi, Ahmad ibn Salih (d. 1746). 'Rihla ila Halab wa'l-Sham', ed. 'Abd al-Qadir al-Maghribi, *Majallat al-Majma' al-'Ilmi al-'Arabi* 7 (1927), 299–314, 346–58, 549–52. Repr. in Fuat Sezgin, ed., *Texts and Studies on the Historical Geography and Topography of Syria* (Frankfurt: Institute for the History of Arabic-Islamic Science, 1993).

Anonymous. *Anonim Osmanlı Tarihi (1099–1116/1688–1704)*, ed. Abdülkadir Özcan (Ankara: Türk Tarih Kurumu, 2000).

Anonymous. 'Mémoire pour le Roi relatif aux Maronites, aux Druses, et aux Amédiens (entendre aux Chiites), habitants du Liban', Bibliothèque Nationale Ms. Français 32926 fols. 93a–100a, published in Nasser Gemayel, *Les échanges culturels entre les Maronites et l'Europe: Du Collège de Rome (1584) au Collège de 'Ayn-Warqa (1789)* (Beirut: 1984), 808–22.

Anonymous. *Tarikh al-Umara' al-Shihabiyyin bi-Qalam Ahad Umara'ihim min Wadi Taym*, ed. Salim Hasan Hashshi (Beirut: al-Mudiriyya al-'Amma li'l-Athar, 1971).

D'Arvieux, Laurent (d. 1702). *Mémoires*, ed. Antoine Abdelnour (Beirut: Dar Lahad Khatir, 1982).

al-'Aynturini, Antuniyus Abu Khattar (d. 1821). *Mukhtasar Tarikh Jabal Lubnan* (Beirut: Dar Lahad Khatir, 1983).

Blackburn, Richard, ed. *Journey to the Sublime Porte: The Arabic Memoir of a Sharifian Agent's Diplomatic Mission to the Ottoman Imperial Court in the Era of Suleyman the Magnificent* (al-Nahrawali, Qutb al-Din (d. 1582)) (Würzburg: Ergon, 2005).

al-Budayri al-Hallaq, Ahmad (d. after 1762). *Hawadith Dimashq al-Yawmiyya, 1741–1762* (2nd edn, Damascus: Dar Sa'd al-Din, 1997).

Burayk, Mikha'il (d. after 1782). *Tarikh al-Sham, 1720–1782*, ed. Ahmad Ghassan Sabanu (Damascus: Dar Qutayba, 1982).

Duwayhi, Istfan (d. 1704). *Tarikh al-Azmina 1095–1699*, ed. Fardinan Tawtal (Beirut: Catholic Press, 1951).

*Tarikh al-Azmina*, ed. Butrus Fahd (3rd imprint, Beirut: Dar Lahad Khatir, 1976).

al-Ghazzi, Najm al-Din (d. 1651). *Lutf al-Samar wa-Qatf al-Thamar* (Damascus: Culture Ministry, 1982).

al-Hurr al-'Amili, Muhammad ibn Hasan (d. 1692). *Amal al-Amil fi 'Ulama' Jabal 'Amil* (Beirut: Mu'assasat al-Wafa', 1983).

Ibn al-Himsi, Ahmad ibn Muhammad (d. 1527/8). *Hawadith al-Zaman wa-Wafayat al-Shuyukh wa'l-Aqran*, ed. 'Umar Tadmuri (Sidon: Maktaba al-'Asriyya, 1999).

Ibn Kannan al-Salihi, Muhammad (d. 1740/1). *Yawmiyyat Shamiyya: Min 1111 hatta 1153h – 1699 hatta 1740m*, ed. Akram Hasan al-'Ulabi (Damascus: Dar al-Tabba', n.d.).

Ibn Nujaym, 'Awn Kamil (d. 1696). ''Nubdha min Tarikh Lubnan fi'l-Qarn al-Sabi' 'Ashar', *al-Mashriq* 25 (1927), 810–20.

Ibn Tawq, Ahmad ibn Muhammad (d. 1509). *Al-Ta'liq: Yawmiyyat Shihab al-Din Ahmad ibn Tawq: Mudhakkirat Kutibat bi-Dimashq fi Awakhir al-'Ahd al-Mamluki 885–908 h / 1380–1502 m*, ed. Ja'far al-Muhajir (Damascus: IFÉAD, 2000).

Ibn Tulun, Muhammad (d. 1546). *Mufakahat al-Khillan fi Hawadith al-Zaman*, ed. Khalil al-Mansur (Beirut: Dar al-Kutub al-'Ilmiyya, 1998).

*Hawadith Dimashq al-Yawmiyya: Ghadat al-Ghazw al-'Uthmani li'l-Sham 926–951 h.: Safahat Mafquda tunshir li'l-marra al-ula min Kitab Mufakahat al-Khillan fi Hawadith al-Zaman*, ed. Ahmad Ibish (Damascus: Dar al-Awa'il, 2002).

Ibn Yahya al-Buhturi, Salih (d. 1436). *Tarikh Bayrut* (Beirut: Dar al-Mashraf, 1969).

al-Isfahani, Mirza 'Abdallah (d. c. 1718). *Riyad al-'Ulama' wa-Hiyad al-Fudala'* (Qom: Matba'at al-Khayyam, 1980).

Karama, Rawfa'il ibn Yusuf (d. 1800). *Hawadith Lubnan wa-Suriya: Min sanat 1745 ila sanat 1800*, ed. Basilus Qattan (n.p.: Jarrus Pars, n.d.).

al-Khalidi al-Safadi, Ahmad ibn Muhammad (d. 1624/5). *Lubnan fi 'Ahd al-Amir Fakhr al-Din al-Ma'ni al-Thani*, ed. Asad Rustum and Fu'ad Afram al-Bustani (Beirut: Lebanese University, 1969).

Korte, Jonas (d. 1747). *Reise nach dem weiland Gelobten, nun aber seit siebenzehn hundert Jahren unter dem Fluche liegenden Lande, wie auch nach Egypten, dem Berg Libanon, Syrien und Mesopotamien* (3rd edn, Halle: Johann Christian Grunert, 1751).

al-Makki, Muhammad (d. after 1722). *Tarikh Hims*, ed. 'Umar Najib al-'Umar (Damascus: IFÉAD, 1987).

al-Muhibbi, Muhammad Amin Fadlallah (d. 1699). *Khulasat al-Athar fi A'yan al-Qarn al-Hadi 'Ashar* (Beirut: Dar Sadir, n.d.).

al-Munayyir, Hananiyya (d. 1823). *Al-Durr al-Marsuf fi Tarikh al-Shuf*, ed. Ighnatiyus Sarkis (Beirut: Jarrus Bars, n.d. [1984]).

al-Nabulusi, 'Abd al-Ghani (d. 1731). *Al-Tuhfa al-Nabulusiyya fi'l-Rihla al-Tarabulusiyya*, ed. Heribert Busse (Beirut: Franz Steiner, 1971).

'Hullat al-Dhahab al-Abriz fi Rihlat Ba'labakk wa-Biqa' al-'Aziz' in Stefan Wild and Salah al-Din Munajjid, eds., *Zwei Reisebeschreibungen des Libanon* (Beirut: Franz Steiner, 1979).

*Al-Haqiqa wa'l-Mujaz fi Rihla Bilad al-Sham wa-Misr wa'l-Hijaz*, ed. Riyad 'Abd al-Hamid Murad (Damascus: Dar al-Ma'rifa, 1989).

Naima Mustafa Efendi (d. 1716). *Târih-i Na'îmâ*, ed. Mehmet İpşirli (Ankara: Türk Tarih Kurumu, 2007).

Raşid, Mehmed Efendi (d. 1735). *Tarih* (Istanbul: 1865/6).

De La Roque, Jean (d. 1745). *Voyage de Syrie et du Mont-Liban*, ed. Jean Raymond (Beirut: Dar Lahad Khatir, 1981).

al-Rukayni, Haydar Rida (d. 1784). *Jabal 'Amil fi Qarn, 1163 h.–1247 h.*, ed. Hasan Muhammad Salih (Beirut: Dar al-Jihan, 1998).

al-Sabbagh, 'Abbud (eighteenth century). *Al-Rawd al-Zahir fi Tarikh al-Zahir* (Irbid: Mu'assasat Hamada, 1999).

al-Sabbagh, Mikha'il Nikula (d. 1816). *Tarikh al-Shaykh Zahir al-'Umar al-Zaydani Hakim 'Akka wa-Bilad Safad*, ed. Qustantin al-Basha (Harisa, Lebanon: Matba'at al-Muqaddas Bulus, 1935).

Sarı Mehmed Paşa, Defterdar (d. 1717). *Zübde-i Vekayiât: Tahlil ve Metin (1066–1116/ 1656–1704)*, ed. Abdülkadir Özcan (Ankara: Türk Tarih Kurumu, 1995).

Schulz, Stephan (d. after 1756). 'Reise durch einen Theil von Vorderasien, Aegypten und besonders durch Syrien, vom Jahr 1752 bis 1756' (first published in Halle, 1774), in Heinrich E. G. Paulus, ed., *Sammlung der Merkwürdigsten Reisen in den Orient* (Jena: Wolfgang Stahl, 1801), vol. VI.

al-Shihabi, Haydar Ahmad (d. 1835). *Tarikh al-Amir Haydar Ahmad al-Shihabi*, a.k.a. *Al-Ghurar al-Hisan fi Akhbar Abna' al-Zaman* (Cairo: Matba'at al-Salam, 1900).

2nd and 3rd parts from another manuscript published as *Lubnan fi 'Ahd al-Umara' al-Shihabiyyin*, 3 vols, ed. Asad Rustum and Fu'ad Afram al-Bustani (Beirut: Lebanese University, 1969).

Silahdar Fındıklılı Mehmed Ağa (d. 1723/4). *Silahdar Tarihi*, 2 vols. (Istanbul: Orhaniye Press, 1928).

al-'Urdi, Abu'l-Wafa' ibn 'Umar (d. 1660/1). *Ma'adin al-Dhahab fi'l-A'yan al-Musharrafa bi-him Halab* (Aleppo: Dar al-Milah, 1987).

al-'Utayfi, Ramadan ibn Musa (d. 1684). 'Rihla min Dimashq al-Sham ila Tarabulus al-Sham' in Stefan Wild and Salah al-Din Munajjid, eds., *Zwei Reisebeschreibungen des Libanon* (Beirut: Franz Steiner, 1979).

Volney, C. F. (d. 1820). *Travels through Egypt and Syria in the Years 1783, 1784, and 1785* (New York: Evert Duyckinck, 1798).

Wood, Robert (d. 1771). *The Ruins of Balbec, otherwise Heliopolis in Coelosyria* (London: 1757).

Zahir, Sulayman. 'Safha min al-Tarikh al-Shami lam Yudawwan Aktharuha', *Majallat al-Majma' al-'Ilmi al-'Arabi/Revue de l'Académie Arabe de Damas* 17 (1942), 445–50.

Zinda, Aghustin (d. after 1738). *Al-Tarikh al-Lubnani (1714–1728)*, ed. Juzif Qizzi (Kaslik, Lebanon: Jami'at al-Ruh al-Muqaddas, 1988).

Zughayb, Jirjis (d. 1729). *'Awdat al-Nasara ila Jurud Kisrawan*, ed. Bulus Qara'li (Beirut: Jarrus Bars, 1963), partially translated by Haifa Mikhael Malouf-Limam as 'A Troubled Period in the History of Kisrawan from an Original Lebanese Manuscript', *Arab Historical Review for Ottoman Studies* 11–12 (1995), 145–77.


## Secondary sources

'Abd al-Nur, Antwan (k. 1982). *Tijarat Sayda' ma'a'l-Gharb: Min Muntasaf al-Qarn al-Sabi' 'Ashar ila Awakhir al-Qarn al-Thamin 'Ashar* (Beirut: Lebanese University, 1987).

Abi-'Abdallah, 'Abdallah Ibrahim. *Milaff al-Qadiyya al-Lubnaniyya min khilal Jubayl wa'l-Batrun wa'l-Shamal fi'l-Tarikh: Mahd al-Mawarina wa'l-Usar al-Ma'adiyya wa'l-Faghaliyya wa'l-Bajjaniyya wa'l-Ghalbuniyya wa-Sawaha mundhu ba'd al-Kawan hatta al-Yawm* (al-'Uqayba, Lebanon: Matba'at al-Dakkash, 1987).

Abi-Haidar, Rabâh. 'La société chiite des Bilad Jebayl à l'époque de la Mutasarrifiyya (1861–1917) d'après des documents inédits' (Sorbonne-Paris IV doctoral dissertation, 1976).

Abi-Ibrahim, Bulus Ruhana (d. 1893). 'Makhtut Qadim 'an 'Abrin wa-Bajja wa-Usarihima', *Awraq Lubnaniyya* 3 (1957), 231–7, 291–4, 344–8.

Abisaab, Rula. 'The Ulama of Jabal 'Amil in Safavid Iran, 1501–1736: Marginality, Migration and Social Change', *Iranian Studies* 27 (1994), 103–22.

'Shi'ite Beginnings and Scholastic Tradition in Jabal 'Amil in Lebanon', *The Muslim World* 89 (1999), 1–21.

*Converting Persia: Religion and Power in the Safavid Empire* (London: I. B. Tauris, 2004).

Abou-El-Haj, Rifaat Ali. 'The Ottoman Vezir and Paşa Households 1683–1703: A Preliminary Report', *Journal of the American Oriental Society* 94 (1974).

Abou-Nohra, Joseph. 'Le rôle des ordres monastiques dans les transformations économiques et sociales au Mont-Liban au XVIIIe siècle' in Daniel Panzac, ed., *Histoire économique et sociale de l'Empire Ottoman et de la Turquie (1326–1960)* (Paris: Peeters, 1995), 75–87.

Abu-Husayn, Abdul-Rahim. 'The *Iltizam* of Mansur Furaykh: A Case Study of *Iltizam* in Sixteenth Century Syria' in Tarif Khalidi, ed., *Land Tenure and Social Transformation in the Middle East* (American University of Beirut, 1984), 249–56.

'The Ottoman Invasion of the Shūf in 1585: A Reconsideration', *al-Abhath* 32 (1985), 13–21.

*Provincial Leaderships in Syria, 1575–1650* (American University of Beirut, 1985).

'The Feudal System of Mount Lebanon as Depicted by Nasif al-Yaziji' in Samir Seikaly, Ramzi Baalbaki and Peter Dodd, eds., *Quest for Understanding: Arabic and Islamic Studies in Memory of Malcolm Kerr* (American University of Beirut, 1991), 33–41.

'Problems in the Ottoman Administration in Syria during the Sixteenth and Seventeenth Centuries: The Case of the Sanjak of Sidon-Beirut', *International Journal of Middle East Studies* 24 (1992), 665–75.

'The Shiites in Lebanon and the Ottomans in the Sixteenth and Seventeenth Centuries' in *La Shi'a nell'Impero Ottomano* (Rome: Accademia Nazionale dei Lincei, 1993), 107–19.

'Duwayhi as a Historian of Ottoman Syria', *Bulletin of the Royal Institute for Inter-Faith Studies* 1 (1999), 1–13.

'The Unknown Career of Ahmad Ma'n (1667–1697)', *Archivum Ottomanicum* 17 (1999), 241–7.

*The View from Istanbul: Ottoman Lebanon and the Druze Emirate* (London: I. B. Tauris, 2004).

Ahlwardt, Wilhelm. *Verzeichniss der arabischen Handschriften der Königlichen Bibliothek zu Berlin* (Berlin: A. Asher, 1889).

Ajami, Fouad. *The Vanished Imam: Musa al Sadr and the Shia of Lebanon* (Ithaca: Cornell University Press, 1986).

Akyol, Taha. *Osmanlı'da ve Iran'da Mezhep ve Devlet* (Istanbul: Milliyet Yayınları, 1999).

Al Safa, Muhammad Jabir (d. 1945). *Tarikh Jabal 'Amil* (2nd edn, Beirut: Dar al-Nahar, 1981).

Al Sulayman, Ibrahim. *Buldan Jabal 'Amil: Qila'uhu wa-Madarisuhu wa-Jusuruhu wa-Murujuhu wa-Matahinuhu wa-Jibaluhu wa-Mashahiduhu* (Beirut: al-Da'ira, 1995).

Al-Tikriti, Nabil. '*Kalam* in the Service of the State: Apostasy and the Defining of Ottoman Islamic Identity' in Hakan Karateke and Maurus Reinkowski, eds., *Legitimizing the Order: The Ottoman Rhetoric of State Power* (Leiden: Brill, 2005), 131–49.

Allouche, Adel. *The Origins and Development of the Ottoman–Safavid Conflict (906–962/1500–1555)* (Berlin: Klaus Schwarz, 1983).

Aluf, Mikha'il. *Tarikh Ba'labakk* (Beirut: 1904).

Alyan, Juzif. *Banu Sayfa: Wulat Tarabulus 1579–1640* (Beirut: Lahad Khatir, 1987).

al-Amin, Muhsin (d. 1952). *Khitat Jabal 'Amil* (new edn, Beirut: Matba'at al-Insaf, 2002). *A'yan al-Shi'a*, 11 vols. (2nd edn, Beirut: Dar al-Ta'arif, 1996).

Anderson, Benedict. *Imagined Communities: Reflections on the Origin and Spread of Nationalism* (new edn, New York: Verso, 2006).

Arslan, Hüseyin. *Osmanlı'da Nüfus Hareketleri (XVI. Yüzyıl): Yönetim, Nüfus, Göçler, İskânlar, Sürgünler* (Üsküdar: Kaknüs Yayınları, 2001).

al-Atat, Faysal. *al-Shu'a' fi 'Ulama' Ba'labakk wa'l-Biqa'* (Beirut: Mu'assasat al-Nu'man, 1993).

Atlagh, Ryad. 'Paradoxes d'un mausolée: Le tombeau du sceau des saints à Damas', *Autrement: Collection Monde* 91/2 (1996) '*Les hauts lieux de l'Islam*', 132–53. Republished in English in the *Journal of the Muhyiddin Ibn 'Arabi Society* 22 (1997), 1–24.

Babayan, Kathryn. *Mystics, Monarchs and Messiahs: Cultural Landscapes of Early Modern Iran* (Cambridge, Mass.: Harvard Center for Middle East Studies, 2002).

Bakhit, Adnan. *The Ottoman Province of Damascus in the Sixteenth Century* (Beirut: Librairie du Liban, 1982).

Barbir, Karl. *Ottoman Rule in Damascus, 1708–1758* (Princeton University Press, 1980).

Barkey, Karen. *Bandits and Bureaucrats: The Ottoman Route to State Centralization* (Ithaca: Cornell University Press, 1994).

Bayat, Fadil. *Dirasat fi Tarikh al-'Arab fi'l-'Ahd al-'Uthmani: Ru'ya Jadida fi Daw' al-Watha'iq wa'l-Masadir al-'Uthmaniyya* (Tripoli, Libya: Dar al-Madar al-Islami, 2003).

Beldiceanu-Steinherr, Irène. 'Les Bektaşī à la lumière des recensements ottomans (XVe–XVIe siècles)', *Wiener Zeitschrift für die Kunde des Morgenlandes* 81 (1991), 21–80.

de Bellefonds, Y. Linant. 'Kafāla' in *Encyclopedia of Islam*, 2nd edn (Leiden: Brill, 1978).

Beydoun, Ahmed. *Identité confessionnelle et temps social chez les historiens libanais* (Beirut: Université Libanaise, 1984).

Beydoun, Ibrahim *et al. Safahat min Tarikh Jabal 'Amil* (Beirut: Dar al-Farabi, 1979).

Birge, John. *The Bektashi Order of Dervishes* (repr. London: Luzac, 1994).

Brinner, W. M. 'The Harāfīsh and their "Sultan"', *Journal of the Economic and Social History of the Orient* 6 (1963), 190–215.

Broadbridge, Anne. 'Apostasy Trials in Eighth/Fourteenth Century Egypt and Syria: A Case Study' in Judith Pfeiffer and Sholeh Quinn, eds., *History and Historiography of Post-Mongol Central Asia and the Middle East: Studies in Honor of John E. Woods* (Wiesbaden: Harrassowitz, 2006), 363–82.

Bulaybil, Luwis. *Tarikh al-Rahbaniyya al-Lubnaniyya al-Maruniyya*, 3 vols. (vols. I–II Cairo, 1924; vol. III Beirut, 1959).

CERMOC. 'Guide des centres de recherche en sciences sociales au Liban (1975–1992)', *Cahiers du CERMOC* 11 (1995).

Cevdet Paşa, Ahmed (d. 1895). *Tarih-i Cevdet* (Istanbul: Matbaa-i Osmaniye, 1891/2).

Charles-Roux, Fr. *Les Échelles de Syrie et de Palestine au XVIIIe siècle* (Paris: Geuthner, 1928).

Chevallier, Dominique. *La société du Mont Liban à l'époque de la révolution industrielle en Europe* (Paris: Geuthner, 1971).

Cohen, Amnon. *Palestine in the Eighteenth Century* (Jerusalem: Magnes Press, 1973).

Cole, Juan. *Sacred Space and Holy War: The Politics, Culture and History of Shi'ite Islam* (London: I. B. Tauris, 2002).

Daghir, Sharbal. *Tannurin fi 'l-Hiqba al-'Uthmaniyya: Hajar, Bashar, 'Amir wa-Dat[h]ir* (Beirut: al-Furat, 2006).

Dahir, Mas'ud. *Al-Judhur al-Tarikhiyya li 'l-Mas'ala al-Ta'ifiyya al-Lubnaniyya, 1697–1861* (Beirut: Ma'had al-Inma' al-'Arabi, 1981).

*Al-Intifadat al-Lubnaniyya didd al-Nizam al-Muqata'aji* (Beirut: Dar al-Farabi, 1988).

Darwish, 'Ali Ibrahim. *Jabal 'Amil bayna 1516–1697: Al-Hayat al-Siyasiyya wa 'l-Thaqafiyya* (Beirut: Dar al-Hadi, 1993).

Eberhard, Elke. *Osmanische Polemik gegen die Safawiden im 16. Jahrhundert nach arabischen Handschriften* (Freiburg i.Br.: Klaus Schwarz, 1970).

Ende, Werner. 'The *Nakhāwila*, a Shiite Community in Medina: Past and Present', *Die Welt des Islam* 37 (1997), 267–91.

Fahd, Butrus. *Tarikh al-Rahbaniyya al-Lubnaniyya: Bi-Far'ayiha al-Halabi wa 'l-Lubnani, 1693–1742*, 9 vols. (Jounieh, Lebanon: Matba'at al-Karim, 1963–9).

Farhat, Yahya Qasim. *Al-Shi'a fi Tarabulus: Min al-Fath al-'Arabi hatta 'l-Fath al-'Uthmani* (Beirut: Dar al-Milak, 1999).

Faroqhi, Suraiya. *Der Bektaschi-Orden in Anatolien (vom späten fünfzehnten Jahrhundert bis 1826)* (Vienna: Institut für Orientalistik der Universität Wien, 1981).

Finkel, Caroline. *Osman's Dream: The Story of the Ottoman Empire, 1300–1923* (New York: Basic Books, 2006).

Fleischer, Cornell. *Bureaucrat and Intellectual in the Ottoman Empire: The Historian Mustafa Âlî (1541–1600)* (Princeton University Press, 1986).

'Mustafâ Âlî's *Curious Bits of Wisdom*', *Wiener Zeitschrift für die Kunde des Morgenlandes* 76 (1986; Andreas Tietze Festschrift), 103–9.

Goudard, Joseph (d. 1951). *La Sainte Vierge au Liban* (Paris: Feron-Vrau, 1908).

Goudard, Joseph and Henri Jalabert. *Lebanon: The Land and the Lady*, trans. Eugene Burns (Chicago: Loyola University Press, 1966).

Göyünç, Nejat. 'Einige osmanisch-türkische Urkunden über die Abū Rīš, eine Šeyh-Familie der Mawālī im 16. Jahrhundert' in Holger Preißler and Heide Stein, eds., *Annäherung an das Fremde: XXVI. Deutscher Orientalistentag vom 25. bis 29.9.1995 in Leipzig* (Stuttgart: Franz Steiner, 1998), 430–4.

Griswold, William. *The Great Anatolian Rebellion 1000–1020/1591–1611* (Berlin: Klaus Schwarz, 1983).

Halaçoğlu, Yusuf. *XVIII. Yüzyılda Osmanlı İmparatorluğu'nun İskan Siyaseti ve Aşiretlerin Yerleştirilmesi* (Ankara: Türk Tarih Kurumu, 1988).

Halawi, Majed. *A Lebanon Defied: Musa al-Sadr and the Shi'a Community* (Boulder: Westview Press, 1992).

Hamada, Sa'dun. *Tarikh al-Shi'a fi Lubnan* (Beirut: Dar al-Khayyal, 2008).

al-Hamud, Nawfan Raja. *Al-'Askar fi Bilad al-Sham fi'l-Qarnayn al-Sadis 'Ashar wa'l-Sabi' 'Ashar al-Miladiyyayn* (Beirut: Dar al-Afaq al-Jadida, 1981).

Harik, Ilya. *Politics and Change in a Traditional Society: Lebanon, 1711–1845* (Princeton University Press, 1968).

Hathaway, Jane. *A Tale of Two Factions: Myth, Memory and Identity in Ottoman Egypt and Yemen* (Albany: State University of New York Press, 2003).

al-Hattuni, Mansur Tannus. *Nubdha Tarikhiyya fi'l-Muqata'a al-Kisrawaniyya*, ed. Nazir 'Abbud (n.p.: Dar Nazir 'Abbud, [1986]).

Havemann, Axel. *Geschichte und Geschichtsschreibung im Libanon des 19. und 20. Jahrhunderts: Formen und Funktionen des historischen Selbstverständnisses* (Würzburg: Ergon, 2002).

Haydar Ahmad, 'Ali Raghib. *Al-Muslimun al-Shi'a fi Kisrawan wa-Jubayl: Siyasiyyan, Tarikhiyyan, Ijtima'iyyan, bi'l-Watha'iq, 1842–2006* (Beirut: Dar al-Hadi, 2007).

Heidemann, Stefan. *Die Renaissance der Städte in Nordsyrien und Nordmesopotamien: Städtische Entwicklung und wirtschaftliche Bedingungen in ar-Raqqa und Ḥarrān von der Zeit der beduinischen Vorherrschaft bis zu den Seldschuken* (Leiden: Brill, 2002).

Heyberger, Bernard. *Les chrétiens du Proche-Orient au temps de la réforme catholique: Syrie, Liban, Palestine XVIIe–XVIIIe siècles* (Rome: École Française, 1994).

*Hindiyya: Mystique et criminelle (1720–1798)* (Paris: Aubier, 2001).

Hitti, Philip. *Lebanon in History: From the Earliest Times to the Present* (London: Macmillan, 1957).

Hiyari, Mustafa. 'The Origins and Development of the Amirate of the Arabs during the Seventh/Thirteenth and Eighth/Fourteenth Centuries', *Bulletin of the School of Oriental and African Studies* 38 (1975), 509–24.

Holt, P. M. *Egypt and the Fertile Crescent 1516–1922: A Political History* (Ithaca: Cornell University Press, 1966).

Hourani, Albert. 'From Jabal 'Āmil to Persia', *Bulletin of the School of Oriental and African Studies* 49 (1986), 133–40.

Hublus, Faruq. *Tarikh 'Akkar al-Idari wa'l-Ijtima'i wa'l-Iqtisadi 1700–1914* (Beirut: Dar al-Da'ira, 1987).

al-Humsi, Subhi Nahdi. *Tarikh Tarabulus: Min khilal Watha'iq al-Mahkama al-Shar'iyya fi'l-Nisf al-Thani min al-Qarn al-Sabi' 'Ashar al-Miladi* (Beirut: Mu'assasat al-Risala; Tripoli: Dar al-Iman, 1986).

Hütteroth, Wolf-Dieter and Kamal Abdulfattah. *Historical Geography of Palestine, Transjordan and Southern Syria in the Late sixteenth Century* (Erlangen: Palm und Enke, 1977).

Imber, Colin. 'The Persecution of the Ottoman Shiites according to the Mühimme Defterleri, 1565–1585', *Der Islam* 56 (1979), 245–73.

*Ebu's-su'ud: The Islamic Legal Tradition* (Stanford University Press, 1997).

Inalcik, Halil. 'Centralization and Decentralization in Ottoman Administration' in Thomas Naff and Roger Owen, eds., *Studies in Eighteenth Century Islamic History* (Carbondale: Southern Illinois University Press, 1977), 27–52.

'Military and Fiscal Transformation in the Ottoman Empire, 1600–1700', *Archivum Ottomanicum* 6 (1980), 283–337; repr. in *Studies in Ottoman Social and Economic History* (London: Variorum, 1985).

'Tax Collection, Embezzlement and Bribery in Ottoman Finances', *Turkish Studies Association Bulletin* 16 (1992), repr. in Inalcik, *Essays in Ottoman History* (Istanbul: Eren, 1998), 173–91.

Ismail, Adel. *Histoire du Liban du XVIIe siècle à nos jours* (Paris: G.-P. Maisonneuve, 1955).

Jaber, Mounzer. 'Pouvoir et société au Jabal Amil de 1749 à 1920 dans la conscience des chroniqueurs chiites' (Sorbonne-Paris IV doctoral dissertation, 1978).

Joudah, Ahmad Hasan. *Revolt in Palestine in the Eighteenth Century: The Era of Shaykh Zahir al-'Umar* (Princeton: Kingston Press, 1987).

Jouplain, M. (pseudonym for Bulus Nujaym). *La question du Liban: Étude d'histoire diplomatique et de droit international* (Paris: Arthur Rousseau, 1908).

Kafadar, Cemal. *Between Two Worlds: The Construction of the Ottoman State* (Berkeley: University of California Press, 1995).

Karahan, Abdülkadir. 'Fuzûlî', in *Türkiye Diyanet Vakfı İslam Ansiklopedisi* (Istanbul: İSAM, 1996), XIII:240–6.

Karam, Butrus Bishara. *Qala'id al-Marjan fi Tarikh Shamali Lubnan* (Beirut: 1937).

Karamustafa, Ahmet. *God's Unruly Friends: Dervish Groups in the Islamic Later Middle Period, 1200–1550* (Salt Lake City: University of Utah Press, 1994).

Kawtharani, Wajih. *Al-Faqih wa'l-Sultan* (Beirut: Dar al-Rashid, 1989).

Khalifa, 'Isam. *Abhath fi Tarikh Shamal Lubnan fi'l-'Ahd al-'Uthmani* (n.p.: 1995).

'Al-Iltizam fi Shamal Lubnan min khilal ba'd al-Watha'iq al-'Uthmaniyya' in *Lubnan fi'l-Qarn al-Thamin 'Ashar: Al-Mu'tamar al-Awwal li'l-Jam'iyya al-Lubnaniyya li'l-Dirasat al-'Uthmaniyya* (Beirut: Dar al-Muntakhab al-'Arabi, 1996), 201–19.

Khalil, Fu'ad. *Al-Harafisha: Imarat al-Musawama, 1530–1850* (Beirut: Dar al-Farabi, 1997).

Kohlberg, Etan. 'Some Imāmī-Shī'ī Views of *Taqiyya*', *Journal of the American Oriental Society* 95 (1975), 395–402.

'The Term "Rāfiḍa" in Imāmī Shī'ī Usage', *Journal of the American Oriental Society* 99 (1979), 677–9.

Köprülü, M. Fuat. *Islam in Anatolia after the Turkish Invasion (Prolegomena)*, trans. and ed. Gary Leiser (Salt Lake City: University of Utah Press, 1993).

Kunt, Metin. *The Sultan's Servants: The Transformation of Ottoman Provincial Government, 1550–1650* (New York: Columbia University Press, 1983).

Kurd 'Ali, Muhammad (d. 1953). *Khitat al-Sham* (Damascus: Maktabat al-Nuri, 1983).

Lammens, H. 'Les "Perses" du Liban et l'origine des Métoualis', *Mélanges de l'Université Saint-Joseph* 14 (1929), 23–39.

Laoust, Henri. 'Remarques sur les expéditions du Kasrawan sous les premiers Mamluks', *Bulletin du Musée de Beyrouth* 4 (1940), 93–115.

van Leeuwen, Richard. *Notables and Clergy in Mount Lebanon: The Khazin Sheikhs and the Maronite Church (1736–1840)* (Leiden: Brill, 1994).

Legrain, Jean-François. 'Réalités ottomanes en Palestine d'aujourd'hui: Bethléem 1996 et 2005' in Gérard Khoury and Nadine Méouchy, eds., *États et sociétés de l'Orient arabe: En quête d'avenir 1945–2005* (Paris: Geuthner, 2007), II:371–89.

Lewis, Bernard. 'Some Observations on the Significance of Heresy in the History of Islam', *Studia Islamica* 1 (1953), 43–63.

'Ottoman Land Tenure and Taxation in Syria', *Studia Islamica* 50 (1979), 109–24.

Longrigg, Stephen. *Four Centuries of Modern Iraq* (Oxford: Clarendon Press, 1925).

Lowry, Heath. 'The Ottoman Tahrîr Defterleri as a Source for Social and Economic History: Pitfalls and Limitations' in Lowry, *Studies in Defterology: Ottoman Society in the Fifteenth and Sixteenth Centuries* (Istanbul: Isis Press, 1992), 3–18.

Maalouf, Amin. *Le rocher de Tanios* (Paris: Grasset, 1993).

McGowan, Bruce. 'The Age of the *Ayan*s, 1699–1812' in Halil Inalcik and Donald Quataert, eds., *An Economic and Social History of the Ottoman Empire, 1300–1914* (Cambridge University Press, 1994), 637–758.

Majdhub, Talal. 'Masadir Tarikh Lubnan fi'l-Qarn al-Thamin 'Ashar' in *Lubnan fi'l-Qarn al-Thamin 'Ashar: Al-Mu'tamar al-Awwal li'l-Jam'iyya al-Lubnaniyya li'l-Dirasat al-'Uthmaniyya* (Beirut: Dar al-Muntakhab al-'Arabi, 1996), 23–41.

Majer, Hans-Georg. 'Fundstücke aus der vor Wien verlorenen Kanzlei Kara Mustafa Paşas (1683)' in Klaus Kreiser and Christoph Neumann, eds., *Das osmanische Reich in seinen Archivalien und Chroniken: Nejat Göyünç zu Ehren* (Istanbul: Franz Steiner, 1997), 115–22.

Makdisi, Ussama. *The Culture of Sectarianism: Community, History and Violence in Nineteenth-Century Ottoman Lebanon* (Berkeley: University of California Press, 2000).

Makki, Muhammad 'Ali. 'La politique chi'ite au Liban du XIe au XIVe siècle', *Cahiers de l'École Supérieure des Lettres: Colloque 'Ashura'* (Beirut) 5 (1974), 22–45.

*Lubnan 635–1516: Min al-Fath al-'Arabi ila'l-Fath al-'Uthmani*, 4th edn (Beirut: Dar al-Nahar, 1991).

Makki, Muhammad Kazim. *Al–Haraka al-Fikriyya wa'l-Adabiyya fi Jabal 'Amil* (Beirut: Dar al-Andalus, 1982).

al-Ma'luf, 'Isa Iskandar (d. 1956). *Tarikh al-Amir Fakhr al-Din al-Ma'ni al-Thani*, ed. Riyad al-Ma'luf (Beirut: Catholic Press, 1966).

*Tarikh Zahla*, 2nd expanded edn (Zahle, Lebanon: Manshurat Zahla al-Fatat, 1977).

*Diwani al-Qatuf fi Tarikh Bani al-Ma'luf* (1st edn 1908; new edn Damascus: Dar Hawran, 2003).

Matthee, Rudolph. *The Politics of Trade in Safavid Iran: Silk for Silver, 1600–1730* (Cambridge University Press, 1999).

Mazzaoui, Michel. *The Origins of the Ṣafawids: Šī'ism, Ṣūfism and the Ġulāt* (Wiesbaden: Franz Steiner, 1972).

Mélikoff, Irène. 'Le problème Kızılbaş', *Turcica* 6 (1975), 50–67.

*Hadji Bektach, un mythe et ses avatars: Genèse et évolution du soufisme populaire en Turquie* (Leiden: Brill, 1998).

Melville, Charles. '"Sometimes by the Sword, Sometimes by the Dagger": The Role of the Isma'ilis in Mamluk–Mongol Relations in the 8th/14th Century' in Farhad Daftary, ed., *Medieval Isma'ili History and Thought* (Cambridge University Press, 1996), 247–63.

Mohasseb-Saliba, Sabine. 'Monastères doubles, familles, propriétés et pouvoirs au Mont Liban: L'itinéraire du couvent maronite de Mar Challita Mouqbès (XVIIème–XIXème siècles)' (Université de Provence Aix-Marseille I doctoral thesis, 2006).

Moore, R. I. *The Formation of a Persecuting Society* (Oxford: Blackwell, 1987).

Moosa, Matti. *Extremist Shiites: The Ghulat Sects* (Syracuse University Press, 1988).

Mordtmann, J. H. 'Sunnitisch-schiitische Polemik im 17. Jahrhundert', *Mitteilungen des Seminars für orientalische Sprachen an der Friedrich-Wilhelms-Universität zu Berlin, 2. Abteilung (westasiatische Sprachen)* 29 (1926), 112–29.

Mouton, Jean-Michel. *Damas et sa principauté sous les Saljoukides et les Bourides 1076–1154* (Cairo: Institut Français d'Archéologie Orientale, 1994).

Mufarrah, Tuni. *Lubnan al-Asil laysa Ta'ifiyyan: Dirasa Tarikhiyya, Siyasiyya, Ijtima'iyya* (Jubayl: Santar al-Harf, 1999).

al-Muhajir, Ja'far. *Al-Hijra al-'Amiliyya ila Iran fi'l-'Asr al-Safawi: Asbabuha al-Tarikhiyya wa-Nata'ijuha al-Thaqafiyya wa'l-Siyasiyya* (Beirut: Dar al-Rawda, 1989).

*Al-Ta'sis li-Tarikh al-Shi'a fi Lubnan wa-Suriyya: Awwal Dirasa 'Ilmiyya 'ala Tarikh al-Shi'a fi'l-Mintaqa* (Beirut: Dar al-Milak, 1992).

*Sittat Fuqaha' Abtal: Al-Ta'sis li-Tarikh al-Shi'a 2* (Beirut: Higher Shiite Islamic Council, 1994).

Muhammad 'Amru, Yusuf. 'Nazra 'ala Madi wa-Hadir al-Shi'a fi Bilad Kisrawan wa-Jubayl', *al-'Irfan* 72–2 (1984), 62–73.

Muruwwa, 'Ali. *Al-Tashayyu' bayna Jabal 'Amil wa-Iran* (London: Riad al-Rayyes, 1987).

Naff, Alixa. 'A Social History of Zahle, a Principal Market Town in Nineteenth-Century Lebanon' (UCLA doctoral dissertation, 1972).

Nakash, Yitzhak. *The Shi'is of Iraq* (Princeton University Press, 1994).

Nasrallah, Hasan 'Abbas. *Tarikh Ba'labakk* (Beirut: Mu'assasat al-Wafa', 1984).

*Tarikh Karak Nuh* (Damascus: al-Mustashariyya al-Thaqafiyya li'l-Jumhuriyya al-Islamiyya al-Iraniyya, 1986).

Newman, Andrew. 'The Myth of the Clerical Migration to Safawid Iran: Arab Shiite Opposition to 'Ali al-Karakī and Safawid Shiism', *Die Welt des Islams* 33 (1993), 66–112.

Ocak, Ahmet Yaşar. *La révolte de Baba Resul: La formation de l'hétérodoxie musulmane en Anatolie au XIIIe siècle* (Ankara: Türk Tarih Kurumu, 1989).

*Osmanlı Toplumunda Zındıklar ve Mülhidler (15.–17. Yüzyıllar)* (Istanbul: Türkiye Ekonomik ve Toplumsal Tarih Vakfı, 1998).

Orhonlu, Cengiz. *Osmanlı İmparatorluğu'nda Aşiretlerin İskanı* (Istanbul: Eren, 1987).

*Osmanlı İmparatorluğu'nda Derbend Teşkilatı* (2nd expanded edn, Istanbul: Eren, 1990).

Öz, Baki. *Aleviğin Tarihsel Konumu* (Istanbul: Der Yayınları, 1995).

Philipp, Thomas. *Acre: The Rise and Fall of a Palestinian City, 1730–1831* (New York: Columbia University Press, 2001).

Poliak, A. N. *Feudalism in Egypt, Syria, Palestine, and the Lebanon, 1250–1900* (Philadelphia: Porcupine Press, 1977).

Rafeq, Abdul-Karim. *The Province of Damascus, 1723–1783* (Beirut: Khayats, 1966).

(Rafiq, 'Abd al-Karim). *Bilad al-Sham wa-Misr min al-Fath al-'Uthmani ila Hamlat Nabuliyun Bunabart (1516–1798)* (Damascus: 1967).

Repp, R. C. *The Müfti of Istanbul: A Study in the Development of the Ottoman Learned Hierarchy* (London: Ithaca Press, 1986).

Rida, Ahmad with Shakib Arslan. Two contributions entitled 'Al-Matawila aw al-Shi'a fi Jabal 'Amil', *al-'Irfan* 2 (1910), 237–42, 286–9, 330–7, 381–92, 444–50.

Ristelhueber, René. *Traditions françaises au Liban* (Paris: Libraire Félix Alcan, 1918).

Röhrborn, Klaus. *Untersuchungen zur osmanischen Verwaltungsgeschichte* (Berlin: Walter de Gruyter, 1973).

Sabbagh, 'Abbas Isma'il. *Tarikh al-'Alaqat al-'Uthmaniyya al-Iraniyya: Al-Harb wa'l-Salam bayna'l-'Uthmaniyyin wa'l-Safawiyyin* (Beirut: Dar al-Nafa'is, 1999).

Salamé, Michel. 'Une tribu chiite des montagnes de Hermel (Liban): Les Nacer ed-Dine', *Revue de Géographie de Lyon* 32 (1957), 117–26.

Salati, Marco. 'Ricerche sullo Sciismo nell'Impero Ottomano: Il Viaggio di Zayn al-Dīn al-Šahīd al-Tanī a Istanbul al Tempo di Solimano il Magnifico (952/1545)', *Oriente Moderno* 70 (1990), 81–92.

*Ascesa e caduta di una famiglia di Asraf sciiti di Aleppo: I Zuhrawi o Zuhra-zada (1600–1700)* (Rome: Istituto per l'Oriente C.A. Nallino, 1992).

'Toleration, Persecution and Local Realities: Observations on the Shiism in the Holy Places and the *Bilad al-Sham* (Sixteenth–Seventeenth Centuries)' in *La Shi'a nell'Impero Ottomano* (Rome: Accademia Nazionale dei Lincei, 1993), 123–32.

'Presence and Role of the *Sādāt* in and from Ğabal 'Āmil (Fourteenth–Eighteenth Centuries)', *Oriente Moderno* 79 (1999), 597–627.

'Shiism in Ottoman Syria: A Document from the Qāḍī Court of Aleppo (963/1555)', *Eurasian Studies* 1 (2002), 77–84.

Salibi, Kamal. 'The Buhturids of the Ġarb: Mediaeval Lords of Beirut and of Southern Lebanon', *Arabica* 8 (1961), 74–97.

*The Modern History of Lebanon* (London: Weidenfeld & Nicolson, 1965).

'The Lebanese Emirate, 1667–1841', *al-Abhath* 20–3 (1967), 1–16.

'Northern Lebanon under the Dominance of Ġazīr (1517–1591)', *Arabica* 14 (1967), 144–66.

'The Muqaddams of Bšarrī: Maronite Chieftains of the Northern Lebanon, 1382–1621', *Arabica* 15 (1968), 63–86.

'The Sayfās and the *Eyalet* of Tripoli 1579–1640', *Arabica* 20 (1973), 25–52.

'The Secret of the House of Ma'n', *International Journal of Middle East Studies* 4 (1973), 272–87.

*A House of Many Mansions: The History of Lebanon Reconsidered* (Berkeley: University of California Press, 1988).

'Mount Lebanon under the Mamluks' in Samir Seikaly, Ramzi Baalbaki and Peter Dodd, eds., *Quest for Understanding: Arabic and Islamic Studies in Memory of Malcolm Kerr* (American University of Beirut, 1991), 15–32.

Salzmann, Ariel. 'An Ancien Régime Revisited: "Privatization" and Political Economy in the Eighteenth-Century Ottoman Empire', *Politics & Society* 21 (1993), 393–423.

*Toqueville in the Ottoman Empire: Rival Paths to the Modern State* (Leiden: Brill, 2004).

al-Samad, Qasim. *Tarikh al-Danniyya al-Siyasi wa'l-Ijtima'i fi 'Ahd al-'Uthmani* (n.p.: Mu'assasat al-Jami'iyya, n.d.).

'Nizam al-Iltizam fi Wilayat Tarabulus fi'l-Qarn 18 min khilal Watha'iq Sijillat Mahkamatiha al-Shar'iyya' in *al-Mu'tamar al-Awwal li-Tarikh Wilayat Tarabulus ibana 'l-Hiqba al-'Uthmaniyya 1516–1918* (n.p.: Lebanese University, 1995), 59–95.

'Muqata'ajiyya al-Zanniyya wa-Mawqifuhum min al-Sira 'ala al-Imara al-Shihabiyya' in *Lubnan fi'l-Qarn al-Thamin 'Ashar: Al-Mu'tamar al-Awwal li'l-Jam'iyya al-*

*Lubnaniyya li'l-Dirasat al-'Uthmaniyya* (Beirut: Dar al-Muntakhab al-'Arabi, 1996), 161–78.

al-Shidyaq, Tannus (d. 1859). *Akhbar al-A'yan fi Jabal Lubnan*, ed. Fu'ad Afram al-Bustani (Beirut: Lebanese University, 1970).

Sohrweide, Hanna. 'Der Sieg der Safaviden in Persien und seine Rückwirkung auf die Schiiten Anatoliens im 16. Jahrhundert', *Der Islam* 41 (1965), 95–223.

Soueid, Yassine. *Histoire militaire des Muqâta'a-s libanais à l'époque des deux émirats* (Beirut: Université Libanaise, 1985).

Stewart, Devin. 'Notes on the Migration of 'Āmilī Scholars to Safavid Iran', *Journal of Near Eastern Studies* 55 (1996), 81–103.

'*Taqiyyah* as Performance: The Travels of Bahā' al-Dīn al-'Āmilī in the Ottoman Empire (991–93/1583–85)' in D. Stewart, B. Johansen and A. Singer, *Law and Society in Islam* (Princeton University Press, 1996) (also Princeton Papers in Near Eastern Studies 4 (1996)), 1–70.

'Ḥusayn b. 'Abd al-Ṣamad al-'Āmilī's Treatise for Sultan Suleiman and the Shī'ī Shāfi'ī Legal Tradition', *Islamic Law and Society* 4 (1997), 156–99.

*Islamic Legal Orthodoxy: Twelver Shiite Responses to the Sunni Legal System* (Salt Lake City: University of Utah Press, 1998).

Stoyanov, Yuri. 'On Some Parallels between Anatolian and Balkan Heterodox Islamic and Christian Traditions and the Problem of their Coexistence and Interaction in the Ottoman Period' in Gilles Veinstein, ed., *Syncrétismes et hérésies dans l'Orient seldjoukide et ottoman (XIVe–XVIIIe siècle): Actes du Colloque du Collège de France, octobre 2001* (Paris: Peeters, 2005), 73–118.

al-Subayti, 'Ali (d. before 1914). 'Jabal 'Amil fi Qarnayn', *al-'Irfan* 5 (1914), 21–5.

Süreyya, Mehmed (d. 1909). *Sicill-i Osmanî*, ed. Nuri Akbayar and Seyit Ali Kahraman (Istanbul: Türkiye Ekonomik ve Toplumsal Tarih Vakfı, 1996).

Suwaydan, Ahmad Mahmud. *Kisrawan wa-Bilad Jubayl bayna al-Qarnayn al-Rabi' 'Ashar wa'l-Thamin 'Ashar min 'Asr al-Mamalik ila 'Asr al-Mutasarrifiyya* (Beirut: Dar al-Kitab al-Hadith, 1988).

Taha, Ghassan Fawzi. *Shi'at Lubnan: Al-'Ashira, al-Hizb, al-Dawla (Ba'labakk-al-Hirmil Namudhajan)* (Beirut: Ma'had al-Ma'arif al-Hikmiyya, 2006).

al-Tayyah, Butrus. 'Risala Tuhaddithu Thawra fi Tarikh Lubnan', *Awraq Lubnaniyya* 8 (1957), 359–65.

Tekindağ, M. C. Şehabeddin. 'XVIII. ve XIX. asırlarda Cebel Lübnan Şihâb-Oğulları', *Tarih Dergisi* 13 (1958), 31–44.

'Yeni Kaynak ve Vesikaların Işığı altında Yavuz Sultan Selim'in İran Seferi', *Tarih Dergisi* 22 (1967), 49–78.

Tezcan, Baki. 'Searching for Osman: A Reassessment of the Deposition of the Ottoman Sultan Osman II (1618–1620)' (Princeton University doctoral thesis, 2001).

Touma, Toufic. *Paysans et institutions féodales chez les Druses et les Maronites du Liban du XVIIe siècle à 1914* (1st edn 1971; Beirut: Université Libanaise, 1986).

Tucker, Ernest. 'Nadir Shah and the Ja'fari *Madhhab* Reconsidered', *Iranian Studies* 27 (1994), 163–79.

Üstün, Ismail Safa. 'Heresy and Legitimacy in the Ottoman Empire in the Sixteenth Century' (University of Manchester doctoral dissertation, 1991).

'Uthman, Hashim. *Tarikh al-Shi'a fi Sahil Bilad al-Sham al-Shamali* (Beirut: al-A'lami, 1994).

Veinstein, Gilles. 'Les premières mesures de Bâyezîd II contre les Kızılbaş' in G. Veinstein, ed., *Syncrétismes et hérésies dans l'Orient seldjoukide et ottoman (XIVe–XVIIIe siècle): Actes du Colloque du Collège de France, octobre 2001* (Paris: Peeters, 2005), 225–36.

Venzke, Margaret. 'The Ottoman Tahrir Defterleri and Agricultural Productivity: The Case for Northern Syria', *Osmanlı Araştırmaları* 17 (1997), 1–13.

Winter, Stefan. 'Shams al-Dīn Muḥammad ibn Makkī 'al-Shahīd al-Awwal' (d. 1384) and the Shi'ah of Syria', *Mamluk Studies Review* 3 (1999), 159–82.

'Shiite Emirs and Ottoman Authorities: The Campaign against the Hamadas of Mt Lebanon, 1693–1694', *Archivum Ottomanicum* 18 (2000), 209–45.

'The Shiite Emirates of Ottoman Syria (mid-17th – mid-18th Century)' (University of Chicago doctoral dissertation, 2002).

'Un lys dans des épines: Maronites et Chiites au Mont Liban, 1698–1763', *Arabica* 51 (2004), 478–92.

'Les Kurdes de Syrie dans les archives ottomanes (XVIIIe siècle)' in *Études Kurdes* 10 (2009), 125–56.

'The Province of Raqqa under Ottoman Rule, 1535–1800: A Preliminary Study', *Journal of Near Eastern Studies* 68 (2009), 153–68.

Woods, John. *The Aqquyunlu: Clan, Confederation, Empire* (2nd edn, Salt Lake City: University of Utah Press, 1999).

Yahya, Hasan. 'Ahammiyyat Wilayat Tarabulus al-Idariyya wa'l-Siyasiyya fi'l-Nisf al-Awwal min al-Qarn al-Thamin 'Ashar min khilal al-Watha'iq al-'Uthmaniyya wa-ghayriha min al-Watha'iq' in *al-Mu'tamar al-Awwal li-Tarikh Wilayat Tarabulus ibana 'l-Hiqba al-'Uthmaniyya 1516–1918* (n.p.: Lebanese University, 1995), 25–58.

Zahir, Sulayman (d. 1960). '(Asma') Qura Jabal 'Amil', *al-'Irfan* 8 (1922), 260–4, 343–9, 431–40, 521–7, 591–3, 651–9, 759–75.

*Qala'at al-Shaqif*, ed. 'Abdallah Sulayman Zahir (Beirut: al-Dar al-Islamiyya, 2002).

*Tarikh al-Shi'a al-Siyasi al-Thaqafi al-Dini*, 3 vols., ed. 'Abdallah Sulayman Zahir (Beirut: al-A'lami, 2002).

Zarinebaf-Shahr, Fariba. 'The Ottoman Administration of Shiite *Waqf*s in Azerbaijan' in Faruk Bilici, ed., *Le waqf dans le monde musulman contemporain (XIXe–XXe siècles): Fonctions sociales, économiques et politiques* (Istanbul: Institut Français d'Études Anatoliennes, 1994), 233–6.

'Qizilbash "Heresy" and Rebellion in Ottoman Anatolia during the Sixteenth Century', *Anatolia Moderna* 7 (1997), 1–15.

al-Zayn, 'Ali. 'Adwa' 'ala Tarikh al-Iqta'iyya al-'Amiliyya', *Awraq Lubnaniyya* 3 (1957), 420–7, 463–72.

*Li'l-Bahth 'an Tarikhina fi Lubnan* (Beirut: 1973).

*Fusul min Tarikh al-Shi'a fi Lubnan* (Beirut: Dar al-Kalima, 1979).

Ze'evi, Dror. *An Ottoman Century: The District of Jerusalem in the 1600s* (Albany: State University of New York Press, 1996).

# Index

# Cambridge Studies in Islamic Civilization

*Other titles in the series*

POPULAR CULTURE IN MEDIEVAL CAIRO *Boaz Shoshan*

EARLY PHILOSOPHICAL SHIISM *The Ismaili Neoplatonism of Abū Yaʿqūb al-Sijistāni* *Paul E. Walker*

INDIAN MERCHANTS AND EURASIAN TRADE, 1600–1750 *Stephen Frederic Dale*

PALESTINIAN PEASANTS AND OTTOMAN OFFICIALS *Rural Administration around Sixteenth-Century Jerusalem* *Amy Singer*

ARABIC HISTORICAL THOUGHT IN THE CLASSICAL PERIOD *Tarif Khalidi*

MONGOLS AND MAMLUKS *The Mamluk–Īlkhānid War, 1260–1281* *Reuven Amitai-Preiss*

HIERARCHY AND EGALITARIANISM IN ISLAMIC THOUGHT *Louise Marlow*

THE POLITICS OF HOUSEHOLDS IN OTTOMAN EGYPT *The Rise of the Qazdağlis* *Jane Hathaway*

COMMODITY AND EXCHANGE IN THE MONGOL EMPIRE *A Cultural History of Islamic Textiles* *Thomas T. Allsen*

STATE AND PROVINCIAL SOCIETY IN THE OTTOMAN EMPIRE *Mosul, 1540–1834* *Dina Rizk Khoury*

THE MAMLUKS IN EGYPTIAN POLITICS AND SOCIETY *Thomas Philipp and Ulrich Haarmann (eds.)*

THE DELHI SULTANATE *A Political and Military History* *Peter Jackson*

EUROPEAN AND ISLAMIC TRADE IN THE EARLY OTTOMAN STATE *The Merchants of Genoa and Turkey* *Kate Fleet*

REINTERPRETING ISLAMIC HISTORIOGRAPHY *Harun al-Rashid and the Narrative of the ʿAbbāsid Caliphate* *Tayeb El-Hibri*

THE OTTOMAN CITY BETWEEN EAST AND WEST *Aleppo, Izmir,* and *Istanbul* *Edhem Eldem, Daniel Goffman,* and *Bruce Masters*

48334455R00124

Made in the USA
Middletown, DE
15 September 2017